The Royal Gold Cup.   *B.M.*

METALWORK AND ENAMELLING

A PRACTICAL TREATISE ON GOLD AND SILVERSMITHS' WORK AND THEIR ALLIED CRAFTS

HERBERT MARYON

Technical Attaché, Research Laboratory,
British Museum, 1945–1963

Line Drawings by
Cyril Pearce

**FIFTH
REVISED EDITION**

DOVER PUBLICATIONS, INC.
NEW YORK

Published in Canada by General Publishing Company, Ltd.,
30 Lesmill Road, Don Mills, Toronto, Ontario.
Published in the United Kingdom by Constable and Company,
Ltd., 10 Orange Street, London WC 2.

This Dover edition, first published in 1971, is an unabridged
and revised republication of the fourth edition of the work as
published in 1959 by Chapman & Hall Ltd., London (first
edition, 1912).

International Standard Book Number: 0-486-22702-2
Library of Congress Catalog Card Number: 76-130881

Manufactured in the United States of America
Dover Publications, Inc.
180 Varick Street
New York, N. Y. 10014

This edition

is dedicated to the memory of

HERBERT MARYON, O.B.E., F.S.A.

1874-1965

The death of Herbert Maryon coming just after his successful survival of two cataract operations was a blow to his many friends. His wonderful reconstruction work on the Sutton Hoo treasure in the British Museum will ever remain a cenotaph to his memory but this same work may well have cost a high proportion of his sight. His erudition, skill and above all his vast experience were a combination not readily replaced. When her Majesty the Queen invested him with the Order of the British Empire, she asked him what he spent his time upon. He answered, "Well, Ma'am, I am a sort of back room boy at the British Museum." And now, as one of his old friends, I have to say farewell to Herbert Maryon, O.B.E., F.S.A.

LT.-COM. ALEX. R. NEWMAN
British Museum, London

PREFACE

TO THE FOURTH EDITION, 1959

IN THIS BOOK I have discussed metalworking and enamelling, as practised to-day, primarily from the practical and technical point of view. And, where evidence exists for some more primitive methods of working, employed by the craftsmen of early Sumeria, Egypt, China or Europe, where I felt that they were likely to prove of value to a modern worker, I have given details of those methods.

I have so planned the book that soldering, casting, raising, stone-setting, enamelling and the other branches of the craft of the metal-worker are treated in separate sections, and all that I have to say on each is grouped in one or more consecutive chapters. Further, I have discussed in some detail the production of certain notable examples of fine metalwork where they demonstrate the practical application of the process under discussion. In this way I have been able to treat each subject in a more comprehensive and, I believe, more useful manner than if details of its working had been spread in fragments throughout the book. The chapters on soldering, for example, give a more complete and practical account of this important subject than can be found elsewhere. They may appeal, therefore, to workers in other crafts than those to whom they are primarily addressed, as also may the chapters on design, metal casting, raising, setting out, the making and sharpening of tools, and so on. In the last chapters I have assembled various tables and standards which are in general use, and I have attempted to bring into useful order the many gauges employed in measuring the metals and other materials of the craft.

I have, in every case, described the method which I have personally employed—the best method known to me—but it is probable that in some cases better methods than those described here may be practised.

I wish to thank the many friends who have assisted me in the preparation of this new edition of a work originally published nearly fifty years ago. Particularly to Dr. H. J. Plenderleith and my other colleagues in the British Museum, whose vast knowledge of the craftsmanship of many lands has been freely placed at my disposal; to the keepers of museums and other collections in many parts of this country and abroad who have given me facilities to study works in their care; to the instructors in the Central School of Arts and Crafts, London, and of the Municipal School of Art, Birmingham, who have given me of their knowledge; to the Goldsmiths' Company, Goldsmiths' Hall, London; to the History of Technology (Imperial Chemical Industries), for permission to reproduce the drawing of the mould of an early Chinese vase; to Messrs. Johnson, Matthey & Co., and, above all, to the craftsmen of many lands who, down the ages, have left fine works in metal and in enamel, making us all their debtors.

HERBERT MARYON

PREFACE

TO THE FIFTH EDITION, 1971

THIS FIFTH EDITION, published nearly sixty years after the original, has been amended and brought up to date in areas where technology has completely superseded the systems and materials in use in 1912. Where, however, the older methods and approaches are still viable, they have been retained to maintain the character of the original volume, even though their use may be confined to the laboratory or teaching institution.

This edition also incorporates the bulk of the extensive emendations and revisions which my late father noted in his personal interleaved copy of the fourth edition.

JOHN MARYON

CONTENTS

Chapter   *Page*

I MATERIALS AND TOOLS   1
   Platinum, gold and silver. Care of material. Assay. Copper and
   brass. Other metals and alloys. The workshop. Various tools.

II SOLDERING   5
   Definition of soldering. Influence of high temperatures. Unsolder-
   ing a joint. Hard and soft solders. Gold and its alloys. Solders
   for gold. Ancient solders. Rediscovery of the ancient methods.
   Silver and its alloys. Silver solders. Solders for copper and brass.
   Preparing and casting solders.

III SOLDERING (*continued*)   17
   Binding work for soldering. Soldering in plaster. Use of a flux.
   Application of a solder. The soldering hearth. The jeweller's
   charcoal and wig. Management of the flame. Various hints.
   Removal of borax by pickling. Unsoldering a piece of work.
   Composition of pickles. Antidote for acid burns. Pickling.
   Brazing.

IV SOLDERING (*continued*)   27
   Gas. Jeweller's jet. Blowpipes. Bellows. Management of the
   blowpipe flame. Spirit lamps. Blowlamps. Coke fire. Charcoal
   fire. Furnace.

V SOLDERING (*continued*)   35
   Soft solders. Composition of soft solders. Fluxes. Soldering bits.
   Various hints. Removal of soft solder.

VI FILIGREE AND OTHER SMALL WORK   41
   Wiredrawing. Square and other wires. Tube or "chenier."
   Tools. Jeweller's bench.

VII FILIGREE (*continued*)   53
   Grains. Bosses. Rings. Leaves. Filigree wire. Soldering.
   Boiling out. Granulation. Filed solder.

VIII THE SETTING OF STONES   63
   Tools required and their use.

IX THE SETTING OF STONES (*continued*)   70
   The Coronet setting. The Cut-down. Millegriffe. Thread or
   Thread-and-grain. Use of foil. Star, Gothic or Tulip. Pavé.

CONTENTS

Chapter		Page

X THE SETTING OF STONES (*continued*) 80

Gipsy or flush. Roman. Band or Rubber-over setting. Cramp setting. Pin setting for pearl. Drop stones. Other settings.

XI RAISING AND SHAPING 87

Tools. Stakes. Raising hammers. Planishing and collet hammers. Sinking and Raising. Problems in raising. Annealing. Shaping. Planishing. Various hints. Difficult shapes. Flutes. Other shapes. Sinking.

XII SPINNING 104

The lathe. The pattern or forme. Sectional chuck. Other chucks. Early spinning. Followers. Tools. Spinning. Lubricants. Metal for spinning.

XIII REPOUSSÉ WORK 113

Definition. Methods. Supporting the metal. Mildenhall treasure. Materials and tools. Pitch. Lead or zinc. Board work. Composition of pitch. Removing pitch. Repoussé and chasing tools. Snarling iron.

XIV REPOUSSÉ WORK (*continued*) 123

Transferring the design. Lettering. Patterns on bowls. Work in the round.

XV MOULDINGS 127

Folded edges. Wired edges. The drawswage. Making the dies. The drawbench. Swaged mouldings. Turned mouldings. Bending strip metal. Running plaster mouldings for casting.

XVI TWISTED WIRES 135

Their value. Analysis of each pattern.

XVII HINGES AND JOINTS 140

Chenier joints. Joint tool. Various hints. Soldering. Brooch joints.

XVIII METAL INLAYING AND OVERLAYING 148

Decorative effect. Piercing the recesses. Punching them. Islamic work. Persian inlays. Overlaying. Engraving. Tools. Etching. Etching grounds. Transferring the design. Needling. Mordants. Biting. Fusing the inlay. Electro-deposition. Hammering it in.

XIX NIELLO 161

Mycenæ and Enkomi. Theophilus. Cellini. Bolas. Spon.

Chapter   *Page*

XX JAPANESE ALLOYS AND STRATIFIED FABRICS   166
Banded alloys. Wood grain. Mixed alloys.

XXI ENAMELLING   169
Definitions. Composition of enamel. Early examples. Various classes of enamels. Tools and materials.

XXII ENAMELLING (*continued*)   175
Cloisonné enamels. The backing of an enamel. Its purpose. Preparing and fixing the cloisons. Preparation of the enamels. Charging the cells. Firing an enamel. Polishing an enamel.

XXIII ENAMELLING (*continued*)   182
Plique-à-jour enamels. Preparation of the cloisonné frame. Charging and firing.

XXIV ENAMELLING (*continued*)   184
Design for champleve enamels. Preparation of the ground-plate. Champlevé enamel.

XXV ENAMELLING (*continued*)   186
Bassetaille enamel. Definition. History. Method of working. Two outstanding examples. Some modern work. Cast work.

XXVI ENAMELLING (*continued*)   190
Encrusted enamels. Methods of support. Protection of soldered joints.

XXVII ENAMELLING (*continued*)   192
Painted enamels. Preparction of plaque. Backing. Grinding colours in mortar. Applying the enamel. Drying. Firing. Foil. Grinding colours on slab. Painting. Gold. Alterations. Grisaille, etc.

XXVIII METAL CASTING   200
Primary metal casting. Materials for moulds. Stone, clay and bronze moulds. The pattern. Casting a sword. Cuttlefish-bone casting. Casting a relief. A Chinese vase. Piece-moulding. Materials. Throwing the core. Wax model. Pour, runners and vents. The mould. Cire perdue casting. Statuette. Plaster cast. Plaster piece-mould. Irons. Core making. Wax cast. Chaplets. The descending and the ascending principles. Compo cire perdue mould. Pouring and finishing.

XXIX METAL CASTING (*continued*)   216
Casting in sand. History. Preparation of sand or loam. Casting flasks. The piece-mould.

Chapter   *Page*

XXX METAL CASTING (*continued*)   219
*Cire perdue work. Definition. The wax. Preparation of wax
cast. Lining the mould with wax. Preparation of core. Fixing
pour and gates. Casting a standing figure. Material for mould.
Making the mould. Cellini's method. Firing the mould. Pouring
the metal. Cire perdue in Central America, Ashanti, Scandinavia.*

XXXI METAL CASTING (*continued*)   228
*Cire perdue. Recent developments. Rubber moulds. Materials
for investment. Centrifugal casting.*

XXXII METAL CASTING (*continued*)   233
*Furnaces. Metals. Melting and pouring. Low melting alloys.
Breaking down the mould. Finishing the casting.*

XXXIII CONSTRUCTION   237
*Hollow handles. Compound mouldings. Fitting a moulding to a
tapering vessel. The folding iron. Square and round trays.
Buckling in sheet metal. Fixing a tablet to a wall. Inkpot tops.*

XXXIV SETTING OUT   245
*Tools. Transferring drawings to metal. Measurements. Various
geometrical problems. Inscriptions. Rectangular ring for small
work.*

XXXV POLISHING AND COLOURING   256
*Polishing. Firestain. Avoidance of firestain. "Firefree"
silver. Metal colouring. General rules. The colouring of
gold. The gilding of silver. The colouring of silver. The colouring
of copper and brass.*

XXXVI THE MAKING AND SHARPENING OF TOOLS   267
*Carbon steels. Alloy steels. Forging. Hardening. Tempering.
Grinding. Sharpening. Stropping.*

XXXVII DESIGN   274
*The craftsman, ancient and modern. His training and opportuni-
ties. Design. Unity. Growth. Line. Modelling a design.
Mouldings. Importance of the "jewel."*

XXXVIII BENVENUTO CELLINI   285

XXXIX ASSAYING AND HALLMARKING   287
*Gold. Preliminary assay. Final assay. Silver. Hallmarking.
Maker's, standard, city and year marks. Irish hallmarks.
Foreign plate.*

Chapter		*Page*
XL	Various Tables and Standards	294
XLI	Gauges	309
	Bibliography	318
	Notes on the Plates	319
	Workshop First Aid	325
	Index	327

LIST OF PLATES

Figs. 238–43. A sampler of twisted wire patterns (1–72), *between pp.* 136–137.

Plates

The Royal Gold Cup, *Frontispiece.*

1 The " King John " Cup, King's Lynn, Norfolk.

2 Candlestick of Bronze inlaid with Silver.

3 Silver Dish by Omar Ramsden.

4 The Bell Shrine of St. Conall Cael.

5 Golden Cover for a Copy of the Gospels.

6 The " Bacon " Cup, 1574.

7 The Birdlip Mirror.

8 The Ramsay Abbey Incense Boat.

9 The Valence Casket.

10 Standing Cup in Rock Crystal.

11 Silver Cup.   Nuremberg.

PLATES

12   A Fine Golden Dagger Handle from China.

13   Two Japanese Sword Guards.

14   Enamelled Bronze Trappings from Polden Hill, Somerset.

15   Anglo-Saxon Buckles from Taplow.

16   The Tara Brooch.

17   Gold Bowl. Etruscan. *Circa* 600 B.C.

18   An Inscribed Ewer. Made at Mosul in A.D. 1232.

19   Two Golden Shoulder-clasps from the Sutton Hoo Ship Burial.

20   A French Wine Cup of the Sixteenth Century.

21   Shoulderpiece from a Cuirass. Greek. *Circa* 400 B.C.

22   Silver Bowl from Chaource. Roman.

23   The Central Link of the Chain of Office made in 1887–88 for the Mayor of Preston.

24   The Kingston Down Brooch.

25   A Panel in Champlevé Enamel and Millefiori Work.

26   Cire Perdue Work.

27   Two Brooches. Etruscan.

28   A Sampler of Granulation Work.

29   The Towneley Brooch.

(*Plates 1–29 are inserted between pp.* 320–321.)

CHAPTER I

MATERIALS AND TOOLS

Platinum, gold and silver. Care of material. Assay. Copper and brass.
Other metals and alloys. The workshop. Various tools.

PLATINUM, GOLD AND SILVER may be purchased from dealers in jewellers' materials, either in the pure or the alloyed state, in sheet, wire and granular form. Sheet silver is generally kept in a coiled strip, perhaps 6 or 12 inches wide, and of considerable length; but sheets may be rolled to any size or thickness. The surface is generally free from scratches and blisters. Wire may be obtained of almost any size and section. Gold and silver are sold in the granular form for casting or alloying. They may also be had in the form of tube or " chenier." This can be obtained with a soldered join up the side or seamless: the latter variety being very useful for joints and hinges. Solid or hollow mouldings and extrudings, hollow beads, chains, snaps, swivels, mounts, settings for stones, blanks for rings and other similar things are kept in many different designs and in several qualities.

Owing to the cost of the material a number of precautions are taken in the workshop against the loss of any portion of it, however small. The bench is swept several times a day with a hare's foot, which forms a convenient little brush to which the gold will not adhere. All filings—lemel is the technical name for them—are carefully preserved. The residue from the polishings, the dust from the floor and even the sediment from the water in which the men wash their hands are carefully dealt with. The mud and dust are taken to a refiner's, and he recovers the precious metal from them.

There are several methods of ascertaining the quality of the gold in any article. Two methods are in general use. The first is by means of the "touch" or "blackstone." This is a hard black stone or a piece of black unglazed pottery. The gold to be tested is rubbed against it, leaving a streak. The colour of the streak, or "touch," is compared with that made by a small bar, or "needle," of known quality, known as a "touch needle." Touch needles

1

are made for every carat. The streaks on the blackstone are, after examination, washed over with nitric acid and again compared. The quality of the gold may in this manner be roughly ascertained.

A more accurate method generally employed is that of assaying. A description of this process is given in Chapter XXXIX, page 287. A third, very delicate, method of ascertaining the presence of even a trace of gold (or any other metal) is by means of the spectroscope, but this method is more useful for strictly scientific analysis.

The following notes on metals and alloys may be found useful, though detailed descriptions of the methods of working them will be found at intervals throughout the book and their chemical compositions will be found on page 304.

Copper and Brass. These materials are supplied in rolls, many yards long, of any width up to 12 inches or more. They are also kept in sheets measuring 48 × 24 inches. Their surface varies much in quality, some sheets being badly scratched and blistered. Perfectly smooth metal may, however, be procured. The sheets may be had in soft annealed finish, half-hard, hard-rolled, or burnished. For raising or repoussé work the first should be chosen. Copper and brass are supplied also in the form of strip, wire and rod. There is hardly any limit to the size or variety of shape in which these are made. Seamless copper tubes up to 6 inches or greater diameter are to be met with. They are useful for a number of purposes where a join up the side of a vessel would be objectionable. A length of the tube can, of course, be hammered and shaped in the manner described in Chapter XI; a considerable saving in time may be thus effected. Mouldings and hollow beads of various shapes are kept ready made. Gilding metal and the many bronzes and brasses may be had in a variety of forms.

German Silver. Good white colour. It is a hard, springy material to work in.

Nickel. Greyish-white colour. It spins well. Has a strong magnetic property.

Aluminium. Good for raising and spinning.

Pewter and Tin. Very soft and easy to work, but both now very expensive.

The arrangement of the workshop varies considerably according to the kind of work to be undertaken. For large work the bench should be about 2 feet 10 inches high, the top being of hardwood and at least 2 inches thick. It should be firmly fixed. The vice should weigh not less than 65 lb., for, if lighter, it will vibrate too much when raising is being done. The soldering hearth is described in Chapter III. The gas supply pipe should measure not less than

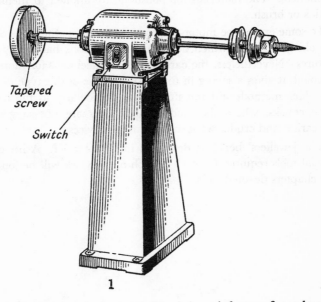

Tapered
screw

Switch

1

$\frac{1}{2}$ inch clear bore. A pipe with $\frac{3}{4}$ inch bore is better, for unless you get a good supply of gas you may have difficulties in getting the work hot enough. Get a good-sized blowpipe also. Fletcher's No. 5 bellows are large enough for most purposes. The lathe is mentioned in Chapter XII. It need not be back-geared. A slide rest, a drill chuck, and a face-plate with dogs make it an extremely handy tool for the many odd jobs which turn up in the course of the work. A number of wooden chucks should be provided. A surface plate is a rather expensive tool, but it is useful in trueing up work which has to stand or fit accurately. A good piece of plate glass will make an excellent substitute, however. The grindstone should be mounted with motor and drip can. A large, smooth slab of stone is useful for grinding smooth the rims of bowls and other vessels after they have been filed as truly as possible. The kind of stone does not seem to matter much. A smooth York paving stone answers very well. The drawbench is described in Chapter XV. The polishing lathe now in general use has an electric drive and is sturdily built (Fig. 1). The mandrel is screwed to take various mops, brushes and other grinding or polishing appliances. The materials for polishing are applied to them with a stick or brush.

To some extent the motor-driven carborundum wheel has ousted the old grindstone, which despite its dirty habits had many good features. Nevertheless, the carborundum wheel calls for more skill although it gives a saving in time. In the case of this type of work the older methods still remain in use, particularly in the case of lathe chucks, where the modern appliances are not so good as the earlier and cruder wooden homemade devices.

The jewellers' bench is described in Chapter VI. A list of the special tools required for each branch of the work will be found in the chapters devoted to it.

CHAPTER II

SOLDERING

Definition of soldering. Influence of high temperatures. Unsoldering a joint. Hard and soft solders. Gold and its alloys. Solders for gold. Ancient solders. Rediscovery of the ancient methods. Silver and its alloys. Silver solders. Solders for copper and brass. Preparing and casting solders.

SOLDERING IS THE art of joining together separate pieces of metal by running between them a molten metal or alloy which will closely adhere to and even penetrate their surfaces, and, when cooled, will bind them together. The metal or alloy used for this purpose is known as solder. It must have a lower melting point—require less heat to melt it—than the metal of which the work is composed, so that a temperature high enough to melt the solder will leave the work uninjured. But the melting point of the solder should approach as nearly as may be conveniently possible to that of the work, for a more perfect and a stronger joint is thus produced.

In a hard-soldered joint, when the molten solder—the solder when melted—is in contact with the other pieces of metal at a high temperature, it will tend to penetrate the surface of the heated metal: an intimate union of the two thus taking place. The junction is not merely a surface-grip made by an adhesive. It involves the partial absorption of the solder after its initial penetration of the surfaces.

It is because of this penetration—this interdiffusion of the solder and the soldered—that the unsoldering of a hard-soldered joint is so difficult. In such a joint there is no quite sharply-defined line of separation between the two original parts—their outlines have become a little blurred. However, it should be remembered that this effect of the blurring of the dividing lines between the parts depends upon the temperature employed. And, if the soldering temperature has been taken high—to a level approaching that of the melting point of the parts themselves—then the blurring and interdiffusion may be considerable, and the unsoldering of such a

5

joint will be very difficult. When cooled, such a joint may be hard to detect, either optically or chemically.

A soldered joint in ancient gold work which has been buried in the earth for centuries may be very difficult to detect either visually or chemically owing to the leaching away from the surface of the solder of all traces of the alloying metals (copper, silver or zinc) used by the craftsman with pure gold in the manufacture of the solder. This is due to the action of the salts of the earth, which attack the alloying metals and leave only the pure gold. The effect is known as an "enrichment of the surface."

There are many kinds of solder. They are known by such names as platinum solder, gold solder, silver solder, spelter, tinman's solder, plumber's solder, etc. They may be divided broadly into two groups—hard solders and soft solders. Hard solders melt at, or above, red-heat, and are used for materials which can safely withstand such temperatures. Soft solders require comparatively little heat to fuse them, so they can be used for soldering almost any metal or alloy. Joints made with hard solder are considerably stronger than those made with soft. The hard solders are used generally by goldsmiths, jewellers, silversmiths and by other workers for the better class of bronze, copper and brass ware, also for scientific and chemical work. Coppersmiths use both hard and soft solders. It should be remembered that it is impossible, without doing damage to the work, to use hard solder on work upon which there is already soft solder. For, at the high temperature necessary to fuse hard solder the soft solder would have spread so deeply and so far over the work as to seriously damage it.

Before discussing the solders employed for goldwork, a few words are necessary as to the method by which the proportion of pure gold in any article is indicated. The quality of gold is expressed by the number of parts of pure gold out of 24 parts or carats. Thus pure or " fine " gold is 24 carat. If any other metal is mixed with the gold, the latter is said to be alloyed with it. For instance, 22-carat gold contains 22 parts of fine gold and 2 parts of some other metal or metals; 18-carat gold has 18 parts of pure gold to 6 parts of metal, and so on. In recent times gold coinage in Great Britain consisted of 22 parts of fine gold and 2 parts of copper; or, in thousandth parts, 916·66 parts of pure gold to 83·34 parts of copper. This gold was known as " standard " gold. In France, the United

States and most other countries the standard alloy was fixed at 90 per cent. of gold.

The metals generally used to alloy gold for manufacturing purposes are copper and silver. Every increase in the copper content of the alloy results in the lowering of its melting point, until an alloy is reached with 18 per cent. copper, melting at 880° C. Beyond this point any further increase in the copper content of the alloy no longer lowers the melting point, but raises it instead. To produce a lower melting alloy it is now necessary to introduce a percentage of some other metal, silver for choice.

To make a solder for gold it is only necessary to add to a piece of the gold which you are to use a small portion (a fourth, fifth or sixth part by weight) of copper, or of copper and silver. If a small amount is required, melt them together on the charcoal until they are thoroughly mixed. Flatten out the little bead of molten metal as it begins to cool. Drop it into "pickle" (a mixture of 10 parts sulphuric or nitric acid and 90 parts water) and afterwards roll or hammer it out to about size 6 on the metal gauge. A larger amount is best melted in a crucible, cast in a flat sheet and rolled out to the thickness required. For example, you are using 18-carat gold. A pennyweight of it contains 18 grains of fine gold and 6 grains of other metal. If you added 3 grains more then you would have 18 grains of gold and 9 grains of alloy—two-thirds gold, one-third alloy. Now two-thirds of 24 (carats) is 16, so the mixture would be 16 carat in quality. To use 16-carat solder on 18-carat gold is not unusual, but it requires some experience, as their melting points are not so very far apart. To make an easier solder, add to the pennyweight of 18-carat gold, 5 grains of alloy instead of 3 grains. The resulting mixture will be just under 15 carat, and will prove a perfectly safe solder to use on 18-carat gold. In a similar manner the proportion of metal to be added to produce a solder of any quality may be reckoned.

It should be remembered that with copper as the alloying metal, you produce a solder which is richer in colour than one alloyed with silver, but it will not flow quite so easily. So, as a rule, both metals are used together, as in the examples given below, which are for solders made from fine gold. Always choose a solder which is as good as you can safely use on the work.

The hard soldering of gold and silver was as familiar a process to

7

the metalworkers of Sumeria and Egypt as early as the year 2500 B.C. as it is in London or Birmingham to-day. The goldsmiths were making elaborate jewellery in gold with hard-soldered joints; they were making soldered cloisonné ornaments to be set with stones; they were soldering handles to vases, and heads to pins. Many of the works they produced may be seen in our museums.

Now the solder they used was an alloy of gold, probably a mixture of gold and silver or copper. Gold as discovered is rarely quite pure. It is often found to be naturally alloyed with silver or with copper. Electrum, which was so widely employed in the ancient world for jewellery and for coinage, was a natural alloy of gold and silver: pale gold in colour. It makes a good solder for a purer gold. However, if the goldsmith wished to make a useful solder for gold artificially, a smaller amount of copper than of silver would be needed. For a proportion of copper would reduce the melting point of gold more than would a similar amount of silver; it would cause it to melt at a lower temperature. Particulars of a few solders suitable for gold work are given below and demonstrate this point.

Alloyed Golds and Gold Solders

	Gold	Copper	Silver	Zinc	Notes
1	75	5–15	10–20		18-carat gold.
2	63	15	23		Best gold solder.
3	58	14–28	4–28		14-carat gold.
4	55	14	32		Easy melting solder.
5	12	29	55	5·5	Very easy melting solder.
6	50	17	33		12-carat gold.
7	50	35	15		12-carat gold.
8	41	21	37	1	10-carat solder.
9	38	14	40	8	9-carat solder.
10	24·5	20	45	10·5	Easy flow.

It has been observed that when objects made of gold have been buried in the earth for many centuries a change occurs in the metal near the surface of the work. Much of the alloying metal, be it copper, silver or some other metal, is dissolved by the chemical action of the wet earth, leaving a thin film of almost pure gold at the surface of the object. So the colour of the work is enriched —practically pure gold being left at the surface and the unaltered alloyed gold inside. For this reason the solder at the joints of many early works now shows no difference in colour from that of the remainder of the work; the alloying metal has been dissolved.

At first the goldsmiths, when they wished to make a soldered joint, placed little chips of an easy-flowing gold (as a solder) at intervals along the joint, then they heated the work in the charcoal fire until the solder ran. But by 2000 B.C. they had found that to make a delicate soldered joint—one in which the solder did not " flood " the fine wirework or grains—they wanted something more finely divided than chips or filings of solder. They discovered that it needed but a small amount of very finely divided copper, brought into close contact with the heated gold, for the two metals to diffuse together at the surface of the gold, forming a solder there and making a sound joint. Later, the finest examples of wire and gold grain work were produced by the Greek and Etruscan goldsmiths of the eighth to the fifth centuries B.C. from grains measuring as little as one hundred and sixtieth of an inch in diameter, and masterpieces of their art may be seen in the British and other great museums (Plate 17). In the British Museum there is a pair of bracelets of very delicate gold filigree. They are made from exceedingly fine wires without a background, and are soldered without any sign of flooding. They are Etruscan work of the seventh to sixth century B.C. The methods these craftsmen employed continued in constant use up to Roman times.

Pliny, who died in the year A.D. 79, gives valuable information as to the Roman methods of soldering. He describes traditional methods, which probably came down from a remote past. The Roman goldsmiths used copper salts and other materials which provided carbon, and fired the work in a charcoal fire. But in late Roman times the art of making gold grain work went out of fashion, and the method of soldering very fine grains or wires was lost.

In the eleventh century a monk named Theophilus, or Rugerus, wrote a most valuable account of the methods employed by the craftsmen of his day. He tells us how he obtained scales of black copper oxide by heating a sheet of copper till it turned black, and then he quenched it in water so that the scales fell off. This he did repeatedly until he had obtained sufficient copper oxide for his purpose. He used the black oxide with other materials which provided carbon, and with their help he soldered his work.

9

During the Middle Ages knowledge of some of these ancient methods of soldering, such as that which made the finest gold grain work possible, seems to have been lost, though splendid work of every other kind was done. In the nineteenth century innumerable attempts to copy the finest Greek and Etruscan filigree and fine grain work were made, but none were completely successful. In the course of their endeavours the craftsmen evolved an ingenious method of overcoming the trouble caused by the displacement of the grains. They put some borax on a metal plate and heated it. The borax boiled up, subsided, and melted into a hard, glistening substance—borax-glass. This they ground in a mortar to a fine powder. They took a piece of solder and filed it away to powder. They mixed this with an equal bulk of the dry, ground borax-glass, and put the mixture into a little pot (Fig. 48), shaped like a watering can with a straight spout. The upper side of the spout-stay was roughened by making a number of nicks across it with a file. The grains and other work were stuck in their places with gum or rice paste. When dry, the mixed solder and borax-glass from the little pot were sprinkled over the joints. The nail of the fore-finger was drawn repeatedly over the roughened surface of the spout-stay, and the vibration caused a thin stream of the pot's contents to fall upon the work. Heat was applied very gently, from below where possible, in order to avoid the danger of blowing the finer particles out of place. If the work had no background a good deal of the solder and borax might have fallen through and have been wasted. With such work therefore the parts to be soldered might be stuck together with vaseline, to which the powders would adhere.

The search for a better method went on. Then, rather more than forty years ago, an Englishman, Mr. Littledale, was trying to reproduce some of the finest ancient jewellery. He found that there were two major difficulties. The solder, however finely he cut or filed it, continually flooded the fine grain or wire work. And the flux often boiled up and displaced the grains. After many experiments Mr. Littledale decided to divide the solder, not by mechanical but by chemical means. And he dispensed with the flux altogether. He found that copper carbonate was the best salt to use, and mixed it with a glue (seccotine). With this mixture, diluted with water, he stuck the grains or wires in place. When heated, the copper salt turned to copper oxide, and the glue to carbon. The carbon combined with the oxygen in the copper oxide and passed off as carbon dioxide gas, leaving the finely divided metallic copper in the joint. The copper combined with some of the adjacent gold and made a fine film of solder just where it was required. With this the work became soldered. Mr. Littledale's brilliant discovery enabled him to reproduce some of the finest examples from the ancient world, and he has done most beautiful original work by this method in platinum, in gold and in silver.

Pure silver is known as " fine " silver, but it is too soft for general use. It is, therefore, alloyed with copper. The proportion of alloy in what is known as " Standard " silver, or the silver which was used for silverware or for coinage in Great Britain, is 18 parts alloy (copper) to 222 parts of fine silver; or, in thousandth parts, Standard silver contains 925 parts of fine silver to 75 parts of alloy; or 37 fortieths of fine silver; or 11 oz. 2 dwt. of fine silver to 18 dwt. of copper. This is the standard quality for " Sterling silver " and is " Hall-marked " as such. There is another standard, known as the " New Sterling " or " Britannia " standard, in which the proportions are 10 parts alloy to 230 parts fine silver, or 959 thousandths fine silver, or 11 oz. 10 dwt. fine silver to 10 dwt. of alloy, but this alloy does not wear very well, so it is comparatively little used.

Silver solders are usually made by alloying silver with copper or with brass (i.e. copper and zinc). Those alloyed with copper alone are harder but do not flow along the joint quite so freely as those solders of which zinc is an ingredient. On the other hand, solders which contain much zinc are not quite so strong as those made from silver and copper alone, and if heated many times the zinc which happens to be near the surface is burnt away—leaving the surface rough. This may cause trouble in finishing. Solders for work which is to be enamelled should contain little or no zinc. But for ordinary silverwork, where the ease with which a solder will flow is an important consideration, the solder may contain a fair percentage of zinc. The sixth solder overleaf is very hard and, on account of its freedom from zinc, suitable for work which has to be enamelled. The seventh is extremely strong and flows quite easily. It is more expensive than the eighth owing to the greater proportion of silver in it. Brass wire is often used as the alloy for this purpose, not scrap brass, because wire sold commercially is of pretty good quality, while sheet brass may not be. The composition of good brass wire may be about 70 per cent. copper and 30 per cent. zinc. The eighth solder flows very easily indeed, but it is not so strong as the others. And, if made from brass pins, the difficulty of the burning out of the zinc may arise. Pins may contain from 40 to 70 per cent. of zinc. They often contain 60 copper and 40 zinc.

Silver Solders

	Silver	Copper	Zinc	Tin	Cadmium	Notes
1	80	13	6–8			Hard.
2	70–75	20–23	5–7·5			Medium.
3	66	23	10			French.
4	63	30	7·5			Common.
5	40	14	6	40		
6	80	20				Very hard.
7	75	16	8–9			Good and strong.
8	66	22	12			Easy flowing.
9	50	15·5	16·5		18	Very low melting. Use fluoride-base flux. 620°–630°C.
10	60–62	27·5–29·5	9–11			Easy. Use borax flux. 690°–730° C.
11	42–44	36–38	18·5–20·5			Used for brazing turbine blades. Use borax flux. 698°–778° C.

Numbers 9, 10 and 11 are British Standard 206. Grades C, A and B.

These solders may be used also on copper and brass.

Solders for copper, brass and iron are known as spelters, and the process of soldering these metals with hard solders, such as those above and those given in the next table, is known as brazing.

The melting point of these spelters depends largely upon the percentage of zinc present, so that as the percentage of zinc increases the melting point is lowered. Occasionally small percentages of tin or lead are included, but these metals, though lowering the melting point, yet weaken the alloy, so they should be avoided. The composition of some spelters follows.:—

Brazing Spelters

	Copper	Zinc	M.P.	
1	54	46	*c.* 880° C.	
2	50	50	*c.* 875° C.	Strong.
3	33	66	*c.* 820° C.	Weaker and more fusible.
4	66	33	*c.* 930° C.	For iron.

A solder to use with any brass can be made by taking a portion of the brass and adding to it a quarter of its weight in zinc. The best method of making brass solder is to melt the brass or copper first under a layer of charcoal. Warm the zinc to near its melting point and add it to the brass. Use common table salt, pearlash or cream of tartar as a flux. They are better than borax for this purpose. Stir the alloy well before pouring. The solder may be poured from a height into water, passing through a wet broom on its way, to break it into small pieces. Or it may be pounded into powder in an iron mortar immediately it has cooled sufficiently to set. It is a mistake to remelt any hard solder containing zinc for the purpose of obtaining a more regular mixing of the ingredients. Some of the zinc is burnt out each time the alloy is heated, so the fusibility of the solder is impaired, not improved.

A good brazing material for a copper-base alloy is known by the name " Silfos." It is composed of copper 80 parts, silver 15 parts and phosphorus 5 parts. Like other phosphorus-containing alloys it needs no flux on copper-base objects. It must not be used on ferrous articles.

The ingredients for gold and silver solders, with the exception given below, are, when melted, poured into what are known as ingot moulds. These moulds are made in various forms. That

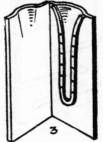

shown in Fig. 2 is suitable for casting rectangular pieces of solder or of the metal itself. These plates or ingots may be rolled out afterwards into long strips if required. This type of mould consists of two iron plates, kept apart by a flange the thickness of the ingot required. By sliding one plate over the other the shape of the mould may be varied. The two plates are kept together by a clamp. Another convenient form of ingot mould is shown in Fig. 3. It is made from two pieces of sheet iron with a former between them made from a piece of iron wire which has been flattened by passing it through the rolls. The wire is then bent to the outline of the ingot required. In this case it is like a capital U, perhaps 3 inches high, with the top ends bent out a little; in thickness rather less than ⅛ inch. By varying the shape and thickness of the bent iron wire, ingots of any form or thickness may be cast (Figs. 4 and 5).

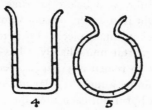

A few nicks made with a 3-square file across the flat sides of the wire will assist the escape of the air when the metal is poured in. The bent iron wire and the two plates are firmly held together by U-shaped pieces of stout iron wire slid on at intervals round the edge of the plates (Fig. 6). The mould used by jewellers for casting ingots is made from a piece of hearthstone—the white stone used for

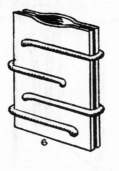

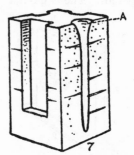

cleaning hearths. A block of this is taken and rubbed quite flat on each side. On each face a hollow is carved to the shape of the ingot required (see Fig. 7). The wide-open mouth or " pour " at *A* is the way the metal is to come in. The opening is made wider here so that none gets spilt outside. Bake dry. Take a slab of charcoal and rub one side of it quite flat on a stone. Near one end of this flattened side dig a little pit large enough to hold the metal when melted. If you now put the piece of hearthstone with the side which has been hollowed out against the flat part of the charcoal you have a complete mould, with only the little opening or " pour " turned so as to be quite close to the little pit in the charcoal. The two parts of the mould—hearthstone and charcoal—may be tied together with wire (Fig. 8). When the metal is melted—and this

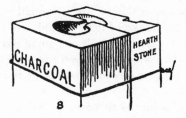

8

is done in the hollow on the charcoal—you have only to tilt the mould so that the molten metal may run into the place prepared for it. These hearthstone moulds may be made in any shape. For wire make them long and narrow, tapering to a point at the end away from the pour. This point is for convenience in getting it through the holes in the drawplate. It saves filing or hammering.

The mould having been prepared, take the ingredients for your solder, cut them into small pieces and put them into a fireclay crucible with a little powdered borax on top. Put the crucible in the furnace or on to a place prepared for it on the hearth. Heat it until all its contents have melted. If you are using a metal mould, warm it well by placing it on the furnace or hearth. Just before you are ready to pour the metal, put a little olive oil into the mould to grease it. Stir the molten metal well with an iron rod. Some of the borax may stick to the rod, but do not, if you can help it, pick up any of the metal. Then lift the crucible with the tongs and steadily fill the mould. Avoid splashing the metal in. Put the

15

crucible back in the furnace if there is any metal yet remaining in it. The metal in the mould will be set in half a minute. The clamps may be knocked off, the metal turned out and the mould got ready at once for the remainder. Be careful that there is not a trace of moisture about the mould when you pour the metal into it, for it would blow up, possibly with serious results. The oil does not matter. Some borax will have collected at the top of the ingot. A sharp blow may bring it off, or the ingot may be scraped clean or boiled in pickle (15 per cent. sulphuric acid in water). Then carefully cut and file off any rough edges or stray branches that may be present on the ingot; for if you use an ingot the edges of which are rough and uneven, with thin projecting pieces, for rolling into sheet or drawing into wire, cracks will be sure to appear in it. Roll out your ingot of solder to a convenient thickness, say, size 8 on the metal gauge, or thinner for very small work.

The exception to the use of ingot moulds, referred to on p. 13, is that in which you wish to make a very small piece of solder. You may melt it on a charcoal block. It will run up into a ball. Flatten this as it cools by pressing any piece of iron on to it. Then hammer it out as required.

That a piece of solder shall never be mistaken for a piece of silver, or vice versa, it is a good plan to scratch a number of lines in all directions across the sheet of solder when it has been rolled to the required thickness. If this is done it can never afterwards be mistaken for sheet silver.

CHAPTER III

SOLDERING (*continued*)

Binding work for soldering. Soldering in plaster. Use of a flux. Application of a solder. The soldering hearth. The jeweller's charcoal and wig. Management of the flame. Various hints. Removal of borax by pickling. Unsoldering a piece of work. Composition of pickles. Antidote for acid burns. Pickling. Brazing.

THE SEPARATE PIECES of metal which are to be hard soldered together should first be bound in position with binding wire. This wire can be obtained in various sizes. No. 20 on the standard wire gauge is a good thickness for general silver or copper work. No. 28 for finer work and jewellery. No. 32 for very fine jewellery. The wire is of iron, and on no account for gold, silver, copper or brass work should it be galvanized or tinned. For the metals with which such wires are coated, when heated, would alloy themselves with the gold or other metal of which the work is composed and make a " burnt " line which would be very difficult to remove. So make sure that you use only plain iron wire. It often has a dull, slightly rusted surface. Both the work and the iron wire expand when heated. But unless both are heated equally the work may expand a good deal before the wire has begun to stretch. As a result you may find that in soldering, say, a square box of thin metal, the wires have cut into the corners. It is not difficult to avoid such an injury to the work. You have but to make a Z-shaped kink in the wires every here and there as they pass round the box. These will allow the work to expand, yet they will not make the wires slack. In soldering the seam at the side of a tapering tube— part of a cone—some difficulty may be met with in keeping the wires which tie it together from sliding towards the smaller end, and so working loose. To prevent this take three lengths of wire and make kinks or knots at intervals. Then put these wires lengthwise of the tube, clipping their extremities round its open ends. Wires tied round the tube will not now slip down, for they cannot pass the kinks.

Sometimes it is impossible to tie work together with binding wire:

17

the shape of the parts may prevent it. For instance, a number of wires or other thin pieces radiate from the point at which they are to be soldered; or grains and narrow cloisons are to be fixed upon a background. In the former case fix the wires accurately in position on a piece of wax. Plasticine or any other material which would tarnish the metal must not be used, for metal so tarnished is almost impossible to solder. Wax can be bought from any dealer in jewellers' materials. When fixing the wires in their positions tuck under each one of them a tiny V-shaped loop of binding wire, leaving the ends of the wire projecting above the wax. These little wire loops should be made from ¼-inch lengths of thin binding wire. Put one of these little loops under each wire or boss as it is being stuck down in position on the wax. When all are arranged paint borax over all the joints which have to be soldered. Then mix a little plaster of paris and pour it over the work. When set, the wax may be removed. The little loops of binding wire, with their ends firmly fixed in the plaster, will keep all the parts in place. Now clear away any plaster which may interfere with your soldering. Thoroughly dry the plaster. Add a little more borax wherever necessary and solder in the ordinary way. Grains or cloisons may be fastened down on to a background with gum. This should be mixed with borax. It is a good plan to keep a lump of gum on the borax slate and rub a thick paste of it for use in sticking down these small pieces. Dry thoroughly. Then go over the joints again with ordinary borax before soldering. For further notes on such work see Chapters VI and VII, on Filigree. There are so many things to think about in wiring up any work for soldering that it is difficult to give general rules. Each case must be decided on its merits.

Something must now be said on the all-important subject of the choice and use of a soldering flux. All the metals used by the jeweller and silversmith, with the exception of pure gold, become oxidized when heated in air. A thin film of oxide forms on the surface. With copper this film can be a dense black scale with a film of red oxide beneath. All the alloys of copper—and they are many—show some trace of oxidation. However, to solder work it is necessary that the surfaces to be joined shall be clean and bright, even when red-hot. To keep them clean they must be covered with some substance which will exclude the air and dissolve the oxide. A substance which does this is known as a flux. Now for hard solders borax performs this duty splendidly. It is generally used in the lump form, not the powder. The lump of borax is rubbed with a little water on a small piece of slate. It grinds up into a white creamy paste which can be applied to the joint with a brush or feather. If several joints are to be soldered at the same heating put borax on them all. Then all of the joints will keep clean until you are ready to solder them. If you put borax only on the first you would have to cool the work down and thoroughly clean the other joints before you could solder them, for unless it is boraxed, a joint will not keep clean when the work is heated. Take care to work the borax well into the crack. Joints should be as close as possible, though the solder will fill a crack as thick as a sheet of writing paper. Should it be necessary, however, to solder up a wider gap it is well to plug it first with a scrap of metal. Borax, when heated, first boils up in a white scum, then it subsides and melts into a hard transparent substance known as borax glass. In certain kinds of work, in which this boiling up of the borax might cause trouble by moving parts out of their true position, the difficulty is got over in another way. Gum tragacanth is mixed with the borax on the slate to assist in keeping the parts in place. Or, instead of lump borax, borax glass is used. It is ground with petroleum jelly instead of water and used in the ordinary way. It hardly boils up at all. The solder will follow the borax, but it will not flow where there is no borax. If, however, there is some place upon which you particularly do not wish the solder to go, you may cover it with rouge, loam, whiting or tripoli, or a mixture of any of these, as an extra safeguard.

With the borax the solder may be applied. It may be cut into pieces of convenient size first. This may be done by making a series of parallel cuts 1 inch long and $\frac{1}{8}$, $\frac{1}{16}$ or $\frac{1}{32}$ inch apart at the extremity of your piece of solder. It has already been rolled down to a convenient thickness. Then, holding one finger against the sheet of solder, touching the ends of all the little strips, make another series of cuts at right-angles to the first set. A number of tiny square or oblong pieces, or " paillons," of metal will be separated at each cut. They would fly all about if you had not your finger against them. Drop them on the borax slate or into a little box specially kept for them Take very great care that no pieces of gold or silver, or any other material than solder, gets mixed with them. It might cause serious trouble. With the tweezers place a number of these little pieces at intervals along the joint or crack to be soldered. They should be sufficient in bulk to fill the crack. Not more, or you would have afterwards to file off the superfluous amount. It would otherwise make the work look heavy. If when the solder has been melted you find that the crack is not sufficiently filled, it is quite easy to add a few more pieces of solder. To do this before the work has cooled down, with the tweezers dip each piece of solder into the creamy borax and place it in position, holding it down until the borax has boiled up. The solder will then keep firmly in position. If you omit to hold it down the borax may carry it, when it boils, right away from the joint.

Another method of applying the solder, much favoured by silversmiths, is that in which the solder is first cut into long strips, perhaps $\frac{1}{8}$ inch wide, and held in the left hand with pliers. When the work is sufficiently heated the point of the solder is touched on to the joint where required. Some of the solder melts instantly and flows into the crack. One advantage of this method is that the solder is not exposed for long to the heat of the flame. For the fusibility of solder is always impaired by long-continued heating, generally owing to the burning out of some of the zinc which it contains. Another advantage is that there are fewer marks left on the work where the solder rested before it melted. " Paillons " of solder generally leave a trace or " ghost " to mark their temporary resting place. But strip solder cannot be used for very small work owing to the danger of disturbing the various parts, a difficulty which does not occur with larger work, which can be firmly tied together. Another form in which solder is used is that of powder, for soldering filigree work (see p. 10).

Large work should be placed on a hearth for the process of soldering. The hearth is an iron tray resting on a stand or bench about 3 feet high. The tray is fixed on a pivot so that it can be rotated when necessary—a very great convenience, for in soldering it is often necessary to turn the work round. The tray is filled with coke or pumice-stone broken to about 1- or $1\frac{1}{2}$-inch fragments. For the reason already given, take care that not even the smallest fragment of soft solder is allowed on this hearth. It is necessary in many cases to have a perfectly level surface upon which to rest the work during the process of soldering. A most convenient slab for this purpose can be made in the following manner. Take a number of pieces of pumice-stone and rub one face of each piece flat on a rough stone. Put all the pieces on a board with their flattened sides downwards, but first give the board a slight coating of oil or thin liquid clay to prevent adhesion. Arrange the pieces as closely together as possible, covering a space 9 inches square. Make a rim round about them from pieces of board 1 inch high. Then mix a bowl of plaster of paris. To do this, fill the bowl one-third full of water. Sprinkle the plaster in by handfuls. Soon it will begin to show above the water in the middle of the bowl. Go on adding more plaster round the edges until the water will only absorb the plaster slowly. Let all the plaster sink in and then thoroughly stir the mixture for a good half minute, taking care to get no more air bubbles into the plaster than you can help. The plaster will now be of uniform and creamy consistency. Take in your hand a little at a time of the liquid and throw it over the lumps of pumice-stone. Try to fill the gaps between the lumps very thoroughly. You must be quick about this part of the work, as the plaster may be set in two or three minutes. When you have filled in all the gaps fill up all over quite level. If you have been quick about the first part of the filling the plaster will still be liquid enough to use. You must not pour the plaster in at first, or the pieces of pumice would float out of their places. Level off the top with a straight piece of wood. Leave the work now and wash out the bowl before the plaster left in it has set hard. In five minutes the slab should be set and feel warm to the touch. When quite hard give the board upon which it rests a few blows with a mallet. The slab of plaster and pumice will then separate from it. Turn the slab over. Next knock off the wooden rim and fix it with plaster, mixed in the same way, into a shallow tray of sheet iron—not wood. You have now a slab with a smooth face of pumice-stone which will last for years. When thoroughly dried you can do upon it all the hard soldering that you wish. Its flat surface gives a very even support to work laid upon it for annealing or soldering. A sheet of asbestos resting on any flat surface may be used instead.

When, however, a piece of work rests flat on a slab, and the flame from the blowpipe cannot reach its underside, the work takes a considerable time to get red-hot. A few pieces of iron wire or, better, broken pieces of piercing saws are laid between, to lift the work clear of the slab. Work, however, which does not require this even support is annealed or soldered on the loose pumice, coke or charcoal in the hearth.

Jewellery, as a rule, is soldered upon a flat piece of charcoal held in the hand or upon a jeweller's "wig" or "mop" (Fig. 34). This is a mass of fine iron wire bound together, with a more or less level surface. It also is held in the hand. Very small work is sometimes placed on a thin piece of sheet iron, perhaps 1 inch square, laid upon the charcoal.

When using any of the hard solders you must bear in mind that the whole work must be made fairly hot before the parts near the joint to be soldered are raised to red heat. For if a considerable part of the work is cold it will take away much of the heat, wherever you may have directed the flame, the exception being that with a long or thin piece of work one can sometimes bring the parts near the joint to the required temperature before much of the heat is dissipated. As a rule the flame is played all over the article while you watch carefully that no thin or exposed part gets too much heat. It is easier to control the heating if you work in a dull light. Move the flame right off the work every now and then. Any red-hot part will show at once. Then, when the work is dull red, with a few sharp blasts, the point of the flame being directed towards the joint, that part is raised to so high a temperature that the solder flows like water along and into it. Cease blowing or move the flame away immediately, or the temperature may rise so high as to melt part of the work also. Remember that a thin or small piece will get hot much quicker than a heavier piece. So if you are soldering large and small pieces together watch carefully lest a small piece gets dangerously hot while the heavier parts are comparatively cool. To solder, say, a light setting on to a large piece of work requires some judgment. For to raise the work to a sufficiently high temperature may take minutes, yet a single sharp blast would be sufficient to melt the setting. The secret lies in keeping the heat away from the smaller piece and in playing on the large piece only. Thin projecting pieces or thin parts may be protected with a coating of loam, rouge, whiting or a mixture of any of these. Remember also that to make a sound joint both parts must be at about the same temperature. Otherwise the solder will flow and hold to only that which is the hotter. It sometimes helps to bank up the hearth with coke or pumice so that heat is reflected back on to the work. In soldering a long joint the tang end of a large file, held in the left hand, can be used to stroke the molten metal along. But as a rule if there is sufficient borax, the solder will flow towards the point which is hottest. Do not forget, in arranging the work on the hearth for soldering, that molten solder is a liquid and therefore runs downwards more freely than upwards. Copper may be raised to nearly a white heat before it will melt; brass, however, runs much sooner —at a yellow heat. Silver looks pink when " red-hot " if the flame has been moved away. It will melt before it gives a white glow. Gold changes colour very little before reaching its melting point, but then it collapses very suddenly. So use considerable care and manage your flame so that no thin part gets a sharp blast. Remember to move the flame right off the work for a fraction of a second every now and then. You will thus be able to see when any part is getting too hot.

To ensure a good joint the one great rule is—cleanliness. All the surfaces should be chemically clean before the flux is applied. In some cases, when, for example, a sheet of gold is to be backed with silver and the failure of the soldering at any place might have serious consequences later on, the work is treated as follows. The surfaces are cleaned by boiling them in diluted acid (sulphuric acid 5 per cent., water 95 per cent.), afterwards in a solution of washing soda and water, and again in clean water. The surfaces should not afterwards be touched by the hand, for that might leave a trace of grease, but they should be immediately painted carefully with the borax solution and tied together with stout iron wire. The solder is laid along one long edge and one side. The work is now heated, and the solder may be drawn right through the joint. When the borax has been removed, the combined sheet is rolled as thin as may be required. If the joint is sound no blisters will be formed between the two parts of the plate.

In soldering a wire on to another part of the work you may have some difficulty in keeping the solder from running on to and thickening the wire. This is a particularly disagreeable habit, for it quite ruins the appearance of a twisted or plaited wire if it is clogged up in this way. To avoid this difficulty you must take care that the heat reaches the wire only through the work—not directly from the blowpipe flame itself. The heat may be applied underneath, for example, so that the flame does not touch the wire at all. The work will then be the hotter of the two, so the solder will not rush to the wire. Another method is that of running solder over the surface of the work where the wire is to come and afterwards putting the wire in place, boraxing and reheating till the solder flows and grips the wire.

Special care is required when it is necessary to solder the two halves of a ball or bead together. Inside, round the rim of each half put borax and solder. Heat each half separately so that the solder flows right round the edge of each half ball. Now rub or file the rims quite level, borax each half, tie the two together and heat until the solder runs through the joint. You may be quite certain that by following this method you will always get a sound joint. Do not forget that you must always leave a hole for the escape of the air when soldering up any bead or other hollow article. If you omit to leave one, the pressure of the heated air inside when soldering may burst the work. Cases have occurred where jewellers have lost their eyesight through neglect of this simple precaution. Leave the hole open; it will do no harm.

To unsolder a piece of work, first think how you can manage to separate the parts when the solder is melted. You may be able to lift or knock off the loose piece with the tongs, or you may so arrange it that the parts will spring or fall open. You may find that instead of lifting the piece off you would lift the whole work instead. In such a case tie the work down and perhaps fix another wire to the loose piece, by which you may pull it off. Paint the joint well with borax and apply loam, rouge or whiting to any parts or joints which are not to be disturbed. Then heat the work till the solder runs and immediately remove the loose piece.

To remove the borax after soldering various " pickles " are used. For gold a solution of nitric acid and water is made to boil in a porcelain bowl, and the work left in it until all the melted borax has disappeared. Eight parts of water to one of acid is a good proportion to use. The boiling solution dissolves also any alloy (copper or silver) which may be present near the surface of the gold. It will also remove lead should any of this material be present. So the work when it leaves the acid has an exterior of pure gold— the alloy having been removed, but to an infinitely small depth. It should be remembered that with continued heating some of the water boils away and the acid solution becomes relatively stronger, so more water should be added to counteract this tendency. For silver or copper a solution of sulphuric acid (vitriol) is used, made by adding 1 part of acid to 6 to 10 parts of water. It is dangerous to add the water to the strong sulphuric or nitric acid, as this is liable to cause spitting. The colour of silver after pickling is pure white. It is well to use brass or nickel tongs to lift your work into or out of the pickling solutions.

In mixing these solutions it cannot be too strongly emphasized that if you pour water into acid you may cause an explosion, with serious consequences, while if you pour acid into a much greater bulk of water nothing will happen except that the water will get warm from chemical action. The sulphuric acid solution is generally put into a copper bowl or pan with the work and heated till it boils, when the borax will have been dissolved. Avoid any splashes, hot or cold, from these solutions. They burn holes in clothes and may make serious burns on flesh. If you receive a splash, flood the part with plenty of water; and in order to neutralize the acidity apply bicarbonate of soda, soap suds or a solution of common washing soda. Then exclude air from the affected part by covering with a thin paste of flour, starch or baking soda. Or you may use an aqueous solution of Proflavine. Avoid grease. After treatment with any of the above, cover with cotton wool or a cloth and bandage lightly. If acid should get into the eye, wash it well, then a drop of castor oil should be applied under the eyelid with a thin glass rod with rounded end, and a doctor should be consulted. Do not use carron oil or tannic acid for severe burns. Simple first-aid kit should be regarded as an essential piece of equipment in every well-run workshop.

It is usual to keep pickle in a large pan of glazed earthware or of lead. The acid solution acts more slowly when cold, but if work is left in it for an hour or two the borax will be gradually dissolved and the work cleaned just as satisfactorily as by using hot solutions. Finish by flushing under a tap of running water. Large work, for which you may not have big enough copper pan, can be cleaned perfectly satisfactorily in this way by cold pickling. You can hasten the process, if desired, by repeatedly heating the work and plunging it while red-hot into the solution, but stand well away from the pickle and do not under-estimate the attendant risk of accident through splashing. The oxides formed on the surface of copper and its alloys are removed by the acid solution.

Work which has been in pickle should always be washed thoroughly in plenty of water immediately it is removed from the solution. If there are any hollow parts to the work it is usual to boil it in soda and water to remove any trace of the acid. If you do not take this precaution, some of the acid which has got inside will dry out and on concentration will cause corrosion, and the salts formed will dry out in crystals and cause trouble later on. Binding wire should always be removed from the work before it is pickled.

It is well to remember that solder will not melt again, even if the work is heated to a dangerously high temperature, unless there is flux in contact with it. So when a work has to undergo several successive solderings—and it may have to " go through the fire " twenty times or more—it is usual to boil it out after each soldering in order to remove the borax from the joints already made. As a further protection a coating of loam, whiting or rouge may be painted over any joint which you wish to remain undisturbed.

To join pieces of copper or brass together by brazing, first fit the pieces together closely and bind them with iron wire. This should not be thinner than that of which an ordinary (brass or steel) pin is made. It may be a good deal thicker if the work is heavy. Apply borax in the ordinary way (p. 19) or in the form of powder. Then put some brass solder or wire on the joint. Brass wire makes a good solder for iron or steel, but it would obviously be unwise to attempt to use it on brass itself, as this would be possible only when the composition of the alloys is known and accurately adjusted. But precise information as to composition is not generally available. Make sure that the wire or spelter will not move away or fall off when the borax boils up. The wire may be bent round the joint or bound in place with iron wire. Build the coke round about the work and heat until it is a bright red but not a white heat. The spelter or wire should melt, follow the borax and run into the joint. Should it not run easily add a little more borax. When cool the borax may be removed by pickling or scraping and the joint filed smooth.

A spelter for use with cast-iron or steel is made from copper 42 to 60 parts, nickel 1 to 10 parts, silicon 3 parts (maximum), zinc balance.

26

CHAPTER IV

SOLDERING (*continued*)

Gas. Jeweller's jet. Blowpipes. Bellows. Management of the blowpipe
flame. Spirit lamp. Blowlamps. Coke fire. Charcoal fire. Furnace.

COAL-GAS IS the simplest and most generally available fuel for the purpose of soldering. It is employed in a rather different manner for small and for large work. For jewellery and other small articles a jeweller's jet and a mouth blowpipe are the tools used, while for large work a blowpipe (Fig. 9) and bellows

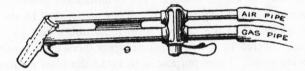

(Fig. 10) are necessary. Very delicate work is sometimes fired in a muffle furnace. The jeweller's jet (Fig. 12) is a small iron stand through which the gas-pipe passes to a horizontal tube, 4 or 5 inches long, pivoted at one end above it. The horizontal tube can be swung right round the pivot, and the gas supply is so arranged that when the tube or jet is in the position for soldering a full supply of gas can pass through it, while as it is turned away from one the supply is automatically cut down until only sufficient remains to keep the jet alight. The end of the tube is cut off at an angle of about 45 degrees. The iron stand is generally fixed to the bench on the right-hand side of the worker. The mouth blowpipe (Fig. 11)

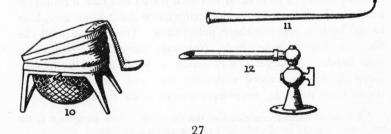

used in conjunction with this jet is a tapering tube of brass about 8 inches long, the smaller end being bent round at right-angles. The tube varies in diameter from about $\frac{1}{4}$ inch down to an opening large enough to just admit an ordinary pin. A second blowpipe with an opening about twice this size is useful for rather larger work. For still larger work, however, the gas-blowpipe and bellows must be used.* The blowpipe in this case consists of two concentric tubes, measuring perhaps $\frac{3}{8}$ and $\frac{1}{8}$ inch in diameter respectively. They are bent round to nearly right-angles at one end like the mouth blowpipe. The outer tube is for gas, the inner for the compressed air from the bellows, the supply of both being regulated by a tap or taps. In choosing a blowpipe see that you get one with plenty of room through the taps. You should have a bore of $\frac{1}{2}$ inch all the way from the main to the mouth of the blowpipe, which, however, may be a little smaller. The bellows most generally used are those known as Fletcher's No. 5. They are worked by the foot. On the underside of the bellows is an indiarubber disc, or rather two discs, covered by a net which prevents them from expanding to bursting point. Their purpose is to make the blast continuous, for one which came in puffs would not be always satisfactory. These rubber discs sometimes burst, and it is well to know how to replace them. It will be found that the net is held on by a wire running round its circumference. Untwist the join and the net will come off. The two rubber discs are fastened on with a twisted wire in the same way. Remove them and see that the valve underneath is working well. Put on the new discs and be careful in fixing the wire that you smooth out every pleat round the edge of the rubber. Remember to bend the ends of the wires out of reach of the discs when they are expanded, otherwise they may be punctured. Replace the net as before.

We come now to the management of the blowpipe flame. Let us take the jeweller's jet first. If you light the jet and turn it round till full on you will have a loose, flickering flame about a foot long, blue at the bottom and elsewhere pale yellow. Turn it down till the flame is about 6 inches high. Now take the mouth blowpipe in your hand. The larger end is tinned, to be clean for the mouth. Keep the cheeks inflated and, controlling with the cheek muscles, try to blow a gentle, continuous stream of air through the pipe.

* Instead of bellows, one can now use pumps of various sorts, such as the small ones that are usually sold for pumping air into fish tanks.

With a little practice the blast need not stop even while you take a fresh breath into your lungs through the nose. Do not blow too hard; quite a gentle blast is required, just as though you were whistling to yourself. When you have had a little practice with the blowpipe move its small end to a position immediately over the horizontal tube of the jet, and about ⅜ inch from the end where the flame is. Turn the blowpipe to such an angle that the flame is blown downwards to the left at about an angle of 45 degrees. The character of the flame will be quite changed. Instead of being nearly white it will be blue, with some flashes of white towards the point. The jet of air has both altered the direction of the gas flame and made it hotter, for it is now burning a good deal more oxygen from the air. This is the cause of its change of colour. If you blow hard you will have a roaring, rough-edged, very hot flame, useful for heating a largish piece of work but rather likely to melt any thin or projecting parts of it. If, however, you breathe gently through the pipe you will have a silent flame with less ragged edges. This flame is not so fierce as the other, but it is hot enough to heat the work up sufficiently and to melt the solder. Now turn the jet round till you have a flame only 4 inches high. Move the point of the blowpipe till it is only ⅛ or ¼ inch from the end of the horizontal tube. (It is cut off at an angle of 45 degrees, but these measurements are taken from the top of the slope). The character of the flame is changed again. You have a sharp spike of flame 3 or 4 inches long, and if you look you will notice that it consists of an outer dark-blue flame, with an inner light-blue one extending about half the way along. Take the wig (Fig. 34) in your left hand and hold it beyond the end of the flame. Gradually bring it nearer. The fine iron wires of which it is composed will quickly become red, then white-hot, and then burn, throwing out bright sparks in all directions. Move the wig away, and try again and again to see which part of the flame will make the wires begin to burn most quickly. You will find that the hottest part of the flame lies just beyond the tip of the inner light-blue cone. You have now learnt what you can do. You can heat the whole work up with the soft, gentle flame, and you can then, by shifting the position of the blow-pipe, direct a sharp, very hot flame on to the solder and the parts near it. This is just what you should do in soldering. If you have sufficiently warmed the whole work with the gentler flame, then immediately the hot, pointed flame touches the solder it will melt

29

and run into the joint. With the large blowpipe and bellows you may get a similar variety of flames: the roaring, ragged flame for heating up and soldering large work; the quieter, gentler flame for smaller, more delicate work, parts of which might become melted in a fiercer flame; and the sharp, intensely hot flame which is so useful in actually melting the solder when the work has been sufficiently heated. You must practise with these different flames, so that you may produce each of them at will and keep them entirely under control. Each type of flame may be produced however high or low the gas may be turned.

It is a good plan when annealing or soldering to move the work every now and then out of range of the flame, even for a fraction of a second. You can then see at once how it is getting on—if any part has become red-hot or is in danger of becoming melted. When using the large blowpipe, of course you move that instead of the work. If you have difficulty in getting the work hot enough, probably more gas is required. But do not use a bigger flame than is necessary, for that is both wasteful and dangerous. You will find that the work will get hot quicker if you can hold it considerably below the jet and direct the flame nearly squarely on to it; while if the flame makes as it were a glancing blow at the work much of its heat is wasted. You will notice this particularly with the large blowpipe when you try to heat some piece of work which is nearly at the limit of the blowpipe's power. Indeed, in such a case it is well to build a temporary wall of coke, charcoal, firebrick, gas-carbon or any other not very fusible material behind the work to catch the flame when it has passed and to turn it back on to the work again.

It often happens that a room otherwise available for metal-working has no supply of gas. This need not, however, prove an insurmountable obstacle, for soldering lamps, burning spirit or oil may be used instead. Work as large as a fair-sized brooch can be soldered by means of the spirit lamp shown in Fig. 13. Resting on a cast-iron foot is a large reservoir for methylated spirit. At a little distance is an inclined tube filled with cotton waste or wick and connected by a tube with the reservoir. The inclined tube should be about ¾ or 1 inch in diameter. When the wick is lighted you have a very good flame. You can regulate it by pulling the wick up or down the tube. The flame is extinguished by dropping on to it the little disc of metal attached to the hinged, curved wire

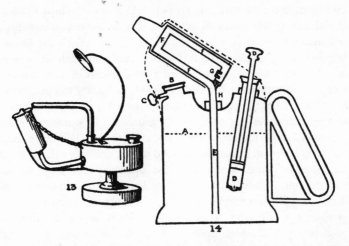

shown above the reservoir. A cap is provided to cover the inclined tube and prevent the escape of the spirit when the lamp is not in use. The lamp is used in conjunction with the mouth blowpipe.

For larger work a lamp burning paraffin would be required.* The Swedish blowlamps known as Ætnas are most useful. Of similar make are the Barthel brazing lamps, their principle of construction being similar to that of the lamps used by house decorators for burning paint off woodwork. The most useful size to buy holds about a quart of oil and will burn for an hour with but little attention. The construction is shown in Fig. 14. A is the reservoir, two-thirds full of paraffin oil, which has been poured in at the screw-cap B. C is a little air-tap. D the pump by which air is forced into the reservoir. E is the pipe for the oil, which runs from near the bottom of the reservoir through the tube F and escapes by a minute hole at G. H is a shallow depression at the top of the reservoir. This little cup is filled with methylated spirit, which, when lighted, heats the tube F so much that any oil within it is turned to vapour. This gas, emerging from the pinhole G, burns with a hot blue flame and rushes forward, keeping the tube F redhot on its way. To start the lamp, open the air-valve C, fill the cup H with spirit and light it. When it has nearly all burnt away, but not before, close the tap C and pump some air into the reservoir. This air will, of course, collect at the top of the reservoir, above the oil. The pressure will force the

* Calor gas may be used instead of the paraffin blowlamp.

oil to escape by the only way now open to it—up the pipe E, through the almost red-hot tube F, where it will be turned to vapour, and out into the air at G, where it catches alight. When the flame has begun to burn satisfactorily it is well to pump as much air as possible into the reservoir, as this will send a good supply of oil to the vaporizer F. To extinguish the lamp it is only necessary to open the valve C. This relieves the pressure and no more oil is forced up the tube E, so the lamp goes out at once. If you begin to pump air into the reservoir before the vaporizer is hot enough, you will drive through the jet G a stream of paraffin instead of gas, and this will burn with a large smoky flame. The remedy is: open the valve, and the flame will go out. Then start afresh by heating the vaporizer with a further supply of methylated spirit. The lamp will burn upside down or in any position, but it sometimes happens, when the oil is nearly used up, that a sudden shake may put the flame out. Dense fumes of paraffin vapour come from the jet instead. A match held near G may light the lamp again. But if the pressure is too great it may blow the match out instead. Therefore relieve the pressure a little by opening the valve C for a second or two. The jet will light up quite easily then. But at any time you can stop the lamp by opening the valve: so you will have no real difficulty with it. As a rule, as soon as the lamp is fairly alight, pump as hard as you possibly can. The lamp will then go for a quarter of an hour or more without any further attention. The flame from an Ætna lamp, quart size, is about 9 inches long, blue in colour and it roars considerably. When you have finished with the lamp and the flame is extinguished always leave the valve open. If you do not and the lamp is warm, oil will slowly rise in the tube E and flow out of the jet. Some of this oil will become burnt inside the vaporizer when next the lamp is lighted and clog the jet. Special needles are provided with the lamp for cleaning, and they should be used if ever the jet seems to have become at all clogged. Should you run out of methylated spirit, the lamp can be lighted by using " meta fuel," or even, though it is not a good way, by holding the vaporizer, till hot, between the bars of an ordinary fire. Then close the valve and pump as usual.

It sometimes happens that one has to deal with a larger piece of work than the lamp can conveniently cope with. The simplest way to overcome the difficulty is to make up a coke fire in an ordinary fire grate and wait until it has burnt clear. Then make a hollow place near the centre and place your work in it. The heat of the fire should be sufficient to make the whole work red-hot, and if the flame from the blowlamp be brought to bear on it while yet in the fire, any part may be sufficiently heated to make the solder run.

The old method of soldering, employed before the introduction of coal-gas, was that in which a charcoal fire, excited by a blast from one or more pairs of bellows, was used. This was the method invariably employed until the middle of the nineteenth century, and in many places, notably the East, it is used to this day. Much of the most beautiful work in existence was executed by its aid. Such a furnace can easily be fitted up for work in any place where ventilation is good. This is important, because with coke or charcoal carbon monoxide gas is evolved. This is exceedingly dangerous in a confined space.

Charcoal may be purchased almost anywhere, or it can be made in small quantities as follows: Fill an iron box—an iron saucepan, for instance—with small logs of wood. Close it to exclude the air and fasten the lid on with stout iron wire. But leave an opening for the escape of the gases. If the lid fits loosely it will do. Place the saucepan on a fire and leave it there until no more gas is driven off. Remove it from the fire and leave it till cold and the charcoal will be found ready for use. Use a cast-iron saucepan, not a soldered or enamelled one—for it would probably fall to pieces in the process. Then make a sheet-iron tray or hearth measuring about a foot across, with sides 2 inches high. It is well to make it work on a pivot, for it is a very great convenience to be able to turn work about while soldering. In the centre of the hearth is a small flat box of sheet-iron in the top of which a large number of small holes have been drilled. This box is connected by a pipe with the bellows. To make the hearth ready for soldering, place a red-hot coal on or near the perforated box and heap the charcoal over it. Blow with the bellows, gently at first, but harder as the fire spreads, just as you have seen a blacksmith do. When a good fire has been obtained, level a space near the centre and there place your work, piling up the hot charcoal all round. Work the bellows till you see the solder flow, then cease blowing and move some of the charcoal away so that the work may cool down. The old workers used to have for small work a thin iron bowl with many holes punched through it from the inside. This

33

bowl they placed over their work and heaped the charcoal right over both. They would leave one of the punched holes uncovered so that they could look in from time to time to see how the work was getting on. The holes in the bowl were punched from the inside with a sharp spike. This left ragged edges on the outside of each hole, which kept small pieces of charcoal from falling in.

A furnace which will require no bellows can be made in the following way. Take some clay and beat it up well with a little sand. With this or with bricks build a circular furnace about a foot in diameter inside, with walls 4 inches thick. Leave a hole 4 inches square at one side near the ground. Just above this put an iron grating all over the floor of the furnace. The air will then be able to enter at the square hole and pass through the grating. Build the walls straight up for about a foot above the grating. Then arch them over the top, leaving room for a piece of 3-inch iron piping for a chimney. This should run into an ordinary house chimney. Leave an opening at one side, 6 inches square, for a door, and close it with a piece of firebrick. Make two or three peepholes through the side of the furnace, closing them with pieces of mica. Put a thick layer of charcoal over the grating and light it by putting some red-hot coals among it.Then close the door. You will get a good draught and can regulate the heat by varying the size of the opening under the grating. The amount of heat produced varies with the wood from which the charcoal was made. That made from birch is said to give the highest temperature. When the furnace is hot the work to be soldered, resting on a piece of thin sheet-iron, is placed on the hot charcoal and the door closed again. It is necessary to watch the work all the while through the mica window. Immediately the solder flows, open the door. This, by stopping most of the draught through the charcoal, will prevent the temperature from rising higher. Remove the work at once with a pair of long-handled tongs. A furnace very similar to this was very widely used in olden times, though instead of the long chimney bellows were often employed to provide a forced draught. It was used also for enamelling. The grate under the ordinary scullery boiler or copper is arranged in a very similar manner.

It is well to remember that the fumes given off by hot charcoal are injurious, so they should be led into a chimney or into the open air.

CHAPTER V

SOLDERING (*continued*)

Soft solder. Composition of soft solders. Fluxes. Soldering bits. Various hints. Removal of soft solder.

W E NOW COME to the soft solders. They melt at a comparatively low temperature, so they may be used for soldering almost any metal or alloy. Soft solders consist chiefly of tin and lead, though other metals are added sometimes to lower the melting point or for other purposes. Mixtures of tin and lead fuse at a temperature lower than the melting points of either tin or lead. So a suitable alloy—that is to say, a mixture of tin and lead—may be used as a solder for either of those metals. It has been found that an alloy containing 2 parts of tin to 1 of lead, or, more precisely, 63 per cent. of tin to 37 per cent. of lead, has a lower melting point than alloys made in any other proportion. It fuses at 183° C. It is also nearly the hardest of all the lead-tin alloys. As the two qualities generally reckoned the most desirable in a soft solder are (1) a low melting point and (2) strength, this alloy forms one of the best soft solders known. An alloy containing 46 per cent. tin, 54 per cent. lead and $\frac{1}{4}$ to $\frac{1}{2}$ per cent. antimony is actually the strongest of the so-called soft solders.

There is another alloy of tin and lead much used by plumbers. They employ it for " wiping " joints in lead pipes. It consists of 2 parts of lead to 1 of tin; its melting point is about 250° C. This alloy undergoes a prolonged pasty stage on cooling, and it is on this property that the plumber depends. At temperatures above 183° C. the mass consists of granules of solid lead-rich alloy floating in a liquid which is almost identical with the 63/37 solder mentioned above. The mass continues in a pasty state until it has cooled down to about 180° C. This and the 63/37 solder are the two soft solders in general use. Occasionally a solder or an alloy for casting is required with a much lower melting point. For this purpose either bismuth, cadmium or mercury is added to the tin and lead. Thus an alloy composed of 2 parts bismuth and 1 part each of tin and lead will melt in boiling water. For further particulars of these fusible alloys see Chapter XXXII.

Soft solder may be bought in sticks or it can be made from its constituent metals. When melting them it is well to use a deep narrow-mouthed vessel rather than a shallow wide-mouthed one, for the metals oxidize rapidly when heated and exposed to the air. A layer of lead and tin oxides forms on the surface. This effect can be largely prevented by putting a little fat or resin on the surface of the molten metal, which it covers on melting and so protects the alloy from the action of the oxygen in the air. The metal should be thoroughly stirred with a stick of green wood before pouring. The gases liberated by the charring of the wood assist in bringing the dross to the surface. This should be skimmed off and the metal poured at once. A good mould may be formed from a piece of angle iron propped up level on the floor at such an angle as to form a long, narrow trough the ends of which can be stopped up with little heaps of sand or clay. Pour the solder into the trough to a depth of about $\frac{1}{4}$ inch, starting at one end and moving towards the other. When cool the solder will be in a long triangular stick ready for use. Soft solders, complete with one or more cores of flux, may be purchased wound in coils like cotton. They are convenient to use and may be applied with an electric iron or an ordinary copper soldering-bit. Soft solder does not seem to have come into general use before the fourth century B.C., when in Greece it was employed in soldering the handles on to bronze vases and for similar work; but at least one example is known from Al Ubaid, Sumeria, dating from the third millennium B.C.

An extremely useful proprietary solder is that known as Fryolux Solder Paint. It consists of a mixture of finely powdered solder and an active liquid flux. It is usually applied with a brush, just like paint. It can be worked into any space, large or small, while cold; and when heated the solder flows and makes the joint. Any flux residue left after soldering may be removed by washing in water or by wiping with a damp cloth. One could hardly wish for a more conveniently-handled soft solder.

The tools required for soft soldering are few and inexpensive: a soldering bit or other heating apparatus and some pieces of solder, with some zinc and acid to make a flux. The flux employed may be zinc chloride (" killed spirit ")—prepared in the manner

described below—sal-ammoniac, resin or tallow. The purpose of
the flux is to keep the air away from the heated metal and to assist
the flow of the solder by dissolving the oxide. For iron or steel
" killed spirit " is used as a flux. But for copper and its alloys and for
the more precious metals there are various alternatives, though zinc
chloride is still generally employed. To make " killed spirit," i.e.
a solution of zinc chloride, take 8 oz. of hydrochloric acid (known
sometimes as muriatic acid, or spirit of salts) and put it in a strong
dish, such as a 2-lb. jam jar, in the open air. Add to it pieces of clean
zinc cut small. The acid will boil violently, getting quite hot,
splashing all around and giving off unpleasant fumes. Do not,
therefore, add too much zinc at a time or the acid may get hot
enough to crack the dish. Go on adding zinc till no more gas is given
off. The acid now is said to be " killed." When quite quiet the
liquid, which is now zinc chloride, is ready for use as a flux. Pour
the clear liquid into a bottle. You can use a stick, a brush or a
chicken's feather to apply it to the joint. A flux for soft soldering can
be made in the form of paste in the following manner. Take some
petroleum jelly, to 1 lb. of this add 1 oz. of chloride of zinc, prepared
as described above. Mix well, and the flux is ready for use. Prepared in this way it has the advantage of not spattering. Wash the
work thoroughly after soldering. Powdered sal-ammoniac mixed
into a paste with water also works excellently. A flux which may be
used on any metal except aluminium is made of the following ingredients: ½ pint spirit of salts, zinc enough to kill it, ¼ oz. sal-ammoniac
and 2 oz. water. Tallow, powdered resin or resin and olive oil are
largely used by plumbers as a flux for making joints in lead pipes.
Activated resin fluxes, e.g. " Alcohre " are now available and are
very effective.

The soldering bit (Fig. 15) has a copper head and an iron shank.
The head is formed from a bar of copper, either pointed or flattened
out to a chisel shape. The shape shown in Fig. 16, with the head
fixed at right-angles to the shank, is a most convenient form. In
buying or making a soldering bit be sure that the copper head is
not less than a pound in weight. Smaller ones do not hold sufficient
heat to warm up any but the smallest pieces of work. Before using
the bit its edge must be " tinned," that is to say, coated with a thin
layer of solder. To do this, heat the bit in the flame of a gas-ring
or in a red fire—not a smoky one, for that would make it dirty and

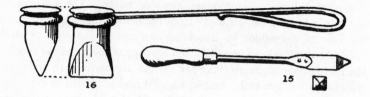

16   15

unusable. It must not be allowed to get red-hot, as it would become coated with oxide. It should feel decidedly warm when held 4 inches from the cheek. Put a small piece of soft solder and a lump of sal-ammoniac on a piece of metal cut from a tin canister. By the way, a tin canister is made of thin sheet-iron with a coating of tin on each side. Rub the soldering bit on the tin. Some of the solder will melt and stick on to the bit wherever the sal-ammoniac also touches it. Rub the bit about till a coating of solder is spread all over its working edge—the part farthest from the handle. The bit is now ready for use. It is a convenient but not, however, an essential tool, for the blowpipe can be employed equally well to melt the solder.

The work must be prepared by scraping the parts which are to be joined. They should be quite bright and clean. Any loose pieces may be tied into their places with wire. Put some flux along the joints. Heat the bit, then, holding it in the right hand, rub the edge on the piece of tin canister before-mentioned in order to ensure the cleanliness of the working edge. Then take a stick of solder in the left hand and dip the end of it into the flux. Slide that end up against the edge of the bit. In a second some of the solder will melt and flow on to the bit. At once rest the bit against the joint, taking care that the metal on both sides of the crack gets equally heated. The solder will run off the bit, following the flux into the joint as soon as the work is hot enough. If it does not flow easily, reheat the bit and add more flux to the joint. Any pieces of solder which fall on the bench should be picked up by touching them with the hot bit. The solder turns dull as it sets, therefore the work should not be moved till this change has taken place, or the liquid solder may not hold and the parts may be displaced. When all the joint is soldered, you may reheat the bit and run it all along the joint in order to spread the solder quite evenly, though you must be careful not to allow the parts to move before the final setting of the solder. It will be much easier to scrape off any superfluous solder now than if it had been left in uneven patches.

When flat surfaces have to be soldered proceed as follows. Clean them thoroughly and work all over each surface separately, using flux and soldering bit or Fryolux Solder Paint; or you may apply flux and lay a sheet of tinfoil between the parts. Then tie them together with binding wire and heat till the solder runs. You may add a little additional solder if necessary.

In joining together pieces of pewter, tin or lead, it is possible to do without solder altogether by melting or " burning " the pieces together. The bit should be used while very hot and the work done quickly, for if the tool were allowed to rest for more than a second or so a hole might be burnt right through the metal. Should such an accident occur, the hole, if large, may be plugged with fresh metal and the joint made while the plug is held in place by a pad of cloth or a piece of wood. Flux must be applied just as though solder were being used. Any superfluous metal can be filed or scraped off afterwards. In making lead tanks for some purposes, where chemical action might be set up between the lead and any solder used, all the joints are made or " burnt " in this way. The work is done with a blowpipe burning hydrogen, and a strip of clean lead is held against the joint in such a manner that it fuses together with the edges of the work. Roman lead water pipes were made from sheet lead coiled round a bar, with the two longitudinal edges bent upwards; and a mould of wood or clay was made and molten metal could be added to fuse the edges together. This made a perfectly watertight joint.

Soft solder, if heated to much above its melting point, will penetrate deeply into gold, silver, copper or brass. It forms a dark, spongy alloy with gold, silver or copper, as the case may be, which can be got rid of only by cutting the whole affected piece out. It will be clear, then, that no hard soldering can be done on any piece of work on which there is any soft solder whatever. You must either remove every trace of it first or abandon your intention of using hard solder.

To remove soft solder from gold or silver work, scrape off as much of the solder as possible. Then take:

3 vols. of Glacial Acetic Acid, and
1 vol. of Hydrogen Peroxide (20 vols.).

Put the work in the solution and warm it. Do not allow it to boil.

This solution dissolves the lead in the solder, and it leaves the tin on the surface of the work in the form of powder which may be removed with a scratch brush. The solution works slowly.

Another method is to take a boiling solution of

4 oz. Hydrochloric Acid (20 per cent.), and
½ oz. Ferric Chloride.

This solution removes the solder, but attacks the silver, putting a thick film of silver chloride over the work. To remove this, brush the surface of the silver with a concentrated aqueous solution of thiourea, applied with a " Rotaprint " glass brush. The silver chloride is dissolved and the surface may be brushed smooth.

Fluxes for Soldering

Material	Flux for hard soldering	Flux for soft soldering
Aluminium .		Stearin.
Brass . .	Borax.	Resin, sal-ammoniac or zinc chloride.
Copper .	Borax.	Zinc chloride, or activated resin.
Gold . .	Borax.	
Iron . .	Borax.	Zinc chloride, or activated resin.
Lead . .		Tallow. Resin.
Pewter .		Resin. Sweet oil or Gallipoli oil.
Silver . .	Borax.	
Steel . .	Borax.	Sal-ammoniac.
Tin . .		Tallow. Resin.
Zinc . .		Zinc chloride.

CHAPTER VI

FILIGREE AND OTHER SMALL WORK

Wiredrawing. Square and other wires. Tube or " chenier." Tools. Jeweller's bench.

QUITE A NUMBER of tools are required for this work, though most of them are not very expensive. Drawplates, pliers and soldering materials are perhaps the most important, so we will discuss these first. The usual form for a drawplate is that of a piece of steel several inches long, 1 to 2 inches wide and perhaps $\frac{1}{4}$ inch thick. The steel plate is pierced by several rows of holes. Drawplates are made with holes of various shapes—round, square, oblong, triangular, half-round, star and so on. The holes vary in size in regular order, the largest on a plate measuring perhaps $\frac{3}{16}$ inch in diameter, the next a very little less, and the twentieth or thirtieth hole perhaps $\frac{1}{16}$ inch. On another plate the series of holes may commence at about $\frac{1}{16}$ inch and go down to $\frac{1}{32}$ inch. On another the smallest holes may be so fine as to be almost invisible at their smaller end. All these holes are widened out considerably towards one side of the plate. In the construction of these drawplates the holes are drilled first and widened out at one end. Then a long tapering mandrel of the required section (round for round holes, square for square ones, etc.) is driven into each hole in succession, but to a different depth in each, with the result that each hole tapers slightly and is a little larger or smaller than its next-door neighbour. After the holes have been thus graded the plate is trued up, hardened and tempered. The drawplate is used in reducing wire to a smaller diameter or in altering its section —changing a round wire into a (smaller) square one, for example. It may be held in a vice or by cleats on a bench. Suppose that you have a piece of round copper wire $\frac{1}{16}$ inch in diameter which you wish to reduce to $\frac{1}{32}$ inch. At one end file a point about an inch long. For gold or silver wire you would not file the point, but produce it by hammering.

Gold, silver, copper or brass wires measuring up to $\frac{1}{16}$ inch may

41

be drawn down by hand, but for larger sizes a drawbench is necessary. A description of this tool is given on p. 131. Take the wire in your left hand with its pointed end towards you, and hold a pair of drawtongs (Fig. 17) or large pliers in your right. The end

of one handle of the drawtongs is bent round to give a better grip. Try the wire through various holes in the plate, putting the point into one after the other from the far side till you find a hole through which the wire (and not only the point) will just pass. Put the wire into the next smaller hole, and the point will come some distance through it and will then jam. Seize the projecting point with the drawtongs and firmly pull the whole length of the wire through the hole. If the length is considerable you may, after the first yard or two, hitch the wire round your body and pull without the aid of the drawtongs. The wire, by its forcible passage through the tapering hole in the plate, will have become smaller in diameter, longer and slightly harder. Pull it through the other holes in succession until you have reduced it to the required size. It is usual to oil or grease the wire, or the holes in the plate, to reduce the labour. Oil, tallow, vaseline or even soap may be used. Grease from a paraffin-wax candle acts well. Olive-oil soap is used by some professional wire-drawers. It is a good plan to wrap a rag soaked in the lubricant round the wire at the far side of the draw-plate when long lengths of wire have to be drawn down.

When the wire has passed through a number of holes it will become hard and springy. If you do not anneal it, it may break. Wind it into a close coil to as small as it will conveniently go; for small sizes, perhaps an inch or two in diameter, for thicker wire 6 inches, more or less. With thin wire be sure that no ends or bows are allowed to project, for they would almost certainly be melted in the annealing, so bind the coil with fine binding wire, if necessary, to prevent this. Then place it on the wig or charcoal and gently warm it with the blowpipe until it reaches a dull red heat. It is not necessary that it should be red-hot all round the coil at the same time, but you must make sure that every part of the wire has been made red-hot once. Use the soft, more gentle flame for this work, not the roaring or the pointed flame (p. 29). Small wire can be made into a coil, bound with binding wire and annealed by hanging the coil on the end of the jeweller's blowpipe and swinging it round and round over the jet until it is hot enough. Cool the wire in water, not pickle, and remove the binding wire. If you put silver and iron in contact into any sulphuric-acid pickle which has been in contact with copper, or into fresh pickle in a copper pan, a thin film of copper will be deposited on the silver, and it may cause trouble. The copper may be removed in a 20 per cent. solution of silver nitrate. Silver crystals will be left in place of the copper, and may be brushed off. The wire is now annealed and all the springiness has gone out of it. In reducing large wire to small it may be necessary to anneal it several times—whenever it gets hard, in fact. Wire-drawing is not a difficult task but it is well to buy wire as near as possible to the size you require and so save the labour of drawing it down.

When a comparatively small amount of wire is required, it can be made from scraps of metal in the following manner. Take an ingot mould of suitable form—that is to say, one with a long, narrow recess tapering to a point at the end opposite the pour (Fig. 7). Melt the scraps in a hollow in the charcoal and tilt the molten metal into the mould (see p. 15). Larger pieces may be obtained by cutting a strip from the edge of a thick sheet of metal, but in either case take great care to remove all projecting edges or loose pieces from the ingot or strip before you draw it down. You must at any cost avoid longitudinal folds or pleats, for they would produce cracks running down the wire. So, by means of a hammer, file or scraper, true up your ingot that no cracking or scaling can take place. Also examine the wire from time to time while you are drawing it down. To draw wire which is not circular in section requires a little more care. In making square wire, for example, there is some risk in the earlier stages—before the corners have become sufficiently developed—that the wire may become twisted in its passage through the plate, with the result that the corners are damaged or the wire broken. To avoid this, feed the wire into the hole quite truly, holding it with pliers if necessary. Another plan is to allow it to pass between the jaws of a wooden clamp or between two boards screwed closely together before it reaches the drawplate. Every precaution must be taken to avoid twisting.

Wire oblong in section can be made from square wire either by flattening it with the hammer or by passing it through the rolls. The rolls, or flattening mills, are a pair of hardened steel rollers, worked by a wheel or handle and adjusted by screws. Sheet metal or wire may be reduced to any thickness by flattening it between the rollers. Oblong wire of any size can be produced in this way by using wire of suitable size to commence with. This is a convenience, for drawplates do not always give the exact shape you require. In feeding wire through the rolls to flatten it, take care that it goes through exactly the same place between the rolls and at right-angles to the rolls all the while. If allowed to creep from side to side while being rolled it will emerge as a distorted ribbon of irregular width.

Half-round wire may be produced with the aid of a round-hole drawplate. To do this, take a piece of wire and slightly flatten it, either with the hammer or by passing it through the rolls. Fold the flattened wire in half. Make the point at the double end, soldering the two strips together for a short distance if they seem inclined to separate. Anneal the whole length of the strips. Then pull them through the round holes in the ordinary way. Take care that the two pieces do not get twisted as they go through the holes. Keep them true by holding the blade of a knife between them close up to the drawplate. Of course, two lengths of half-round wire are produced instead of one piece of round wire. In the same way oblong wire with the section of half a square may be produced with the square-hole drawplate, but be careful that it does not wind.

Hollow wire or tube can be made from strips of sheet metal. To make a tube $\frac{1}{8}$ inch diameter take a strip about $\frac{3}{8}$ inch wide. Mark off the strip from the edge of the sheet of metal with the dividers, holding that tool so that one leg runs along the bench against the metal while the other scratches the line on its surface (Fig. 18). This plan must, however, be followed only if the edge of the metal is true. Cut the strip off and see that its edges are true and parallel. Make a point at one end by cutting a small piece off each side of the strip (Fig. 19). Now take a piece of hardwood in which a number of grooves of different sizes, semi-circular in section, have

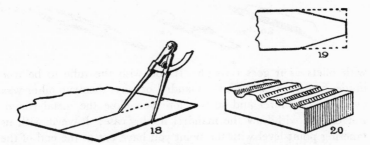

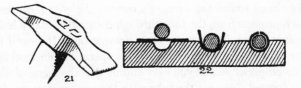

been cut; or a metal swage of the same form (Fig. 20). See that the sharp top edges of the grooves are rounded off. With a narrow hammer (Fig. 21), for example, tap the strip into the groove,

commencing near the edges. Or you may hold a mandrel (a length of round steel wire) in the line with the centre of the strip and drive both into the swage with a hammer which has a slightly convex face (see Figs. 22 to 24). It is most important that the metal near the edges of the strip shall be curved well, otherwise the sides of the tube may work thin near the joint. Turn the strip a little in the groove and by carefully placed blows tap the metal still further round the wire. It is indeed possible to close the metal completely round so as to form a tube. Should you do this, however, it is well to take the precautions of slightly oiling the wire to facilitate its withdrawal, completely closing the tube for a few inches only at a time, and gradually withdrawing the wire towards the as yet uncompleted end of the tube.

If the work is to be finished by the drawplate the strip is tapped round a certain distance in the swage, and the process is completed by inserting the prepared end in the drawplate and pulling through just as though it were wire. But to keep the opening in the tube to the same side (it might otherwise wander round spirally) hold the blade of a knife firmly in the gap just as it passes through the draw-plate; or, if the join has already got twisted round, hold it true

with pliers as it goes through. If you wish the tube to be true inside, first file a point on the mandrel or wire, then rub oil or wax over both mandrel and strip before you close the metal round. But do not withdraw the mandrel in this case; leave it with its tapering point level with the point you have cut at the end of the tube. The mandrel must be longer than the strip of metal (tube). Pull them through the drawplate together again and again until the outside of the tube has been drawn quite true and it has been reduced to the desired size. Fig. 25 shows the tube before it is completely closed round the wire. To remove the wire push the end of it which projects from the tube through the small end of a hole in the drawplate which just fits it. Then draw it out. It is well to use a copper rather than a steel wire for this operation, for steel is practically incompressible and you may unduly thin the metal of which the tube is formed. Anneal the tube with the copper wire inside it and drop it into oil before you attempt to separate it from its mandrel. The tube may be soldered up the side now if necessary. Hollow half-round wire can be made from strip. It should be first swaged nearly to shape and then put through a drawplate which has half-round holes, a pointed burnisher of suitable size being held in the hole in the drawplate against the strip. Hollow wire of almost any section can be made from tube or strip metal in one or other of the ways described above. Another kind of drawplate, not very frequently met with, is the ruby plate. It is used for extremely fine wire. As its name implies, the drawhole for the wire is pierced through a ruby. A moulding of any form, however heavy it may be, can be made by means of the draw-swage. A description of this tool may be found in the chapter on Mouldings, p. 129.

To straighten a length of wire, first anneal it and then stretch it tightly. If this is not sufficient, rub it while tightly stretched over the corner of the bench pin; this should take out any kinks. Another plan is to put a number of stout wire nails in a row in the bench and to bend the wire in a zigzag fashion to the left of one nail, to the right of the next, to the left of the third, and so on, then to pull the whole length of wire through the nails. The zigzag bending which it gets when passing the nails pulls the wire straight.

After drawplates and swages, pliers are the next essential tools for filigree work. Of these you will require several pairs: round-nosed pliers (Fig. 26), one pair quite small and one a larger size; snipe-nosed pliers (Fig. 27), two pairs, 4-inch; flat pliers (Fig. 28), one pair; tapered bell pliers (Fig. 29), one pair. A hand vice (Fig. 30),

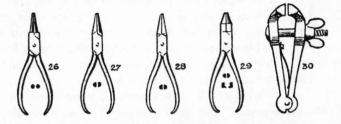

a pair of slide tongs (Fig. 33), beechwood or boxwood clamps (Fig. 32), a pin vice or universal holder (Fig. 31)—this is a four-jaw chuck fitted with a handle. It is useful for holding mandrels, wire, files, etc. Get all these tools of good quality. As the jaws of cheap

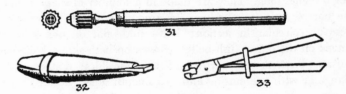

pliers either break or bend apart, so that you get no grip, avoid them. The inside surface of the jaws of pliers is scored to keep the work from slipping. But the roughening may be such that the work would be badly scratched. It is well to smooth down the extreme roughness by rubbing the jaws on fine emery paper until they can grip well without damaging the work. Avoid making them too smooth. To hold work firmly with ordinary pliers requires considerable effort. If, however, you take any ordinary flat-nosed pliers and cut the jaws down to, say, one-third of their ordinary length you will find that the strength of their grip is tremendously increased. In this way a use may be found for broken-jawed pliers.

Materials for soldering come next. First the jeweller's jet and mouth blowpipe. These are the tools generally used, though a few jewellers prefer to have a small hand blowpipe with bellows. If gas is not available the spirit lamp may be used instead. Jeweller's wig (Fig. 34). Charcoal. Some small pieces of thin sheet-iron. A

little plaster of Paris. Borax, slate and brush. Tweezers for picking up pieces of solder or parts of the work; it is well to have a pair of these of brass, for they can be used for lifting small articles into or out of pickle. Steel tweezers are not suited for this work. A very efficient pair of brass tweezers can be made from a strip of hard sheet metal, 7 inches long by $\frac{3}{8}$ inch wide, size 10 on the metal gauge. The strip has only to be folded in half, hammered a little, and the loose ends cut and filed to a point. Binding wire; this is best charcoal iron wire. The small sizes required can be obtained in $\frac{1}{4}$-lb. reels. Get Imperial Standard Wire Gauge Nos. 28 and 32. A little sulphuric acid (vitriol) for making pickle. A small copper boiling-out pan. For gold you use nitric acid pickle in a porcelain pan. The use of these pickles is explained on pages 24 and 61.

You will also require: (1) Needle files. These are slender files, 5 or 6 inches long. They are made in a number of shapes: flat— one narrow side is sometimes left smooth or " safe "; rat-tail— these are circular in section; half-round—flat on one side and convex on the other; fish-belly—convex on both sides; knife-edge —triangular with one narrow and two wide sides; donkey-back— triangular with one cutting and two smooth sides; square; three-square—in section an equilateral triangle. (2) A small, very sharp chisel for cutting filigree wires. It should have a small ball handle. Wires often have to be cut through at, say, an acute angle. To file them thus would be wasteful, but if you rest the part to be cut on a piece of brass or bronze (a worn halfpenny will do) you may cut it cleanly with the chisel. (3) A pair of straight snips or nail scissors. Japanese filigree workers fasten a loop to the handle of these, through which they slip finger or thumb. The tool is therefore kept on, if not in, the hand all the while. (4) Some scorpers. Get a few of these, flat and round, $\frac{1}{16}$ inch across the face, and one knife-edged. (5) Piercing saw frame (Fig. 35), 3 or 4 inch. (6) Saws, No. 00. The easiest way to put a saw in is to fasten it first in the top jaw— that farthest from the handle. When necessary, thread the saw next

48

through the hole prepared for it in your work. Then press the top jaw firmly against the bench so as to shorten the span for the blade. While the frame is thus compressed fasten the loose end of the blade in the lower jaw. When the pressure is removed the saw will be stretched tightly. The teeth should point towards the handle so that the saw cuts when it is pulled, not like a carpenter's saw—when pushed. (7) Drillstock and drills. The former is more useful if fitted with a universal chuck. (8) Cutting punches (Fig. 36) These

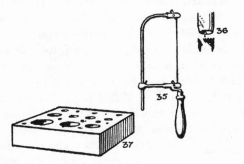

are steel punches with a sharp circular edge. They are for cutting out small discs from sheet metal. Be careful in using them not to let the sharp edge of the punch come in contact with a steel stake. Always put a piece of brass between the metal from which you cut the discs and the steel stake upon which you cut them. Give the punch a smart blow at first. Then if the metal is not quite cut through hold the punch firmly in the circular mark already made and give it a few lighter taps, rocking the tool gently from side to side as you do so.

It gets through easier so. A cake of lead or zinc is often used instead of the steel stake for cutting discs upon. Of course no brass is required in this case. The discs when cut will be slightly convex, but to boss them up more a doming block (Figs. 37 and 38) and set of doming punches are useful. (9) The doming block is a square or oblong piece of brass or steel in which is

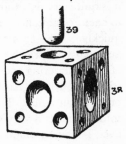

cut a series of hemispherical hollows. These cup-shaped recesses vary in size from $1\frac{1}{2}$ inches to $\frac{1}{32}$ inch. The doming punches (Fig. 39) fit the hollows. To produce a rounded boss or half-bead from a disc o metal, drop it into a hollow which is rather larger in diameter. Set the disc level in the recess. Take a suitable punch and place it quite centrally on the disc. Give it a good blow with a hammer and the metal will be driven into the hollow. If necessary, it may now be shifted to a smaller hollow and made into a complete half-ball by using the punch which corresponds with the hollow. You may even file off any metal which projects above the block before you remove the half-bead. You can make a half-bead of any size by taking a disc of metal one-third larger in diameter. If the metal gets hard, anneal it. If you wish to dome up a disc only slightly you have but to drop it into a hollow of considerably larger diameter and use a large punch. A doming block is not, however, an essential tool. Suitable hollows may be hammered in a cake of lead, tin or zinc or any other material which is hard and tough enough for the purpose. It is well, however, to put a sheet of thin paper between the disc and the block to prevent the transference to the boss of any trace of tin or lead or zinc, as the case may be. (10) A sandbag (Fig. 40).

(11) Triblets. These are tapering rods or mandrels, generally of steel. They are used for " setting " rings or collets true or for enlarging them after they have been soldered. To do this you slide the ring on to the triblet as far as it will go. Holding the large end in your hand, rest the narrow end of the triblet upon the bench so that the ring is pressed against its front edge. Tap the ring gently with the mallet, turning the triblet all the while. Keep the triblet pressed as far through the ring as it is able to go. When the ring fits the triblet it is quite circular, though it may yet require enlarging. If you wish to enlarge the collet, use a steel hammer. This will stretch the metal quickly. Take care though that your blows are placed regularly and that you stretch both edges of the collet equally. If on account of the hammering one side of the band grows convex as it rests on the triblet, you must hammer on the middle and the concave side to bring it true again. Triblets are made in various sizes. An old cotton spindle makes a very good small one, for it tapers from about $\frac{1}{8}$ to over $\frac{1}{4}$ inch in diameter. Oval, oblong or square triblets also are used. You should have others which go up to $\frac{1}{2}$ or $\frac{3}{4}$ inch in diameter. For sizes larger than this it is usual to true up a ring on the bickiron or sparrowhawk. The arms of these tools are not always truly

circular, but you slide the ring along the arm as far as it will go and turn the ring while tapping it instead of turning the stake. When a ring has been trued up on the triblet or bickiron it will be circular, but it may not be quite flat. So a flat stake will be required. This is a piece of steel 3 or 4 inches square, perhaps an inch thick, and quite smooth and true on top. The domestic flat-iron makes a very good substitute. Blocks of wood should be fastened each side of the handle so that it will stand firmly face upwards. (12) The jeweller's hammer (Fig. 41) has one flat and one rounded face. It weighs only a few ounces. To flatten work without marking it in any way a horn mallet (Fig. 42) or a fibre-faced hammer (Fig. 43) should

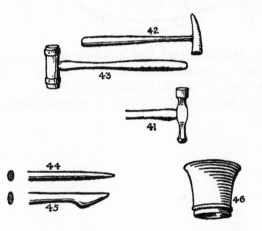

be used. The mallet is much the lighter tool of the two. (13) A steel burnisher or two (Figs. 44 and 45). (14) A jeweller's eye-glass (Fig. 46). If you take a length of piano wire, form a loop at one end for the glass and bend the remainder into a curve to fit round the back of the head, the glass may be kept in position without effort. The jeweller's bench (Fig. 47) has a large semi-circular piece sawn out of the top in front. From the centre of this curved recess a piece of wood projects. It is known as the " pin." It is a piece of hardwood, perhaps 4 inches long, with a sloping top, and it is let into the front edge of the bench. Work is held on or against it while it is being filed or otherwise proceeded with. To catch the filings a large piece of sheepskin is fastened under the top of the bench. It extends below the pin, across the

recessed front of the bench from arm to arm. The soldering jet is fastened on the right-hand arm, near its extremity. The lamp is so arranged that a ray of light is concentrated on the pin, at which so much of the jeweller's work is done, so that the job is always well illuminated.

CHAPTER VII

FILIGREE (*continued*)

Grains. Bosses. Rings. Leaves. Filigree wire. Soldering. Boiling out.
Granulation. Filed solder.

THE PRINCIPAL " motifs " used in filigree and other jewellery, besides representations of the human figure or animals are (1) jewels and their settings; (2) architectural forms, ships, crowns, crosses, shields and other symbolic or heraldic devices; (3) the leaves, fruit and stalks of plants; (4) Wires—plain twisted or plaited; (5) rings; (6) bosses and grains.

We will take grains, the simplest form, first. They have considerable decorative value, especially if they are arranged in groups. Mr. R. L. B. Rathbone, in his little book on *Simple Jewellery*, illustrates many beautiful arrangements. Grains also have an important constructional value, for when soldered close up to the point of contact of two other forms, the grain strengthens the joint considerably.

If you put a tiny fragment of silver or gold on the charcoal, and allow the tip of the bright blue flame from the blowpipe to touch it, it will melt instantly, and run up into a ball, or " grain." This little bead of metal will be slightly flattened where it rests on the charcoal when cooling. If you wish to make truly spherical grains, and it is worth while so doing, first make a number of little pits in the surface of the charcoal block. These pits can be made by pressing the head of a round-ended repoussé tool of the correct size into the charcoal. The pits should be about the size to take the lower half of the grain. Then lay the piece of metal which is to form the grain just over the hollow. When the metal melts it will form a practically perfect sphere and it will not run about on the charcoal as a grain formed on a flat surface will. With a little practice you can make grains pretty quickly in this manner. To produce a large number of grains of approximately the same size clamp a piece of silver in the vice and spread a cloth or paper beneath it to catch the filings. Take a file, the choice of which must be determined by experience, and with firm, even strokes file some of the silver away. The filings will all be of approximately the same size and weight. And each fragment, when melted, will become a grain. If after melting a few of the filings you find that the grains are not of the size you desire you must change your file, or your method of filing, till the filings you are producing fuse into grains of the size you want. But if you wish to produce hundreds or thousands of them all exactly the same size there is another quite reliable method. Take some fine wire and make from it, in the manner described below, a sufficient number of little wire rings, all of the same size. Now these rings, being of the same diameter and from the same wire, must have exactly the same amount of metal in each. Therefore when melted they will form grains of equal size. Take a little box made of sheet iron. Put a layer of powdered charcoal over the bottom of it. Then arrange rows of the little rings, side by side, but not touching each other. When the floor of the box is covered shake over the rings another layer of powdered charcoal. On that arrange another series of little rings. Go on with these alternate layers of charcoal and rings until the box is filled. Tie the lid on with stout iron wire, and put the box in the fire. Let it get bright red-hot. Then take it out and cool it in water. Wash the charcoal away. You will find that all the rings have changed into grains. When you have made the grains it is well to boil them in pickle to clean them, then to wash them in water to get rid of any traces of the acid, and afterwards to keep them in a little tin box for safety. It will be found convenient to have all the grains that you make, in whatever manner, accurately graded. So that you may employ on your work grains of any desired size. To do this you must devise some means of sorting them. Perhaps the simplest method is to provide yourself with a series of small sieves. To prepare these, purchase a few packets of sewing needles of various thicknesses. Through a sheet of cork drive a dozen of the needles, all of the same size, perhaps $\frac{3}{32}$ inch apart, allowing the points to project some $\frac{1}{2}$ inch. Drop some sealing wax over the eye ends of the needles and the back of the cork, so that the needles cannot work loose. Take a piece of sheet copper a few thousandths of an inch thick and lay it on a pad formed from several thick sheets of blotting paper. Over an area which could be covered by a penny, punch a great many holes in the foil with the needle-pad. You will find that the size of the holes may be controlled by pressing the needles a longer or a shorter distance through the foil—for the needle-points taper. Prepare a number of these discs, each with all its holes of one size, but each disc with different sized holes from those in the other discs. Take a sheet of thin sheet brass or copper, $\frac{1}{2}$ inch in width, and from it cut off a number of strips of different lengths. Let the first be 4 inches long, the second $4\frac{1}{4}$, the third $4\frac{1}{2}$, and so on, till you have one for each perforated sheet. Turn each into a circle and solder its ends together. Then on the bickiron (Fig. 113) hammer each into a true circle, and adjust their sizes till each one will nest easily into its larger and smaller neighbours. File the top and bottom edges level. Now take the piece of perforated foil which has the smallest holes, and stand the largest ring upon it. Soft solder them together. Cut off any superfluous metal and file up tidily. Do the same with all the rings and perforated sheets in order. In this way you will have made a series of nesting sieves with which you may sort your grains into groups of equal size. Keep each group in a box of its own.

Grains $\frac{1}{8}$ inch in diameter or larger can be made in this way, but when big they use up so much material that it is better to make hollow bosses instead. Little discs of metal may be formed from grains by flattening them on a stake with the hammer. If the grains should show signs of cracking round the edges before they are sufficiently flattened for your purpose, they must be annealed. Then you may proceed with the hammering. Flat discs form a valuable contrast to more rounded forms in a design. Should you wish to do so you can boss them up in the doming block, or even in the lead cake. But to boss up flattened grains is to go a long way round, for if you have a set of cutting punches (see Fig. 36) you can cut the discs from sheet metal. If you have not got the punches you can cut the discs out with shears, and file them up truly. It is not always necessary to raise bosses very high. A slight convexity is often sufficient to catch the light. Concave discs also make an effective contrast with the wirework among which they are placed.

Rings of wire have many uses. They are both decorative in themselves and valuable as a means of linking up different parts of the work. The rings can be made from wire of any section, plain or twisted. And the links themselves may be of round, oval, square, oblong, diamond, hexagonal, or almost any other plan. The usual way to make them is to take a mandrel, a piece of wire or tube, the section of which is that of the opening through the rings required.

55

Thus, you wish to make a number of rings, oval in section, measuring $\frac{1}{8}$ by $\frac{3}{32}$ inch inside. Take a piece of steel, iron or brass wire of the required section, cut a strip of thin paper, $\frac{1}{2}$ inch wide, and paste or gum one side of it. Wind this paper spirally round the wire, taking care not to allow any overlapping. Next take some of the wire you are to use and, after seeing that it has been annealed, grip one end of it against the paper-covered mandrel with the hand-vice, slide-tongs or any other convenient tool. Then wind the wire closely and evenly upon the mandrel, turning the latter with the right hand, and keeping the wire tightly strained with the left. The wire should be wound quite straight round, not diagonally across the mandrel. If the coils take this diagonal direction they will turn out larger than you wished. Wind as many coils on the mandrel as you wish to make rings. You may then anneal the coiled wire while it is on the mandrel, if that is a tool whose temper is of no importance. The strip of paper will be burnt away in the process and the wire may be afterwards slipped off the mandrel without any trouble. It is not necessary to use the paper strip when winding small circular rings—they will generally slide off easily enough if you have not a very long coil. But with other shapes the wire is found to grip the corners of the mandrel so tightly that the coils can only be withdrawn from it with difficulty. So use the paper except for circular rings.

You now have a close spiral of wire. To cut it into rings you can either grip the coil in the clams, gently, not to crush it; or hold it in the hand-vice, first putting in a piece of leather to protect the coil from the roughness of the jaws, and then cut through one side of each coil with the piercing-saw. It is well to use a fine saw too. The rings, as they are cut through, may drop out of the clams. They are safer so, for otherwise they might get in the way of the saw. A quicker way of cutting off the rings is that of using the snips or scissors. It is only necessary to watch that you cut straight up the coil—you might otherwise get more or less than a complete ring. The extremities of rings which have been cut with the snips do not come together quite so neatly as those of rings which have been cut with the saw, but if you are making the rings only to melt them into grains this will not matter. There is yet another way of cutting the rings from the coil. Take a piece of steel wire, the size of the mandrel upon which you wound the wire. Insert at one end a small piece of clockspring, leaving part of it, sharpened to a knife edge, projecting on one side. Slide the coiled wire down until its last turn rests against this spur. Put the other end of the iron wire through the small end of a hole in the drawplate, which will just admit it. One end of the coiled wire therefore rests against the drawplate, and the other against the sharp spur. If the iron wire is now pulled through the drawplate, the spur on its further end will cut through each coil of the wire in succession. There are two precautionary measures which should be taken first, however. Slide a milk bottle over the coil of wire. The rings, when cut off, will fall into the bottle instead of flying all over the place. Put a brass washer on the wire before it goes through the drawplate. The washer will keep the spur from injuring itself against the drawplate when it has cut through the last coil. Rings other than circular should be cut through at some part of their circumference which will not show much in the completed work.

The extremities of rings cut from a spiral coil do not quite meet. Before using them in your work, they must be straightened. Rings made from fine wire may be flattened by pressing them on a flat stake with the face of a hammer, but stouter rings should be gripped on either side of the joint by two pairs of snipe-nosed pliers. With a very little manipulation the ends may be brought opposite each other. If the ends do not quite meet, the ring should be gripped right across its diameter with the pliers, and a gentle pressure applied. This compression should be repeated in one or two directions across the ring to make it truly circular, care being taken not to press too hard, for the ring might then collapse entirely. The joints may now be soldered, though many workers prefer to leave the soldering until the work is being put together. A large thin ring is more difficult to solder than a small one. The ring may be bent until its ends spring past each other, and so are able to hold together when placed in contact; or the ring may be stood up on the charcoal against some support, its ends resting downwards in a scratch made on the surface of the charcoal to keep them from slipping; or it may be soldered after being pegged down on to the charcoal.

If you hold the end of a piece of fine wire near the tip of the bright blue blowpipe flame, it will melt and run up into a bead. This little mass at the end of the wire may be hammered out flat on the stake, and then filed into the form of a little leaf, the wire forming its stem. The end of the wire will melt easier if you dip it first into borax. To make a larger leaf, melt upon the charcoal a fragment of the metal you are using, and when it is quite liquid, heat the end of a wire in the flame and thrust it into the mass. Directly they unite, stop blowing. The bead of metal will remain molten for some seconds, so you have time to press it flat on the charcoal with, say, the flat side of the tweezers. This will save trouble in beating out. A larger leaf still would be made from sheet metal with perhaps a wire soldered on for a stalk. Branches can be made by uniting a number of leaves made as above, or by beating them up from a sheet of metal by repoussé work. Fruit and flowers are made in a similar manner. The old method by which seed pearls are used to represent grapes is also worthy of remembrance.

The making of various patterns of twisted wires is discussed in another chapter. It is not necessary here to emphasize the great decorative quality of this material, which is to be found on a large proportion of the objects made by jewellers and silversmiths. It is a pity, however, that of the many beautiful varieties of this work made by the old goldsmiths, so few, perhaps half a dozen altogether, are used now. Wires used for filigree proper are generally flattened, not round, for wire which measures less in one direction across the section than in the other is easier to bend. It also keeps flatter on the background, if it has one. In filigree work a tracing of the design is fixed on to a flat stake with a few little pieces of wax. The wire to be used is bent to fit the curves with a pair of pointed pliers or tweezers. It is cut where required by resting it on a piece of brass, and then pressing the point of a very sharp chisel through it. The chisel cuts cleaner than a pair of shears or snips, however finely they may be set. Each piece of filigree wire after shaping may be stuck into its place on a thin piece of sheet iron with the gum solution. If, however, it is very important that it, or any other light piece of work, shall accurately retain the exact curves given it, it must be annealed before it is fastened into its place. This annealing is done either on or in a metal pattern made to the required shape.

It is not very easy to put twisted wires on to work neatly, for the solder has a great tendency to run to the wire and clog it. You must try to keep the flame from the wire until the remainder of the work is hot enough to melt the solder. You manage this as a rule by applying the heat to the underside of the work, or at any rate in such a manner as to keep the wire cooler than the part of the work to which it is to be soldered. If you allow the wire to get very hot it will stretch and refuse to go back to its correct dimensions again. It was in overcoming such difficulties as these that the experience of Mr. Littledale, referred to on p. 10, has proved so valuable.

If a ring of wire is put round a setting it is well to join the ends first, for it is easier to keep in place so. If it goes on a plain tube you may file a tiny groove round the tube first just to make a home for it.

It is almost impossible to describe in general terms the manner in which the other motifs mentioned at the beginning of this chapter are prepared. The various forms may be stamped, forged, swaged, pierced out, cast, electrotyped, raised, worked in repoussé, or produced by a combination of several of these processes. Each fresh piece of work presents a new problem, and the experience of the worker must guide him in deciding which method he must adopt to solve it. To attempt here to grapple with all the problems which might arise would be futile. But in the various chapters in this book sufficient information may be found to enable the craftsman to do the work in a practical manner. The rest must be left to his ingenuity.

We proceed then to a consideration of how the parts of a piece of jewellery may be brought together and soldered. Let us take first, as a simple example, the soldering together of a group of two, three or four grains. Arrange them on the charcoal block. But, as they will probably roll about more than you wish, you may fix them in position by pressing them a little into the block with, say, the flat side of the tweezers. See that there is some gum mixed with the borax. With the tip of the borax brush moisten each grain where it touches its neighbours. Then with the same tool pick up a tiny piece of solder and place it on the joint. See that the liquid borax quite covers the solder. Do this to each of the joints. Or, using a pair of finely pointed tweezers, dip the paillons of solder into the moistened borax and then place them in position. The solder for such small work may be rolled down to size 1 on the metal gauge, and cut into paillons as small as you like, perhaps $\frac{1}{32}$ inch in each direction for a single joint between grains, but larger for a joint where three grains meet. You must be careful to avoid the use of too much solder on this light work. Of course, sufficient solder must be used to make a sound joint. Any surplus tends to make the work look heavy, and it is almost impossible to remove it afterwards by filing. Think first how much will be required to fill the joint, and put on just that amount. It takes less time to cut a paillon of solder to the correct size than to try to remove any surplus afterwards!

To solder the work, bring a very gentle flame near it, and apply the heat so that the borax boils up very quietly, without disturbing the grains or throwing the solder off. A sharp blast would almost certainly cause one or other of these troubles. When the borax has settled down increase the heat a little. Notice that the pieces of solder, being smaller than the grains, may get red-hot first. If you allow them to melt they will run up into little beads themselves and perhaps fuse on to one of the grains, and they may not make good joints between the grains and the background. If, however, you are careful to heat up the background first, and to let the heat reach the solder sufficiently to melt it only after the grains are red-hot, then the solder may run between and fasten them together, for solder will always flow to the part of the work which is hottest (if it is boraxed, of course). If the solder gets hot too soon, and it may do so, move the work away from the flame for a second or two to let it cool. Then bring the flame to bear on the work in such a manner as to get the background and the grains equally hot. The flame may come almost directly downwards on them. When the temperature of the work has risen sufficiently high, the lumps of solder will suddenly collapse and the molten alloy run like water into the joint. Cease blowing instantly, and let the work cool down. It will be found that it is easier to unite two smaller groups to make a group of four or more grains than to solder them all at once.

If the heat is applied to the upper surfaces of the various parts of the work, they naturally get a little hotter than the undersides, which are in contact with the charcoal. The solder, therefore, will have a tendency to spread over the upper surfaces. To overcome this difficulty it is well, if you can, to encourage the flame to reach the work from its underside. To make this possible rest the work upon short lengths of iron wire or broken saws in order to lift it above the surface of the charcoal. Indeed, the jeweller's wig, Fig. 34, gives probably the best solution to the problem, for the heat penetrates the surface of the wig and flows under the work. Again in soldering bosses or flat discs or other pieces which might be injured by the solder getting on to their outer surface, it is well to do as much as possible of the soldering from the back. Of course, keep all borax away from a surface on which you do not want solder to run. Indeed, you may find it well to paint a little loam or whiting over such a surface, to protect it.

It is usual to " boil out " the work in pickle after each soldering. This process dissolves all the fused borax from the work, and it makes the surface of the work clean again, ready for the next solder-ing. You will remember that gold and silver, as generally used by jewellers, contain some alloy, usually copper, and that some of this alloy gets burnt out from near the surface of the metal each time the work is made red-hot. And that until the burnt matter (usually copper oxide) is removed from the surface, the soldering cannot well be repeated. The solder generally contains some zinc—a fusible metal, some of which is burnt out of the solder each time it is made red-hot. It will be seen, therefore, that " boiling out," or scraping the surface should precede any subsequent solderings if they are to be successful.

In soldering a fresh joint near one previously made it is usual to protect the old joint by painting it with a layer of rouge, whiting or loam made into a paste with water so that the solder does not run again. But you must be careful to keep every speck of such material away from the new joint which you are making, and also from your borax slate, as they prevent the solder from running properly. Further, the pickles used to clean your work will not dissolve them. It is necessary, therefore, to scrape or wash off the protective coating before " boiling the work out." You must also remove all the binding wire before the work is put into pickle, for if even a trace of copper is to be found in it, a thin film of that metal will be deposited on the silver, and such a film is difficult to remove.

Instead of forcing the grains into the surface of the charcoal block for soldering, you may keep them together in another manner. Make a solution of gum tragacanth and fasten the grains or other small pieces into their places with it. Or you can mix the gum with your borax and use them both together. It will be found, however, that a small piece of thin sheet iron forms a more satisfactory surface on which to fasten them with gum than the charcoal block. The iron has this advantage also, that should you wish the work to

61

be curved from side to side, or in any other direction, the thin iron plate on which the various parts are stuck can be made beforehand to take that form. When the grains or other pieces of the work are fastened in their places with gum, the work should be dried in a gentle flame before the joints are painted with borax or the solder applied. It is always a good plan to keep a lump of gum tragacanth on the borax slate, and to give it a rub in the borax solution occasionally. It prevents the solder from moving about so much. When the work is meant to be kept flat, after it has been boiled out, it may be placed on a steel stake and carefully tapped level with a horn or boxwood mallet. Or, if you wish to dome up a piece of work which is flat, you may place it on a sandbag, and boss it up by gentle blows from a convex-faced hammer or repoussé tool.

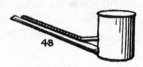

CHAPTER VIII

THE SETTING OF STONES

Tools required and their use.

IN THIS AND THE two following chapters the construction of the settings for various stones is discussed. Their attachment to the works they are intended to decorate is not dealt with here. There are a number of different ways in which stones may be set, though it has been found by experience that certain stones look better in one type of setting than in another. As a general rule, fine stones which are cut in facets (Fig. 49), gems, the beauty of which is largely dependent on the light which passes into and through them, and is reflected from the inner surfaces of the facets, look better in

open settings such as the claw or coronet. For in this setting, not only is the stone separated from its surroundings as a very precious thing, but light is able to pass between the claws to the underpart of the stone, and enter there, making the whole gem look more brilliant. On the other hand, stones which are flat, or which have the smooth rounded shape known as cabochon (Figs. 50 and 51), are generally put into one of the closer settings. But there is no invariable rule. The nature and shape of the stone, its position and importance in the work, should be considered in deciding whether it is to go into a coronet or cut down, gipsy or Roman, thread or rubbed over setting. For stones which are cut flat, or nearly flat, underneath, such as turquoises, half-pearls, opals or carbuncles, no opening need be made through the back of the setting. But stones with a " culet " or point underneath generally go into a setting which has a hole cut right through the metal at the back: this opening being squared out wider underneath the shelf or bearer upon which the stone rests. The widest part of a stone—where its top and underside meet—is called the girdle, waist or shoulder. Part of a setting must support the stone below this point, or the stone would drop through the setting, and part must come above, to hold the gem in. Stones which are not fairly level round the waist, or which are not well bevelled off above it, give rather more trouble in setting, so they should be avoided if possible.

The tools required for setting are:

1. *One or two triblets.* These tapering rods of steel are used for turning up and enlarging collets and rings. An old cotton spindle, as has been remarked, makes a very useful triblet. These spindles measure about 15 inches long, and taper from about $\frac{1}{4}$ inch to about $\frac{1}{16}$ inch in diameter. Other triblets, measuring up to about $\frac{3}{4}$ inch in diameter may be required.

2. *A number of scorpers* (Figs. 52 to 57). These are short cutting 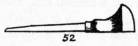 tools, fitting into small round handles. The handle being against the ball of the little finger, the blade of the tool is held between the thumb and first two fingers. Many workers prefer to have a handle for each scorper. But some use a single handle fitted with a screw chuck into which any blade will fit. In this case the scorpers are kept, points upwards, in a row of holes in a small block of wood. The tool required can be found and fitted into the handle in two seconds. Gravers and scorpers which can be bought ready made are generally far too thick at the back. To keep them in order a great deal of time has to be wasted in grinding away the superfluous metal—a third to a quarter of the weight of the blade. The tools must, of course, have sufficient metal in them to be rigid, but any additional weight represents just so much labour thrown away. If you wish to make some scorpers use round tool-steel rods, Nos. 20 to 30, Stubs' Wire Gauge. Forge the tools to shape, harden and temper them, as described in Chapter XXXVI. They are known by various names: " flat " scorpers (Fig. 53); " round " scorpers (Fig. 54) (sometimes

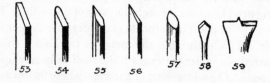

called " half-round "); " spitstickers " (Fig. 55); " knife-edge " (Fig. 56); " bullstickers " (Fig. 57) and so on. They are sharpened to an acute angle on the oilstone. It is usual to try the point on the thumb nail. If sharp, it will not slip at all, but will catch at once. If a bright cut is to be made by the scorper, the tool must first be rubbed quite bright on the blackstone. Should the bright cutting be required on a concave surface, the underside of the tool must be curved also, or the cut will not be clean.

3. *Cement sticks* (Figs. 60, 61). These are pieces of wood 4 inches long, $\frac{1}{4}$ to $\frac{3}{4}$ inch diameter. At one end is a knob of "cement," into which any small piece of work can be stuck. To make the cement,

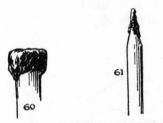

melt some resin and stir into it sufficient brickdust or plaster of Paris to make a thick paste. To fasten a piece of work on to the stick, warm the cement over a gas jet, and press the work into it. It will hold quite firmly when the cement is cold. If the underside of the work is very uneven, with recesses likely to become filled up with the cement, and thus give considerable trouble in cleaning out afterwards, it is well to cover the back of the work with gold-beaters' skin before pressing it on to the cement. Cement sticks are sometimes made to taper like a meat skewer. They are smeared with cement and are useful for holding collets, settings and other small rings.

4. *A wax stick.* This is a conical piece of prepared wax attached to a small, round stick, 1 inch long. It is used for picking up stones to try them in their settings. It is composed of beeswax mixed with (1) Venice turpentine—a viscous sticky material; (2) Venetian red —this colours and dries the mixture; and (3) glycerine—very little of this is required. It prevents the mass from setting too hard.

5. *Drillstock and drills.* The former is the ordinary jeweller's tool (Fig. 62). Its use is almost universal, for, besides its simplicity of construction, it has the great advantage of requiring but one hand to hold and use it, leaving the other free to hold the work. The drillstock should be fitted with a screw chuck, for with this almost any drill may be used. It will be remembered that the drill, when

in use, rotates alternately from left to right and from right to left. The cutting edges of the drill may be sharpened so that in whichever direction the tool may be rotating it will cut (Fig. 58), or both edges of the drill may be sharpened to cut in one direction. For drilling partly through thin metal a flat-bottomed drill is used (Fig. 59). It has a small projecting point in the centre which keeps the drill from wandering. This drill is used to sink holes for half-pearls, turquoises or other stones which are flat underneath. A slight peck is made with a narrow, round scorper in the centre of the space to be drilled, for the point on the drill to go into. But do not make this small hole very deep.

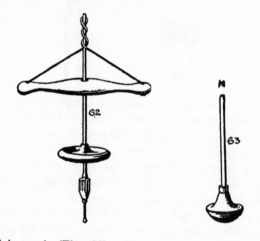

6. *Graining tools* (Fig. 63). These tools are made from short straight rods of steel, one extremity of which fits into a small handle, like that of a scorper. The other ends in a cup-shaped but not very deep hollow; the tool is used to shape any small projecting point of metal into a neat boss or grain, by rounding over its top and edges. The tool is held between the thumb and second finger, the forefinger being on the top of the handle. The hollow point is then placed over the projecting piece of metal, and the tool gently rocked from side to side. It presses the metal into shape. These tools are made by driving a rounded punch (counter-punch) into the end of a piece of steel rod which has been softened. The end of the rod is then filed so as to leave only a narrow rim, like a knife edge, round the hollow produced by the punch. The rim is smoothed

up with fine emery and the tool hardened and tempered. The hollow end may be kept burnished by occasionally working it on a small steel boss or "fion," made in either of the two ways now described. Take a piece of tool steel, measuring, say, 1 inch by 1 inch by $\frac{1}{8}$ inch. Part of an old file will do. Make it quite soft by leaving it in a fire until the fire goes out. Bevel one edge of it to a wedge shape (see Fig. 67). With hacksaw or slotting file make a series of cuts $\frac{1}{16}$ inch deep across the tapered edge of the steel plate, leaving a little square piece of metal between each cut. These squares will, of course, vary in size from nearly $\frac{1}{8}$ inch, down to a very small square peg of metal at the narrow end of the taper. Next round over each of these square pegs neatly with a file. Make each one as smooth and round a boss as possible. Polish them with a buff and fine emery; afterwards with rouge. Then harden the plate (Fig. 68). It is not necessary to temper it. Set it in a small cake of lead so that it will always stand upright. Polish up the little bosses finally with Sheffield lime made into a paste with water. The use of this material enables the highest possible polish to be given to steel articles.

A simpler and quite as effective a way of making fions is the following. Take a piece of steel wire an inch long, file each end to a rounded point, the size that you wish the tool to be, for graining tools and the fions on which they are kept bright are made in various sizes. But half a dozen, running from $\frac{1}{16}$ inch downwards, are perhaps as many as you are likely to require. Make the points as true as you can. Then harden them, but do not temper. Put the tool in the drillstock and rest the point on a fine emery buff. After a few turns of the drillstock the point of the tool will begin to penetrate the buff. Shift to another place. The fine emery will give an almost perfect polish to the point of the tool. You may also polish up the graining tool in the same manner. Another kind of graining tool (Fig. 64), has several, say five, little hollows in a row at its point.

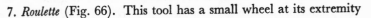

7. *Roulette* (Fig. 66). This tool has a small wheel at its extremity

with a row of shallow depressions round its circumference. These hollows produce a row of small bosses or grains upon any narrow edge of metal along which it is forced.

8. *Push tool.* A short brass tool set in a small handle like a scorper. It is made from a piece of $\frac{3}{16}$ inch brass wire. The point is slightly hollowed. The tool is used to press a stone firmly home into its setting.

9. *The setting or pressing tool* is a short square-ended tool of brass, set in a small handle like the last. It is used to push the tops of the claws of a coronet setting over the edge of the stone. To avoid any danger of the tool slipping it is gripped in a vice and its point roughened by tapping it with a file.

10. *One or two 6-inch lengths of $\frac{1}{8}$ or $\frac{3}{16}$ inch steel rod.* The ends are filed to conical points varying in sharpness. A large cork pushed on to the middle of the mandrel serves as a handle. The use of these tools is described under " Thread " and " Roman " settings.

11. *Clamp* for drilling pearls or other rounded objects (Fig. 65). This is made from a strip of stout brass folded in half. A series of holes, varying in size, is drilled through the two halves. The inner edge of these holes is rounded off to give a safer grip on the object to be drilled, and to prevent any injury being done to it by the sharp edge of the hole. By moving up the sliding ring the pearl can be gripped quite firmly between the jaws.

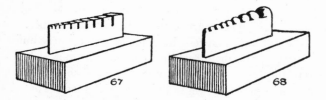

12. *Saw-frame and piercing-saws.*
13. *Several pairs of pliers, flat, snipe- and round-nosed.*
14. *Files of various shapes.*
15. *Shears.*
16. *A pair of spring dividers.*
17. *A punch with a matted surface.*
18. *An oilstone, a blackstone and a rubstone.* The blackstone is used for producing a burnished surface on a scorper after it has been

sharpened on the oilstone, when a bright or burnished cut is required. The rubstone is a flat-topped stone upon which work may be rubbed quite level. In fitting parts together it is a great convenience to be able to grind surfaces which are to come in contact quite flat and true.

19 *Burnishers* (Figs. 44 and 45).

20. *Polishing materials.*

21. *Soldering materials.*

CHAPTER IX

THE SETTING OF STONES (*continued*)

The Coronet setting. The Cut-down. Millegriffe. Thread or Thread-and-grain. Use of foil. Star, Gothic or Tulip. Pave.

THE CORONET OR CLAW SETTING (Fig. 69). Take a piece of silver about size 14. Cut off a strip the height you wish the setting to be, and in length a little over three times the diameter of the stone. With a pair of round-nosed pliers bend the strip into a ring. It is difficult to bend the extreme ends of metal of this thickness, so with the piercing-saw cut the ring as marked (Fig. 70), to obtain a true circle. This is an easier way than that of hammering the ends of the strip into shape on a triblet, or in a

swage or lead cake. The bending of the strip can, however, be done with a pair of pliers, one jaw of which is convex and the other concave. In gold-work the metal used would be thinner, say size 10, and therefore easier to bend. Squeeze the ends of the strip together. They should fit exactly and form a ring, the outside of which is about equal in diameter to that of the stone. Tie the ring together with binding wire and solder the join. Slide the ring on to a triblet and give it a few taps with the hammer to make it quite circular. Pass a file across the top and bottom to true them. When a number of settings have to be made it is quicker to take a piece of chenier, i.e. tube, of the right size, and cut the rings, or collets as they are called, from it. Next fasten the collet on to the cement stick, right in the centre of the cement end. About half the collet to be left projecting from the cement. It is a good plan to use a pointed stick thinly coated with cement and to drive the end firmly into the setting, then to melt the cement. It will hold the collet firmly.

When the cement has set hard, take a bullsticker, and with the outer, more curved part of its cutting edge bevel off the inner edge of the collet (Fig. 72), holding the stick against the bench pin and turning it to meet the tool. Turn the bullsticker in your hand and with the point cut a little shelf all round on the inside of the ring, rather more than $\frac{1}{16}$ inch below the top edge. On this ledge or bearer the stone will eventually rest, though the ring is, at present, too small to allow it to drop in. Be careful to leave sufficient metal in the rim to make the claws strong enough. Only a small ledge is necessary to support the stone, but it must be cut low enough in the collet to allow the rim to stand a bare $\frac{1}{16}$ inch above the edge of the stone when, later on, the stone is resting on the ledge. Should the stone be pointed underneath, the edge of the bearer must be bevelled off to match. In Fig. 73 the stone is shown resting on its bearer, though there would not really be room for it until the claws were cut and bent out. The drawing, however, shows how the top of the bearer must be sloped inwards to correspond with the pointed underside of the stone. Stones vary in the thickness of their edge, or waist, and in the angle to which the culet, or pointed underside, is cut.

The next thing to do is to cut the claws. Their number will depend a good deal on the size of the setting. You may make them any shape you like. Carve them into leaves or waves if you will, using saw, drills, files and scorpers, but take care that they are not too wide and stiff to allow you to bend the tops of them over on to the stone when finished. They must be strong enough to hold the stone and to stand any reasonable usage: $\frac{1}{16}$ inch or less is sufficient for their width.

To make a coronet with straight claws remove the collet from the cement stick. Take the piercing-saw and remove the metal from between the first two claws, commencing the cut just by the soldered seam. Cut right through the metal to about half-way down the collet, and below that point slope the cut outwards down nearly to the bottom (Fig. 74). Consider how many claws there shall be. If an even number, cut next the opening which comes exactly opposite the one you commenced with. Afterwards the two at right angles to these, and so on for an eight-clawed setting. Be careful to make each claw exactly the same size. Then with a fishbelly needle-file narrow the claws towards the top, and

71

with a round scorper (the underside of the point of which is slightly curved, and rubbed bright on the blackstone), true up the spaces between the claws. The lower part of the setting will now appear too heavy for the top, so make a series of cuts with a three-square, i.e. three-cornered, needle-file round the bottom also, one in line

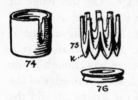

with each claw. Take away sufficient metal to leave only a row of rounded points or teeth round the bottom of the collet. Finish these also smoothly with a fine file. See that the setting will stand up truly—not leaning to one side. Next take a piece of silver, size 14, and cut from it a disc or " bezel," the size of the base of the collet. Take the collet and pass a fine file across all the points at once to make sure that they are of the same length. Tie the disc and collet together. Apply borax with a finely pointed brush, and with the same tool place a tiny paillon of solder by each point. After soldering, drill out the centre of the bezel, then take a three-square file and cut a groove all round its edge. This will make it look lighter. In Fig. 76 it is shown complete, although the groove round its edge is not made till after it has been soldered to the collet. Lastly, choose a round-ended repoussé tool which is a little larger in diameter than the top of the setting and press it gently straight down between the claws. It will force them all outwards and make them wide enough apart to receive the stone. The setting is now ready for polishing. Do this with threads and tripoli. It sometimes happens that several coronet settings have to be soldered together. To make sure that the tops of adjacent claws shall not be joined together in the process, it is well to bend them a little away from each other. They can be straightened up afterwards. A method of preparing a complete finger-ring with its collets ready to receive the stones, by casting it in one piece, is described in Chapter XXXI.

To set the stone, pick it up with the waxstick and try it in the setting. Bend the claws in or out as may be necessary. See that the stone goes fairly down on to the ledge provided for it. Hold it in place with the left thumb-nail, and push the tops of the claws over it with the square, roughened, brass setting tool Claws on opposite sides of the stone should be attended to in succession. See that the stone is level in the setting. Press the claws well down, into close contact with the stone. Then with a sharp scorper cut the point of the claws into a V-shape, cutting each side and the top of the turned-down part of the claws. With the pointed end of a mandrel smooth the metal right down on to the stone so that there shall be no possibility of anything catching in the claw.

Some ring-makers go about the work in a different manner. They make the setting to taper narrower underneath from the first. They make a rough sketch of the coronet, making it large enough at the top, in this case, for the stone to go in, and deep enough to cut the bezel from the same piece of metal. They produce the sides of the sketch downwards till they meet as shown in Fig. 77. Then with A

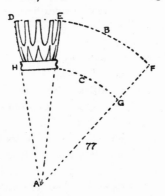

as centre they make the two arcs B and C. They measure along B $3\frac{1}{7}$ times the diameter of the top of the coronet DE. This measurement comes from D to F. Join F and A, cutting C in G. Then DFGH is the shape required. The jeweller cuts this out in the metal he is to use, bends it up for the coronet and solders it. It forms part of a cone, of the exact proportions of the coronet. But only if he is to finish and polish the work himself does he cut the bearer for the stone at this time, for some of the scraping and polishing which they receive might injure the claws if they were left thin at the top. So he leaves the bearer till the stone is ready for setting. With a file he levels the top of the collet, and then makes a mark with the dividers parallel to it, to mark the piece he is to cut off to form the bezel (Fig. 76). With a very fine saw, 0000, he cuts off the bezel from the lower part of the coronet. He then cuts the points below the claws, K in Fig. 75, files these level and the top of the bezel true. He does this so that the upper part of the coronet shall stand truly, without leaning. He then ties them together, solders them and puts the groove round the bezel as described above. He then cuts the claws themselves. After the polishing, the setter holds each claw in turn in a little nick filed in the side of the bench pin, and with a scorper cuts the bearer for the stone. Then with a pair of fine pliers he bends the top of each claw, above the stone, straight up, vertically. Some stones are so shaped underneath that it is not necessary to cut a bearer at all, their undersides being sufficiently supported on the tapering inner side of the claws. The setter now removes the stone and files the sides of the claws to a point. He then replaces the stone and with the pliers bends the top of the claws towards the stone, attending to two on opposite sides first, then to two at right angles to the first pair. He takes great care to keep the stone level on top. When the point of the claw is bent nearly into contact with the stone he files the end to a nice shape. Then with the setting tool he presses it right home.

Setters do not, however, all go about the work in the same manner. Another way of closing down a coronet setting is to use a closing tool. This method is preferred for rather thin coronets—those made from gallery, for example. The tool is shaped almost like a graining tool. It has a deep conical hole at the end, and is large enough to fit over all the claws at once. The tool is pressed firmly down on to the setting and rocked from side to side. It forces the top of all the claws inwards at once. It can only be used when the claws are of fairly thin metal. Coronet settings can be bought ready-made, as also can gallery, the material from which such settings can be made. It is in the form of long strips, variously ornamented, with claws along one edge. A sufficient length is cut from the strip to fit round the stone, and, when soldered and trued up, the coronet is complete.

The Cut-down setting (Fig. 78). This setting is often used for a fine stone, in a tie pin, for example. Cut a strip of silver, size 14, the height you wish the setting to be, and long enough to form a ring a little larger in diameter outside than the stone. Join it up and cut the shelf or bearer for the stone as described above. In this case, however, the setting must be large enough for the stone to fit right down on to its bearer as in Fig. 73. Test the fit of the stone from time to time while cutting the bearer: it should fit accurately. With a pair of dividers make a light scratch round the setting at *M*, and below this scratch bevel off the lower outside corner of the setting, as marked in drawing (Fig. 79). Fix the pin socket or ring, if one is required. All the soldering must be completed now, before the stone is set. If the setting is an open one, polish the inside of it. Put the stone in the setting, and press the edge over with the rough-ended brass setting tool, then rub the rim of the setting down as closely as possible to the stone, using a rough pointed mandrel for

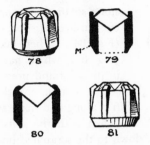

the purpose (Fig. 80). Next take a flat scorper and cut away sections of the rim, leaving narrow ridges standing out at intervals round the setting. The cuts should commence near the stone at the top, and slope outwards to the lower angle of the collet (Fig. 81) at M in the section. Here the cut ends and no metal is removed. The ridges or " points " thus die away to nothing at M, but are the original thickness of the rim at the top. They are separated from each other by a plain surface which slopes outwards from the edge of the stone to the corner M. At first leave the ridges the same width all the way down. It is easier to get them equal and straight thus. But when they are all spaced out equally, taper each one so that it is quite narrow at the bottom (Fig. 78). Round off the outer surface also. Then with a pointed mandrel and with a grain tool work round the upper part of the points, where they overhang the stone, rubbing the metal right down on to it. The setting may now be stoned, polished with threads and crocus, and finished with rouge on a dogwood stick.

A variation from the cut-down setting is known as " Millegriffe " (Fig. 82). In this setting proceed as described for the cut-down setting to the point when the edge of the setting is to be rubbed down on to the stone. A row of little grains separated by minute cuts has now to be formed close round the edge of the gem. Remove the stone and bevel off the top inner corner of the setting with a bright scorper. The cut must not extend far downwards towards the stone. Indeed, it must only just bevel off the inner edge of the rim B (Fig. 83). With the dividers scratch a line parallel to the top edge of the setting to mark the lower limit of the graver cuts, unless

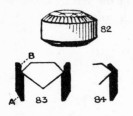

you like to take them down to the corner which corresponds with M (Fig. 79). With the setting tool press the rim in over the stone so that the angle below the bright cut surface, B, keeps the stone in place (Fig. 84). Then take the graining tool (Fig. 64), which has the row of hollows in its point and press it on the top edge of the setting with a slight rocking motion. Mark out and partly form several of the grains. Shift it along and mark some more. Go right round the rim with it. Then with the spitsticker make the cut between each grain, down to the scratched line. True up the tops of all the grains with the graining tool. They should be small and very even, for the slightest irregularity shows. To smooth up the outer sides of the grains take a brightly polished spitsticker and drag it sideways across the ridges. It will bump down into the hollows between them and scrape off any irregularities, leaving both ridges and hollows with a burnished surface. The effect of this setting is very light and dainty.

The " Thread " or " Thread-and-grain " setting (Fig. 85). This type of setting is frequently used when a number of stones are to come close together. Put the work on a cement stick, wet the stones on the tongue and arrange them in their places. The stones must be placed as closely together as you can put them. They should just touch. When all are in order make a mark with a spitsticker between each stone. A hole must now be drilled for each. Make a slight peck in the centre with a narrow, round scorper to make a start for the drill. It is safer to use a drill rather smaller in diameter than the stone, though quicker to use one the exact size, if you are quite sure of it. But it must on no account be too large. For pearls, turquoises and other stones which are flat underneath it is not necessary to drill right through the metal, the rule being that for culet stones—stones which are cut to a point underneath—the settings are always drilled right through. The recess for the stone

76

should be made just a little deeper than the shoulder or " girdle " of the stone. If, however, a pearl or a turquoise is so thick at the edge that it would require a hole deeper than the metal would allow, file the back of the stone. To do this make a small dent or hole in the board pin and turn the stone face downwards into it. Use a fine file and wet it slightly before you begin. If the metal for the setting is thin it is well to use a drill which is nearly flat across at the bottom, with a point in the centre to keep it true (Fig. 59). You can drill with this until the centre point begins to push out the underside of the metal, if necessary. It is well to clear the way for this centre point by first drilling a fine hole for it a little way into the metal. While drilling turn the work to see that you keep the same depth all round. When you have cut deeply enough, open

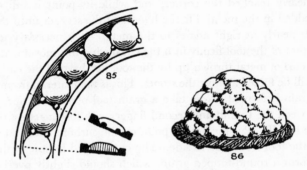

out the hole with the bullsticker, turning the work round and round as you proceed. With the waxstick pick up the stone from time to time and try it in the hole, pressing it in with the thumbnail or against the pin. When the stone fits exactly go on to the next, and so on until all the holes have been opened out. Then if the holes are pierced right through the metal, open out each one underneath, using piercing-saw and three-square files. When the work is backed, that is to say, made of two plates of metal of different qualities, one soldered behind the other, you may drill the holes right through the front plate before the back plate is soldered to it. This method saves time.

To set the stones. With the waxstick put the first in its hole, press it well home either against the pin, or with a brass hollow-ended pushing tool. With a pointed mandrel or the tang of a file, pointed but not very sharp at the end, make a few snicks at intervals round the stone. Each snick on the metal to be made directly towards the edge of the stone. The effect of these snicks is that a tiny scraping of metal is driven up against the stone, holding it in its setting. Go on till you can no longer lift the stone out with the waxstick. Then run the tool once or twice right round the stone, the side of the tool rubbing against it. This will drive up a line of metal all round the stone which will grip it firmly.

The grains are to be put in the corners wherever two or more stones meet. A series of grains, varying in size, can also be put to fill up any tapering spaces where there is not enough room for additional stones. To make the grains. Take a spitsticker and make a deepish cut, about $\frac{1}{16}$ inch long, towards the spot on which you wish to form the grain. At the end of the cut, when the tool has nearly reached the corner, and while its point is still deeply embedded in the metal, lift the handle of the scorper until the tool stands nearly at right angles to the metal. It is necessary to hold the point of the tool firmly into the cut during this movement. The little curl of metal thrown up by the tool just beyond the end of the cut will be forced against the stones. This is the material from which the grain is formed. Now take a grain tool of suitable size. Hold it between the thumb and second finger, with forefinger on the top of the handle. Put the hollow point on the curl of metal and gently rock the tool from side to side. The cup-shaped hollow in the tool will form a round-topped grain, which should slightly overlap the adjacent stones. Do not press the grain down very flat. Keep it high, and smooth, and bright. When all the grains have been finished, true up all the metal near by, cutting downwards to the edge of the stones with a spitsticker. The grains will hold the stones firmly. Finish with a spitsticker which has been rubbed bright on the blackstone. The thread of metal which gives its name to this setting is left as a sort of outline to the group of stones and grains, preserving the shape of the leaf or scroll, as the case may be. It is just a narrow edge of metal, cut smooth on top with a flat scorper. Keep it as close to the stones as possible. Make the scorper bright underneath before cutting. Settings are cut brightly in this way for pearls or soft stones, so it is not necessary to polish them. There would be some danger of ruining the pearls if that were done. A little dry plaster of paris is generally put into the bottom of the setting for a pearl. It makes the white backing which a pearl requires. A small piece of suitably coloured foil may be put at the bottom of the setting to brighten up or tint a stone.

In the fine gold jewellery of the Saxon period the craftsmen were accustomed to place a piece of gold foil beneath each slab of flat, polished garnet. The foil was enriched by an all-over diaper of little pyramidal points which reflected the light which passed through the stone. The points were made by stamping them up from the underside of the foil with an easily made tool. It may be formed from a chisel, the sides of whose cutting edge are inclined to each other at a right angle. A series of nicks is made across the edge with a three-cornered file, leaving a row of little pyramids in place of the original edge. The tool is hardened and tempered. With this punch a single row of pyramidal points may be driven up at each blow of the hammer while the foil rests, face downward, on a paper-covered sheet of lead. With a little care a close, evenly-spaced all-over pattern may be produced—one which brightens up a flat translucent stone.

" Star " setting is a variation from the thread and grain setting. It is used for single stones set in plain surfaces. The grains hold the stone in securely, and the rays of the star radiating from it enhance its importance. In the case of a pearl or other soft stone the rays would be bright cut, but for diamond or other work which will be polished afterwards, bright cutting is not necessary.

Yet another variety is the " Gothic " or " Tulip " setting. Instead of the straight rays of the star a series of scallops is cut round the stone with a round, bright scorper. The stone is kept in place by grains, like the last. In " Pavé " setting (Fig. 86), the stones are arranged as closely together as possible, the grains which keep the stones in place being the only metal left in sight. The work is done in the way described above for thread and grain work.

CHAPTER X

THE SETTING OF STONES (*continued*)

Gipsy or flush. Roman. Band or Rubbed-over setting. Cramp setting. Pin
setting for pearl. Drop stones. Other settings.

THE GIPSY OR FLUSH setting (Fig. 87). In this setting the
metal comes smoothly right up to the stone, without any
claws or grains, the stone looking as though it had grown in
the metal.

Drill and open out this setting as described above for the thread
setting. Make sure that the stone fits very accurately. But it must
not be sunk too deeply. Take a half-round file, and to the depth
of about $\frac{1}{32}$ inch file down the surface of your work, leaving
untouched, however, a little ring of the metal just round the hole
you have been at work upon. The inner edge of this little circular
band of metal, which forms the side of the hole, is, of course,
vertical. The outer edge slopes away, and the bank may be $\frac{1}{16}$ inch
wide at the bottom (Fig. 88). To set the stone, press it well home

87   88   89   90

against the board pin, or with the pushing tool. Then with hammer
and a matt-ended punch drive the metal in the circular bank
gradually towards and on to the stone. In the case of pearls and the
softer stones considerable care must be taken not to chip them. The
punch used has a rough surface, as it is less likely to slip than a
smooth-ended tool. Now burnish the metal right up to the stone.
By the time that the metal has closed down on its edge, the little
circular ridge of metal left round the stone by your filing will have
disappeared, and the surface of your work is fairly level. It should
now be filed true and quite level right up to the stone, leaving no
visible evidence of the manner in which the gem has been fastened
in. If you care to do so, you may with the punch drive the metal
down on to the edge of the stone immediately the hole has been

opened out, leaving the filing until afterwards. In this case the metal round the edge of the stone will be sunk by the punching to a lower level than that further away (see Fig. 90). This is put right when you file all the surface level.

A *seal stone* is set in much the same way. When the stone comes from the lapidary its corner B (Fig. 91) is generally quite sharp. With a corundum file grind off the extreme corner so as to form a new edge, less than $\frac{1}{32}$ inch wide (Fig. 92). Pierce out with the saw the hole in the ring, if it is for a ring. Then with the outer side of the bullsticker bevel off the edge of the hole to the outline of the stone and cut the bearer. When the stone begins to go into the recess you are cutting, it will either jam or rock on some projecting part. If it gets firmly jammed in, push the wax stick firmly on to the stone, then give the stick a sharp blow with the handle of a file. This will generally bring the stone out. To find out how it rests, mix a little crocus and oil, and put a very thin film of it on the underside of the stone. Then press the stone into the setting.

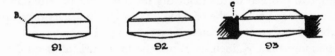

91   92   93

The crocus will show exactly where it touches. Go on cutting until the stone fits firmly on to its bearer. Then with a round scorper cut a channel or gutter C (Fig. 93) on the surface of the metal, all round the hole and quite close up to it. To set the stone, take a mandrel with a blunt point and rub hard with this tool in the gutter C until the ridge of metal between the gutter and the hole for the stone is driven over the edge of the stone, or drive the intervening ridge down with the matted punch. Work with the mandrel until the side of the tool is rubbing against the stone itself. The metal will by this time have completely closed over the little edge made by the corundum stick, and will hold the stone firmly. Rub the metal carefully down just against the stone. With a round scorper true up any inequalities. Polish with slate stone, with crocus, and finally with a dogwood stick and rouge. This setting is known by the name of " Roman."

The " Band " or " Rubbed-over " setting. This can be used for stones of almost any shape, but is more suitable for cabochon cut than faceted stones, for the unevenness of the latter makes the edge of the setting irregular. It is one of the simplest settings to make. Take a piece of sheet silver, size 4 or 5, and cut off a strip a little wider than the height you wish the setting to be. Bend it round (Fig. 96) and cut off sufficient to barely reach round the stone. The ring or " bezel " made from the strip can always be stretched a little by sliding it on a triblet and giving it a few taps with the hammer, but only by cutting a piece out can it conveniently be made smaller. It is therefore better to cut the band too short than too long. Tie the ring together with fine binding wire. Solder and file up the join. Make the ring true on the triblet and see that the stone will slip into it. Level the top and bottom with a few strokes on the rubstone. Then, if the setting is not to be fastened on to a larger piece of work, back it with a thin piece of whatever metal you are to use. Cut the piece rather larger than the ring, and tie the two together with wire. If the ring shows an inclination to get out of shape, or if it is for an irregularly shaped stone, it is better to proceed in the following manner. Put the stone in the ring and place both on the backing. Then with a graver drive up a number of tiny curls of metal against the ring. The graver cuts need not be more than $\frac{1}{32}$ inch long, but the little curls of metal driven up by them will effectually prevent the ring from twisting out of shape during the soldering. Remove the stone and tie the ring and backing together. Borax the joint and put paillons of solder on the backplate where it projects beyond the ring. Then solder. If you are to decorate the setting with a ring of twisted or other wire, do it now. Next boil out in pickle. Afterwards cut off all superfluous metal, using the shears right up against the ring, or the wires if there are any, and file up tidily. If, however, the setting is to be open at the back, either solder in a bearer for the stone to rest on, or back it as already described and cut out with the piercing-saw as much of the back plate as possible, leaving only a very narrow edge for the stone to rest upon. File up the opening neatly.

When a number of settings of about the same size have to be made, it is easier to take a piece of tube of the correct diameter and cut it into suitable lengths, instead of turning up each band separately. In setting stones or other objects which may be irregular in shape at the back, it is sometimes convenient to make the bearer from a ring of wire or a short piece of tubing made to fit the back of the jewel.

To set the stone. If it requires any foil or backing, first put this into the setting, then press the stone well home. See that the top edge of the setting projects $\frac{1}{32}$ inch, or less, above the shoulder of the stone all round (Fig. 94). The top of the rim is now to be pressed over the edge of the stone. This can be commenced with the brass pushing tool and completed with the pointed mandrel.

Take care to rub over an equal amount all round, so as to form a little flat edge close round the stone. Then with a small warding pillar file, with its smooth edge towards the stone, file round the setting to make the little edge quite true (Fig. 95). The work is now ready for polishing. Another way of closing the band setting is that of running a roulette round the rim. This crushes down the edge sufficiently to hold the stone in. Yet another way is that in which a pushing tool, the point of which is rounded from side to side, is used to press portions only of the rim of the setting against the stone (see Fig. 97). In setting a stone thus, it is well to press in a portion of the rim, say, at the two sides of the stone in immediate succession, than at the two ends in succession, and afterwards at the intermediate positions. A flat scorper is then used to true up the wavy top of the rim.

In old work, band settings were often made quite tall and conical. A ring of wire soldered inside near the top acted as bearer for the stone.

" Cramp " Setting. This is a variation on the rubbed over setting, and is much used for fragile objects. Turn up a thin band to fit round the stone, and solder it. Fit a bearer within upon which the stone can rest. The band must be wide enough to project about $\frac{1}{16}$ inch above the girdle of the stone. Parts of the border are now sawn away, leaving claws or " cramps " standing up at intervals round the setting. First with the dividers scratch a line parallel with the top of the setting to mark the lower limit of the claws. Then file away sections of the rim above the scratched line, taking care to leave the cramps strong enough. The spaces between the claws may be filed to a knife-edge on top (Fig. 98), or they may be serrated. In another form of cramp setting the top edge is nicked at intervals with a three-square file, leaving projecting teeth like those on a saw (Fig. 99). To set the stone it is only necessary to press over each cramp or tooth with the setting tool.

An enamel, a cameo or other object upon which you may prefer not to risk the effect of any pressure, can sometimes be set from the back of the work thus (Fig. 102). Take a strip of metal long enough

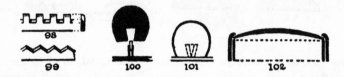

to go round the edge of the enamel, and considerably deeper than its thickness. Make from it a ring or collet into which the enamel will fit, and curl its top edge inwards. Make a second ring which will fit tightly into the first. This second ring is to keep the enamel in its place below, for it will act as a bearer. It may be fastened firmly by short pins passing through both rings, or by means of soft solder. The back of the enamel may be covered with a piece of thin sheet metal, or you may use the frame for a glass, as in a locket.

A pearl (not a half-pearl) is usually drilled halfway through from the back. A pin, notched and roughened, is soldered on to the setting to correspond with the hole in the pearl. The latter is then cemented on to the pin with shellac, mastic, diamond cement or some other adhesive. A screwed pin fitting into a tapped hole in the pearl makes a better job, but great care must be taken not to split the pearl. One side of the screw should be filed flat, for it gives a little clearance in cutting. A split pin is sometimes used instead (Fig. 100). The hole in the pearl is drilled as before and then widened out inside. The pin is made from two pieces of half-round wire, or a round pin is split lengthways with the saw. A small wedge is next made to fit between the two halves of the pin. The wedge must be shorter than the split in the pin, and it must not be so thick at its wider end as to force the two halves of the pin further apart than the widened-out hole in the pearl will permit. To set the pearl it is only necessary to place the point of the wedge between the two halves of the pin, apply the cement, and finally to press the pearl home. The wedge will force the two halves of the pin apart inside the pearl, making it impossible for the latter to be afterwards withdrawn (Fig. 101).

To set a drop stone (Fig. 103). A groove is cut by the lapidary round the upper end of the stone. Into this groove a small ring is fitted, projecting very little above the surface of the stone (Figs. 104

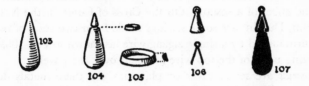

and 105). A mount or cap is now made to fit over the ring and upper part of the stone (Fig. 106). The inner surface of this cap is coated with soft solder—" pewtered." When the cap is placed in position very little heat applied to it is sufficient to firmly unite cap and ring (Fig. 107). A bead or ball pendant is generally drilled halfway through from the top. A roughened wire projects from the cap and is fastened with cement into the hole in the stone.

To set a coin as a pendant (Fig. 109). Make a ring of wire rather larger in diameter than the coin. At intervals round its circumference solder on small clips, projecting each side of the ring. When the coin is put into the ring the clips can be pressed against it on

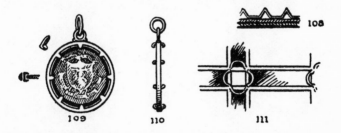

either side. Another way is to solder short lengths of wire across the ring above mentioned. Each end of these short pieces is afterwards curved back with the pliers to rest against the coin and keep it in place (Fig. 110). Do not forget the loop for suspension.

In old work pearls were very often drilled right through and fastened by a fine wire which ended in a tiny coil or bead against the stone.

In the Treasury of St. Mark's at Venice is a Byzantine book-cover decorated with gold filigree, jewels and enamels. It has many oblong stones set in cells of beaded wire with a half-ring of plain wire soldered at each end of the cell. These half-rings are bent sideways over the ends of the stones, and hold them firmly in place. Whenever four stones meet, as in Fig. 111, the four bent half-rings give the effect of a rosette. On the Cross of Cong, in the National Museum, Dublin, are some settings made from two rows of twisted wire surmounted by a single zigzag wire, as shown in Fig. 108. The projecting parts of the top wire are bent over the jewel.

Diamonds are set in silver or platinum, for these metals do not interfere with the colour of the stones as gold would. Silver mounts are, however, backed with gold—which as alloyed for use in a ring is a stronger metal. The openings through the settings under the stones are squared out behind with the piercing-saw; the dividing lines between adjacent stones being finished underneath with a smooth three-square file. The filing is continued until there is only a fine edge of the mount or setting left. But, of course, due regard must be paid to strength. So, in a cluster, alternate holes would be left perhaps with a circular opening underneath. With large pieces of work the craftsman would leave thicker bars here and there, arranging them so as to form a pattern.

CHAPTER XI

RAISING AND SHAPING

Tools. Stakes. Raising hammers. Planishing and collet hammers. Sinking and Raising. Problems in raising. Annealing. Shaping. Planishing. Various hints. Difficult shapes. Flutes. Other shapes. Sinking.

H OLLOW VESSELS of almost any shape may be formed from one piece of sheet metal without a joint. Two of the processes used are those of raising and sinking. Raising means the formation of a bowl form of any shape from comparatively thin metal by hammer blows which force the edge of the disc towards the bowl's axis and contract its mouth. The shape of the body can be altered at will. Sinking means the formation of a bowl form by stretching the metal by hammering either on the inside or the outside of the bowl, thus expanding the body while leaving the mouth comparatively unaltered. In modern workshops, both methods have largely been abandoned in favor of spinning—a method by which the sheet of metal is burnished into shape on a lathe, but for their freedom from limitations and their personal qualities, raising and sinking always hold their own for artistic work.

The tools required for raising are:

A number of stakes. The T-stake (Fig. 112) is an extremely useful one. The raising of work of almost every shape is commenced on this tool, though it may be completed on another. The stake is

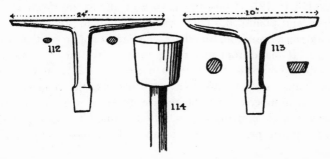

made of iron, steel-faced. The arms are each about 12 inches long, elliptical in section, one measuring about $2\frac{1}{4}$ inches wide by 1 inch deep at the end, the other about $1\frac{1}{2}$ inches by 1 inch. This tool either stands permanently in a large block of wood, or it can be held in a vice. As a substitute for this stake a rod of steel or brass, 12 to 18 inches long and $1\frac{1}{2}$ or 2 inches in diameter, may be used. Its efficiency is increased if one end is slightly flattened on top and the extremity undercut to make an angle of about 70 degrees with the upper surface, as shown on the drawing of the T-stake. Large bowls may be raised even on wood. The bickiron also (Fig. 113) is T-shaped. In this tool one arm is flat on top, and the other circular in section, tapering from about $1\frac{1}{2}$ inch diameter at the shoulder to $\frac{1}{2}$ inch at the end. Bottom stakes (Fig. 114) are flat on top and circular in plan. Three inches and $1\frac{1}{2}$ inch in diameter are good sizes; the shank should be 9 inches long and not less than 1 inch square. These tools are used for levelling the flat bottom of bowls and for other work. Round-headed stakes (Figs. 115 to 117) have

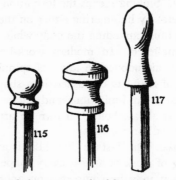

many uses. Some of the most valuable stakes are those shown in Figs. 118 to 121. Upon them work of almost any form may be shaped and planished. These tools can be made by a blacksmith in mild steel, or in iron, from bars which must not be less than 1 inch square. If made from material $\frac{3}{4}$ inch square they are not rigid enough. Another tool is called a horse (Fig. 122); at the end of each arm is a small square hole into which goes the shank of a small stake. A number of small stakes are made to fit on to this horse. They are made in many shapes, fluted or smooth (Figs 123 to 127). The long arms permit them to be applied to almost any part of the work.

A sinking block. This is a piece of wood with several shallow circular depressions cut in it. These hollows may range from about

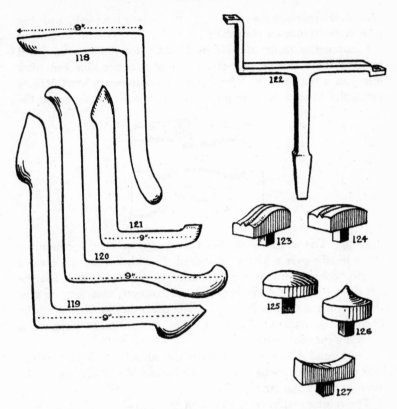

8 inches in diameter and 1½ inches deep, to 2 inches by ½ inch. Pieces of metal can be sunk to a rough saucer shape in these hollows by means of a round-faced mallet or hammer. The sinking block is often made from a piece of tree trunk 2 feet high, with the depressions cut in the top.

A vice. This should weigh not less than 65 lb. It should have jaws at least 5 inches wide. Vices of 50 lb. weight or less are not rigid enough to prevent vibration. The vice should be firmly bolted to the bench, and that to the wall or floor, for it must be quite firm.

Several hammers. It is most important that these should be of the proper shape, as their efficiency is thereby vastly increased.

The raising hammer is shown in Figs. 128, 129. It has two faces, each measuring 1¼ by ¼ inch. They have all the edges and corners well rounded off. This is especially necessary in the case of the front corners, i.e. those furthest from the handle, for if they are not sufficiently rounded they are likely to cut into the work, and thus give more trouble in planishing. For the same reason the face of the hammer is made as wide as $1\frac{1}{4}$ inch, for it has been found by experience that a wide-faced raising hammer cuts the work less than a narrow one. The face of the hammer in most general use is flat in section. The other face is rounded, as shown in the

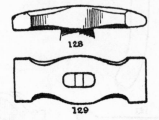

drawing. The weight of the head is about 8 oz.; and the hammer has a handle over a foot long, indeed, 16 inches is not too great a length. Some craftsmen use a hammer with a circular face, like the left side of that shown in Fig. 132. If, however, they were to give the hammer shown in Fig. 128 a fair trial, they would hardly be likely to go back to the other. The straight-faced hammer is certainly the more efficient tool.

The second raising hammer is like the other in all respects except that the thickness of the face is $\frac{1}{8}$ inch instead of $\frac{1}{4}$ inch. The handle may be rather shorter.

The raising mallet (Fig. 130) or a horn tip (Fig. 131) may often be used instead of the raising hammer. The horn tip is the end of a bullock's horn. It is sometimes weighted with lead. The face of

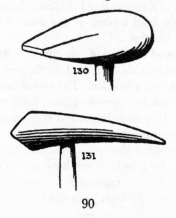

each of these tools is cut to a blunt wedge-shape. The thickness of the wedge at the point is about $\frac{1}{4}$ inch. These tools do not bruise the metal so much as a steel hammer does, so there are fewer marks to remove in the final planishing. Italian coppersmiths seem always to use the mallet in preference to the raising hammer. It may be well to note in this connection that there is one very definite difference between the silversmith and the coppersmith in his manner of holding a bowl-shaped vessel while raising it to shape. The silversmith holds the bowl with its opening turned away from him, as shown in Figs. 139 to 142, while the coppersmith puts his bowl on the far end of the stake with its opening towards him. And each craftsman is certain that his own is the correct way!

The planishing hammer (Fig. 132) has two flat faces. One may be circular, the other square. Beginners may find considerable difficulty in managing this tool properly, for, in unskilful hands, its sharp corners leave marks at almost every blow. The secret of its successful use lies in a certain stiffening of the wrist. Try to bring the hammer down " dead true " each time, and the wildness of aim which

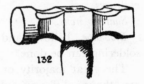

is responsible for the trouble will disappear. But, to begin with, a planishing hammer whose sharp corners have been rounded off should be used.

Collet hammer. Some of these are shown in the illustration (Figs. 133 to 135). They are made in a variety of sizes to suit the very varied uses to which they may be put.

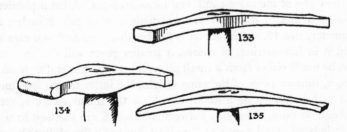

The ball-faced hammer (Fig. 136) is used for bossing work up from the back and for a number of other purposes. So also is the sinking hammer (Fig. 137), whose principal work, however, is that of sinking the central, depressed portions of round trays and other objects. The hammer shown in Fig. 138 is for work inside bowls—levelling the bottom, for example.

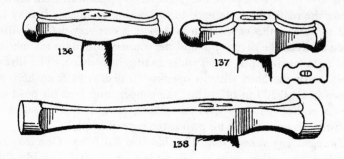

A pair of compasses, preferably with quadrant, and a pair of callipers.

Snarling irons.

Blowpipe, bellows and a hearth upon which annealing and soldering can be done.

The great majority of shapes to be raised—bowls, cups, vases, etc., though differing widely in profile, are all more or less circular in plan. They are, therefore, almost always raised from circular pieces of sheet metal. If the metal is of a fair thickness, say size 12 on the metal gauge, or thicker, it is usual to commence with a disc rather less in diameter than the combined height and width of the bowl you wish to make. Some craftsmen add ½ inch to this measurement. A tall, narrow shape requires less metal than a shallow one of the same combined measurements. A hemispherical bowl 6 inches in diameter can be made from a disc 8 inches in diameter, size 12. If the metal is thicker than this and you care to thin it in hammering, of course, a smaller piece will do. A bowl can be made either from a small piece of very thick metal or from a larger, thinner piece of the same weight, the latter taking less time. But metal thinner than about size 8 on the metal gauge is very difficult to raise. The sizes between 10 and 16 are the best to use. A little bowl may be sunk or " peaned " out of a five-shilling piece: the inscription on the edge being left intact. To do this take a round-faced hammer and strike repeated blows near the centre of the coin, on a flat stake. The metal will go hollow on top, and the hollow can be made deeper and deeper by continued hammering. The work can, after a time, be turned over on the rounded stake and shaped and planished smooth. Do not omit to anneal pretty frequently. Some of the large cauldrons of the Early Iron Age in England were made from bronze plates held together by rivets. The metal is surprisingly thin; sometimes only $\frac{1}{100}$ inch. The thickness of the wall of a bowl may be measured by a specially designed tool with micrometer fitting.

The fruit stand shown in Fig. 165 measures nearly 6 inches high, $7\frac{1}{4}$ inches across the bowl, 5 inches across the foot. Depth of bowl, $2\frac{1}{2}$ inches. Narrowest part of stem, $\frac{7}{8}$ inch. The bowl, being very shallow, will require a disc $9\frac{1}{2}$ inches in diameter. The foot, which is a shape which will take a good deal of hammering, will come out of a disc $6\frac{1}{2}$ inches in diameter. Both discs are of silver, size 14 on the metal gauge. File off the rough edges of the discs, so that they may be comfortable to handle. With the round-faced mallet or hammer sink the discs to a rough saucer shape in one of the hollows of the sinking block. If the metal now feels hard and springy, anneal it.

To anneal is to soften by heat. When a piece of gold, silver or other metal is subjected when cold to hammering, spinning, rolling or other " work," the crystals of which the metal is composed become distorted and break up. As a result the material gets hard, and if the working is continued for long it may cause cracks to appear. More than 4,500 years ago it was discovered that if the metal was heated sufficiently the strains would disappear, and the metal would become soft again. Further, it has been learnt by experience that if some of the non-ferrous metals when red-hot are plunged in water or other cooling liquid, then the sudden cooling or "quenching" may make them about 25 per cent. softer than if they were allowed to cool down in air. It is customary to make sure that every part of a work which has to be annealed has been red-hot for at least a few seconds before it is quenched. Objects made of steel, however, behave differently from those of the non-ferrous metals group; steel becomes hard on quenching.

Standard silver may be safely heated to a dull red (600° to 700° C.). Copper may be taken to a rather higher annealing temperature. If you quench any hot metal in pickle, remember that you risk serious danger from spattering. Take tongs of brass for use in an acid bath, and do not put silver into any pickle which has been used for copper work, for you risk the possibility that a film of copper will spread over the surface. Such a film is difficult to remove.

Take the compasses and round the centre of the convex side of the metal, lightly scratch a circle 5½ inches in diameter on the larger disc and one 1½ inch in diameter on the smaller. From these circles the raising will commence. Place the T-stake in the vice or in its block.

Hold the larger disc of silver with its concave side against the end of the larger arm, with part of the scratched circle opposite the upper corner of the tool. The upper edge of the disc of silver should be held by the left forefinger about ¾ inch above the top of the stake, the forefinger resting against the top or side of the tool. Now, with the flatter side of the raising hammer, strike a sharp blow ¼ inch above the scratched line (Fig. 139). The force of the blow must be sufficient to carry that part of the metal touched by the hammer downwards against the top of the stake (Fig. 140). It is

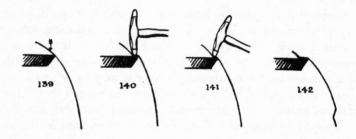

essential that the metal be driven right against the stake, so a second blow must be given in the same place if the first has not been completely successful. A sharp click or ring from the stake will announce that the blow has got right home. Turn the metal a little, still keeping the scratched circle opposite the upper corner of the stake, and strike another blow beside the first. Continue this process right round the circle, taking care that at each blow the hammer gets home. The front edge of the hammer face should produce a very definite groove, or rather angle, between that part of the metal with which it has been in contact and that further from the centre of the disc. To ensure this it is well to hold the elbow

94

rather high and to notice from time to time that the front edge of the hammer face is doing its work properly. Fig. 141 shows the bad effect of holding the hand too low—the edge would come in very slowly if you did not make the front corner of the hammer do more work. Continue the hammering in a spiral round and round the bowl to the edge, the distance between the coils of the spiral being rather less than the thickness of the hammer face, nearly $\frac{1}{4}$ inch. Before the hammering has reached the rim the latter will present a waved appearance (Figs. 143, 144). This is quite correct, but care

must be taken to prevent any folding of the metal, for folds are extremely difficult to remove and, if allowed to remain, they develop later into cracks. To remove a pleat or deep wave remember to anneal first and to strike blows always at its narrow extremity— where it begins to rise above its surroundings. If you strike at the wider end you may, indeed, remove the fold, but your bowl is making no progress. You would only commence at the wide end if the metal had begun to form an actual pleat at the narrow end, which had to be got out at any cost. Anneal first. If, after annealing, you intentionally bend the metal into waves, similar to those shown in Fig. 144, but carried right down to the corner from which you are raising, you will find that you can make greater progress and get the edge in quicker than if you go on as before. The waves should be as strong as, or stronger than those shown in Fig. 144. Of course you look out for, and stop, any tendency to pleat.

When the hammering has reached to the edge of the disc, the metal will feel very hard and springy. It must be annealed before you go over it again. But if you wish the edge of the bowl, when completed, to be very thick and strong, it is well to put the work on a sandbag and hammer straight down on to its edge all the way

round, before annealing. Do this after every course of raising, and by the time the bowl has been completed the edge of the metal will have grown considerably thicker. When you have given the metal its first course (of raising), its shape will be that of a shallow bowl about 9½ inches diameter and perhaps 1 inch deep (Fig. 146). Each successive course should increase its depth and decrease its diameter by about ⅜ inch. Beginners sometimes find considerable difficulty in inducing the bowl to become smaller at the top. They obtain a form something like Fig. 152. They have failed to keep the edge of the metal a sufficient distance above the top of the stake, and they have not seen to it that the front edge of the hammer face did its work properly by making the very definite angle, mentioned above, between that part of the metal which has been struck and that which has yet to be. The remedy for this state of things lies in keeping the elbow high and in listening for the sharp click which tells that the hammer has gone home. In some cases, when the metal is thin, for example, the other raising hammer (with face 1¼ by ⅛ inch) may be used to advantage. This hammer touches a smaller piece of metal at each blow, so the force applied is able to do its work more effectually. But progress is slower.

The different forms passed through in raising a bowl like Fig. 151 are shown in the series Figs. 145 to 151. It will be noticed that to reach a shape with a narrow mouth it is usual to shift the place from which raising is done from the bottom corner to B in Fig. 148.

This will enable you to reach a form like Fig. 149, from which it is not difficult to produce the shape required. The raising should be continued until the neck of the bowl is rather less in diameter (⅛ inch or so) than the diameter actually required. Fig. 157 shows at C and D the points from which the raising would be done for a shape like Fig. 156.

To return to the work upon the fruit stand (Fig. 165). The centre of the bowl may be hammered down to the correct curve with a round-faced hammer, while the work rests on a sandbag. Should a bowl when being raised grow too deep, place it face downwards on

the bench and tap it in all over with a flat-faced hammer, watching
the curvature and taking care not to make any large dents. The
pressure of the corner of the stake will have produced a projecting
ridge at the scratched line mentioned above, or the corners *B* (Fig.
148), *C* and *D* (Fig. 157). The ridge or ridges may be removed by
hammering them smooth on a suitable stake. You generally raise a
shape in approximately straight lines, filling out the curves when
shaping and planishing. These processes come next. They go on
more or less concurrently—bossing out, with rounded hammer or
snarling iron, any part that is too hollow; and planishing, that is to
say, hammering the work quite smooth all over—leaving a regular
series of hammer marks everywhere. For the marks left by the raising
hammer are irregular in position and uneven in size and depth.
Anneal the work first. Find a stake which will fit the required curve.
Hold the stake against the drawing to make sure. Probably it will
fit only a part, so use the stake for that part of the work only, and
another for the remainder. See that the stake is clean and smooth,
rubbing it bright with emery paper if necessary. With the planishing
hammer commence at any convenient spot and hammer out all the
uneven marks. After doing a little piece, look inside. If the corresponding part there does not look smooth you must strike harder or
use a heavier hammer. Go round and round in a long spiral, leaving
a regular series of hammer-marks all the way. If the stake does not
fit very well do not work straight round, but planish little patches
perhaps $\frac{3}{4}$ inch in diameter first, each following on and blending with
the others. Watch the outline and remember that the work you are
doing now will expand the bowl a little. For if you continue to strike
hard on any place which is solidly supported underneath, the metal
between hammer and stake must stretch, and, being stretched, must
go somewhere, so your hammering will tend to raise a bump.
Bearing this fact in mind, you will be able to shape your bowl as
required. Should you wish to enlarge any part considerably you can
boss it out with the snarling iron, as described later. Raising and
planishing being completed, anneal, then work the flutes, as they are
quite simple ones, by filling the bowl with pitch and putting the
lines in with chasing tools. In any case, whether the bowl be plain
or fluted, when the hammering is completed, if you find that the edge
is not very true scratch a line round it with the compasses, just
touching the lowest indentation in its edge. Then, with the open

part of the bowl turned towards you, cut the edge true with the shears. Let them travel round the upper edge of the bowl towards your left hand. It is easier to cut in that direction. Then file the top of the bowl level and give it a rub on the flat stone to make quite true.

The raising of the foot (Fig. 153) must now be taken in hand, though many workers would carry on both bowl and foot alternately. The arm of the T-stake is too wide at the end to go inside the foot, so work should be commenced on a rod of iron about 1¼ inch in diameter. It may be held in the vice. Take no notice at present of the angle near the bottom of the foot, but raise the foot to the shape shown in the dotted line B (Fig. 153). The size of the

top of the foot, where it is to join the bowl, must be gradually reduced from 1½ inch to the correct diameter—about an inch at the top—the narrowest part of the stem being a little lower down. It is not well to commence raising from so small a circle, for the smallness of the stake required, ¾ inch or so, makes the shape more difficult to raise, and the strain and wear on so small a part of the disc are rather severe. The point of the bickiron may be used for this part of the work when you have carried it as far as possible on the 1¼ inch iron rod, but it is well to see that the point is not so sharp as to cut the metal. Should the foot not be growing tall enough, use the rounded side of the raising hammer, but not quite close to the scratched circle, as the metal is apt to work thin there. The rounded side of the hammer stretches and drives the metal inwards and upwards, making taller the shape which is being raised. On the other hand, if the shape seems to be growing too tall, use the flat side of the hammer and hold the silver so that the point of the bick-iron, or other tool upon which you are working, does not press against the top of the foot. If, however, this does not stop the growth, scratch another circle round the foot about half-way between the top and the rim. Then, on the T-stake, work from this line instead of from the smaller circle until you have reduced the rim to rather less (⅛ inch or so) than the required size. Your work will look like Fig. 155. Now continue the raising process, using the T-stake for the beginning of each course (near the rim), and the bickiron for that part of the foot which is too narrow for the T-stake to reach into. Place the T-stake and the bickiron with the point turned away from you, and raise from the rim to the top instead of from the top to the rim as at first. Still use the flat face of the hammer. Now that the rim is of the correct size there should be no difficulty in getting the top in also. When, by the eye and the callipers, you find that the shape is correct down to the little shoulder B (Fig. 153), planish down to there, and lightly scratch a circle to mark the corner. Then on the T-stake work down the lowest ¾ inch of the foot to the correct angle and planish that part also. The bottom edge of the foot may be turned outwards like A (Fig. 153), or a separate moulding soldered on as in Fig. 165. To do the former you must cut the lower edge of the foot true after the planishing of the surface below B has been completed. Then hold the foot upside down against the side and upper edge of some rectangular stake, and tap over the little flange at the bottom. Then see that the bottom is quite level, so that it will stand on a piece of plate glass without rocking, yet touching all round. Afterwards file the edge.

When raising a tall, narrow shape you may find that the work has a tendency to lean over to one side. But if for each course you reverse the direction in which you rotate the silver while raising, the work will keep straight.

Should you wish to make a hexagonal foot, proceed as above, as far as the turning down of the last ¾ inch. In this case turn it down rather more steeply than the drawing shows, for the difficulty later will be to keep the base narrow enough. Anneal the work. Then divide the rim into six equal parts and draw lines very carefully to the top. These lines show where the corners are to come, so take great care to ensure their looking true to the eye as well as measuring truly. Cut out the little piece which forms the top of the foot. On any convenient stake flatten each of the six spaces with a mallet. Draw straight lines from corner to corner, crossing the lower part of each of the six spaces and forming a regular hexagon. Then, on a flat-sided stake, turn downwards all the metal which projects beyond the lines last drawn. Planish all over, taking great care to keep all the edges true. The bottom will now be uneven, and must be cut level. If the six sides of the foot, instead of being straight, are foiled like Fig. 158, then the parts below the angle *B* (Fig. 153) are made separately and soldered on, as described in Chapter XXXIII. Solid drawn copper tube is sometimes used instead of sheet metal when a tall shape has to be made. The tube may, of course, be hammered and shaped just as the sheet metal can.

The raising of a shape like Fig. 156 proceeds in precisely the same way as that described for the bowl (Figs. 145 to 151). Raise to the

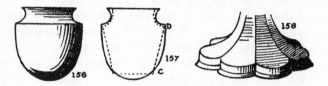

shape shown by the dotted lines. Shapes like Figs. 159 and 161 are formed similarly. Raise as shown by the dotted lines and afterwards fill out to the proper form, using a snarling iron where necessary. For a description of this tool see p. 122. Note in Figs. 159 and 161 that while the bowl is being raised its diameter is kept in every part a little less than that finally required. There is no difficulty in reducing the diameter at any point while the raising is in progress. When this is completed and the shaping and planishing have commenced, the whole work fills out a little. Any reduction now is rather more troublesome, for you have the planishing to do over again. The flutes in Fig. 160 are set out by scratching in the

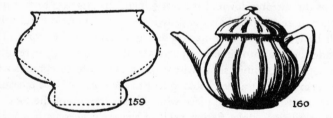

lines of the ridges, taking great care to get them true and regular. The hollows are then tapped in with collet hammers on to stakes (Figs. 123, 124), fluted to the required shape. The flutes are planished on shaped stakes. By another method the bowl is filled with pitch and the flutes worked in with repoussé, modelling or chasing tools (see page 125). In modern commercial work the flutes would be struck out in dies. The lower bosses in Fig. 161 are worked out with the snarling iron, as described on p. 122. The upper bosses can, however, be reached with a round-face hammer, and may be bossed out on the lead cake. They are all finished, however, with the planishing hammer on suitably shaped stakes. Or the bowl may be filled with pitch and the shapes finished with chasing tools.

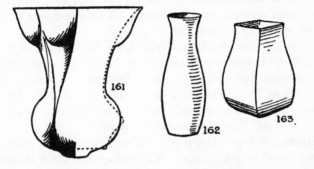

Bowls oval in plan, their long and short diameters having the ratio of about 3 to 2 (Fig. 164), may be raised from circular pieces of metal. An elliptical line is scratched round the centre of the disc of metal (instead of a circular one as in the case of a round bowl). The metal near $A B C$ and $D E F$ will, in the course of raising, stretch more than the metal $F A$ or $C D$. The reason is that on a curve of small radius (as the ends of the ellipse in this case) the metal gets hammered rather more severely, and naturally stretches to a corresponding degree. The unequal space between the edge of the metal and the scratched line is thus compensated for, and the bowl

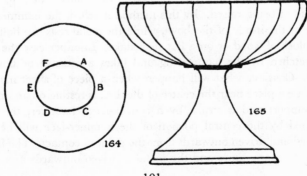

101

rises to an equal height all round. For an elliptical bowl, of which the ratio between the longer and shorter curves is greater than 3 to 2, it is necessary to cut the metal elliptical also.

The lack of a sufficient variety of stakes will make the work more difficult, but if you have a new stake made when you find the need for it, or alter a useless shape into a good one, a good working set will soon be accumulated. Remember that you have a very useful set of small stakes in your hammers. Of these a dozen to twenty will be gradually accumulated.

At the Japanese exhibition held at the White City, Shepherd's Bush, in 1911, there were shown lions 3 feet high raised from one piece of sheet iron—without a join. They give an idea as to what can be done by careful work in this difficult material. Very fine pieces of raising may be seen in some of the mediæval morions and tilting helmets. These, of course, are of steel.

Although it is possible, it is not always desirable to make every hollow vessel in this manner. The soda-water bottle shape (Fig. 162) can be so produced, but it would be more reasonable to make it from a piece of solid drawn tube with a piece soldered on at the bottom. The narrow-mouthed square vase (Fig. 163) could, if necessary, be raised in one piece, but it could be made much more easily if joins were permitted. Again, there is some difficulty in raising very small articles—they are so difficult to hold. Indeed, bowls of less than $1\frac{1}{2}$ inch diameter may be struck in dies or between suitably shaped punches and a cake of lead or zinc. But with these exceptions, raising may be resorted to for the production of almost any shape.

There is an alternative method of making a bowl from sheet metal. The work may be " blocked " or " sunk " or " peaned " instead of being raised. By this method much of the hammering is done in the inside of the bowl, while the metal rests in a hollowed-out block of wood or on a flat steel stake. In either case the metal is stretched by the hammering and takes a concave or bowl-like form. Consider what will happen when a piece of sheet metal, in this case a piece near the centre of the disc, is resting on an unyielding support and is struck by a convex-faced hammer, the metal touched by the central portion of the hammer-face will be compressed and driven outwards from the point of contact. The blow is repeated many times and the metal is driven outwards in a gentle

102

curve. No hammering is done near the edge of the disc, which takes first a saucer and then a bowl shape. If the hammering is continued the metal is stretched still further and the bowl becomes deeper. The work may be varied by holding the bowl on a convex stake and hammering it from the outside. In any case the work will need planishing, and that can be done best from the outside. One important distinction between the work of raising a bowl and that of sinking one is that in raising the diameter of the original disc of metal is reduced, and a bowl of any shape can be made from it. On the other hand, in sinking a bowl the diameter is hardly altered at all, but the metal is thinned and expanded to form the bowl. To raise a bowl of any given size one may take a large, relatively thin, disc of metal; and to sink a bowl of that size one would take a smaller, thicker disc.

CHAPTER XII

SPINNING

The lathe. The pattern or forme. Sectional chuck. Other chucks. Early spinning. Followers. Tools. Spinning. Lubricants. Metal for spinning.

THE BOWLS, stems and feet of cups, and hollow vessels of almost any profile may be produced from discs of sheet metal by burnishing them to shape on a lathe. This process is known as spinning. It is applicable to shapes which are circular in plan: though the form of the work produced may, of course, be afterwards altered by the use of snarling irons, or by shaping and planishing it on a suitable stake. Thus, the general form of Fig. 161 could have been produced on the spinning lathe, the flutes or lobes being afterwards snarled and hammered out. But, primarily, spinning is employed for shapes which are circular in plan, whatever their profile may be. The process is in very general use among manufacturing silversmiths, to whom the ease with which a number of exactly similar copies of a shape may be produced is of importance. It has, however, little interest for the artist, for to him variety and a less mechanical form than that so generally adopted commercially will naturally appeal.

The principal tools employed are the lathe, the pattern or forme, and the burnisher or spinning tool. We will look at these each in order and afterwards see how they are used.

Considerable speed being necessary, backgearing is not required in the spinning lathe. Almost any single-geared lathe which is large enough may be used. Small work may be spun with a foot lathe, but, as in wood-turning, any diameter greater than about 5 or 6 inches means very hard work unless you have power. A speed of from 800 to 1,200 revolutions per minute is necessary for the metals with which we are dealing. The thicker the metal, the less the speed required. The rest employed is like the ordinary T-rest of the wood-turner (Fig. 175). It has, however, a row of holes drilled in its top edge, into any conveniently placed one of which a stout steel peg, known as the " pin," is dropped. Its use is explained below. The tailstock is similar to that used for turning, but it is often fitted with a revolving centre. In this case the centre, which is not tapered, rests against one or two hardened steel buttons which take up most of the friction (Fig. 166).

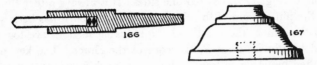

The forme, pattern or chuck upon which the metal is spun plays a very important part in the work. It is a block of wood or metal of the exact shape of the bowl required; though it is made smaller than the design by just the thickness of the metal employed for the bowl. When the shape of the bowl is such that the pattern can be withdrawn from it when the spinning is completed, Fig. 167 for example, the pattern is made in one piece. But if the shape would not allow of this, and you do not wish to destroy the pattern after it

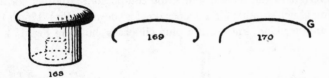

has done its work, a section chuck must be employed instead. The forme or pattern is generally of well-dried maple. The block from which it is made is bored and tapped to fit the nose of the lathe, and then turned to fit a templet which has been set out from the drawing. Due allowance is made for the thickness of the metal which is to be used for the bowl.

For a shape like Fig. 171 a sectional chuck would be used. It would be made as shown in section in Fig. 172. The part *A* is fitted

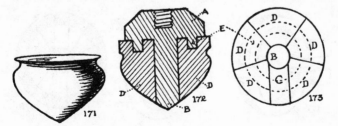

to the nose of the lathe by the screw shown in the drawing and extends as a thick, parallel-sided pin B to the bottom of the bowl. Round it, completing the shape of the bowl, are a number of movable pieces D (Figs. 172, 173). At least one of these, a " key " section, C (Fig. 173), has parallel sides. It is always rather thinner than the pin or core of the chuck B. When a bowl has been spun on to the chuck, the bowl and the movable sections are together pulled lengthwise from B, the core of the chuck. The key piece may then be wriggled free. It has room to shift now that the core has been removed. The remaining sections come out easily, and are replaced at once round the core, and the chuck is ready for the next bowl. Sometimes patterns are made with more than one key piece, but unless at least one is provided the radial pieces could not be removed. The projecting ring E on piece A fits into a groove in the movable sections and keeps them together. The shape, or " stock," or " shell," as the bowl is sometimes called, would be spun up as far as possible on another (a simple pattern), before being transferred to the section chuck for completion. Another form of section chuck suitable for a deeper bowl is shown in Figs. 176 to 179. Yet another kind, known as a plug chuck, is shown in Fig. 174. It

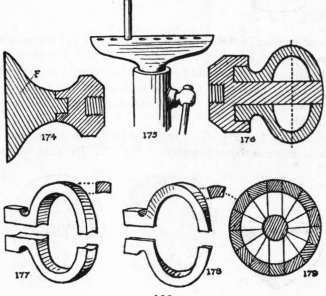

174   175   176

177   178   179

is used for shapes which are constricted in the middle and open at each end. The bottom of the shape spun on Fig. 174 must, of course, be cut out before the movable section *F* of the chuck can be removed. A shape like this would, however, be more easily spun from a tapered tube than from a disc.

Yet another kind is the nailhead chuck (Fig. 168). It is made from a hardwood, such as boxwood. This chuck is used for turning inwards the lip of any small bowl or dish. It thus saves the expense of making a sectional chuck for a shape like Fig. 169. The diameter of the chuck must be less than the mouth of the complete bowl. The chuck is rubbed with powdered pumice and water to make it grip the work. The latter, which has already been spun as far as possible on another chuck, is slipped over the nailhead and kept in position with the finger. With a little trouble the edge *G* (Fig. 170) may be worked round to the curve shown in Fig. 169.

A bowl such as Fig. 180 can be made without the aid of a section

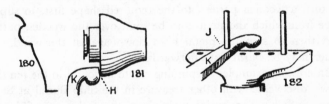

chuck. It is spun on an ordinary pattern which fits it from the bottom to as far as the angle *H*. By the time that the bowl has been spun thus far the rim will have taken a curve something like that shown by *N* (Fig. 188). A hooked tool *K* (Figs. 181, 182) is now clamped firmly to the rest or to the lathe-bed. Seen from above the rounded end of the tool " takes up " or continues the curve of the pattern beyond the corner *H*. The tool, of course, does not rotate, as the pattern does, but it remains permanently near the corner H, and so supports the bowl against the pressure of the spinning tool. The bowl can, therefore, be spun to the required shape just as though it were on a section chuck. In some cases a hole is drilled through the shank of the tool at *J*, and the tool slipped over an extra pin in the T-rest. It may be held in place by an assistant.

A shape like Fig. 167, say, for the base of a cup, can be spun without difficulty. Even if the mouldings are undercut, as in Fig.

183, it would not be impossible. If the pattern were required
again it would be necessary to cut away first those parts of it which
would bind when the metal was spun over them. The metal at
those places would be spun without support, " in the air " as it is
called.

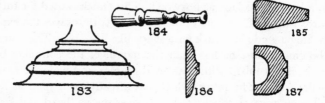

The decoration of a bellows pipe, such as Fig. 184, can be effected
by holding the tapering pipe or tube between centres or arbors, and
spinning it to shape without any further support inside. The
baluster stem of a cup may be spun in the same way. But it is better
to turn a wooden pattern to the required shape first, to slip the
tube from which the stem is to be spun over the wooden pattern,
and then to spin the metal hard down against the wood. The
latter may be burnt out afterwards.

Interesting examples of spinning are to be found in the ten silver
bowls discovered with other treasure in the Ship Burial at Sutton
Hoo, Suffolk. The burial took place about the year 655. The
bowls measure 9 inches across by 2 inches deep. They were spun
in the following way. Over a recess of the correct shape turned
in the face of a block of wood on the lathe, the sheet of silver from
which the bowl was to be made was fastened, probably by a series
of nails fixed just beyond the line of the rim. The silver was then
spun into the hollow pattern behind it by long stroking movements
of the tool.

The disc of metal from which a bowl is spun is kept in position
against the forme by a small block of wood known as the " follower."
The latter in its turn is supported by the revolving centre of the
tailstock. This is shown in Fig. 188, where L is the head of the
lathe, M the forme, N the blank or disc of metal which is being spun,
O the follower, P the revolving centre, R the tailstock, S the rest,
T the pin, and V the tool. Followers are made in different shapes,
with flat or hollow faces (Figs. 185 to 187). The important thing to

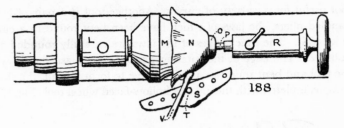

188

notice about them is that as large a follower as possible is always chosen. With a large follower the disc of metal is not so likely to jam and stop rotating; for the grip of a large follower is so much greater than that of a small one. Nevertheless, some difficulty is frequently met with in spinning a shape like Fig. 189 as so small a part of the pattern would be in contact with the disc of metal at first. Spinners frequently flatten the bottom of the forme like Fig. 190, just to give a better grip. They also rub pitch or powdered pumice on it for the same reason. Another way to obtain the same result is to raise a good-sized bump in the centre of the disc of metal to be spun. This bump may be pressed almost flat again between the forme and the flat follower by screwing the tailstock tightly, and the extra pressure obtained in this way will naturally give a better grip.

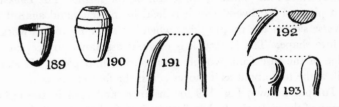

The tools are longer and heavier than those used by wood-turners. Including handle, they measure from 2 feet to 3 feet in length, and may be from ½ inch to 1 inch in thickness. They are forged from tool steel, hardened, tempered and polished very brightly. They are made in a number of shapes, but that shown in Fig. 191 is perhaps the most convenient for general use. It, like all spinning tools, has a smooth, highly polished surface with no sharp angles or corners which might cut or tear the metal. Fig. 192 is a similar tool, but with flat face for smoothing up. Fig. 193 is a ball tool which goes into curves rather well. Fig. 194 is a hook tool useful for a variety of curves. Another tool is a pair of long-handled pliers, the jaws of which have been bent round in a curve (Fig. 196). The inner edges of the jaws are carefully rounded and polished. The edge of the rotating disc may be seized lightly with the tool and bent round in a quick curve to form a bead, the shape being completed with the aid of a hollow-faced wheel tool (Fig. 197),

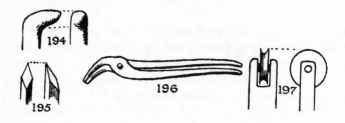

which is known as the beading tool. The diamond-point (Fig. 195), made from a square bar of steel, is useful for cutting the edges of the work true. It is the ordinary metal-turner's hand tool. If the metal which is being spun is thick enough, shallow mouldings and lines are sometimes turned in it, and its surface smoothed up with a sharp-edged turning tool. The work may also be smoothed with emery cloth and polished, while still on the forme. The backstick is a piece of hardwood which is held in the left hand against the reverse side of the rotating disc when the spinning tool is working it into shape. The backstick is of great assistance in keeping the edge of the disc from wobbling or getting into pleats. It should follow the tool about as it moves across the face of the work.

To spin a bowl, Fig. 189 for instance, first turn in the lathe a forme of the right shape, but flattened at the bottom a little to give a better grip (Fig. 190). Rub a little pitch or resin on the flat part of the pattern for the same reason. Take a disc of metal of suitable size and grip it between the flattened end of the forme and a suitable follower; centre the disc by holding a piece of hardwood against it as it rotates. When true, screw up the tailstock tightly and clamp it. See that the centre is kept well oiled. Slide the rest to a convenient position and clamp it also. Take a tool (Fig. 191) and hold it to the left side of the pin in the rest against the metal disc close to the follower. Starting from that place, slowly and very firmly press against the disc as it rotates, stroking it from near the centre to the edge again and again. Try to force it against the forme. Considerable pressure is necessary in spite of the great leverage you have against the pin. You will have no difficulty in pressing the metal in near the centre, but the rim will give you some trouble. As in raising, the most difficult part of the work consists in getting the edge to come in and in preventing it from becoming waved or pleated. As the tool approaches the edge little pleats will begin to form, and they become largish waves at last. If you press hard the disc will just go out of shape and buckle or wave, or even pleat badly. To prevent this you must steady the edge of the metal by holding the backstick against it. This will do something to counteract the pressure of the tool on the outer surface of the bowl, and it will keep the edge true. The secret of success in spinning consists in catching the pleats when and where they are small, just as they begin to rise above the surface of the metal. Press them out there. If, however, they will not disappear and the work is getting uneven, remove it from the lathe. It has probably got hard, so anneal it and then hammer it true on a stake. Whenever the work becomes hard and springy it must be annealed. When part of the metal has been spun right down on to the pattern, take the diamond-tool and turn the edge true. Be careful how you hold this tool, for if held carelessly it is liable to run in and cut your work badly. It is well always to keep the edge of the disc trued up in this way, for it will spin better. When the shape is correct, slip the work off the forme and boss out the bottom with a mallet on a sandbag. It will require but little planishing. Of course, if the bottom of the bowl is not very pointed there will be no need to flatten the forme as described here.

To lessen the friction it is necessary to lubricate the work well. Use a mixture of tallow and oil. Keep it in a covered pot and dip the tool into it from time to time. Silver and gold can be spun with oil alone, but for brass, tallow is almost essential, though beeswax or soap is sometimes used instead.

The sheet metal taken for spinning may give trouble. For the effect of the ordinary rolling out in one direction only of the sheet of silver, brass, or German silver, as the case may be, is that the grains of which the metal is composed acquire a directional quality through their repeated stretchings lengthwise as the sheet passes through the rolls. Such metal may spin unevenly. A good means

111

of overcoming this difficulty is to arrange that during the final rolling each alternate course shall be taken at right angles to the last, the metal being cut into squares to facilitate this operation. In this way the metal is rolled equally in both directions and should spin quite truly.

CHAPTER XIII

REPOUSSÉ WORK

Definition. Methods. Supporting the metal. Mildenhall treasure. Materials and tools. Pitch. Lead or zinc. Board work. Composition of pitch. Removing pitch. Repoussé and chasing tools. Snarling iron.

REPOUSSÉ IS A GENERAL term to describe ornamental work produced by modelling sheet metal with hammer and punches. It differs from cast ornament and from stamped work both in design and in treatment. Upon the visible traces of its method of production some portion of the charm of repoussé work depends. The thoughts which the craftsman was able to put into his work supply the remainder. The surface of the work should bend to and fro to catch the light at different angles. Some parts of the ornament may be lower in relief than the rest and fade into the background. The thing to avoid in this and all other relief work is the effect of ornament which has been made from a different piece of metal and has been stuck on to the background. It should be obviously of one piece, but with surfaces tilted about to play with the light: an ornamentation of, rather than a decoration applied to, the metal.

A good example of such a tilting of the surfaces may be seen in the " King John " Cup at King's Lynn (Plate 1). In this splendid work the craftsman wished to make the light on certain surfaces twinkle, instead of being reflected steadily. He therefore chased what would otherwise have been an even surface into one composed of many small waves. The effect of this chasing is that as one's glance passes down, say, the stem of one of the trees, the light ripples over the surface in a very charming way. Strictly speaking, repoussé is that part of the work which is done from the reverse side of the metal— the bossing up of the lines or patterns from the back; chasing is the part which is done from the front. But in modern times the term repoussé has been extended to cover all work in relief, whether done from the back or the front. The term chasing is applied also to the touching up and finishing of cast work with hand-held punches.

When a raised pattern is to be produced on the surface of the work, the metal is placed face downward on a pad of some material which will yield sufficiently to the force of the blows given, but which will at the same time support the metal nearby and prevent it from being disturbed. For this purpose it is necessary that the supporting material shall be in continuous contact with the underside (really the face) of the work. Now the best material for this purpose is pitch, prepared as described below. Pitch being an adhesive material, too much so sometimes, it will remain in contact with the metal, even after a considerable amount of hammering; and, owing to the even support given to the metal, a sharp impression will be made of the shape of any tool used, especially if the pitch is allowed to get cool and hard. A tool, however, is generally moved about while being struck by the hammer, so that an impression of its exact shape is rarely visible.

To obtain any considerable amount of relief it is necessary to work while the pitch is warm and soft. It sets fairly rapidly. A support of lead, tin or zinc, will give a clear, sharp impression, and these materials have the advantage of being clean to work with. Not, however, being of an adhesive nature, they do not keep in close contact with the work. So, after a small amount of hammering some parts of the metal will be found to be unsupported, and therefore unsafe to work upon. A cake of one of these metals is most valuable as a backing where a small amount of bossing up is required, as in knocking up little discs or leaves. Care must, however, be taken to remove any particles of zinc or tin or lead, which may have transferred themselves to the work, for they would cause serious damage if it had to be heated afterwards. Linoleum and wood are two other materials which can be used as a backing, but pitch is the best all-round material.

Patterns in relief can be, and often are, obtained by beating down the background of the design from the front instead of by raising the ornament above the level of the background by working on the underside of the metal.

Among the various ways of holding the metal, the simplest is that of fastening it to a board with nails. This method is only suitable when outline work, or very low relief is required, as on a tea-tray. It has the advantage, which pitch has not, of being quite clean to use. The best nails are 1-inch oval sprigs. They are driven into the wood, at intervals of 2 to 3 inches, all round the sheet of metal to be worked upon. The nails are not placed close up to the edge of the metal, but about ¼ inch beyond it. They are driven about ⅜ inch into the wood and the remaining portion is then knocked over sideways on to the metal. The nails, being oval in section, bend easily, but care should be taken that their heads are not hammered into the metal, for the little marks they make are difficult to get rid of. In tracing a large piece of work, the central parts should be done first. These must be tapped down till the metal there rests on the wood, it being almost impossible to work on the metal where it is not firmly supported. It will be found that the most convenient tools for this purpose are a mallet or a levelling tool—a piece of boxwood ¾ inch square by 4 inches long, used as a repoussé tool. In this and in nearly every other case where tools are used to drive sheet metal flat, the section of the tool, where it touches the metal, should be flat with rounded edges and corners (Fig. 198). The reason for this rule is that when the force

of the blow carries forward that part of the metal with which it comes in contact—disturbing the adjacent metal very little—a square-edged tool would leave a sharply defined mark, or cut, round its outline. The tool with rounded edges, however, would bend the metal there without cutting it.

When the outlining is completed the work can be backgrounded, if necessary, where it is. In this part of the work it is well to commence near the traced lines and work towards the more open parts of the background, and not from the middle of the open spaces towards the pattern. For by working in the last-named direction a little hill of metal will be driven up near the traced line, and this will be difficult to remove neatly.

Very interesting examples of elaborate relief work, done entirely by chasing from the front, are to be found in the well-known Mildenhall Treasure. Here, in the great " Neptune " dish, for example, the work was done in the following manner. The whole

115

of the design was outlined with the tracer while the sheet of silver rested on an anvil, a stone, or some other rigid ground. The modelling of the surface of the figures and other details of the design, and the driving down of the background were effected entirely from the front of the sheet: no work at any time being done from the back. If the work is examined closely it will be seen that the background dips steeply downwards near the outline of the figures. The craftsman was satisfied when he had obtained that amount of contrast in relief. He did not attempt to produce a level background. To do that would have entailed a great deal more work than he was willing to give to it. Or perhaps he preferred a background like this: one which, within a short distance from their outlines, rose to the same height of relief as that of the figures. For on such a generally level surface glasses and other drinking vessels would stand firmly. The hammering down of the ground near the outline of the figures caused the metal to expand laterally, with the result that the figures became slightly convex in section: for their sides were driven inwards, and they bent the only way possible to them, upwards. No repoussé work was done from the back. After the chasing had been completed, the whole of the background, and the back of the dish were made fairly smooth with scrapers. The maximum height of reliefs is $\frac{1}{16}$ inch.

The backgrounding of a design is generally done with punches, which may be of any shape, or with levelling or other flat-faced tools. Again, matt-surfaced tools are employed sometimes where a texture or fine grain is required.

The hammering given to the background with any of these tools drives it downwards, leaving the pattern in relief. This relief varies with the thickness of the metal employed, and with the weight of the hammer blows. For a tray about 20 inches by 9 inches, size 10 on the metal gauge, the relief would be about $\frac{1}{16}$ inch. For a tray 24 inches across, size 12, the relief would be rather less. Size 15 is too thick for it to be possible to produce much relief by this method, except by very heavy hammering such as was employed on the Mildenhall dishes on an unyielding stake.

By the time that the backgrounding is completed, the whole work will be found to have stretched, perhaps $\frac{1}{4}$ inch to the foot. Hence the necessity of placing the nails in the first instance at some distance from the edge of the metal. Woods with a strong grain, such as oak, pitch-pine, etc., are not suitable for repoussé boards, as after some use the harder part of the grain of the wood is left standing in ridges. Among the materials required for repoussé work will be:

1. *A board* of some hard, close-grained wood such as sycamore, measuring, say, 24 by 12 by 1 inch, for use as above described.

2. *Pitch.* As a ground upon which to do repoussé work pitch allows of far greater possibilities in the way of relief and texture than are attainable with other materials. The pitch generally used is that known as Stockholm, or Swedish, pitch. It is dark brown in colour, and can be obtained from any dealer in jewellers' requisites. Pitch is too brittle to use alone, and it must be mixed with some other substance to make it tougher. For this purpose tallow and plaster of Paris, mason's dust, bathbrick dust or resin, may be used.

Take:

(i)	Pitch	.	.	.	.	.	10 lb.
	Brickdust.	.	.	.	.	.	20 „
	Resin	.	.	.	.	.	4 „
	Tallow	.	.	.	.	.	2 „
or (ii)	Pitch	.	.	.	.	.	6 parts.
	Brickdust.	.	.	.	.	.	8 „
	Resin	.	.	.	.	.	1 part.
	Linseed oil	.	.	.	.	.	1 „
or (iii)	Pitch	.	.	.	.	.	14 lb.
	Resin	.	.	.	.	.	14 „
	Plaster of Paris or brickdust	.	.	.	.	.	7 „
	Tallow	.	.	.	.	.	8 oz.

Melt the pitch, or the pitch and resin in an iron pan. When quite liquid add the plaster of Paris or brickdust by handfuls, stirring well all the while. Put in the tallow last. Its effect is to soften the composition, so rather more tallow may be required in cold than in warm weather. Linseed oil is sometimes used instead.

3. *A pitch board.* This is a rough wooden tray 1 inch deep, filled with pitch. It should be made as large as you are ever likely to require. To fasten a piece of work upon it, warm the surface of the pitch with a blowpipe, taking care not to set it alight, for that would be dangerous. The cinders of burnt pitch would behave as air-bubbles, and you would not get an even support for the metal. With blowpipe and a rod or spatula level the surface sufficiently, removing any burnt pieces. Then lay the metal upon the pitch and press it down with the handle of a hammer. Place weights on it until the

pitch has set. Any bubbles left under the metal can be located by the hollow sound which the metal over them will give when tapped. Heat any such place with the blowpipe, or by placing a piece of red-hot iron on it, and press down again.

To remove the work from pitch. If the pitch is quite hard a repoussé tool driven under the edge of the metal, between it and the pitch, will often give sufficient leverage to crack the metal off. But if the pitch still holds, or there is any danger of injury to the work, it is safer to warm the metal with the blowpipe. The heat melts the pitch in contact with it, and will allow the work to be lifted off with pliers. The metal is then made a little hotter, though not hot enough to set the pitch alight, but just enough to induce the pitch still adhering to it to flow easily. The work can now be wiped clean with cotton waste or a brush dipped in paraffin. Paraffin readily dissolves partially melted pitch. But should the pitch get chilled before it can be all removed from the metal, it may be necessary to warm the latter again. Care must be taken in this case not to set everything alight. Burnt pitch is difficult to remove. Indeed, the simplest way to get rid of it is to anneal the work thoroughly and plunge it into water. It may be necessary to do this twice to remove all traces of the burnt matter. Molten pitch is very sticky, but it can be handled with impunity, when it is not too hot, if the hands are kept wet.

4. *A pitch bowl and ring* (Fig. 199). The bowl is hemi-spherical, of cast-iron, 9 inches in diameter and about ½ inch thick. Filled with pitch it weighs about 20 lb. The weight is of importance, for if the bowl is much lighter it will be likely to dance about when you work on it. It stands on a ring, which may be of leather or of coiled rope. The bowl can be turned about or tilted to any angle as the work proceeds, all the while standing firmly in its ring.

5. *Two hammers.* One weighing about 16 oz., and which may be of almost any shape if it has a flat face. It is used with the larger repoussé tools. A light hammer is unsuited for such work. The second hammer is the chasing hammer shown in Fig. 200. The head weighs 3 or 4 oz., and the handle is about 9 inches long. Its rounded end makes it easy to hold, and use. A wooden mallet can be used instead, and it makes less noise.

6. *Chasing tools.* Although a considerable amount of ornamental work could be done with a couple of punches—a tracer and

a backgrounding tool—yet one would soon find their limitations.
Fifty to seventy repoussé and chasing tools make a useful set,
though a professional worker may have several
hundred. Out of these he has perhaps a dozen
favourites. The tools are all about 4 inches
long, but they vary in thickness. The smaller
ones are generally forged thicker in the middle
of their length, as they are then easier to hold.
Tools with sharp angles or rings on the shank
hurt the fingers, so they should be avoided. It
is better and cheaper for the worker to shape
the points of his tools as he may need them;
for the tools he can buy are rarely the exact
shape that he requires. Unfinished tools, called
blanks, can be bought ready forged. They only
require the points to be shaped and hardened,
and are then ready for use. The tools being
all very much alike except at the point, the
description given below refers to that part of
them which actually touches the work. Although
no two in a set are alike, the tools fall naturally
into a few groups, known by the following
names: Tracers; bossing, cushion, modelling
and chasing tools; matts and liners; ring,
number and letter-punches.

200

A clear distinction should be recognized at this stage between
the work done by a tracing tool and that done by an engraving tool
(a "graver" or "burin"). In an engraved line (see Chapter XVIII)
the material which originally filled the site of the groove is entirely
removed from the work save perhaps a little roughness or burr alongside and at the end of the groove. In the traced line, however, no
material is removed, but a trench is formed by the hammer blows
on the tracer, which compress and drive aside the metal which
hitherto filled the site of the trench. The groove so formed is often
mistaken for an engraved line by those who have not taken the
trouble to recognize the distinction between the two entirely different techniques. As a result of this, about half the descriptive
labels for works in our museums and galleries are wrongly described.
Whether there will be any evidence of the tracing work on the reverse

side of the material depends partly on the thickness of the metal on which it is being done and partly on its manner of support. Traced work on thin metal which rested upon a foundation of pitch will be clearly visible as a softly rounded line but that on thick metal firmly supported, say on a hard stake, will have a bruised appearance. On the other hand, an engraved line on the front of the work will not show on the back at all.

Tracers are like rather blunt chisels, and are used chiefly for outlining. Their working edges vary from about $\frac{1}{100}$ inch in thickness by $\frac{1}{16}$ inch long, to perhaps $\frac{1}{8}$ inch wide by $\frac{3}{4}$ inch long (Figs. 201 to 204). The last one is curved as shown in the section. A very useful size is about $\frac{1}{40}$ inch thick by $\frac{1}{8}$ inch long.

Tracers and all the other tools are held in the same way—between the thumb and the first two fingers of the left hand. The third, and sometimes the fourth, fingers rest on the work to steady the hand (Fig. 215). The tracer is held nearly perpendicularly, but leaning back a little from the direction in which it is to travel. The front corner is thus lifted a little above the metal. If a blow is now struck with the hammer on the upper end of the tool, the corner of the tracer, known as the heel, will be driven into the metal. The tool will, at the same time, move forward slightly. The blow is repeated again and again, the edge of the tool slowly sliding forward and cutting itself a channel in the metal. Some of the material displaced goes to form a little ridge on either side of the traced line. Some of it, if the metal be not too thick, is driven up in a ridge on the underside of the metal. Some difficulty may be found at first in getting

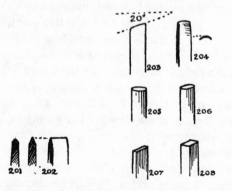

a tracer to work properly. If held too nearly perpendicular it will

120

not move along at all, but will dig into, and perhaps cut through, the
metal. If held at too great a slope, the point will slide away, making
merely a scratch on the surface. The correct angle to hold it can be
ascertained only by trial, and it varies with different tracers. In
making curves of small radius it is necessary to tilt the tracer back
further than usual, so that only the heel touches the metal; for if
held at the usual angle, it would be likely to make a series of tangen-
tial marks round the outside of the curve. The tracer is much more
likely to slip away when so held, so it must be gripped very firmly.
Curved tracers (Fig. 204) are sometimes used, but with a little
practice curves of any radius can be, and generally are, worked with
a straight tracer. At whatever angle the tracer may be held to the
metal, the blow from the hammer should always fall in a direct line
with the axis of the tool. Beginners frequently make the mistake of
striking the head of the tool at an angle instead of fairly on the top—
with surprising results! If the point of the tracer is dipped occasionally in oil it will move more freely. The edge of the tracer which is
to touch the work is not invariably made just at right angles to the
shank of the tool, as in the case of an ordinary chisel. It may be
sloped like a skew chisel, and vary as much as 20 degrees from a
right angle (Fig. 203). If made so, it will travel easier. The heel
of the tracer is sometimes rounded off a little. The bottom of the
groove made in the metal should not show " stitches." It should
be nearly smooth.

Bossing and cushion tools (Figs. 209 to 214) are made in various

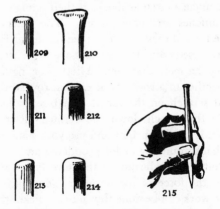

shapes—round, tapering, square or oblong, but they are all alike in

121

this—their sharp edges are rounded off. For the purpose of this group of tools is to drive the metal up in bumps or ridges, and any sharp corners on the tool would be likely to cut or tear the work. Bossing and cushion tools are therefore more or less circular in section at their working ends. Modelling and chasing tools (Figs. 205 to 208), on the other hand, being used on the front surface of the work, are, as a rule, much flatter. Many of them are quite flat at the point, though sometimes the extreme edges are rounded off. It will be clear, however, that to obtain a rounded or a level surface on the work, one would not use a very rounded tool on the face. It is on this very point that so many ready-made tools fail: they are not flat enough. The ideal chasing tool for truing up a convex or a flat surface is flat in the centre, though it may have its corners and edges rounded off a little, as in Fig. 198.

Lining and matting tools are used in order to give variety of texture to the work. Liners have a number of shallow lines, or grooves across them; the others are hatched in different manners. The function of this whole group of tools has been much abused. Texture is often relied upon to produce changes of light and shade which should have been caused by changes of plane. It is better to produce the desired effect by modelling the surface than by altering its texture. These tools are employed also for touching up cast work. A very finely grained matt tool can be made by nicking a rod of hard steel all round, then breaking a piece off and using the broken end.

Ring tools make a circular mark, as their name implies. Number and letter punches are made in sets. The letters or figures are reversed, like type, if they are to be used on the surface of the work; but are not reversed when the punches are to be used on the underside. It may happen that several letter or figure punches are employed together in a row. To keep that row straight it is well to make a light scratch on the metal as a base or head-line for the letters. Slide the punch down the surface till it catches in the scratch. Hold it firmly upright and use your hammer.

Tools for backgrounding or for producing an " all over " texture are so held that they can be moved about freely just above the surface of the metal, the force of the hammer blows bringing them into contact. The work can be done thus much quicker than if the tool is brought to rest upon the surface of the metal, and the blow then given.

7. *One or two snarling irons* (Figs. 219 and 220). These are rods of iron perhaps a foot long by about ½ inch square. One extremity is held in the vice, and the other ends in a rounded knob set at right angles to the axis of the rod. These tools are often made Z-shape, as shown in Fig. 220 (p. 125). They are used to produce bumps or bosses on the outside of tubes, bowls or other vessels which are too narrow in the mouth to allow the insertion of a hammer, or repoussé tool, for that purpose. One end of the tool being in the vice, the bowl or other work is so held that the knob on the tool is pressed firmly against the underside of the place where the boss is to be produced. A sharp blow is now given to that part of the snarling iron which is near the vice. The rebound from the blow causes the knob to strike sharply against the metal opposite to it. The blow is repeated again and again, until a sufficiently large bump has been produced on the work. It may be necessary to anneal the work should it get hard before this result is attained. The pattern, having been roughly bossed up in this manner, can be finished from the front with chasing tools. An iron bar should be used to strike the snarling iron. It is easier to manage than a hammer.

8. Two or three cakes of zinc, lead or tin, weighing 3 to 10 lb., for use as described above.

CHAPTER XIV

REPOUSSÉ WORK (*continued*)

Transferring the design. Lettering. Patterns on bowls. Work in the round.

TO TRANSFER a design to sheet metal the simplest method is that of tracing it with carbon paper. Part of a knitting-needle set into a wooden handle, as the lead in a pencil, makes a good stylus. The point of the needle should be ground quite smooth and round. When buying carbon paper see that the marks it will make on metal do not rub out very easily. Paper which is prepared on one side only should be chosen. To a convex surface, such as the side of a bowl, or to any domed-up piece of metal it is nearly impossible to transfer a design in the manner just described. It should be drawn freehand in pencil, the proportions being checked by measurement with dividers. To make corrections in the drawing, first rub out the part that is wrong. This is best done by fine emery paper used with a circular stroke, then re-draw with pencil or ink. Ink-lines may be trued up with the point of a knife. Another method is that of laying the design upon the metal, and then lightly pricking out the principal masses with a pointed punch. The little marks showing through on the other side of the metal will serve as guides for knocking up the parts in relief.

Inscriptions may be worked from either the back or the front of the metal, or by a combination of the two processes. It all depends on the form and section of the letter which you wish to use. A letter which is round-topped in section (Fig. 216) can be worked entirely from the back. For a square-topped letter (Fig. 217) some chasing on the front may be necessary, as also for a

216   217   218

form such as Fig. 218, where the top of the letter is hollowed. It is important to remember that when inscriptions are worked from the back alone, each individual letter will work out taller and wider than the drawing, to the extent of about double the thickness of the sheet of metal from which it is beaten. The letters in the inscription will therefore appear to be crowded closer together than in

123

the design. When working from the underside of the metal, allowance must therefore be made for this thickening of the letters, by tracing them, to the extent indicated, slenderer and shorter than they are shown in the drawing. They will then work out the right size in front. When letters are outlined from the front, of course, no such allowance has to be made. It is hardly necessary to point out that inscriptions must be reversed, right and left, on the back of the metal if they are to come out the right way round in front.

When letters are to be outlined from the front, the metal may be either fastened down on wood with nails, or the work may be done on pitch. The outlining is done with a tracer. The metal is then turned face downwards on to the pitch board. The work done with the tracer in front will show through on the back of the metal as a ridge round the outline of the letters. This will serve as a guide for the embossing. Each letter is now knocked up, piece by piece, first with a tool shaped like Fig. 214 and afterwards with others like Figs. 205 to 208. Should a square-topped letter be intended, a traced line is put in from the back a little within the ridge just mentioned. This traced line will outline the top of the letter. All the metal within it must now be driven down to the level of the deepest part of the line. Before all the letters have been embossed the edges of the sheet of metal will probably have risen high enough to break loose from the pitch. They must be kept down with heavy weights. Care must be taken to work on no parts of the metal which are insufficiently supported. Should any such be found, the metal must be warmed and pressed down into contact with the pitch before the work can proceed. When all the letters have been worked, remove the metal from the pitch and clean it as described above. The driving up of the letters will be found to have forced the background forward a little also. Lay the work on the bench and go over it carefully with a mallet, straightening the sheet and driving the letters bodily a little towards the background. Owing to the hammering which they have already received, the letters will be harder than the background, so if treated carefully they will not be injured. Put the work on the pitch board again and finish up the lettering from the back. Remove it from the pitch, clean and level it as before. If the letters are now to be chased from the front, turn the work face downwards on the bench and fill all the hollows at the back of the letters with broken pieces of pitch. Heat the work till the pitch runs in and fills up all the hollows. Let it cool a little. Warm the pitch on the board with the blowpipe. Lift the work and put it face upwards on the pitch board, and leave it under weights until cool. It can now be tooled over as required.

To work a pattern on a bowl, first anneal the work, then fill it with pitch, inserting at the same time a piece of wood 1½ inch diameter (not less), and long enough to project several inches above the top of the bowl (Fig. 221). When the pitch has set, grip the

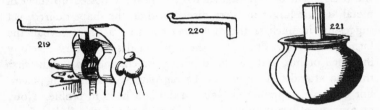

projecting piece of wood in the vice, tilting it to any convenient angle, and the work can proceed. Another method is to fill the work with pitch and to lay it on its side on a sandbag. A stirrup or rope, passing over the bowl, through holes in the bench to the foot can be used to steady the work while the chasing proceeds. When the chasing has been carried far enough, warm the work with the blowpipe until the pitch can be turned out. If the metal is hard anneal it again. Should the mouth of the bowl be large enough to allow the use of repoussé tools inside, put the side of the bowl on to a pitch board and boss up the pattern from the inside, turning the bowl on the pitch board when necessary. If the mouth of the bowl is too small, boss up the pattern with snarling irons. When sufficient relief has been obtained, anneal the work, refill with pitch as before, and finish from the outside.

Repoussé work has sometimes to be done almost in the round. Fine examples of such work may be found in Greek bronzes, and mediæval steel armours. They were executed partly by raising or sinking and partly by repoussé work. The metal was first raised to about the desired relief either by bossing it up from the back with round-faced hammers, the snarling iron or by punches; or by raising the shape with a hammer on a stake, just as a bowl is formed; or by a combination of these two methods. As a rule the great difficulty is to keep the metal approximately the same thickness all over. It is well to work alternately from the front and back, gradually arriving at the highest relief and the lowest undercutting. Remember to anneal the work whenever it gets at all hard. Any cracks must be joined up with hard solder (unless you are working on a metal such as pewter which will not allow of its use). When the right relief has been arrived at, anneal the work, fill the hollow with broken pieces of pitch and melt them in, taking great care to leave no bubbles. Then put the work on the pitch bowl. At this stage the design will be represented by an unevenly bossed up sheet of metal, a little larger in every direction than the shape desired, yet suggesting it much as the dust-sheet covering a statue reveals the form underneath. Then draw the figure or design in very carefully in pencil or ink, and go ahead with your chasing tools. The first thing to attend to is to get all the big planes in their right places. For example, suppose that you are doing a head in profile. Now, no amount of beautiful work on the nose and mouth will be of any use if these parts are left the same height above the background as, say, the ear or the hair. They should be in lower relief. They must go down or the ear and hair must come up, and in like manner through the whole work the planes must be correct. It is only when this is achieved that work looks well from the side view as well as from the front, and then the finer details should be put in. Whenever the metal gets hard in the process of working, it must be taken off the pitch, cleaned, annealed, and filled with pitch again, before the work can proceed—otherwise it may crack badly.

CHAPTER XV

MOULDINGS

Folded edges. Wired edges. The drawswage. Making the dies. The draw-bench. Swaged mouldings. Turned mouldings. Bending strip metal. Running plaster mouldings for casting.

PERHAPS THE SIMPLEST form of moulding is that produced at the edge of a piece of sheet metal by folding it upon itself or over a wire. The turned-down piece thus forms a little border or moulding (Fig. 223). The tool used for this folding of the edge is known as a " turning-over tool " (Fig. 222). It is just a flat piece of steel or iron measuring perhaps 5 inches by 2 inches by $\frac{3}{16}$ inch. An old plane iron can be turned into a very good one. Soften it in the fire. Leave the end nearly sharp, bevel one long edge to rather less than $\frac{1}{8}$ inch thick, and file all the sharp edges off it and off the other long edge, which should be left, however, to the full $\frac{3}{16}$ inch thickness. The top of the iron, where the hammer used to strike it, should be rounded for use on curves, and all its sharp edges smoothed off. If a moulding like Fig. 223 is required, put the

tool in the vice with its thin end upwards. About $\frac{1}{2}$ inch of the tool must project above the jaws of the vice. If more, the tool will vibrate more than you wish. Mark a line on the metal parallel to its edge, either by ruling it with a straight-edge or, if you are sure of the truth of the edge of the metal, by setting a pair of dividers to the correct span and running it along the edge; one leg of the dividers sliding along on the bench against the edge of the metal, the other resting on and marking its surface (see Fig. 18, p. 45). Of course, curves may be drawn in the same way. Hold the metal so that the scratched line comes over the turning-over tool and tap the edge down with a mallet, or with a hammer which has no sharp

127

edges to its face. Remember that whenever metal is bent with a hammer, the face of the tool should have rounded edges, otherwise it will mark the metal badly. The edge of the metal should be tapped over the tool until it is bent to about right angles to its original position. Then lay the work on the bench with the bent edge of the metal sticking up. Carefully and evenly tap the edge down on to the sheet, making sure as you do so that an equal amount is turned over all along, and that the folded edge makes a true line, not a waved one. To do this neatly requires a good deal of care, though the work itself is very simple.

If it should be necessary to hide the actual edge of the metal you may fold the edge toward the side which will not show on the completed article. When the edge has been tapped down evenly, place the work with the folded piece downwards on a flat stake. Take the hammer and a piece of boxwood shaped like a square-ended repoussé tool, its sharp corners having been removed, and tap down to the stake that part of the metal which is a little further from the folded edge than the turned-in part extends (Figs. 224, 225). The double thickness at the edge will become a moulding, raised a little above the surface. If a large moulding is required the metal may be folded over a wire, which may itself be of almost any section. To cover a wire properly it is very important that the correct amount of metal should be allowed for the purpose. Too much is worse than too little, for the superfluous amount crumples up untidily, and is very difficult to remove. First see that the edge of the metal is true. Then make a pencil mark parallel to it distant three times the diameter of the wire. Thus, for $\frac{1}{4}$-inch wire mark the line $\frac{3}{4}$ inch from the edge. Put the turning-over tool in the vice with its rounded edge upwards, and turn down the edge of the metal from the mark. Tap the metal well over the tool, so as to form as much as possible of the hollow to receive the wire. But give it as few blows as will do the work, for much hammering would stretch the edge of the metal, and you do not wish that. Now rest the metal on a flat stake, the bench, or a smooth cake of lead, and hold the wire into the hollow with pliers while you tap the edge of the metal right round it. Cut the wire only when it is nearly all covered in, for the exact length can then be easily decided—not an easy matter otherwise on a curve. See that you leave no sharp edges when you cut the wire, or they may work their way through the metal later on. The wired edge may be brought forward in the same way as the folded one (Fig. 226), or the work may be held face downwards on a stake with the wire and folded edge of the metal on top, the wire overhanging the edge of the stake as shown in Fig. 227. The wired edge may be hammered down to

the position shown in the next drawing. This is an excellent way of bringing a wired edge forward. The edge of the stake may be rounded if a sharp corner is not desired. Of course, it must be quite smooth and true.

Mouldings of almost any section may be produced by means of the drawswage (Fig. 233). This tool consists of a strong rectangular frame with movable dies, which are pressed together by a screw. A groove of the exact section of the required moulding is filed in the adjacent edges of the dies. Then a strip of metal is repeatedly drawn through it, till, the dies having been gradually pressed closer together by the screw, the strip of metal is forced to take the required shape. The frame and dies should be quite rigid, therefore the former should be made from metal not less than $\frac{3}{4}$ inch wide. It will be seen from the illustration that on the two long sides of the frame the metal projects inwards in a V-shaped ridge, A. This ridge is, however, cut away at the left-hand end of the drawing, so that the dies, into which it fits, may be removed. Each die has a V-shaped groove at either end corresponding to the projecting ridges on the frame. The whole arrangement is very similar to the stock and dies by which screws are cut. Indeed, a very useful drawswage can be made from an old screw stock, especially if it be of large size.

Suppose you wish to make a length of moulding like Fig. 230. Remove the dies by withdrawing the screw and lifting them out of the frame at the gap. On the upper face of C, file a groove to the exact section of the moulding required. The shape of the groove may be tested while you are filing it by hammering a piece of lead or other soft piece of metal into it. The lead will take the exact shape of the groove. Modelling wax may be used instead. Alternately file and test the shape of the groove in this way till you are

129

satisfied with its form. You must now widen it out towards each side of the die that the groove may taper, as the holes in a drawplate are tapered. In a drawplate, however, the tapering is towards one side only, but in the die it is in both directions from the centre. But you must leave the centre of the die untouched. Take great

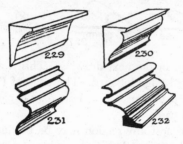

care to prevent any scratch or other roughness being left on the die near the centre, for every mark will be reproduced in the moulding. Nor should any sharp edges or corners be left at the extremities of the groove, for they would cut or tear the moulding instead of quietly pressing it into shape. Take the die B and round off its lower edge on both sides. If B and C are now put together and held to the light, the groove should look exactly the right section in the middle, but be wider towards the front and back edges of the dies. They may now be hardened and tempered, but this is not necessary unless a good length of the moulding has to be drawn. Put the dies in the swage. Take a length of wire or strip metal of the nearest to the required section that may be available. It is sometimes possible to save the swage a little work by first flattening the wire or roughly hammering the strip to shape. Anneal it, grease or oil it, and put it between dies B and C. Tighten the screw till the dies grip the strip. Then on the drawbench pull it through the swage to within $\frac{1}{2}$ inch of the end. Screw the dies a little closer, and pull back again in the reverse direction. Repeat the process again and again, annealing occasionally, greasing frequently and screwing the dies closer every time. The strip will gradually assume the desired shape.

Mouldings 229 and 230 are solid and are flat at the back. But frequently a moulding is required the back of which follows the contour of the front. Less metal is used in this way. Such

130

mouldings are made from strips of sheet metal instead of wire. The dies are so made that part of C projects into the groove D. If the metal for the moulding is thin, the dies must be made to match each other accurately, and careful attention given to any projecting ridges, which might cut through the strip.

Small mouldings, up to ⅛ inch, can be drawn by hand, the draw-swage being held in the vice. But for larger work some mechanical help must be had. The drawbench (Fig. 233A) is the most generally

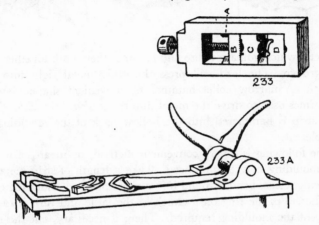

convenient tool. It is a low bench 5 feet or 6 feet long. At one end is fixed a roller with strong handles to turn it, at the other a pair of cleats to hold the drawplate or swage. A strap is fastened to the roller and ends in an iron ring, triangular in shape. This slips over the hooked handles of the drawtongs. The extremity of the wire which is to form the moulding is gripped in the drawtongs and the swage put into position against the cleats. The ring on the strap is now hooked on to the tongs and the strap tightened by pulling the large handles. Very considerable force is required to turn the handles when a wide moulding is being drawn. Geared draw-benches are made, and the strap is sometimes replaced by an endless chain.

When only a short length of moulding is required, a groove of the required section may be filed into a piece of steel and the strip or wire hammered into it a little at a time (Fig. 234). The tool should be wide enough to take an inch or more of the moulding at once. No sharp corners should be left at the extremities of the groove.

The metal should not be hammered right home at once, but gradually worked down with the hammer along its whole length, no part being finished till the moulding is nearly complete all along. It may be necessary to anneal it first. If the moulding is not a solid one, it is necessary to lay a strip of lead above the strip

of metal which you are to use and hammer them both together into the groove. The lead will press the other metal right into the hollow. A narrow collet hammer of convenient shape may be sometimes used to drive the metal into the groove (Fig. 235). The lead strip is hammered into the hollow back of the moulding to complete it.

The following is a very convenient method, by means of which any moulding may be produced. Take a length of strip metal of convenient size, bend it round into a ring and hard solder the ends together. Fix the ring on a chuck in the lathe and turn it to the shape of the moulding required. Then, if necessary, cut the ring at the join and straighten out the strip.

You will have, of course, no difficulty in bending into a ring a strip of metal measuring, say, $\frac{3}{8}$ inch by $\frac{1}{8}$ inch if you bend it in the direction of its smaller measurement. But if you wish to make a flat ring of it, $\frac{1}{8}$ inch in thickness, you may have some difficulty in getting the metal to bend in that direction. You can, however, do the work in the following manner. Take a piece of hardwood measuring, say, 3 inches by 4 inches by 1 inch and put it end up in the vice. The vice should grip it in the direction in which it measures 3 inches, and 1 inch of the wood should project above the jaws of the vice. Make two saw cuts $\frac{1}{2}$ inch deep, leaving the exact width of your strip of metal between them. With a chisel remove the wood between the saw cuts and round off the vertical corners of the notch (Fig. 236). Anneal the strip of metal and put one end of it, flat side up, into the notch. By using the other end of the strip as a lever you can bend the metal to the curve required. Do not cut the ring from the remainder of the strip until you have got it to

132

the exact curve, for the long strip makes a convenient handle and lever. The ring may try to " buckle " in the process, but a few taps with a mallet on a stake will soon flatten it again. Strip copper up to 1 inch by ¼ inch in thickness may be bent in this way by hand. It goes easier if red-hot. The notch in this case must be lined with sheet metal, or, better still, made in a stout piece of metal instead.

Mouldings are often built up from a number of strips or concentric rings of different sections, soldered one above the other (see Chapter XXXIII).

The simplest way of making a complicated moulding to go round a difficult shape, such as that shown in Fig. 237, is to run it in plaster and then cast it in the metal. First make two brass templates, one to the exact shape of the ground plan, E, the other to that of the moulding, F. Soft solder the first template on to another piece of sheet metal, G, which measures 2 inches larger all round. Solder also a few loops of wire on top to hold the plaster in place; you don't want it to slide off. Fasten the second template to a small wedge of wood in such a manner that when the latter lies flat on the bench the template stands up on its edge. Mix a little plaster, as described on p. 21, and put some of it on the wire loops and all over the plan.

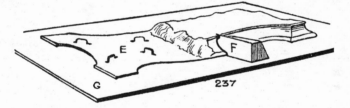

Hold the second template flat on the sheet of metal G, and rest it against the edge of the metal plan, E. You can now slide the template F along the edge of E; it will scrape off any plaster which has come too far. Add plaster wherever required. Slide F again and again round E, washing the former whenever it gets clogged with plaster. Very soon the plaster on E will get firm, and the template will cut it cleanly. Take great care to hold the wedge of wood to which the template F is fastened quite flat on G all the while. To fill up small gaps in the plaster mix a teaspoonful at a time. To mix a small amount of plaster like this, take a bare spoonful of the dry plaster and put it, spoon and all, into a basin of water. When the bubbles have ceased to rise from the plaster in the spoon take it out and beat it up into an even paste. Apply it with a brush, and when setting run the template by again. Keep template F wet when finishing. When the moulding is free from gaps, it is ready for moulding and casting in its final material.

A moulding may be formed in sheet metal by modelling it on pitch with repoussé tools. The work may be done from either the back or the front of the metal. To work a moulding on a large bowl it is usual to bed the side of the bowl in pitch, the bowl being moved round as each section of its circumference is completed. For work done on the outside, fill the bowl with pitch and insert a thick stick by which to hold it in a vice, as described on p. 125.

Large simple mouldings may be worked with hammer alone on suitably shaped stakes or swages.

CHAPTER XVI

TWISTED WIRES

Their value. Analysis of each pattern.

ORNAMENTAL WIRES are used in jewellery, in silversmiths' work, for the decoration of mouldings, and alone, as in bangles. In ancient times many varieties were in use, both goldsmiths and armourers displaying considerable ingenuity in inventing and combining different patterns. But in recent years little thought has been given to them, with the result that the varieties in use are now very few indeed. Curiously enough, the Japanese, to whom their decorative qualities might have been expected to appeal, have never shown any interest in them. Medieval armourers, on the contrary, found in them an unfailing joy, as the numerous wire patterns to be found on sword-grips testify. Medieval silversmiths also, with their keen attention to every detail of the craft, invented and employed many beautiful examples. That numbered 7 below, for example, gives a most charming play of light and shade. That numbered 23 is one of the most beautiful of the whole series. No. 30 was used by the ancient Irish metalworkers for some of the splendid gold torcs now in the Dublin Museum. Six dozen varieties of wire patterns are shown in Figs. 238-243, though the number might have been doubled without difficulty. But enough are given to suggest the wide choice available to a craftsman who wishes to give an unexpected pleasure to anyone who examines his work. Every one of the patterns can be made without difficulty, and the interest excited by its use will well repay the thought put into it.

1. Square wire twisted to right slowly.
2. Square wire twisted to right quickly.
3. Square wire twisted to right quickly, afterwards drawn through round drawplate.
4. Square wire twisted to right quickly, afterwards drawn through square drawplate.

5. Square wire twisted to right intermittently. Grip in hand-vices with leather guards to jaws, or in wood clams.

6. Square wire twisted intermittently to right and left in turn.

7. Square wire twisted alternately to right and left.

8. Flat strip twisted to right.

9. Flat strip twisted alternately to right and left.

10. Four square wires put together and twisted as one.

11. Two round wires twisted together quickly.

12. Two round wires twisted together slowly.

13. Two round wires twisted together and afterwards flattened.

14. Two pieces of square wire each twisted to right, afterwards put together and twisted to right.

15. One piece of square wire twisted to right; this and a piece of round wire put together and twisted to right.

16. Two pieces of square wire, one twisted to right and one to left, afterwards put together and twisted to right. The piece which was originally twisted to left is now nearly unwound owing to the right-hand twisting it has undergone.

17. One piece of small twisted wire (two small wires twisted to right) and two large round wires put together and twisted to right.

18. Four square wires each twisted to right, afterwards put together and twisted to right.

19. Two large round wires twisted to right and two strands of twisted wire (two small round wires twisted to right) wound in the grooves.

20. Square wire twisted to right. A small round wire wound on alternate faces.

21. Square wire twisted to right, one strand of two small square wires twisted right wound on one face.

22. Square wire twisted to right, a strand of small square twisted wire wound on alternate faces.

23. Square wire twisted to right, one round wire between two strands of two small wires twisted together, wound on alternate faces.

24. Two strands of square wire twisted to right, put together and twisted to right; one strand of two round wires twisted left and wound between.

25. Four square wires put together and twisted as one. One strand

TWISTED WIRES
Figs. 238–43

(See pp. 135 to 139)

Fig. 238.   Twisted wire patterns, 1–12.   (See pp. 135–36.)

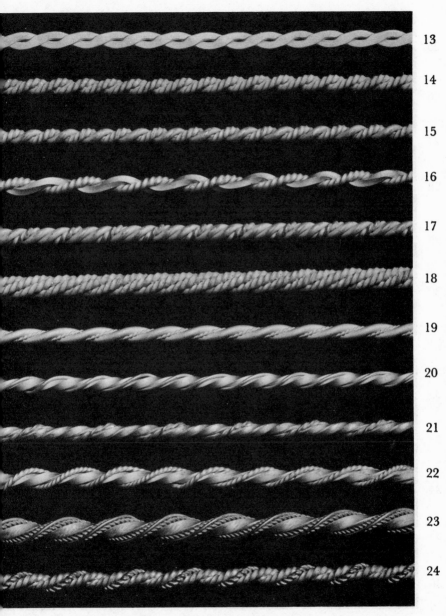

13

14

15

16

17

18

19

20

21

22

23

24

Fig. 239.   Twisted wire patterns, 13–24.   (See p. 136.)

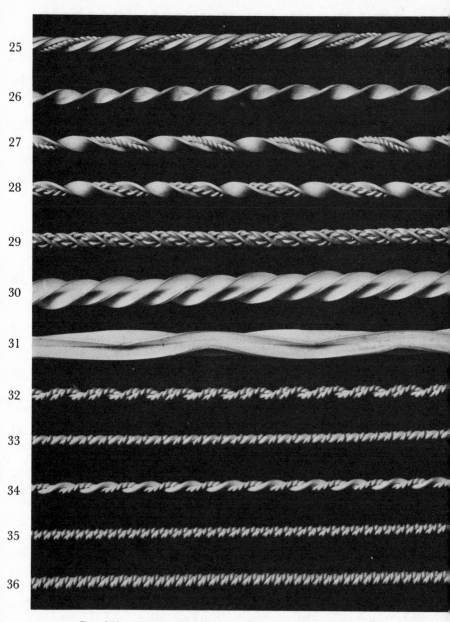

FIG. 240.   Twisted wire patterns, 25–36.   (See pp. 136–37.)

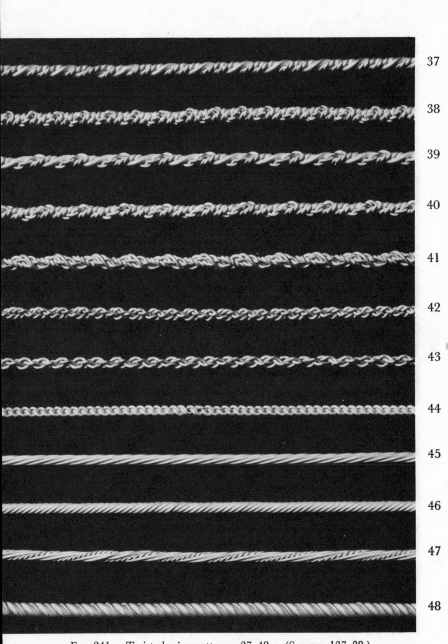

37

38

39

40

41

42

43

44

45

46

47

48

Fig. 241.   Twisted wire patterns, 37–48.   (See pp. 137–38.)

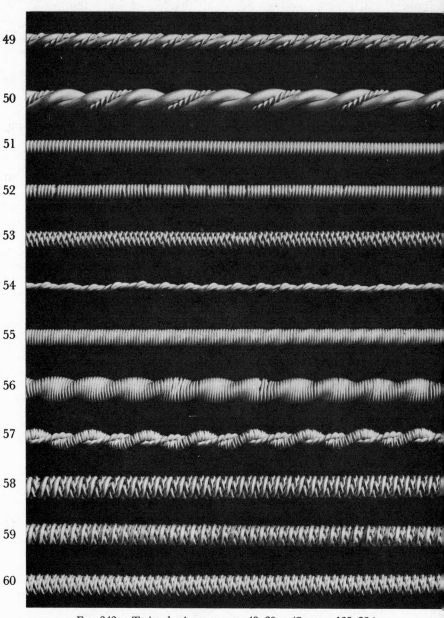

FIG. 242. Twisted wire patterns, 49–60. (See pp. 138–39.)

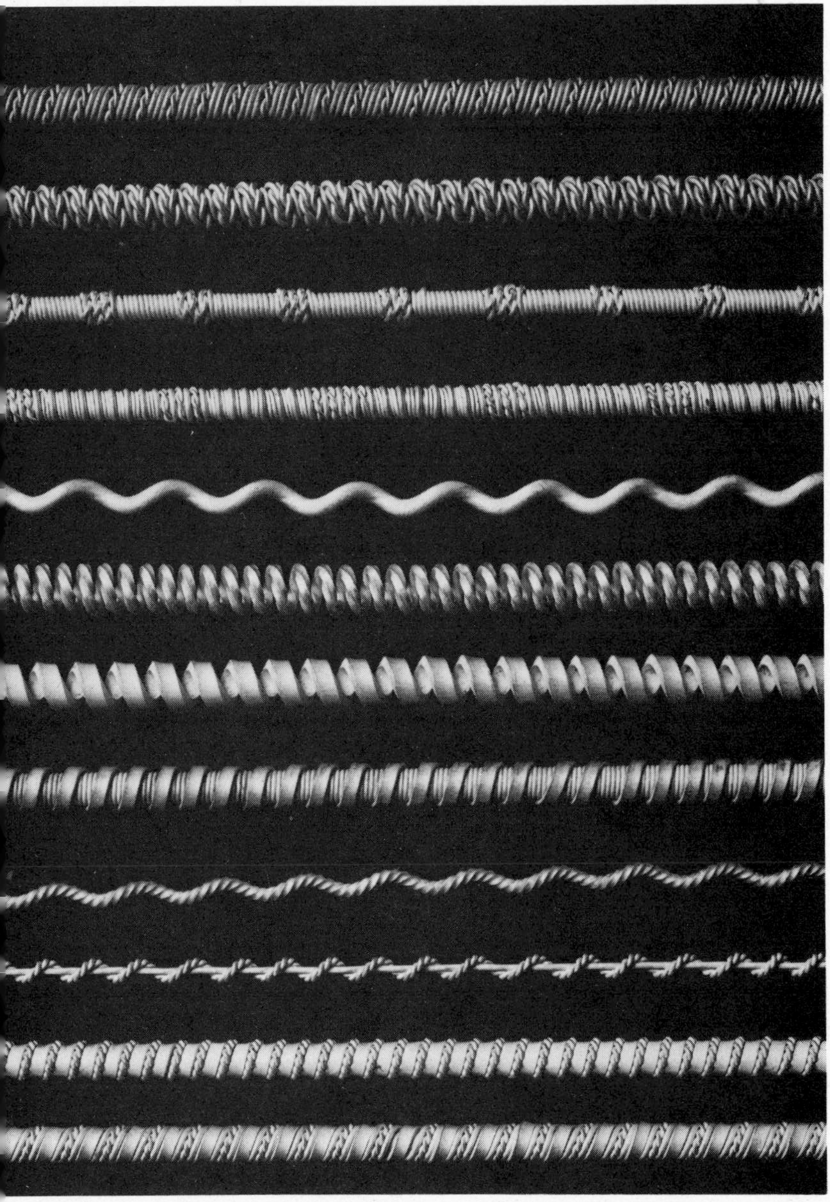

FIG. 243. Twisted wire patterns, 61–72. (See p. 139.)

removed and replaced by a strand of two small round wires twisted left.

26. Flat strip twisted to right.

27. Flat strip twisted to left, one strand of two small round wires twisted left wound on.

28. Flat strip twisted to the left, one strand of two small wires twisted together right wound on.

29. Flat strip twisted to left, two strands each of two small wires twisted together right wound on.

30. Thin strips soldered together to make a strip whose section is a cross (+). A round wire may be laid temporarily in each of the four gaps. The strip and wires are twisted as one mass. The four round wires are then removed. The use of this pattern was familiar to the goldsmiths of Cyprus and Ireland 3,000 years ago. They used it for their earrings and torcs. Some of the latter were constructed without the use of solder. They were forged from a rectangular bar, cut with a chisel nearly halfway through from opposite sides, then hammered to shape, and afterwards twisted. In some examples the extreme edge of the web is thickened by peaning.

31. Thin strips soldered together to make a strip whose section is a cross (+). A round wire is temporarily laid in each gap (four). The wires in this case are gripped in the hand-vice wherever necessary and the twist to right or left made as required.

32. Three strands each of two small wires twisted together right, twisted together right. One strand afterwards removed.

33. One strand of two small wires twisted together right, and one strand of round wire twisted together right.

34. Similar construction but a slower twist.

35. Two strands, each of two small wires twisted together right, twisted together right.

36. Two strands, each of three small wires twisted together right, twisted together right.

37. Two strands, each of two small wires twisted together right, and one larger wire, twisted together right.

38. Two strands, each of two small wires twisted together right and one strand of two small wires twisted together left, twisted together right.

39. A strand of two small wires twisted together right, another

twisted left, and a plain wire twisted together right. It will be noted that the pair of small wires originally twisted left have become partially unwound.

40. Three strands, each of two small wires twisted together right, twisted together right. One strand removed and replaced by a strand of two small wires twisted together left, wound on.

41. Two strands, each of two small wires twisted together right, and one of two small wires twisted together left, twisted together left. A small wire afterwards wound on between the two right-hand twists. Note how the strands with right-hand twist have become partially untwisted.

42. Two strands, each of two small wires twisted together right, twisted together left. Note that they are opening out.

43. Similar material. Further twisting to left. The fabric is now more open.

44. Similar material. The twisting to the left is continued further. The result is an entirely new pattern, triangular in section.

45. Seven equal wires twisted to right loosely.

46. Seven equal wires twisted to right tightly.

47. Seven equal wires, two removed and replaced by strands of twisted wires.

48. Two large round wires twisted together. Two small wires afterwards wound in the hollows.

49. A four-stranded pattern. Two of the strands are of large round wire, the third and fourth of smaller wires twisted right. The four strands are twisted together right.

50. Two large wires twisted together right. One strand of two small round wires twisted right wound on.

51. One small round wire coiled on a larger wire.

52. One small round wire coiled on a larger wire, but the coil is made open at regular intervals.

53. Two small wires twisted right and coiled right on a large wire.

54. A strand of two small wires twisted together right, a single wire wound on.

55. A square wire twisted right and covered with fine wire, wound on.

56. Two round wires twisted together right and covered with fine wire, wound on.

57. One strand constructed like the last and one strand of two wires twisted together right, twisted together right.

58. One strand of round wire and one of two small wires twisted together right, coiled on a large wire.

59. One strand of square wire and one of two small wires twisted right, coiled on a large wire.

60. Similar to No. 58, but here the round wire is smaller than the twist.

61. Three strands of round wire and one of two wires twisted together right, coiled on a large wire.

62. Three strands, one of two wires twisted together right, another with left-hand twist, the third a plain round wire, all coiled on a large round wire.

63. Two small wires coiled on a large round wire for six turns each. Then they are twisted together right for a sufficient distance to make three complete turns round the large wire. The two wires are then again wound six times round the large wire, and twisted together for the next three turns, as before. Any slight irregularity at the end of the twisted coils should be turned to the side of the work which will not be seen.

64. The same as No. 63, with one slightly larger wire wound on afterwards between the coils of twisted wires and between each pair of plain wire coils.

65. Two round wires twisted together. One removed.

66. Square wire twisted right, afterwards coiled openly on round wire which is afterwards withdrawn.

67. Flat strip coiled openly on round wire which is afterwards withdrawn.

68. Small wire coiled right on large round wire. Strip coiled right openly over all.

69. Two strands square wire twisted right. Twisted together right. One strand removed.

70. Two small wires twisted together right. Coiled openly right on small round wire.

71. Strip and a pair of twisted wires coiled right on large round wire.

72. Strip, and one strand of two small wires twisted right, flanked by two small round wires, all coiled right on large round wire.

CHAPTER XVII

HINGES AND JOINTS

Chenier joints. Joint tool. Various hints. Soldering. Brooch joints.

THE HINGE to the lid of a metal box is composed of a number of short lengths of tube, or " chenier," soldered alternately to the box and the lid. A piece of wire, called the " joint pin," running through them all, keeps box and lid together. The strips of metal, or " bearers," soldered on both box and lid, when the metal of which they are composed is not strong enough to bear the strain of the hinge, have the effect of strengthening the joint. If they are put on the outside of the box they sometimes form also a convenient stop, by means of which the lid is kept from opening too far.

To make chenier, take a strip of metal which you are to use, measuring three times the width of the tube you wish to make. Carefully remove any burr or rough edge—if left on it would give you trouble later. Make a point an inch long at one end of the strip by cutting little triangular pieces from the two sides. Lay the strip lengthwise over the groove in a swage block (Fig. 20), or even in a semicircular notch cut across a piece of wood. Tap the strip into the groove with a narrow hammer (Fig. 21), curling the edges up as much as possible—the middle will take care of itself. Then put a drawplate in the vice and draw the strip through a suitable hole. When it has passed through a few holes its edges will meet, and the strip has become a tube. To make sure that the tube is true inside take a piece of copper, brass or iron wire of suitable size, oil it and put it inside the tube. Draw the tube down hard on to it. It is only necessary now to reverse the drawplate and put the end of the wire through a hole which will only just admit its passage, and the wire may be drawn out of the tube. If the chenier is not quite straight it should be annealed, and a number of little nicks made with a needle file along the side upon which the seam comes, for this crack shows very little, and it is important later on that there be no doubt as to which side of the tube it comes on. Roll the chenier on a flat stake till it is quite straight. See also Chapter VI, p. 45.

140

You must now decide whether you will have the hinge projecting from the back of the box, flush with it, or sunk a little way below the surface. In the two latter cases the bearers are soldered inside the box and lid; in the former they are outside. Fit and solder the bearers accordingly. Next make the groove in which the "joints" or "knuckles," i.e. the pieces of chenier, are to lie. Take a good deal of care to make this run truly across the box. If it is inclined ever so little the lid will not look straight when the box is open. The groove is to be cut, partly in the box and partly in the lid, and it must be just large enough to hold the chenier when the lid is in its place on the box. The groove may be cut with a file, followed by a round scorper, and finally trued up with a joint-file. This is a flat file, roughened only on its edges, and these are rounded. Try the chenier in the groove.from time to time. Fig. 244 shows a joint of five knuckles with bearers, *A* and *B*, soldered on outside the box. Fig. 245 is a flush joint, the bearers being soldered inside in this case.

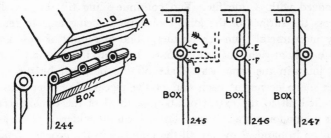

The edges *C* and *D* meet when the lid is opened to about a right angle, and keep it from going back too far. In Fig. 246 the joints are sunk below the surface. The bearers are inside in this case also. The wide edges *E* and *F* form the stop. They are wide because a clear space of at least 90 degrees from the centre of the pin is always necessary to allow the lid to open as far as a right angle to its position when shut. The joint for the back of a watch is of this sunken type. You will notice the wide bevel near the centre. Fig. 247 shows a hinge which would open beyond the right angle. It would go right back, as it has no stopping edges.

When the chenier fits the groove, decide as to how many pieces the joint is to have. An odd number is always chosen; and the box always has one more piece than the lid. If the joint is of three pieces only, it is well to make the one for the lid rather longer than either

141

of the others, that it may be as strong as the two opposed to it. If the joint is of five or more pieces, they are made of equal length. Cut each knuckle just a shade longer than it will be required, using a piercing-saw. The ends of each piece must now be filed quite truly at right angles to its length; otherwise there would be uneven gaps between the different pieces, and the lid of the box would not open smoothly.

To true up the ends of the joints you must use the joint tool (Fig. 252). It is a flat piece of hardened steel, perhaps 1 inch square and $\frac{1}{8}$ inch thick, with a small handle. A triangular or kite-shaped hole is pierced through the middle of the blade. The sides of this hole are filed accurately at right angles to the flat surfaces of the tool. The end of the piece of chenier is put through the triangular hole, and clamped in position with the small set screw provided for that purpose. The extremity of the tube is allowed to project just a shade above the surface. This small amount of metal is now removed with a fine file. You continue filing till the file slides across the surface of the joint tool without being able to remove any more metal from the chenier. The extremity of this is now quite truly at right angles to its axis. Level up the extremities of all the joints in the same way. Take off the burr left by the filing. The sharp corner at each end of the pieces of chenier must be bevelled off to the extent of about a third of the circumference. The reason for this will be seen later, when the soldering of the joints is taken in hand. Now lay all the knuckles in the groove prepared for them, and see that box and lid come together fairly all round. Put a little mark opposite the end of each of the joints. Remove the lid, leaving all the chenier in the groove on the box. Fasten with a clip, or a wire round the box, the alternate pieces which are to be soldered to the box. Remember that the two end pieces always belong to the box, never to the lid. Take particular care that the crack or seam, left up the side of the chenier when you made it, is in each case turned down into the groove, where it will be soldered safely. If you do not attend to this the joint will be liable to open out later on. You can always find the seam if you put the file-nicks in, as suggested above. If you keep the joints which belong to the lid between the others you will be able to see that they are all in their right places.

Now very carefully put borax to each of the pieces which belong to the box. Take care that the borax does not spread, or boil up later, to quite the ends of the pieces of chenier. It might catch the lid chenier, and where it goes the solder will go also. Apply the solder, and fire it just enough to tack the knuckles in their places. Remove the knuckles which belong to the lid, and solder all the others quite soundly. You will now see why the corner of the chenier was bevelled off, as above suggested. The solder has crept round the end of the chenier where it lies in the groove and has filled up the little gap which you made when you bevelled off the corner near the crack in the tube. If you had not done so there would not now be room for the lid knuckles to go home. They filled the whole available space before, leaving no room for the solder to trespass on their ground, as it were. Of course, you would not bevel the corner of the chenier all round, for the knuckles would not seem to touch in that case. You bevel the tube only at the part which fits in the groove. Some workers stop the solder from running too far by painting the work there with rouge, loam, tripoli or whiting. Always put just the correct amount of solder to fill the joint: not too much nor too little. When the soldering is completed, boil out the box in pickle. See that none of the knuckles have shifted. Then fix and solder the lid knuckles in the same way; and boil that out. Then carefully put box and lid together and run a wire through all the joints. See that everything goes truly. You may like to smooth out the inside of the joint with a broach. Smooth up the chenier both inside and outside the box. Finally take a brass wire which fits, wax it, and push it home. If the box is a silver one it is usual to plug the extremities of the joint with pieces of silver wire; the brass wire being shortened as necessary. In a good joint the lid should close itself when tilted. It should not stick or drop. To make sure that all the knuckles are in a direct line with each other, it is a good plan to run an oiled steel wire through them all, and to leave it in while the soldering is proceeding. You will find this steel wire a great help when wiring the knuckles in their places. Many craftsmen remove the chenier belonging to the lid before they solder the knuckles on the box.

For a lightly made box the bearer is often made from a section of the tube called the port-chenier or the counter-chenier. You proceed as follows. Draw down a piece of tube till it will fit tightly round the chenier from which the knuckles are to be cut. Force the chenier inside and anneal both together. They will then fit each other exactly. See that they are quite straight. Roll them on a piece of plate glass to ensure this. Then withdraw the chenier. Split the other tube in half lengthwise with the piercing-saw, and file the edges of each piece true. When doing this you must file away a good portion of the port-chenier in order to allow the hinge to open. Cut the joints from the other chenier, true them all in the joint tool, and bevel their corners near the crack. Lay them in place within the two halves of the split tube, taking care that the cracks in the knuckles in each case are turned against the split tube, where they will be safely soldered. You may now tie all together with binding wire and solder each alternate knuckle to its own piece of the split tube. In applying the borax take great care to prevent its spreading from one knuckle to another, for it would take the solder along also when the work was heated. Fire the work till each knuckle is just tacked in place by the solder, then separate the two halves of the joint and thoroughly solder all the knuckles. Boil out before you try to put the two halves together again. When the joint is complete you may solder each half in place on the box.

A brooch joint can be made in a number of different ways. We will take the chenier joint first. As a rule, several of these are made together. Take a piece of metal, size 6 on the metal gauge, and make from it a tube which you draw down till it is about $\frac{1}{16}$ inch in diameter. With a fine saw make a number of cuts beginning on the side where the crack is and extending two-thirds the way through the tube. The cuts to be $\frac{3}{32}$ inch apart. You have now a number of tiny lengths of tube all attached to one another at one side. With the saw cut away as much as possible of the second, fifth, eighth, eleventh, fourteenth, and so on, but do not weaken the strip so much that it breaks apart. Your tube now consists of a short length of tube, a gap, two short lengths, another gap, two short lengths, a third gap and so on, all connected on one side (Fig. 248). Next take a strip of metal size 6, as long as the tube, and $\frac{1}{8}$ inch wide. Tie the tube on to this with its cut side against the strip. Solder the two together, taking care that every one of the pieces of tube remaining is soldered safely. After boiling out, cut away with the saw all the pieces which join the lengths of tube together (Fig. 249). You would have had a good deal of filing to do if you had soldered

144

the whole length of tube to the strip, instead of making the saw cuts and removing every third length, or rather as much of it as was possible. Cut another strip of metal ⅛ inch wide, size 6, and tie it against the tube at right angles to the other strip. It is to form the bearer or spring, against which the pin of the brooch presses. After soldering it in position (Fig. 250), you can cut your long strip into

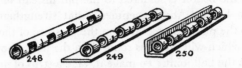

lengths—two pieces of tube with a gap between. This short length represents the part of the hinge which is fastened to the brooch itself. The pin part has yet to be made. In some joints which can be bought ready made, the tube and the bearer are made from the same piece of metal. They are therefore very strong.

To make the pin, take a short length of the same tube which you used for the other part of the joint. Lay it flat on the charcoal with the crack or seam side uppermost. Across it, at intervals of ⅛ inch, lay lengths of the wire which you are to use for the pins. Allow ¼ inch of the wire to project over the tube (Fig. 251). Solder each of the wires to the tube, making sure that the crack or seam down the tube is safely joined in the process. With a fine saw, cut through

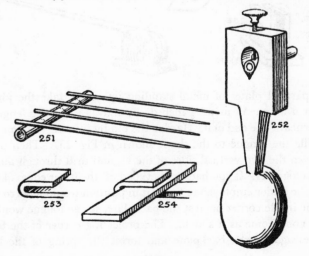

145

the tube between each pin. The soldering will have made the pins soft, so seize both ends of each pin in turn with pliers and twist it until it is quite hard. Then cut off the ¼ inch projecting wire. Very little filing will be required to allow the tube to drop into the gap in the other part of the hinge. The pin or pivot of the hinge can be slipped in and its end expanded with a few taps from a hammer. Sometimes the bearer is soldered to the pin instead of to the other part of the hinge. And sometimes a flat strengthening piece is soldered to the pin to protect it from the pressure of the bearer.

A hinge which will take less room than the joint above described is known as the ball joint. To make it, take a strip of metal, size 10, a full ⅛ inch wide. Grip ⅛ inch of the end of it in the pliers and fold it back on to the strip as much as possible (Fig. 253). Slip another piece of metal of the same thickness between the two parts, and tap flat (Fig. 254). Cut off the U-shaped piece from the strip and bevel off with a file a little of the inner top edges (marked G) of the U (Fig. 255). The U-shaped piece is to be soldered upside down on to a little metal plate, or even directly on to the back of the brooch. The rounded part of the U is now cut off (Fig. 256), and you have

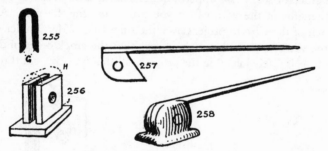

two parallel plates of metal standing up. Now take the pin and solder a tongue of metal ⅛ inch deep, and ³⁄₁₆ inch long lengthwise underneath one end of it. Harden the pin by twisting or hammering it. File the tongue to the shape shown in Fig. 257. Then push it between the two vertical sides of the U, and drill through all three pieces together. If you had not bevelled off the inner edges of the U first, the solder employed in fixing it in position would have rounded off the inside corner against the backplate, so the tongue would not have gone home as it should. The projecting corner of the tongue presses against the backplate and forms the spring of the hinge.

146

With the file, round over the top and sides of what remains of the U, then rivet the pin in. In another kind of ball joint the U-plate is made just as above described, but the curved part of the U is not cut away. It is allowed to remain, and acts as the bearer against which the pin springs. The U-plate is soldered so that the corner *H* (Fig. 256), is turned round to the position marked *J*. The tongue or blade of the pin, of course, has no need of the projecting corner shown in Fig. 257, as the pin springs against the rounded part of the U-plate.

A very safe joint can be made from rings of square wire soldered into position. The join in the rings should in each case be against the backplate. The bearer is added as above described.

The catch of a brooch is generally made from a ring of half-round wire soldered to a backplate. The opening in the ring being in this case at the side, and not against the backplate. In some cases no backplate is used, the catch being made from flattened wire curled up as required and soldered to the back of the brooch.

CHAPTER XVIII

METAL INLAYING AND OVERLAYING

Decorative effect. Piercing the recesses. Punching them. Islamic work. Persian inlays. Overlaying. Engraving. Tools. Etching. Etching grounds. Transferring the design. Needling. Mordants. Biting. Fusing the inlay. Electrodeposition. Hammering it in.

THE PRACTICE of inlaying or overlaying parts of a metal object with patterns formed from wires or plates of a different material is one of considerable antiquity. Beautiful specimens of the craft have come down to us from ancient Egypt, and from the Mycenæan Age of Greece (1400 to 1000 B.C.). Works of the skilful craftsmen of China and Japan, and of the Islamic metalworkers of India, Persia and the Near East are to be found in many museums, and they teach us that a fine piece of craftsmanship need not be made of one material only: there is a charm to be found in the enrichment of a surface by a tastefully designed inlay. And we ask, " May we not bring some colour into our work?" The all-over brilliant polish generally found on our modern silverware is not the only possible finish for a fine piece of craftsmanship. Except in the case of tableware, the obvious cleanness and brightness of which seems to be desirable, the introduction of a surface decoration formed from a different metal would often bring about a true enrichment of the work. Our mediæval craftsmen knew this, and in addition to their use of repoussé or chasing, they employed partial gilding, niello decoration, inlaying or enamelling to enrich their surfaces. Can we not tread the same path, or must the barren assurance of the term " solid silver " forever fetter our imagination?

A simple method of inlaying is that in which the pattern is drawn on a piece of sheet metal and cut out with the piercing-saw. Pieces of the metal which is to form the inlay are sawn to fit the openings, and afterwards soldered in to fill them. The whole work is then polished. If the two pieces of metal which are to form background and pattern are clamped together, the ornament may be sawn out at the same time and by the same cut which pierces out the opening to receive it. But you should allow for the width of the saw cut, for this would leave a little space all round the pattern to be filled up with solder. The best plan is to have the metal which is to form the inlay rather thicker and softer than the background, so that when it is put in place it may be hammered a little and stretched to fill the opening. After the inlay has been soldered in place the surface may be ground or filed smooth and polished.

Parquetry inlays can be made in the same manner as those in wood. A number of narrow strips of the different metals employed are laid edge to edge and soldered together (Fig. 259). The compound strip is then sawn, at an angle to its length (sometimes 90 degrees, but often less), into a number of strips, each the width of the required fillet. The ends of the strips are joined and the edges filed true. You have now a long fillet made up of alternate bands of the different metals employed (Fig. 260).

If two or more wires composed of different metals are twisted together, annealed, drawn a few times through a square drawplate and then flattened by passing them through the rolls, they may be used as a fillet for inlaying, and will look not very different from one made in the manner described above. On some of the Saxon scramsaxes in the British Museum may be seen examples of such inlays, employed to decorate a steel blade.

Inlays which do not go right through the metal into which they are fastened, have the lines or spaces to receive them prepared in one of several different ways. The recesses may be prepared by casting, by stamping, or by chasing. In such work the piece of metal which is to form the inlay is cut to fit the shape of the recess. In some examples its edge is bevelled so that the sheet is narrower towards the front than behind. When the inlay has been pushed into place the surrounding metal is punched, hammered or burnished down against the bevelled edge, so that the inlay is held firmly. The whole surface may then be scraped or ground smooth and polished.

When the outline of the recess is cut with the tracer, such as that shown in Fig. 202, the groove will be a narrow channel, its width corresponding with that of the tool. A slight ridge may have been thrown up on either side of the groove. The craftsman then takes a length of gold or silver wire, of suitable thickness and properly annealed, and lays it along the groove. With a small slightly convex-faced hammer or a similarly shaped punch he drives the wire into the recess. He regulates his blows so that by the time that the little ridges along the sides of the inlaid wire have been driven down to overhang the wire and to grip it in place, the whole surface has regained its original flatness. Some workers like to take a pointed punch and to make a number of deepish punch-marks in the sloping sides of the groove, so that the inlay may dovetail itself into them as a result of the hammering, and so be held more firmly. Or the bottom of the groove may be flattened by going over it with a narrow parallel-sided chase with a flat bottom. The groove produced in this way will be square below, and it will afford a good bed for the inlays.

Should the width of the recess be greater than the wire would fill, then a piece of sheet metal will be needed for that purpose. The shape of the recess is first outlined with the tracer, and part of or the whole of its floor is driven down with flat punches. In much of the beautiful inlaid work produced in the twelfth and later centuries by Islamic craftsmen, the bottom of the recess or depression is not made flat. It is deep only near the outline, and it is often left at its original height everywhere else. It follows that the inlaid sheet metal takes a convex form, being beaten down at the edges but projecting its own thickness higher than the background everywhere else. To do this work a narrow, almost pointed, punch is employed to drive down at the same time both part of the edge of the inlaid metal and part of the little raised bank which surrounds the recess. Work of this kind never has a surface which is quite level, for the central portions of the inlay, lying as they do on parts of the original surface of the vessel being decorated, are always at a higher level.

If, however, the floor of the recess is lowered all over, either by driving it down with flat-faced punches, or by cutting it down with scorpers or other cutting tools, then the inlay may be quite level and its surface will be even with the background. During a few centuries before and after the birth of Christ, the silversmiths of Persia and the neighbouring lands worked in a slightly different way. They took a thin sheet of silver and worked by repoussé and chasing the heads of the figures or other parts which they wished to have in high relief, with which they wished to decorate, say, a dish. After working the heads in relief they cut them out of the sheet and filed their edges smooth and level. They laid them in place on the dish and scratched a line closely round them. With the tracer they outlined the head

150

and with chisels they cut away the ground for a short distance within the traced line, leaving at its original level the centre of the space within the outline. The head being in high relief did not touch this part of the ground, but its sides dropped into the chiselled-out hollow within the traced line. It was carefully fitted there and the metal outside was driven down with punches to grip it in its recess. The heads were thus in high relief, and the remainder of the figures were put in with the tracer alone. Sometimes part of the work was gilded. This method of making a piece of high relief work associated with low relief was not a success. For by repeated cleaning some of the high relief work was worn into holes, and eventually it worked loose and was lost.

Craftsmen of many lands have practised a method of decorating their work by overlaying it with lines, or wider spaces, of gold or silver. The craftsman makes a series of cuts, with a sharp chisel, all over the surface to be decorated. The cuts may be $\frac{1}{50}$ inch or less apart. Sometimes several series of cuts are made, each series lying at a different angle from the first. If a great number of cuts are made, the whole surface to be decorated is transformed from a smooth to a roughened area. An annealed wire is held in position by tweezers and given a tap with a hammer which has a very small blunted point. The blow drives the wire down on to the spiky, roughened metal, which grips the gold or silver firmly. The wire may be turned in any direction to form the desired pattern, and fastened firmly by light blows.

To cover a surface with gold or silver the craftsmen discovered that all that was necessary was to lay, one at a time, a series of wires side by side across the pattern and to tap them down on the roughened ground. Under the blows the metal spread out a little on either side of the wire and made a complete overlay of the original hatched ground. Another method was to lay a sheet of gold foil, or several layers of gold leaf, one after the other, over the surface, burnishing each in turn down on to the hatched ground.

Oriental armourers employed, and still freely employ, these methods in order to decorate with a surface of gold parts of their weapons and armour. By careless writers this method and that in which the gold wires are laid in grooves cut specially for them, are sometimes called " damascening in gold." But the term is misleading, and has no true connection with damascening. For that

151

term can be properly employed only in relation to the structure of a piece of steel. " Damascening " is the production of a watered pattern in the very fabric of the steel, a craft practised in India, Persia and the Near East from the seventh century onwards, and probably earlier. At the time of the Crusades (eleventh to thirteenth centuries) returning warriors brought back from the Holy Land some of the rich stuffs and other products of the East. Weapons and metal vessels, embroideries and woven materials, all alike have been called damask or damascened, after Damascus, the capital city of the Saracens. But it is a mistake to pick out works which are

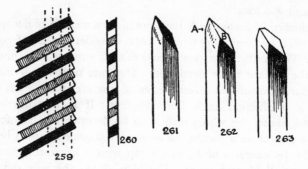

inlaid or overlaid with gold, and to describe them by a name which belongs strictly to another craft.

Metal to be inlaid, if thick, may be supported on a heavy stone or metal slab, and the recesses cut with hammer and chisel. The chisels used are of various shapes. Some are lozenge shaped or triangular at the point, like gravers (Fig. 262), and are employed to outline the pattern. Others are straight (Fig. 264), perhaps $\frac{3}{16}$ inch

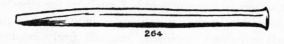

wide, for chipping away the material. They are made about 6 inches long. To sharpen the lozenge-shaped tools, lay one of their lower sides flat on the stone. Then lift the hand a little, and rub until there is produced a facet on the tool. Do the same on the other long side of the tool. The side view of the point thus produced is shown in Fig. 262. The ridge separating the two facets must be in line with the ridge which separates the undersides of the tool. The little angle *A*, where the facets meet the undersides of the tool, is very valuable in practice, for the tool slides along on it as the point cuts its way. Next rub down the back of the tool *B*, keeping the original angle. The sharpness of the point may be tested by touching it lightly against the fingernail. It should stick at once without slipping. If a wide line is required, the graver may be made to cut it by sharpening the tool on the underside or belly, grinding away the lowest angle of the diamond for perhaps $\frac{1}{8}$ inch along the ridge. A tool so sharpened is called a lozenge scolloper (Fig. 263). But scollopers or chisels with parallel sides are made also; they are sharpened on front and back, and are made in several different widths.

For the smaller work done by engravers the hammer is not required. The tools used have a small round handle, held in the palm against the ball of the little finger. They are known in this case as the graver or " burin," and scorpers. The latter are made in various shapes—flat, round, knife-edged, etc. (see p. 64). Engravers hold their work in various ways, much depending on its shape. (1) On a sandbag. This is a round pad of sheepskin, crammed very tightly with sand or whiting, or a mixture of whiting and plaster of Paris. This is better than sand, for there would be no danger of scratching the work should any of the contents escape. The work is held by the left hand on top of the bag and turned about as required. (2) In a chuck or clam (Fig. 265). (3) On a pitch bowl (see Chapter XIII, p. 118). (4) On a cement stick. (5) On a triblet or ring stick (Fig. 270).

The design is drawn on the metal as described on p. 242. The work being then held firmly, the engraver either outlines the pattern with the graver and afterwards removes the ground with scorpers, or cuts the ground away at once without troubling to outline it. The point of the graver should be pushed along just below the surface of the metal, firmly and without jerks. Or the work may be turned or pushed against the point of the graver, while it is held more or less still. A deep line may be cut by going over the same ground a second time. The graver may be made to cut a line of varying width. To do this it is only necessary to rotate the tool on its axis a little. The graver being diamond-shaped in section, this rotation brings part of one of the sides rather than only a corner into contact with the metal, and a wider cut is the result. If a flat scorper is rotated quickly from side to side and at the same time pushed forward, it will make a curious " wriggled " or zigzag cut (Fig. 266). This is a quick way of removing the ground, and it leaves the surface of the metal very rough. This is an advantage in some processes of inlaying—when a " well-keyed " ground is required.

The third method by which recesses for inlaying may be prepared is that of etching. Silver, copper, brass, bronze, iron or steel may be treated by this process. The work is first covered with a specially prepared wax or varnish " ground," and the design drawn on it with a steel point or " needle." The ground is in this way scratched through wherever the lines which form the design or pattern come, and the metal exposed. If some dilute nitric acid is then poured over it, the acid attacks the metal wherever it is not protected by the varnish and eats or bites a furrow wherever the needle has gone. The depth to which the lines are " bitten " depends a good deal on the strength of the acid solution, and on the time the work remains in the " bath," for the longer a line is exposed to the action of the acid the deeper and wider is it bitten. It will be seen then that a design may be etched in lines of varying thickness, for it is only necessary to " stop out," i.e. cover up with varnish, any lines which are sufficiently bitten, and then to put the work into the bath again till the remaining lines are finished. Or the deep lines may be drawn and etched first and the faint ones drawn in afterwards and bitten only for a minute or two. The length of time required to etch the pattern may be but a few minutes, or it may be an hour or two.

Rhind's is perhaps the best-known etching ground. It may be purchased from all dealers in etching materials. Another good etching ground (Bosse's), very widely used, is made as follows:—

White wax	10 parts.
Gum mastic	6 „
Asphaltum	3 „

Melt the wax first in an oven. Stir in the other two. The ingredients must be very thoroughly mixed. The stirring must be continued long after any streakiness in the mixture has disappeared. This ground is quite black, though a thin layer of it is semi-trans-

154

parent. If the asphaltum is left out the ground is quite transparent, but not quite so strong. Another ground is made of:—

Yellow beeswax	.	.	.	.	2 parts.
Asphaltum	.	.	.	.	2 ,,
Burgundy pitch	.	.	.	.	1 ,,

Mix as above described.

When cool roll the ground into balls about 1½ inches in diameter. For use, a ball of ground is tied up in a double thickness of thin silk, blue-bag fashion. Beeswax, paraffin-wax, or shellac, dissolved in alcohol or chloroform, may also be used for a ground or for stopping out any part of the work which has been bitten deeply enough. Remember that lines get wider the longer they remain in the acid.

To ground a plate or other piece of work. Clean it thoroughly. Then heat it until it is rather too warm to hold. It may be held in a hand-vice over a gas- or spirit-flame, or laid on a piece of sheet iron and the heat applied below. When quite uncomfortably warm to the touch lay the plate on a table and dab or rub the ground all over its face. To spread the ground evenly it is usual to either roll a rubber squeegee in every direction over the surface of the plate or to use a dabber (Fig. 267). This is made of horsehair covered

with cotton-wool, and finally with one or two layers of silk or kid. The edges of the silk or kid are brought over a disc of cardboard and bound together with string in the centre of the disc, above, to form a handle. The dabber is patted over the work until the ground is spread quite evenly. It may be necessary to reheat the plate before this can be effected. The ground having been spread evenly over the plate, its surface is now blackened by moving it about a few inches above a bundle of lighted tapers. These give off a good deal of smoke and soon darken the ground. When cool its surface should have a quite smooth, blackened, half-polished

155

appearance, and lines scratched by the needle should show up brightly in contrast. Work which by reason of its shape cannot be grounded in this manner may be dipped into a vessel containing some of the etching ground, melted; or the ground may be dissolved in oil of lavender or chloroform and painted over the work. It is well to remember that the whole of the work except the scratched-in design must be protected from the action of the acid, so the underside and edges must be protected as well as the face. The old copper-plate etchers, however, used to make a little wall of wax round the edge of the plate which was to be bitten, thus turning the plate itself, with its wax rim, into a kind of trough, into which the acid could be poured. The back of the plate did not then require protection.

Designs may be transferred to the etching ground in the following way: Take a thin sheet of paper and go all over it with a soft black-lead pencil. Use the side of the point of the pencil, for it will make a broader mark. Cover the paper with close lines in several directions, till it has a grey, shiny surface all over. Lay this side of the paper on the etching ground, and put the paper on which your drawing is, above. Then go over all the lines of the drawing with a fine point, pressing firmly, but not hard enough to penetrate the paper. The black lead from the lower sheet of paper will be transferred all along the lines to the wax ground, and show up in contrast with its blackened surface. If you have an etching press, it is only necessary to put your lead-pencil drawing, or a tracing of it, face downwards on the ground and pass work and drawing together through the press. The drawing will be reversed in the process, and care must therefore be taken with lettering.

The needle used to scratch through the ground is just a pointed piece of steel. An ordinary sewing needle, with its point rounded off, set in a handle does very well. For broad spaces in the design, a chisel-shaped tool may be used instead. Or, a number of lines drawn so closely together that the acid may work its way from one to the other. A low wooden bridge laid over, but not touching the plate, forms a convenient rest for the hand. When the design has been gone over with the needle, the plate is ready for biting. But first see that every part of the metal, except the scratched-in design, is protected from the action of the acid. Paraffin wax or Brunswick black may be used to cover any exposed parts.

The acid or mordants used for the different metals are given below. They should be got ready at least an hour before they are wanted—the ingredients taking some time to mix properly.

Mordant for gold
Hydrochloric acid . . . . 8 parts.
Nitric acid . . . . . 4 ,,
Perchloride of iron . . . . 1 ,,
Water . . . . . . 40 to 50 parts.

For silver
Nitric acid . . . . . 1 part
Water . . . . . . 3 or 4 parts.

For copper, brass, etc.
Nitric acid . . . . . 1 part.
Water . . . . . . 1 ,,

Sir Frank Short, R.A., the well-known etcher, gave the following mordants for copper plates:

Nitric acid . . . . . 1 part.
Water . . . . . . 1 ,,
Or
Nitric acid . . . . . 1 part.
Water . . . . . . 2 parts.
Or
Dutch mordant
Chlorate of potash . . . 2 parts.
Hydrochloric acid . . . . 10 ,,
Water . . . . . . 88 ,,

Or perchloride of iron. This bath consists of a 40 degrees Baumé solution of perchloride of iron in water.

The Dutch mordant is much slower in its action than the others, and the line bitten by it does not spread so much in width.

Mordant for iron or steel
Hydrochloric acid . . . . 2 parts.
Water . . . . . . 1 part.

In mixing these solutions remember that the acids should be poured into the water, not the water into the acids.

Lay the work face upwards in a porcelain dish and pour the mordant over it to a depth of $\frac{1}{4}$ inch. Bubbles of gas will immediately form all along the scratched lines. Rock the dish gently from side to side or wipe the bubbles away with a feather. If they are allowed to remain the line will not be etched evenly, for the gas in them keeps the acid away from the work. As stated above, the time required to etch the pattern may be a few minutes or an hour or two. Watch the plate and with a needle try the depth of the biting from time to time. To stop out any part which is sufficiently bitten, remove the plate from the acid, rinse it in water and paint some of one of the grounds, described above, over the parts which are bitten deeply enough. When the biting is completed, remove the plate, rinse it in water, warm it and then thoroughly clean with turpentine. Then wash with hot water and soap. Dry in hot sawdust. Or, after the turpentine, the work, if not composed of iron or steel, may be boiled out in sulphuric acid pickle as described on p. 25. Etched patterns are often trimmed up with the graver.

The recesses having been prepared in one of the ways described above, the inlaying must now be considered. There are three entirely different methods by which the pattern may be filled in. By the first the inlay is fused into the hollows. By the second it is deposited in them by the electroplating or the amalgamation process. And by the third it is hammered or burnished in. The first two are the most satisfactory, for the intimate union between inlay and inlaid, like that between a solder and the work soldered, ensures a perfect and permanent hold for the inlay. Any metal or alloy which can be used as a solder for another metal can be used as an inlay for it. Thus brass or silver solder may be used to fill recesses in copper; brass or gold in iron, etc. Flux must be used just as in soldering. To fill large spaces, pieces of sheet metal or wire may be soldered in. When all the lines and spaces have been filled up and fired, all superfluous inlay and solder can be cleared away with a fine file, and the work polished smooth. The Irish craftsmen in the centuries before the time of Christ made gold penannular hair-rings, about an inch in diameter, which they sometimes decorated with a spiral band of silver or niello. They wound a thread spirally round the ring, with from eight to twenty turns, and scratched a line on each side of it. They then depressed the surface between the scratches, either by cutting it down or punching it down with chasing tools. They filled the hollow thus produced with silver solder or niello, and fired it. Then they filed or ground the surface smooth. Soft solder may be used in a similar manner for the decoration, say, of copper.

By electroplating, any metal or alloy which can be electro-deposited may be used for inlaying, those parts of the work on which the deposit is not required being protected by a coat of wax or varnish. In recent years the demands for vanity cases and costume jewellery ornamented in permanent colours have led to many interesting developments in surface decoration. Enamelling over engine-turned or stamped relief has been followed by the use of translucent plastics and lacquers, which serve the same purpose but are cheaper to produce. Liquid inlays fill recesses which formerly would have held a metal inlay, a niello or an enamel, and there is a wide range of colours from which to choose.

Silver may be inlaid with gold in the following manner. Fine gold is filed to very fine powder and kneaded with an equal weight of mercury in a mortar until an evenly mixed amalgam is obtained. The engraved silverwork is rubbed with " grey powder " (mercury with chalk). This slightly amalgamates the surface. The gold amalgam is piled into and over the recesses, and the work left for a day or two. The amalgam should be pressed down in the hollows occasionally. The work is next placed on a warm hob so that the mercury may evaporate slowly. Its fumes are very poisonous, even at room temperature. This gentle heating may go on for many hours, but the work must be heated at last to low redness to drive off every particle of mercury. Then burnish the gold well, scrape down and polish the work.

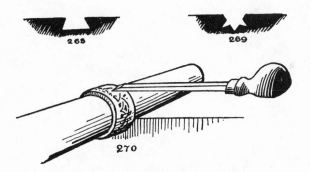

When wire is to be used for the inlay, the groove into which it is to be hammered is more efficient if it is wider below than at the surface of the work (Fig. 268). This undercut form may be produced by widening out the deep part of the groove first cut, or little additional grooves may be cut with a knife-edge scorper at each side of the bottom (Fig. 269). These afford a very efficient key to hold the wire when it has been hammered in. An etched line, though rather uneven at the bottom, is not always deep enough to hold the wire safely. If necessary it may be widened out like the other. The gold or silver wire for inlay should be of pure metal if possible. It is softer than alloyed metal, and it has a better colour.

CHAPTER XIX

NIELLO

Mycenæ and Enkomi. Theophilus. Cellini. Bolas. Spon.

MEDIAEVAL CRAFTSMEN seem to have had a keener realization than have their modern representatives of the æsthetic value of touches of colour or of black in their gold and silverware. They employed rock crystal and agate, precious stones and enamel, ivory and niello to an extent unknown to-day. Their niello was generally composed of a mixture of metallic sulphides. It provided that strong note of black or dark-grey which is found to be so valuable in a lighter colour scheme.

The earliest nielloes come from sites in Greece, Egypt and Cyprus. The work on the Mycenæan dagger-blades is well known. That from Cyprus is seen best on a silver cup from a grave at Enkomi. It dates from about 1400 B.C. It was a pioneer work, and two different techniques are employed in making it. The niello seems to have been composed of copper and silver sulphides. Round the rim of the cup is a recessed band decorated with gold discs set in a ground of niello. The discs were cut with a chisel from a sheet of gold. The chisel cut left the lower edge of the disc slightly wider than the top, and it was not trimmed up. The craftsman set out the position of each disc by scratching a little circular mark round it. He probably stuck each disc in position with gum and then filled in the niello. This overlapped the slightly inclined sides of the discs and held them in place when the niello was fired. The other nielloed pattern is a series of flowers cut out in gold foil and embedded in a layer of niello which fills the recess under them. After firing, the gold flowers were firmly gripped by the layer of niello beneath them. Any rough surfaces on the niello were then ground smooth.

No later examples of niello seem to have survived until we come to Roman times, when a new variety of niello came into fashion. This niello was composed of silver sulphide only: a material which becomes plastic at a temperature far below its melting point. In powdered form it may be filled into recesses in a work, and, after gentle heating, it may be moulded and burnished to its final level.

About the eleventh century A.D. there came a change in the composition of the niello employed by the goldsmiths. A description of the method of making the material and of its use is given by the eleventh century monk Theophilus. His treatises on gold- and silversmiths' work, translated by Robert Hendrie, may be met with occasionally, and a more recent version entitled "On Divers Arts," translated by John G. Hawthorne and Cyril Stanley Smith, is now available. In the earlier book he gives a delightful account of the manner in which he and other goldsmiths of his time did their work. In the chapters on niello, quoted below, he is describing the decoration of a two-handled chalice (Book III, Chapters XXVIII, XXIV, XXXII and XLI).

" Take pure silver, and divide it into two equal weights, adding to it a third part of pure copper. When you have placed these three into a cast metal cup, weigh as much lead as half of the copper which you have mixed with the silver weighs, and taking yellow sulphur break it very small, and put the lead and part of this sulphur upon a small copper vessel, and place the rest of the sulphur in another cast metal cup. And when you have liquefied the silver with the copper, stir it evenly with charcoal, and instantly pour into it the lead and the sulphur from the small copper cup, and again mix it well with the charcoal, and with quickness pour it into the other molten cup upon the sulphur which you had put into it, and then putting down the small vase with which you have poured out, take that into which you have cast it and place it into the fire until (the contents) liquefy, and again stirring it together pour into the iron crucible. Before this cools beat it a little, and warm it a little, and again beat it, and do this until it is quite thinned. For the nature of the niello is such that if it is struck while cold it is immediately broken and flies to pieces, nor should it be made so warm as to glow, because it instantly liquefies and flows into ashes. The niello being made thin, put it into a deep and thick cup, and pouring water upon it, break it up with a round hammer until it becomes very small, and taking it out, dry it, and put that which is fine into a goose quill and close it up, but that which is coarser place again in the vessel and bruise it, and being again dried, put it in another quill.

" When you have filled many quills take the gum which is called parahas (borax) and grind a small piece of it with water in the same vase, so that the water is made scarcely turbid from it, and first moisten the place which you wish to blacken with this water, and taking the quill rub off the ground niello with a light instrument upon it carefully, until you have covered the whole, and do this over the whole. Then gather excessively hot coals (charcoal) and placing the vase in them carefully cover them, so that no coal be placed, nor can fall, over the niello. And when it is liquefied hold the vase with the pincers and turn it from every side on which you see it flow, and in thus turning it round take care that the niello does not fall to the ground. But should it not be completely perfect at the first heating, again moisten it, and superpose (niello) as before, and take great care that no further work is required.

" When you have mixed and melted the niello, take a portion of it and beat it square long and slender. Then take the handle (of the chalice) with the pincers and heat it in the fire until it glows, and with another forceps, long and thin, hold the niello and rub it over all the places which you wish to make black until all the drawings (engraved spaces) are full, and carrying it away from the fire carefully make it smooth with a flat file until the silver appear, so that you can scarcely observe the traits and so scrape it with the cutting-iron, carefully cut away the inequalities, and you will gild what remains. . . .

" . . . Scrape all the parts carefully which are blackened with the niello, with the cutting instrument. Afterwards you have a black and soft stone, which can easily be cut and almost scraped with the nail, and with it you rub the niello, wetted with saliva, carefully and smoothly everywhere, until all the drawings are plainly seen, and it is quite smooth. You also have a piece of wood from the lime tree, of the length and thickness of the smallest finger, dry and smoothly cut; upon which you place this wet powder, which comes from the stone and saliva in rubbing, and with this wood and the same powder you rub the niello a long time and lightly, and always add saliva, that it may be wet, until it is made brilliant everywhere. Then take wax from the hollow of your ear, and when you have wiped the niello clean with a fine linen cloth, you anoint it everywhere, and with goat or hart's skin you will lightly rub it until it is made quite bright."

Benvenuto Cellini, in his treatise on goldsmiths' work, describes the making of niello. He uses a good deal more lead than the amount given by Theophilus. But this is no improvement, for lead is not a good material to associate with the precious metals. Cellini used silver 1 part, copper 2 parts, lead 3 parts with the powdered sulphur. The silver and copper were first melted together and the lead added to them. The crucible was then removed from the fire and the liquid metal stirred well with a piece of charcoal held in the tongs. The scum caused by the oxidation of some of the lead was skimmed off, and the stirring proceeded with until the three metals were thoroughly blended. A narrow-necked earthenware flask, about as big as the fist, was half-filled with powdered sulphur. Into this the molten metal was poured. The mouth was closed with damp clay; and the flask, held in a piece of stout canvas, thoroughly shaken. When it had cooled, the flask was broken open, and the metal, which had now combined with the sulphur, was found in the form of little black grains. These were melted in a crucible with borax, cast into an ingot, and again broken up. This operation was repeated several times before the niello was considered to be properly mixed.

Mr. Bolas, in his little book *Etching on Metals*, described " an easily fusible niello " in which he introduced antimony as an ingredient. He gave:

Native sulphide of antimony, finely ground . . .	2 parts.
Native sulphide of lead (galena), finely ground . .	1 part.
Sulphur in small fragments or powder	8 parts.

These ingredients should fill less than half of a fireclay crucible. Heat gently and stir all the while with the stem of a pipe. If the mixture is overheated or not properly stirred it will become thick and stiff. When properly fused it may be poured out on a slab of stone. The niello is then coarsely powdered. A less fusible niello of finer black colour, and specially suitable for small articles in silver or gold, was described by Mr. Bolas. It is composed of:

Silver	2 parts.
Copper	3 „
Antimony	1 part.
Lead	1 „
Sulphur.	

Melt the silver and copper together, add the antimony and lead, and cast into an ingot. Reduce it to powder by filing it with a smooth file. Mix the filings with twice their weight of powdered sulphur. Drop this mixture, a teaspoonful at a time, into a crucible maintained at a low red heat. Allow the crucible to cool, break it, and with pestle and mortar finely powder the black sulphide. Mix the powder with twice its weight of sulphur and melt it again. Then

break up the niello—into small grains rather than to fine powder.
The work should be thoroughly cleaned before the niello is
applied. Mr. Bolas recommended that the final cleaning shall be
with a stiff brush and some gritty powder, such as bathbrick dust—
care being taken to brush it all out. Etched silver work should be
rubbed with a fine wire scratch brush to remove any silver oxides
which may have been left in the recesses. Fill all the hollows with
the small grains of niello, and pile a little on top to make up for the
smaller space which the fused material will occupy. Drop over it a
little powdered borax—very little. Heat the work until the niello
melts, and at this time, go over it with a hot iron spatula (or a pipe
stem made hot), to assist in completely filling the recesses. Be careful
not to allow the work to get red-hot, or even to remain hot for longer
than you can help, or the lead, which is one of the components of the
niello, will rapidly corrode the silver or gold of which the work is
composed. If the work is not flat, the niello may be dropped into the
recesses of the heated metal as it is turned about, and worked into
place with the hot spatula. Now remove any superfluous niello
with a file. But before you have quite got down to the surface of
your work, heat it again till it is rather too hot for the hand to bear,
and with a steel burnisher and a little oil burnish well the surface
of the niello. The object of this burnishing is to stop up any little
bubble holes which may have come in the process, and which would
otherwise spoil the surface of the work. Then scrape the surface of
the work true and polish in the ordinary way.

Spon in his *Workshop Receipts* gave another formula:

First crucible—Flowers of sulphur . 27 oz.
              Sal-ammoniac . . $2\frac{3}{4}$,,
Second crucible, which after fusion is poured into the first—
             Silver . . . $\frac{1}{2}$ oz.
             Copper . . . $1\frac{1}{2}$,,
             Lead . . . . $2\frac{3}{4}$,,

Add a little sal-ammoniac to the mixture. Reduce to powder,
mix with a small proportion of a solution of sal-ammoniac for use.
Spread the niello on the work. Heat in a muffle till the composition
solders the metal. Polish level as above.

Niello of the composition given by Theophilus works well in
practice. In all probability it is the safest kind to use, for it has less
lead in it than those made to the other formulæ.

CHAPTER XX

JAPANESE ALLOYS AND STRATIFIED FABRICS

Banded alloys. Wood grains. Mixed alloys.

SOMETHING AKIN to inlaying is the Japanese work in banded alloys. The late Sir W. C. Roberts-Austen was the first in this country to describe the work, in valuable papers read before the British Association and the Society of Arts more than seventy years ago. But it is still little known or practised.

The Japanese workman takes thin plates of various metals or alloys—gold, silver, copper, and various alloys of these metals—and solders them together. In the thickish plate thus produced conical holes are bored, or grooves cut, as shown at the right half of Fig. 271.

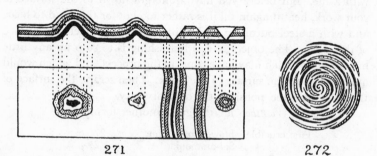

271   272

These cuts penetrate the various layers and expose them in rings or bands. The plate is then turned face downwards on to a stake, and hammered until the depressions in the front surface are levelled out. The banded pattern, looking like contour lines on a relief map, is not obliterated by the levelling of the surface. By another method a many-layered plate, prepared as before, is hammered or rolled out. It is then beaten up irregularly from behind with repoussé tools as shown at the left half of Fig. 271. The bumps in front are then filed flat and parts of the various layers of which the plate is composed become visible in front. The different strata exposed form an irregular marbled pattern. Of course, an inscription or some other controlled pattern may be formed in this manner. The first example of such work produced in this country was the chain for the Mayor of Preston, Lancashire, made by the late Sir Alfred Gilbert (Plate 23). Another variety of banded alloys employed by Japanese craftsmen is that known as " mokume," or wood-grain.

Work of this kind can be used to give interest and colour to an otherwise plain surface. It is not difficult to produce. The various sheets of metal to be used should be rolled down to size 1 on the metal gauge, or even thinner. They should then be boiled out in pickle, again in a solution of washing soda and water, and lastly in clean water. They should then be held by the edges only—for to touch their flat surfaces with the hand might leave a trace of grease, which would interfere with the soldering. Now paint all their surfaces with borax and tie the plates together with wire. Use silver solder and heat till the solder has run through all the joints. The plate may now be folded on itself to make it double the thickness, and the two halves soldered together. It will, of course, have twice as many layers as it had at first. This process of doubling the plate and soldering it may be repeated as often as desired. The resulting thick plate may be rolled out afterwards. It will consist of a large number of thin layers of the various metals used, all united by solder. The back of the plate can now be beaten to drive up bumps in front. These may form regular patterns if desired, or be quite irregularly shaped. Holes may be drilled into the plate or channels cut, exposing the various layers. The filing down of the bumps has a similar result. Should you file right through the plate at any of these places it will not matter much, for pieces of metal may be soldered on the back to fill them. The plate may then be hammered or scraped flat. It may require annealing. Its surface will be composed of irregularly shaped bars, stripes, rings and spots of the various metals employed, giving a delightful mottled appearance.

An interesting variety of this work can be produced as follows. Take thin wires of various metals and twist them to form a cord. Coil this upon itself into a spiral. Solder the coils together. Beat or file the surface flat. The pattern produced is a curious spiral of various coloured metals (Fig. 272).

The Japanese use a number of alloys for this and other work. The two principal ones are known as:

1. *Shaku-do*. This is composed of copper with $\frac{1}{2}$ to 4 per cent. of gold, and traces of silver, lead, etc. The addition of this small proportion of gold enables the copper to take a beautiful purple colour when pickled.

2. *Shibu-ichi*. It is composed of 49 to 86 parts copper, 13 to 51 parts silver, and traces of gold and iron; or of about equal parts of copper and silver and a trace of gold. It takes a fine silver-grey colour. The use of these alloys, each of which is made in several different shades, gives to the Japanese craftsman a much wider range of colour than is generally open to his European brother. For to the Japanese artist the intrinsic value of the material employed counts but little in comparison with its æsthetic or colour value. To him, fortunately, hall-marking is unknown.

CHAPTER XXI

ENAMELLING

W E MAY DEFINE an enamel as a vitreous coating fused to a metallic base. Fundamentally the surface layer is a kind of glass, and the base is of gold, silver, copper, bronze or iron. There is, however, a variety of enamel ware in which the base is not of metal, but of a hard glass. In such work, as in the beautiful Arab mosque lamps of the thirteenth century, and in some decorated glassware from other countries, the body of the vessel is of glass, and it is ornamented by patterns in more fusible glass painted upon it and fired in a furnace. Such works are best described as being of enamelled glass rather than as enamels.

Let us look at the material itself. Enamel is generally a comparatively soft glass, a compound of flint or sand, red lead and soda or potash. These materials are melted together and produce an almost clear glass, with a slightly bluish or greenish tinge. This almost colourless material is known as flux or frit. It is made in different degrees of hardness—those kinds which contain more lead and potash are more brilliant, but softer. Soft enamels require less heat to fire them, and are, therefore, convenient to use, but they do not wear so well. So for any work which has to stand friction, hard enamels are essential. Clear flux or frit is the base from which coloured enamels are made—the colouring matter being metallic oxides. The inclusion of 2 or 3 per cent. of one of these oxides in the molten flux is generally sufficient to produce a useful colour. The enamel, after being thoroughly stirred, is poured out on to a slab in cakes 4 or 5 inches in diameter. For use, it is broken up, ground in a mortar to a fine powder, thoroughly washed, and spread on to a piece of metal. The work is placed in a furnace until the powdered enamel fuses and adheres to its metal base. Such in its simplest terms is an enamel—a vitreous substance fused on to a metallic background.

Enamel being so nearly related to glass, it is interesting to seek for its earliest appearance in history. From early dynastic times in Sumeria (before 2500 B.C.) and Egypt, craftsmen had inlaid pieces of coloured stones as an enrichment of their finger-rings, bracelets and pendants. Sometimes they used pieces of coloured pottery among their lapis, carnelian or chrysophrase inlays. They set them in little cells. These were formed from the upturned edges of the thin gold plates from which the jewel was made, or by the use of little cloisons—strips of sheet gold, set on edge and soldered to the back-plate. The coloured stones or pieces of pottery seem always to be held in position by cement or by the grip of the inturned edges of the cloisons. It does not seem to have occurred to the craftsman that he might fill his cells with pieces of coloured glass and fuse them in position.

It was not until about the thirteenth century B.C. that a goldsmith in Cyprus made that discovery, and not until nearly a thousand years later that the use of enamel became fairly generally known. In 1952 there was discovered in a Mycenæan tomb at Kouklia, Cyprus, six gold rings which were decorated with what seem to be the earliest examples of enamelling yet discovered. They are pioneer works, and they differ technically from nearly all later examples of the craft. The rings themselves are of chased gold, ornamented with twisted square wires, and the enamels are mounted within band settings surrounded by rows of gold grains. It is not known whether each enamel had a foundation plate, but within a slender cloison masses of coloured glass, some fragments measuring $\frac{1}{8}$ inch across, were packed closely. It is possible that the craftsman fired this layer before going further. Above this foundation layer he arranged a simple design of curved gold cloisons, which spread right across the disc, and filled the cells with an upper layer of variously coloured opaque glass fragments. He then fired the whole mass. The fused material settled down and flowed into all but the narrowest gaps between the cloisons, holding the gold bands firmly in its grip. The molten glass locked within itself a number of air-bubbles, some of which were cut into when the whole domed surface was ground smooth. In the finished work there are areas in which pieces of several different coloured enamels appear in a cell unseparated by a cloison, where their edges meet they make so clean a line that it is evident that they could not have been in the form of

170

powder when they were fused together. For had the different colours been in a powdered condition when placed in the recess, they would have fused with an irregular line of junction. The joint, however, examined under a microscope, is quite true, proving that they were smooth-edged masses laid down side by side before fusion.

On some of the Greek jewellery of the fifth century B.C. there is unmistakable evidence that enamel was coming into favour. In the Birmingham Museum is a hair ornament of gold and silver of that time, on which the decoration of gold cloisonné shield shapes round the lion's neck is enamelled. There is in the British Museum a golden sceptre of the fourth century, from Tarentum, in which the cylindrical shaft is covered with a network of fine filigree, and at each crossing of the wires a tiny spot of blue enamel appears, with quite magical effect. The Greeks used enamels sparingly, and no large Greek enamels are known.

When Cæsar conquered Britain in the first century B.C. he found that the Celtic inhabitants of the island were decorating their bronze horse trappings, their armour and their jewellery with enamel. Many examples of their work have survived. Some show spots of red enamel fired in recesses cut in the cast bronze of a horse bit or of a mirror such as that beautiful example from Birdlip, in the Gloucester Museum (Plate 7). Later, the Saxon hanging bowls, such as those from the Sutton Hoo Ship Burial in the British Museum, are some of the most beautiful examples of champlevé work in existence (Plate 25).

Enamel is applied in a number of different ways. For closer examination it will be well to divide enamels into groups according to the structure of their metallic base, and their relationship to it.

The first group is that known as *cloisonné*. This, as we have seen, is the most primitive form. Each mass of powdered glass is placed in a separate compartment, formed from strips of metal, to which, and to the background if it has one, the enamel is fused. If there is no background, and the enamel is translucent, like a strained-glass window, the work is known as *plique-à-jour*.

In the second group the enamel is fused into cells, which are sunk with chasing tools, carved, stamped or cast in the metal baseplate. These enamels are known as *champlevé*. A subdivision of this group is known as *bassetaille enamel*. In it, over a design in low relief, a level-topped layer of enamel is fused. The modelled surface below

171

is clearly visible, and gradations in the height of the relief are reflected by variations in the depth of colour in the enamels above it. Another subdivision of this group is formed by *encrusted enamels*. These are employed to decorate irregular surfaces, such as the shoulders of a finger-ring; or to ornament the mounts of a crystal cup. Or the enamel may cover, say, a figure in high relief formed by repoussé work and chasing.

Enamels of the third group are provided with a plain foundation of sheet metal, generally slightly domed. As a rule the whole surface on both sides of the metal is covered with enamel. The group comes under the general classification of *painted enamels*; although, as with colours painted on canvas, sometimes the material is applied with a palette knife.

The tools required for enamelling are not many, the furnace being the principal one (Fig. 273). Furnaces are made in many

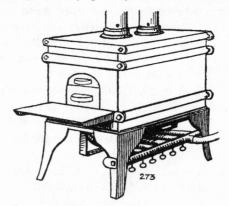

273

patterns and are heated by gas, electricity, coke or oil. Gas-heated furnaces are the most generally used. They consist of a muffle surrounded by a casing of specially prepared fireclay. Fletcher gives 1 part fireclay to 3 or 4 parts sawdust, moistened, worked into form and burnt, as the material from which furnace casings are made. Heat is supplied to the furnace by a row of Bunsen burners underneath. To avoid the heat radiated by the chimney it is well to fix a shield before it. Some enamellers use also a hanging glass screen as an additional protection. A small enamel may be fired in an ordinary clay crucible heated by the blowpipe, or even in a piece of iron folded in half; but the enamel should not be exposed

172

to the direct blast of the flame, or it may be discoloured. This method, however, is rather dangerous for firing small silver articles—they melt so easily. Iron scales or iron rust will discolour clear glass flux or frit, so the enamel must be protected against any accidental flaking of the iron support on which it is fired. A pair of tongs about 2 feet long, with slender handles and jaws, is necessary (Fig. 276). One or two palette knives, with blade about a foot long, are useful for lifting the work on and off the metal plate on which it rests for firing.

A set of boxes, or of wide-mouthed bottles, to hold the enamels should be numbered to correspond with the printed list of colours as supplied by the makers. It is a good plan also to have a set of samplers of the different colours, prepared in the following manner. Take a number of plaques of thin copper, measuring, say, $1\frac{1}{2}$ inch by 1 inch. Dome them up as described on p. 176. Coat one-third of the surface of each with white enamel, one-third with clear flux and the remainder with the enamel you wish to test. Fire them. Then lay a strip of silver foil, prepared as described on p. 195, across the three stripes as indicated in Fig. 274. Cover the foil, the white,

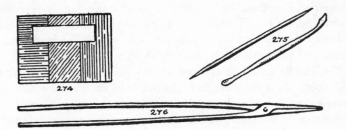

and the flux with a coating of the coloured enamel; and fire the plaque again. You will now have a sampler which shows how the colour will look when fired directly on to copper; and when fired on flux, on white, and on foil. The colour will look quite different on each. It will be most brilliant on the foil, next on the white or the flux, and deepest on the copper. It is only necessary now to paint the number on the sampler, and a figure to indicate if it is a soft, hard, or very hard colour. You decide this by arranging on a plaque small pieces of all the enamels you wish to test, and noticing the order in which they fuse when in the furnace. You should take care in doing this that all the colours are ground equally fine, and that the heat of the furnace reaches them all to the same degree.

In addition to the above, the following will be required—one or two porcelain pestles and mortars (Fig. 277); a small agate pestle and mortar, and one or two small spatulas (Fig. 275); a set of little china pans to hold the enamels when ground (Fig. 278); a slab of plate glass and a glass muller (Fig. 279), for grinding colours for

painting with; a corundum stick, and polishing materials; tools for engraving and repoussé work; rouge or whiting to protect any solder on the work from the heat of the furnace; some gum tragacanth dissolved in water. Cunynghame, in his book on *Enamelling*, says that the best way to dissolve the gum is to powder it well and wet it with alcohol before putting it in water. A porcelain dish and some hydrofluoric acid (in wax, rubber, or lead bottle). Nitric and sulphuric acids complete the list.

The metals usually employed for enamelling are copper, silver, and gold. As a rule, enamel will not hold on commercial brass, though it will on some bronzes. Iron can be enamelled, as we know to our sorrow, for enamelled iron advertisements are fairly plentiful. And of course, the softer metals—aluminium, tin, zinc, etc., will not stand the heat necessary for the fusing of the enamel. But in gold, silver and copper we have three splendid metals for our purpose.

174

CHAPTER XXII

ENAMELLING (*continued*)

Cloisonné enamels. The backing of an enamel. Its purpose. Preparing and fixing the cloisons. Preparation of the enamels. Charging the cells. Firing an enamel. Polishing an enamel.

CLOISONNÉ ENAMEL

IN THIS WORK the recesses to be filled with enamel are formed from narrow strips of metal, bent to shape and soldered or otherwise fastened to the groundplate (Plate 18). Some of the finest examples of cloisonné enamel were made by Byzantine craftsmen between the sixth and the twelfth centuries. They worked generally in gold, and with opaque colours. The wire they employed was thin, about $\frac{1}{100}$ inch in thickness and $\frac{1}{50}$ to $\frac{1}{32}$ inch in height.

Though not absolutely necessary, it is well to provide a cloisonné enamel with a backing of enamel on the underside of its groundplate. To understand the reason for this, consider what would happen if the enamel were put on one side only. When the work was put into the furnace the metal would expand, and the enamel, when fused, would settle down into close contact with it. When the work was taken from the furnace and cooled, both metal and enamel would contract. But the metal would contract much more than the enamel, for such is its nature. The result of this unequal shrinkage would be that a considerable strain would be put on the rather brittle enamel, which might splinter off, particularly if it were jarred in any way. Also, at the second and subsequent firings the metal, being a better conductor of heat than the glass, would expand sooner, and, as it happens, further than the glass, and again vary the stress. To avoid these dangers it is well to cover both sides of the metal with enamel. The metal now, on cooling, cannot curl away from the enamel as it did before. Nor can it contract more than the enamel, for it is gripped firmly on both sides. It must therefore remain in its expanded state, and it adapts itself to the new conditions. It has grown longer and wider than before. That this is actually the case may be proved by measuring an enamel before and after firing it, say, a dozen times. It will be found to have grown perhaps $\frac{1}{8}$ inch in 6 inches. For this reason the settings for large enamels should be made only when the firing has been completed.

The backplate should rise in a gentle curve towards the centre (Fig. 284). Its edges should turn rather quickly downwards, like a convex watch glass, like Fig. 285, not like Fig. 286. The plate may be shaped by running a burnisher repeatedly round the metal about $\frac{1}{8}$ inch from the edge while the plaque is held at an angle of 45 degrees to the stake or bench. Then the burnisher is rubbed across the plate from side to side in every direction until the centre is raised sufficiently. It may require annealing. Instead of using the burnisher the plaque may be shaped on a suitable stake by hammer alone. In any case it is well to anneal the plaque when the shaping is finished. The edge should be filed so that the plaque will stand truly on a surface plate, or on a piece of plate glass. The file may leave a little burr all round the edge. This should be left, as it will help to keep the first coat of enamel in place. The aim of this doming operation is the production of a plaque from which the counter-enamel will be protected from any contact with the iron plate on which it rests when firing. Should the counter-enamel at the edge touch the iron it would probably fuse to it, and it might break away locally from the rest of the work.

Transfer the design to the metal, and scratch in the lines with a steel point. If you have no oblong drawplate, draw down the wire for the cloisons till it is about $\frac{1}{32}$ inch thick, and flatten it between the rolls till it is about 1 or 2 on the metal gauge. Anneal it. Then, with tweezers bend each piece to the shape required, trying it from time to time against the design. Cut it off where necessary with a sharp chisel against a piece of brass. Do not use shears. With the chisel you can cut the end at exactly the angle you wish. If there are many cloisons you may gum them on to a piece of card or glass to keep them safely. When all are prepared clean the backplate and fasten down each cloison with borax in which a little gum tragacanth has been mixed. This will keep the cloisons in place when the borax boils up. The solder used should be as hard as possible, composed, say, of 4 parts silver to 1 of copper for silver work. The solder should be free from zinc, for this ingredient tends to burn out during the firing, and may show as a dark stain through the enamel. It may even cause the enamel about it to flake. It is well therefore to allow as little of the solder as possible to flow on to the background.

It is not essential that all, or indeed any, of the cloisons be soldered. Some workers, the Japanese among them, fasten the cloisons with paste or gum and proceed at once to fill in the enamel. When this is fired it holds the cloisons firmly. However, it is a good plan to solder down at least some of the cloisons, say, the outside ones and the principal divisions. But watch that the solder does not spread much over the ground, for it may affect the colour. Any solder which would be exposed to the direct heat of the furnace must be covered up with rouge or whiting before each firing. If this precaution is omitted the solder may run and cause trouble. When all the soldering is done the work may be boiled out in pickle to remove the borax and any other waste material. Background and cloisons should now be scraped clean, and not again touched by the fingers, which might leave a trace of grease. If the work must be left for a while it should be put in a vessel of distilled water and covered up. In this and all other processes of enamelling absolute cleanliness is essential.

The enamels have next to be ground. If a large amount of this material has to be prepared at once it is well to lay the lumps of enamel on an iron plate and put them into the furnace till they are quite hot, but not fused. Then drop them into a bowl of clean water. The lumps of enamel will crack all over and break up very easily in the mortar. A porcelain mortar 4 or 5 inches in diameter may be used, though an agate one is better, but much more expensive. A small agate pestle and mortar are extremely useful for fine work. Put some of the enamel into the mortar and cover it with water. Set the mortar on a pad of cloth or on a sandbag. Hold the pestle vertically with its lower extremity resting on the enamel, and with a mallet strike the top of the handle to crush the lumps. Keep the pestle away from the sides of the mortar. The water will keep the fragments of enamel from flying about. When all the larger pieces are broken, hold the pestle in the right hand and the mortar with the left, still on the pad, and grind the enamel to powder.

Now the coarser the enamel is ground the more brilliant it will be when fired. But if it is ground very coarsely indeed, it will not cover the metal very well, nor go into narrow spaces, and it will retain

177

air-bubbles when melted. The existence of these spots, where the metal is not completely covered by enamel, results in the surface becoming oxidized, or a hollow may appear in the otherwise level surface of the enamel when fired. Also when you are dealing with enamel work on copper the exposed spots will turn black. For these reasons the enamel must not be left very coarsely ground. As a rule the coarsest you can leave it at is about the size of silver sand. The water will by this time have become milky. This discoloration is due principally to extremely fine particles of enamel, and to some extent to the grinding away of the pestle and mortar, if of porcelain. But it must be entirely got rid of. So pour it away, add fresh water, stirring the enamel about. Directly it settles pour off the water. Do this again and again until quite clear water comes away. With translucent enamels this thorough washing is essential if their brilliance is to be preserved, but it is not so necessary for opaque enamels. The cleanly washed enamel should be kept under water in a covered vessel. Very coarsely ground enamel will keep for years, in water, in stoppered bottles, but finely ground enamel rapidly deteriorates if exposed to the air.

To return to the cloisonné panel. Lay it face downwards on a piece of blotting paper, and spread the counter-enamel all over it with a spatula. Dry it by pressing a layer of blotting paper firmly on it. Turn the plaque over, replace any loose cloisons, which you may stick down if necessary with a little gum. Fill each cell with enamel, taking great care to work it into all the corners and evenly along the sides of the recesses. The Japanese use a pointed piece of cane for their cloisonné ware. Keep the enamel off the top of the dividing lines. Press it down firmly, leaving its surface level, but rather above the top of the cloisons. When all the cells are filled the work is ready for the furnace.

To fire an enamel. Have ready a piece of sheet iron or nickel, a little larger than the enamel itself, upon which it may rest while in the furnace. It must be of such a shape as to support the work evenly. Not more than about an inch of the edge of an enamel should go unsupported, or it may sag when heated. A number of holes may be bored in this furnace-plate to allow the heat to get at the back of the enamel quite freely. To keep the enamel from sticking to the iron plate the latter is sometimes coated with rouge, whiting or plaster of Paris. A little alum, gum, or borax mixed with these materials will help to keep them from crumbling when heated. With continued heating thick scales form on iron, and sometimes come off at inconvenient times. They make black specks in the enamel if they get on to it, so see that the plate is in good order each time before you put the enamel on to it. It may be cleaned with a hammer. Nickel does not scale. Copper, of course, will not do at all. Lay the enamel on the plate, and rest them on the top of the stove to dry. Take great care that this is done thoroughly, for if any moisture remains when you put the work in the furnace, it may boil up and blow your enamel about. When quite dry grip the plate firmly with the tongs, and taking great care not to shake or jar it in any way—for the enamel is in a very fragile condition now—you may put it in the furnace. Do not put it down, but hold it there for a second or two, and then withdraw it. If any steam rises from it, it is not dry enough for firing. If any enamel falls off, withdraw the work instantly and put it in a cool place. Moisten it with water and repair the damage. You may add a drop or two of the gum solution. Then dry the work again. When quite dry put it down in the furnace without shaking it in any way, and close the door. It may occasion surprise that the enamel on the underside of the work does not fall off. Some workers like to add a drop or two of gum to the water in the counter-enamel, or even a drop of saliva. But these aids are unnecessary. If the enamel is dry and you have a steady hand, the work is safe.

While the work is in the furnace do not put the tongs down or attend to any other matter whatever—it requires all the attention you can give it. The time required to fuse the enamel varies from a few seconds to several minutes. Open the top of the furnace door and watch it carefully. When once it has begun to melt you may remove it for a second or two to see how it is getting on. It should be returned immediately. But for certain special effects, such as the obtaining of a clear coating of flux of bright golden colour on copper, it is essential that the firing be completed as soon as possible. The hotter the furnace the better for this purpose, If you move the tongs or a long palette knife about over the enamel while it is in the furnace you will be able to tell when the enamel is fused, for the reflection of the tool will be visible on the shining surface of the work. When this is so, withdraw the work immediately. Put it in a warm place, free from draughts, to cool down. When fused, the powdered

179

enamel will occupy less space than before. It may not now completely fill the cells. If it has drawn away from any part of a cloison or from the background, scrape that part bright with any sharp tool. Then pack enamel tightly against those places, and fill up any others where the enamel is not thick enough.

For the second and all subsequent firings the plate upon which the enamel rests should be made red-hot before the enamel is put on to it, and it should be replaced in the furnace with the enamel upon it, before it has time to get cool. The enamel may be conveniently lifted from the place where it has dried on to the red-hot plate by means of a large palette knife. But this is a rather delicate proceeding, if, as described later on, there is unfired enamel on the underside of the work. At the second and later firings the enamel may crack as the heat reaches it, and fuse together again when it gets red-hot. The plate is heated to enable the enamel to reach this high temperature with as little delay as possible. You may repeat the firing again and again, remembering always to cover up any exposed solder. If it is convenient to do so, after the last firing, you may turn out the gas and when the furnace has cooled a little, you may replace the work so that it may cool down with the furnace. This slow cooling will leave the enamel nicely annealed, and any subsequent cracking will be unlikely. Of course it is not absolutely necessary to do this, for an enamel may be taken straight from the furnace and cooled almost immediately under a stream of water. But not every enamel will stand such treatment, and one hardly likes to risk a valuable one.

The surface of the enamel after the last firing will be rather uneven. To smooth it, hold it when cold under a tap of running water, and grind the surface down to the level of the surrounding metal with a corundum stick, not with a file. This will give you a smooth, unpolished surface. To regain the shining surface of the enamel you may either replace the work in the furnace and fire it again, or polish it. The latter is the better, though slower way. But if you decide to refire it for any reason—a piece chipped out in the grinding to be filled up, for instance—you may first wash a little hydrofluoric acid over the face of the work. For though the running water has carried away nearly all the material ground off by the corundum, yet some has worked its way into the surface. When the work was fired again this would show up as a milky film. But the hydrofluoric acid, which has the power of dissolving glass, will remove it. The acid must be kept in a lead or gutta-percha bottle, for it attacks nearly everything else.* But the better way to regain the bright surface of the enamel is to polish it. Go over it with a fine corundum and water; afterwards with water-of-ayr stone and water; then with crocus powder on a strip of leather, and finally with rouge and wash-leather. You will in this way obtain a most brilliant surface, which will bring out the precious quality of the enamel. With some of the Chinese and other Eastern opaque enamels, however, this part of the work is not carried quite so far— the work being left with an egg-shell polish, which is very beautiful.

The polishing of the enamel will have smoothed the metal also. If there are any large plain spaces of metal left, a light pattern may be engraved on them now. It will help to bind the enamelled and the metal parts of the work together æsthetically. If the work is of copper the metal parts should also be gilt. Great care should be taken during this process to prevent the work from being subjected to any sudden changes of temperature, which might cause the enamel to crack. To ensure safety in this respect, gild it yourself by the mercury process. It is not safe to put the work into a hot gilding solution.

* Now polythene or other suitable plastic containers are used instead of gutta-percha.

CHAPTER XXIII

ENAMELLING (*continued*)

*Plique-à-jour enamel. Preparation of the cloisonné frame. Charging and
firing.*

ENAMELS of this type have no background. They are like
miniature stained-glass windows, the lead lines in the windows
being represented by the metal cloisons in the enamel. A
useful cloison for this work may be formed from an oblong-sectioned
wire. To make such a wire you have only to flatten a piece of
square wire, say, $\frac{1}{32}$ inch diameter, by passing it between the rolls
or by hammering it on the stake. Then you have a four-sided
strip of metal which will bend easily to shape. The filigree wire
pattern which is to hold the enamel is built up in the ordinary
way (see p. 176), or the framework may be a plate, pierced with
holes of suitable shapes (Fig. 280). Those parts of the work to which

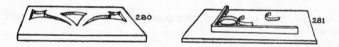

the enamel is to hold are scraped bright and clean. The work is
then, with U-shaped iron-wire clamps, fastened down temporarily
on to a sheet of some material to which enamel will not stick. Now
there are several such materials—aluminium-bronze or mica—
which leave the underside of the enamel clean and smooth after
firing; and tripoli, fireclay or pumice—which do not. Take, say,
a sheet of aluminium-bronze, size 10, a little larger than the work,
burnish one side and lay the wire network on to it. Tie or clamp the
wires down, so that they will not move while you are filling in the
enamel (Fig. 282). Before firing always cover up any exposed solder
with whiting or rouge. Fill up any hollows with fresh enamel and
refire as often as necessary. Then when the enamel is cool, remove
the clamps. A few light taps on the bronze will release the work.
The underside of the enamel may then be polished if necessary. If

you use mica for a temporary background it is well to lay it on a piece of iron, and to clamp the wires round that. If the enamel is to take a curved shape, the aluminium-bronze backing-plate must first be hammered to that shape, and the wirework made to fit. This plate should not have any undercut forms, or the completed work could not be removed from it. However, should an undercut form be required, the shape may be hammered up in thin sheet copper, like any other

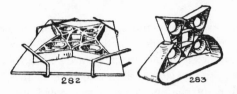

bowl. The cloisons, which should be of gold, are fastened to it with gum, and the cells filled with enamel. The work is fired in the usual manner, and, when all the cells are satisfactorily full, the copper bowl is dissolved in dilute nitric acid, say 2 parts water, 1 part acid: the gold and enamel being unaffected. There is yet another manner in which plique-à-jour work may be done. The metal framework is pierced out of a sheet of metal of suitable thickness. The web between the cells may be filed down to any degree of fineness. The metal framework can be supported in a vertical position on the iron plate which goes into the furnace (Fig. 283). Each cell is then filled with enamel, with which is mixed a little gum tragacanth. The work is carefully dried, and fired in a very hot furnace. It must be removed before the enamel has had time to run down. Any gaps may then be filled in and the firing repeated. Plique-à-jour enamel may be employed with the most delicate filigree, and will suggest that a film of translucent colour had settled upon the wires. The plique-à-jour process should be employed with restraint. It is not suitable for spoons, or for objects which are subject to rough handling.

CHAPTER XXIV

ENAMELLING (*continued*)

Design for champlevé enamels. Preparation of the ground-plate. Champlevé enamel.

IN CHAMPLEVÉ WORK the enamel fills cells which are cut or otherwise recessed in a stout metal plate. We have already seen that beautiful examples of this craft are known from Celtic and Anglo-Saxon Britain (Plate 25). Another centre from which great quantities of champlevé work proceeded was the town of Limoges in Central France, whence in the twelfth, thirteenth and later centuries thousands of reliquaries, crosses, altar vessels and other works were sent to all parts of Europe. In most of the early work from Limoges each decorated space is filled with broken opaque colours, often blues and greens, touched with creamy white. The ground is generally gilded. And the head of a figure is often made by repoussé work in fairly high relief from a separate piece of copper or bronze, gilded, and riveted on.

The design for champlevé work should be so arranged that the pattern formed by the lines of metal between the enamelled cells is itself well related to the plainer, undecorated body of the work. The line pattern should grow out of its background of broader masses, and thus hold the whole design together in a larger unity.

The metal used for champlevé work should be fairly stout, size 14 on the metal gauge, or even thicker for large work. The methods by which the recesses for the enamels may be prepared have already been discussed under "inlaying," p. 149. Champlevé enamels are rarely backed, but to ensure a good grip for the colours it is customary to leave the floor of the recesses rough. Should translucent enamels be used, the walls of the recesses may cast unpleasant shadows across the coloured areas. However, as opaque colours are usually employed in champlevé work, this difficulty does not often arise. The depth of the recess may be anywhere between $\frac{1}{50}$ and $\frac{1}{20}$ inch. A greater depth than this is not desirable, for the enamel is likely to flake off if it is thick.

When the engraving is completed, the metal must be thoroughly cleaned. If there is any pitch or jewellers' cement on it, it may be removed with paraffin. If the metal is slightly warmed the work is easier. It should then be washed in hot soda and water, the face being finally cleaned with methylated spirit. On no account should the work be boiled out in pickle, for this would dull all the clean cutting, so that you would have to go over it again. Nor should you touch the engraved surface with the hands, as they might leave a trace of grease. If the work must be left for a while it should be put into a vessel of distilled water and covered up. In this and all other processes of enamelling absolute cleanliness is essential.

The charging of the cells with enamel, the firing of the work, and the subsequent operations upon it have already been discussed under " cloisonné work " above.

CHAPTER XXV

ENAMELLING (*continued*)

Bassetaille enamel. Definition. History. Method of working. Two out-standing examples. Some modern work. Cast work.

BASSETAILLE ENAMEL

IN THIS WORK the metal groundplate is chased (or sometimes engraved) in such a way that its modelled surfaces beneath the enamel form an essential part of the design. If figures are employed, the folds and other undulating surfaces of their robes are visible through the enamel which covers them, and take an important share in producing the final effect. Again, the enamel, though level on its outer surface, takes a richer tone over the more deeply recessed folds, as the light there has to pass through a greater thickness of enamel. As a result, if the work is turned about in the hand, the light plays enchanting tunes in its chosen medium—colour. It may be noted also that, once he has achieved the general form of the modelled surface, the craftsman may give us also a little rippling of the metal surface here and there. For he knows that such undulations cause the light which reaches them through the coloured enamel to twinkle or sparkle more brightly than it does on smoother surfaces.

It was customary in the fourteenth century, when the bassetaille process was in great favour, to prepare the ground for the enamel by chasing: not by engraving as has been so generally presumed. Such preparatory work is not very difficult, and an examination of a number of early examples, say, in the magnificent collection at South Kensington, will show that the quality of the chasing necessary for such work is not always very high. Usually it is well within the capacity of a craftsman who has learnt how to manage a tracer. Seldom indeed is there evidence in the old work of the hand of a die-sinker. The first important step is the provision of a good silhouette. Then the whole of the area to be enamelled must be sunk a little distance, say, $\frac{1}{50}$ to $\frac{1}{20}$ inch, beneath the level of the background. This sinking may be done by degrees as the craftsman works over the figures and models the forms bit by bit with chasing tools. He will find it a good plan to run a little water-colour paint over the work from time to time while it is in progress. The relief, showing through the colour, will give him a good idea of the progress of his chasing. A young craftsman need not be afraid to tackle such a problem. Let him first provide himself with a design which forms an interesting pattern, for that is essential if he wishes to produce a worthwhile work: a few shillings' worth of silver; and then with a few chasing tools, used as described elsewhere in this book, he may do the rest. He should take silver about size 10 on the metal gauge for a 2-inch panel. The chasing should be done on pitch. When completed, the work should have enamel on both sides, and its surface should be polished flat.

Many examples of bassetaille enamel on silver may be found in our museums, particularly in that at South Kensington. Elsewhere there are two examples of outstanding merit, unsurpassed in any collection. They are the Royal Gold Cup in the British Museum, in which the enamelling is on fine gold; and the " King John " Cup at King's Lynn, Norfolk. This is a silver-gilt cup, and the enamels are on silver. There are some interesting technical differences between them. The King's Lynn cup is the earlier of the two. It dates from about 1325, and its enamels are technically nearer the early champlevé work of Limoges and the cloisonné work of yet earlier times than is the more sophisticated workmanship of the Royal Gold Cup. In the " King John " Cup slender traceries of silver, which run through each figure, divide it into a number of associated panels of colour. But the lines are not heavy enough to cut the figure into awkward-shaped masses. They frame each panel, and the coloured ground behind the figure leaves it as a pleasant silhouette, tied to the silver elsewhere in the panel by a cloisonné-like tracery (Plate 1).

The Royal Gold Cup is the only surviving example of the enamelled secular gold plate of the fourteenth century. All other examples of the same scale and quality have disappeared. Technically and æsthetically it is an infinitely finer piece of craftsmanship than the much-praised gold and enamel salt-cellar which Cellini made for Francis I, and is now at Vienna. With the Ardagh Chalice at Dublin it stands in a class by itself: a verdict which certainly could not be passed on Cellini's work. The Royal Gold Cup in its original condition stood on a stand of gold, similarly decorated. It was made about 1350, probably in Burgundy or Paris, and is decorated with scenes from the life of St. Agnes. The whole of each figure, tree, scroll or piece of furniture represented there is covered from side to side with enamel, which extends as a level surface right across them. Each is thus shown in silhouette against the gold background. The enamels being translucent, all the detailed modelling of the faces, the hands, the folds of the dresses and the other objects is seen through the enamel; the deeper depressions naturally appearing richer in tone than their shallower neighbours (Frontispiece).

In this cup the different coloured enamels are not separated by metal cloisons: the different colours meet side by side. Now, if some wet, powdered enamel is to be laid down beside another patch which is still wet, care must be taken that the boundary line between them does not become irregular. The most convenient way to prevent this is to add a little gum tragacanth to each batch of enamel, and to allow the first colours to dry before the next are laid alongside them. They will not then spread much on to their neighbours' territory.

In many mediæval works executed by the bassetaille process, the enamel extends right across the panel, with no metal surface left exposed. In panels with figures even the flesh is covered with a layer of clear enamel, which allows the modelling of the face and hands to show through.

Sometimes a panel produced primarily by chasing is touched up by a certain amount of work done by engraving tools. Some traces of such work may be seen on the St. Agnes Cup, although the major portion of the relief was executed by chasing. It should be remembered that in a bassetaille enamel, because so much of its effect depends upon the modelling of the metal beneath it, the enamel itself must have a level and well-polished surface. All depressions in the enamelled surface should be filled up and refired, and the surface ground level and polished. The metal background may be diapered, and gilt.

Recently some very fine and technically perfect work has been produced by a few skilled workers in England and France, in which, over elaborately involved machine-cut patterns in low relief, delicately coloured enamels are fired. Such work demonstrates that when our skilled craftsmen produce, on a commercial scale, work whose technical perfection excels that on the most important examples in our national collections, they may yet, with inspired design, give us finer works than the world has yet seen.

Cast metal work may be enamelled, though, unless it is properly annealed after its last firing, the enamel has a tendency to flake off—days or perhaps months after the work is completed: but a careful preparation of the ground will considerably lessen this danger. The edges of the recesses may be slightly undercut; the whole ground pecked over regularly with the graver—to give the enamel a good key; and the work, when done, is very carefully annealed, by being allowed to remain in the furnace while it cools down, as described above.

CHAPTER XXVI

ENAMELLING (*continued*)

Encrusted enamels. Methods of support. Protection of soldered joints.

ENCRUSTED ENAMELS

ENCRUSTED ENAMELS are those which are employed to decorate irregular surfaces, surfaces which, in the sixteenth and some later centuries, the craftsmen delighted to enrich with unexpected touches of colour. Some of the fine jewels of the Renaissance, the gold mounts for crystal cups, the sword hilts and scabbards so freely decorated by Indian and Persian craftsmen, teach us the value of these touches of precious colour, which gleam so brightly on silver or on gold. The opportunities for the employment of such jewels of enamel are so varied that no general rules for the work can be made. One of the principal problems arising from it concerns the manner in which the object may be supported during the firing. An elaborately constructed finger-ring may have a number of soldered joints—joints which must not be exposed unprotected to the heat of the furnace. Or, a pendant jewel, built up from a number of separately formed members held together by solder, may have enamelled decorations on surfaces inclined at many different angles. The enamelling itself may differ but little from that on examples already discussed, but the method of supporting the work in the furnace varies infinitely. In some cases a metal support such as that shown in Fig. 283 will be sufficient, but any soldered joints must be protected by painting them with rouge or whiting. For more elaborate work it is sometimes necessary to provide a support made from plaster of Paris. The plaster is made to envelop large portions of the work, leaving exposed only those parts on which the enamel is to come. When all the soldering and cleaning up has been finished, and the work is ready for the enamelling, it is set up on an iron furnace-plate. Plaster of Paris is mixed in a spoon as described on p. 133, and is spread over the work with a spatula. Every part may be covered with plaster except those surfaces which are to be enamelled. The work may be fired again and again if necessary, but at no time must a soldered joint be left unprotected.

Yet another kind of enamelled work may be found on some of the jewelled book covers of the sixteenth century. The covers of a small book were made from plates of gold or silver, very elaborately and minutely worked with historical scenes in repoussé, and then richly enamelled. There is one such book cover in the British Museum, which belonged to Queen Elizabeth; and another at South Kensington. Similar work on a slightly larger scale may be seen on the stems of some mediæval chalices. Little figures, worked almost in the round from sheet metal, are decorated by enamelling. Cellini's golden saltcellar, which he made for Francis I of France, and which is now at Vienna, is of similar work.

CHAPTER XXVII

ENAMELLING (continued)

Painted enamels. Preparation of plaque. Backing. Grinding colours in mortar. Applying the enamel. Drying. Firing. Foil. Grinding colours on slab. Painting. Gold. Alterations. Grisaille, etc.

PAINTED ENAMELS

CLOISONNÉ AND CHAMPLEVÉ enamels had been made for many centuries before it was discovered that the metal outlines between the different colours were not essential to the permanence of the work, valuable though they were from the decorative point of view. Towards the end of the fifteenth century the craftsmen at Limoges in France, who did a good trade in enamelled shrines, caskets, croziers and other decorated metalwork, began, in the enamelled pictures which they fitted into the work, to leave out the metal divisions altogether. The way in which they worked has been followed, with little variation, by enamellers ever since. It is this—you wish to make an enamelled plaque with a design painted on it. Take a sheet of copper, or of whatever metal you are to use, measuring say, 3 inches by 2 inches, size 6 and dome it up slightly in the middle (Fig. 284), as described on p. 176. If

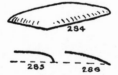

the plaque is not to be covered all over with the same enamel at first, but with a number of different colours to form a pattern, you must now draw the design on the metal. Transfer it with carbon paper and carefully scratch it in with a steel point. You may now boil the plaque in sulphuric acid pickle (water 20 parts, acid 1 part) or leave the plaque in the cold pickle for an hour. Next scrub thoroughly with a nailbrush both the under and upper surfaces with pumice powder and water. Leave the plaque in a covered dish of clean water, and get the enamels ready.

Grind the enamels you are to use, wash them thoroughly, and put them into covered vessels with a little water. When washing translucent enamels always go on until the water which is poured off is quite clear from the milky tinge mentioned above (p. 178). Fill the mortar with water, and wait a few seconds for the enamel to settle, then pour out the water. Repeat this as often as necessary. Do not throw away the sediment which will be found at the bottom of the vessel into which the water is poured. It is composed principally of finely ground enamel. It is quite good enough to use on the underside, or back, of the work. If an agate mortar is used the enamels require less washing: but agate mortars are expensive. Sets of little china pans, fitting one over the other, such as are sometimes used for water-colours, are useful for keeping small quantities of ground enamel free from dust. Ground enamel should always be kept wet.

Lift the plaque by its edges (do not touch the face) and lay it, concave side upwards, on a piece of clean blotting paper. Take some of the sediment from the washings, or any finely ground enamel which you wish to use up, and spread it evenly over the plate. You may add a drop or two of a solution of gum tragacanth or of saliva to assist in keeping it from falling off when the plaque is turned over, though if the work is handled carefully it will do without them. You may apply the enamel with a brush or spatula. It must be spread evenly, and be just thick enough to hide the metal. As a rule the enamel on front and back of the plaque should be equal in thickness. Dry the backing by pressing a piece of blotting paper firmly upon it. Turn the work over and stand it on the table or on a dry piece of blotting paper; not a sodden piece, or some of the backing may come off. The design—scratched in before the plaque was cleaned—will still be visible. Fill it in with the proper colours, taking care to keep the edge of the ground enamel exactly to the drawing. If you put a drop of the gum tragacanth solution into the enamel on the plaque it will help to keep it together. Dry each patch of colour by touching its edge with blotting paper. Let it get nearly dry before you put the next colour up against it. The water will naturally run from the wet enamel into the dry, but you get a truer line between the colours if one is pretty dry first.

You may, of course, mix the colours together as much as you like if they are all of the same hardness. The enamel should be spread evenly all over, but should not be thicker than is necessary to cover the surface completely. Do not let it get wet enough near the edges of the plaque to run on the table. When the plaque is completely covered, dry off the water with clean blotting paper. Lift it with the palette knife to the iron plate on which it goes into the furnace. Put both upon the top of the furnace to dry. Keep the work free from dust. When it is quite dry fire it.

When the enamel comes from the furnace and has cooled down, look it over carefully. Some of the back may have fallen off. If so, it must be repaired. Scrape the metal quite clean at all bare places on both front and back, washing over the scraped edges with hydrofluoric acid to avoid milkiness. Wash clean with water, then fill up the gaps and fire again.

If you give the copper plaque a coating of clear flux first, and then put the coloured enamels over that, they will show up much more brilliantly. Copper, with a coating of clear flux over it, looks a bright golden or a pink coppery colour according to the composition of the flux used and to the temperature at which it was fired. Silver seen through flux looks like white satin. The colour of gold hardly changes at all. Any drawing on the metal, whether scratched in with a steel point, or drawn with a lead pencil, will show clearly through the flux. The surface of the flux may, however, be roughened, then washed over with hydrofluoric acid to avoid milkiness in the colour (see above) and the design transferred to it. The coloured enamels are then applied in their proper places.

You have now the plaque with its first coat of coloured enamel fired on to it. The colours may require modifying, shading may be necessary; you may want to use some gold or silver foil to make a more brilliant patch of colour somewhere; you may wish to put an outline round parts of the design, or touches of gold. Some or all of these things may be necessary. Now, as already stated, enamels vary in their hardness, some requiring much greater heat to melt them than others. The hardest colours should therefore be put on first, the softer ones for a later firing. A plaque may be fired a dozen or more times, but the enamel put on for the later firings should not require heat enough to disturb the harder enamel put on first. So you must find out which colours require the most heat.

194

To do this you take a little of each of those you wish to use and arrange them in a row on a clean plaque and put it in the furnace. Then you note carefully the order in which they melt as the plaque gets hot; then you can go ahead.

Gold leaf or foil may be employed in various ways in enamel work:

(a) It may be used to cover part of the background, say, of a figure, as in some primitive Italian and other paintings. For such work it is well to provide a foundation of translucent yellow enamel over which the gold may be laid. It is a good plan to moisten the surface before laying the gold, and to breathe on the film of gold while applying it. A temperature high enough to just fuse the enamel is sufficient to fix the gold. Should any defects appear, brush the gold with a glass brush, put another layer of gold over the first to cover the gaps, and fire it. It is not necessary to put enamel over the gold.

(b) Stars, fleurs-de-lis, rosettes or other devices may be stamped out in low relief in gold foil and laid on a foundation layer of enamel, to form diaper or other patterns. They are overlaid with a coating of translucent enamel, and the work fired. Translucent colours look brighter when fired on a background of gold or silver than on copper, or on the black or dark blue background employed by many mediæval enamellers. To obtain any especially bright touches of colour you may use small pieces of gold or silver foil, covered with translucent enamel, for that purpose. For use on a curved surface the foil or leaf may be prepared by nicking it at intervals before laying it down. It should be then brushed or stroked into place on the enamelled surface of the work with the glass brush or a burnisher. See that no undesigned gaps appear. As gold leaf is very fragile, it may be laid between two sheets of tissue paper, after making them slightly greasy by rubbing them over one's hair. The tissue will adhere to the gold and it may be handled without difficulty. Patterns may be traced on to the paper and cut out with scissors. Then the tissue may be floated off in a saucer of water. The gold shapes are lifted with a brush and arranged on the enamelled surface. A thin layer of translucent enamel may be laid and fired over the gold. But as the edge of such a " paillon," as the fragment of gold is called, may form too hard a line, it may be necessary to soften it by shading. Iridium black may be used for this purpose, or enamel, ground up as described below, is employed as paint. Glass half-pearls and other devices in relief are occasionally employed to decorate an enamel. The glass pearl will sink a little way into the surface on firing, and obtain a good hold. A little ground enamel can be employed to glaze and retain other devices.

(c) Haloes, sun-bursts and other decorations in gold may be painted on to an enamel surface, using as paint gold leaf ground to a powder in an agate mortar and mixed with a little oil of spike lavender or honey. It does not require a very high temperature to fire it. Oil of spike lavender is a good medium for either under or over-glaze painting, but as it has to be all burnt away in the firing, as small an amount as possible of the medium is used in painting.

To obtain an even coating of enamel some workers sift the powdered enamel, dry, on to the metal ground, in two or three layers, rather than in a single, wet, thicker layer.

For shading, you must use enamel ground finely enough to paint with. Take a slab of plate glass, a foot square, and a glass muller (Fig. 279). See that they are both clean, and put a little of the colour you wish to use in the middle of the slab. In making the choice remember that the grinding will cause the enamel to appear lighter in colour. You have now to grind it finely enough to use as paint. This will take time, but you must go on grinding till there is not a trace of grittiness to be seen in the colour where, near the edges of the slab, it is getting dry. Add a little water when necessary. The finely ground enamel must now be washed. It is not easy to do this without losing a good part of it. But most of the milkiness must be got rid of, or it will show up on the work. Keep that part which is nearest in colour to the enamel before it was ground. You may now add to it a drop or two of oil of spike lavender.

You use the finely ground enamel to paint with, the oil of lavender mixed with the colour helps it to flow fairly smoothly from the brush if they have been evenly mixed. You may add a little fat oil of turpentine if the paint dries too soon in hot weather. But the addition of a large proportion of medium of any kind will tend to make the colour bubble up in the furnace, so use as little as possible. Put in all the shading necessary. Then stand the enamel in a warm place to dry off as much of the medium as possible before the work goes into the furnace. Some of the shading sinks in each time the enamel is fired, so you must strengthen it where necessary. Black enamel, ground finely, turns rather grey, so if you require a very strong black line you should use iridium black. This can be bought ready prepared.

When all the painting is completed the surface-gold may be put on. This can be bought in bottles from dealers in china colours. Or the liquid gold can be made from the following ingredients:

Lavender oil	900 parts.
Gold chloride	100 „
Bismuth subnitrate	5 „

Wash the enamelled plate with spirit before putting on the gold. The latter must be well dried before firing. Not much heat is required to fix it.

It sometimes happens that an enamel curls out of shape during firing. It can be straightened in the following manner. Have ready two large, stiff palette knives. See that they are quite clean and free from dust. With one of the knives lift the enamel straight from the furnace on to a flat stake or smooth slab of stone. Instantly push down any projecting corners, using both knives near the edges of the plaque to press the work into shape. Hold the edges down till the red glow has quite gone from the work. The enamel will be quite soft when it comes from the furnace, but in a few seconds will have set hard—when any pressure would have disastrous results.

To remove a part of the enamel after it is fired is not so difficult a task as it looks at first sight. You can either dissolve the enamel at the offending spot with hydrofluoric acid, or you can boldly cut it out with a graver. In the latter case it is well to wash the spot afterwards with hydrofluoric acid to avoid any subsequent milkiness in the colour. Remember that after using the acid, every trace of it must be washed off the work with plenty of water: otherwise it will do damage.

Throughout all the work, absolute cleanliness of all the tools and materials is essential if you are to produce enamels free from specks.

It is not unusual to employ china colours for the final touching up of an enamel. But this practice is not to be recommended, as the colours have not the same quality as enamel itself. They are principally composed of mineral oxides, without flux. They may sink into the enamel and become incorporated with it, but as a rule they must be covered with a thin film of soft flux to protect them from the action of the atmosphere.

In the sixteenth and seventeenth centuries a large amount of work was done in grisaille on blue or black grounds. The copper was first covered all over with the dark-coloured ground. Then the designs were painted in monochrome, by successive layers of white enamel. Many coats of this were fired one over the other, till the light was sufficiently strong. The shading was given by the dark ground showing through the white. Sometimes, over the dark ground an even layer of overglaze white was spread or powdered on. Any portion not required was scraped off, and the remainder fired on. Additional coats of white enamel were painted on wherever the pattern needed strengthening. Sometimes little touches of colour were added, and gold. Much of the work shows wonderful technical ability, for the drawing and shading are excellent in spite of the difficulty of the medium. But, of course, the principal motif for the use of enamel, the recognition of its glorious quality of colour, is often absent.

A ground of hard white enamel may be spread directly on to the metal, and fired. It is then ground level, and coloured enamels are painted over it. Much work in this fashion was done in the eighteenth century at Battersea and elsewhere. But, dainty though much of it is, it has lost the true quality of enamel—the work being little different from china painting.

Enamelling being so much akin to glasswork, it is not surprising that the two crafts are sometimes combined. For instance, enamel colours are often used on glasswork, as on the beautiful mosque lamps in Arab lands. An unusual method is employed, however, in some of the enamels on the Ardagh Chalice in the National Museum, Dublin. A hemispherical blue glass bead has a recess carved or moulded in its surface. This recess is lined with a grey enamel and afterwards filled up with red. Other enamels on the same cup have a silver cell let into a glass or enamel bead, the cell being filled up afterwards with enamel of a different colour. Yet another method was employed in the first half of the seventeenth century. Gold cells and cloisons were inlaid in the surface of a piece of glass, perhaps for a watch-back or a locket. The cells were afterwards filled with enamel and fired. The surface was ground flat, and polished. The effect is very delicate and jewel-like. Work of this kind was executed to the design of, and perhaps by the hand of Valentin Sezenius about 1723. But probably owing to its difficulty and cost it soon dropped out of production. A collection of this work may be seen in the South Kensington Museum.

An almost similar technique is found in the enamels on the brooch discovered at Carlungie, Angus, Scotland. Some fifty or sixty small opaque blue-glass discs were set in powdered red enamel in recesses in the bronze-work of the brooch. The enamel was fired (at about 685° C.) and adhered firmly both to the glass discs and to the bronze. Other brooches, similarly decorated, came from Belgium in Roman times. There is a curious parallel between this technique and that on the bowl from Enkomi, Cyprus (c. 1400 B.C.), mentioned on p. 161. On this bowl are flowers, cut from gold foil, which were pressed into the powdered niello which filled recesses in the silver bowl. When fired, the gold flowers were held firmly by the niello.

CHAPTER XXVIII

METAL CASTING

*Primary metal casting. Materials for moulds. Stone, clay and bronze
moulds. The pattern. Casting a sword. Cuttle-fish bone casting. Casting a
relief. A Chinese vase. Piece-moulding. Materials. Throwing the core.
Wax model. Pour, runners and vents. The mould. Cire perdue casting.
Statuette. Plaster cast. Plaster piece-mould. Irons. Core making. Wax
cast. Chaplets. The descending and the ascending principles. Compo
cire perdue mould. Pouring and finishing.*

THE CASTING of ingots of simple form has been considered in
Chapter II. Here and in the four following chapters we
make a wider survey. Casting in metal is one of the oldest
arts in the world. Except for the comparatively few works produced
by craftsmen who had access to masses of native gold, copper or
meteoric iron, discovered in a condition suitable for immediate use,
all metal objects have been made from material which at some time
has been intentionally melted and cast. The casting may have been
in the form of sheet or bar or some other shape, from which the
object was to be manufactured. Or a pattern may have been carved
or modelled in the required form, and a mould prepared from it,
into which the metal was cast.

Gold is generally found in nuggets or grains, or as veins in its
native rock. In ancient times jewellery may often have been made
directly from the nugget. But in general the craftsman cast gold
or copper and its alloys into a convenient shape before he used it.

The early workers in metal frequently made their moulds from
slabs of easily cut stone or of baked clay, into which they cut or
scraped the form of the ornament or tool which they wished to make.
For example, the mould for the earliest type of copper or bronze
axehead would be carved or scraped directly into the surface of a
slab of stone: no separate model being necessary. A funnel-shaped
groove, leading from the edge of the slab to the axe-shaped hollow
would form the " pour " or sprue through which the molten metal
entered the mould. A flat piece of stone, laid across the incised
slab, might form the opposite side of the recess, and so complete a

200

closed mould. Many hundreds of such simple moulds for weapons and useful or decorative articles are preserved in our museums. Metal moulds, dating from the Bronze Age in Britain and the Continent, for casting axeheads and other objects also may be found in the museums. They are often made in two pieces, and when a core was needed it was generally made in baked clay. Two finely finished bronze moulds for flanged arrowheads are in the British Museum. Each mould is in four or five pieces, very skilfully fitted together. They date from about 700 B.C., and come from the Near East. In addition to these there are many examples of moulds made in clay from previously prepared models. For instance, a craftsman wished to make a bronze knife-blade. He carved a pattern in wood to the exact shape he required. He then rolled out on his bench a slab of clay of suitable proportions and dusted its surface with soot or any other material which would prevent his pattern from sticking to it. He pressed his wooden pattern into the slab till about half the thickness of the model was sunk below the surface. He made the parting line, where the wooden pattern and the exposed surface of the clay met, quite tidy. And, with a rounded pebble or the end of a stick, he made a series of hemispherical hollows, or "register marks" on the clay surface on each side of his wooden model. He then dusted the exposed clay surface and the model with soot or other powder, as before, and laid a second slab of clay over the first. He pressed it closely on to the model and into the depressions formed by the pebble. Also he trimmed with a knife the outer edges of the slabs, so that they could be replaced at any time exactly one over the other. He lifted the top slab, removed the model and cut a channel to form the pour. He set the mould aside to dry, and when ready, he baked it on the hearth.

Now the model for a knife would be only a few inches long, and no difficulty would have been experienced in lifting off the upper half of the mould without distortion. But in the case of a sword, which, including its tang, might be 2 or 3 feet in length, the lifting of the upper leaf of the mould without damage would be attained with some difficulty. However, a Norse craftsman in Orkney in the Viking period found a simple solution to this problem. He prepared two thin smooth-surfaced sticks, each as long as the model, and greased them. When forming the upper leaf of the mould he laid them on top of the upper slab, allowing them to project an inch or so beyond one end. He worked some of the clay right over them, so that they formed, temporarily, part of the mould. With their help he was able to lift the upper leaf of the mould without distortion. He removed the pattern, cut the groove for the pour, tidied up any defects, and replaced the top slab. He then wriggled the sticks free, and removed them from the work. The mould would shrink, perhaps $\frac{1}{2}$ inch in length while drying, and if the sticks had been allowed to remain in the mould they would probably have caused it to crack. The mould would be allowed to dry slowly. It was fired on the hearth to a brick-like hardnesss, tied together with green withies, buried in the ground in front of the hearth and filled with metal before it had had time to cool down.

Casting in cuttlefish bone is sometimes employed for the reproduction of small reliefs or other articles which have no undercutting. The model must not be in any soft material such as modelling-wax, though sealing-wax may be used. With this limitation it is a very convenient method for reproducing quite small work. Let us therefore consider it before we go on to the more important processes.

Take a sound cuttlefish bone and with a saw split it across into two equal parts. The inner side of the bone is softer than the other. Grind the soft side of each piece quite flat on the rub stone. Flatten also one of the outer sides of the bone, near the thicker end. The reason for this will be given later. Fix three small wooden pegs with conical or pointed ends in one of the flattened faces of the mould. These pegs should be placed as far apart as they may conveniently be. When the two halves of the mould are pressed together the pointed tops of the pegs make depressions which ensure the proper registration of the two pieces whenever they are again put together. Lay the pattern on one face of the mould, say, an inch from the top edge. Press the pattern a little way into the face of the bone. It will give sufficiently to allow this. Now place the second piece of bone exactly over the first, and press it down on to the pegs and the model. Between hands and knees press the two parts firmly together. When the two faces have met, take a rough file and true up the outer edges of the mould while its two halves are in contact. Open it and lift out the model, a sharp impression of which should remain. Make a funnel-shaped opening from the impression to the top edge of the mould. Make also a few small grooves across the face of the mould, radiating from the impression. These grooves form vents through which some of the air escapes as the hot metal enters the mould. The grooves need not reach quite so far as the outer edge of the mould, or rather they should not be wide enough to allow the metal to run right through them and escape. Next paint the face of the mould, where it will be touched by the heated metal, with a strong borax solution. This may be borax ground up on the slate as for soldering, or ground up with paraffin. When this has sunk in, go over the surface with a solution of silicate of soda (water glass)—half water and half silicate of soda. You may, if you wish, put on the borax and the silicate of soda solutions together, half of each. Their purpose is to toughen the face of the mould, so that it may stand the heat of the molten metal better. You may now replace the model very carefully in the mould, seeing that it registers exactly. But slightly oil its surface, or dust it over with French chalk first, lest it stick to the mould. Then put the second part of the mould in place and press the two halves together. This should give you a good impression (see Fig. 287). Remove the

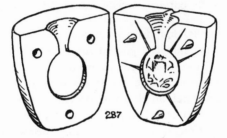

model, tie the two parts of the mould together with binding wire, and dry thoroughly. Take a piece of charcoal and make a hollow in one face of it large enough to hold the metal which you wish to use for the cast. Tie this piece of charcoal against the flattened outer side of the cuttlefish mould, the upper surface of the two being level. Scrape a little channel between the hollow in the charcoal and the funnel-shaped pour in the mould. All being ready, melt the metal in the charcoal hollow. Get it quite hot, and as soon as the brightness disappears and a film is about to form on it, tilt the block and mould so that the metal runs into the latter. You may open the mould immediately the metal has set. If, however, you heat the metal in a crucible, first set the mould in a box of dry (hot) sand.

The clay-slab and the cuttlefish bone methods of casting are alike in that the recess for the metal is made at once—simply by pressure. We now come to other materials which are either painted or poured over the work in a liquid or plastic state, or used in granular form and pressed against the pattern. The two qualities necessary for such a material are: (1) That it be of such consistency that it may be spread over the model in a very finely divided state—so that it may go into every crack, following the form very closely; and give a smooth surface where necessary. And (2) that it be able to stand the heat of the molten metal without melting, powdering or splitting. Moulds are often heated to a bright-red heat to expel the moisture before the metal is poured in, for any water present then would be converted into steam, which would force its way out somehow, even through the liquid metal. You might thus with a damp mould have a serious explosion, with molten metal thrown all about. The surface of the mould must be quite sound and smooth after this heating, so finely ground material must be employed for the first coating next to the pattern, or you would get a rough surface on the cast.

In most industrial foundries greensand moulding technique is used, in which the metal is poured into slightly moist clay-sand mixtures and no attempt is made to dry out the moisture. Sand is permeable, but the escape of the steam is assisted by "venting" with a wire, with which an elaborate system of small holes is made through the sand. But in such work a very fine surface is not required. For fine metalwork it is, of course, necessary.

Should the work be a relief, without any undercutting, it is possible to make one mould do for the front. But as open moulds

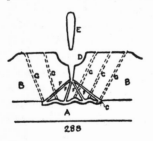

288

do not work very well, a slab of some material is generally required for the back. Moreover, if the model is not to be destroyed, and the work is in the round or undercut in any part, the mould must be made in several pieces. Otherwise you could not remove the model. When a thin flattish casting is to be made it is usual to arrange the work as shown in section in Fig. 288. *A* is the mould for the front of the work. *B* is that for its back. *C* is the cast itself. *D* is a large

204

hollow at the top of the mould, filled at the bottom by the plug *E*. *FFFF* are the inlets or " gates " for the metal, which flows from the hollow *D*, when the plug is removed. *GGG* are vents to allow the air to escape. You will notice that they come from the top of each undulation in the shape of the upper surface of the cast—wherever, in fact, the air might be imprisoned by the molten metal. The inlets *F* run towards the lower parts of the undulations in the form. The air-vents should be as large or larger than the inlets. When the mould has been thoroughly dried, the molten metal is poured into the hollow *D*. The plug is then removed and the metal flows through the various inlets to every part of the mould at once. With a thin casting this is essential, for if there were but one inlet the metal would be likely to set before it reached the extremities of the mould. You would therefore get a faulty casting.

Let us consider the formation of a " piece-mould," such as that required for the " Tsun ": a Chinese wine vessel of the Shang-Yin Dynasty (1766–1122 B.C.), shown in Fig. 289. Many parts of such

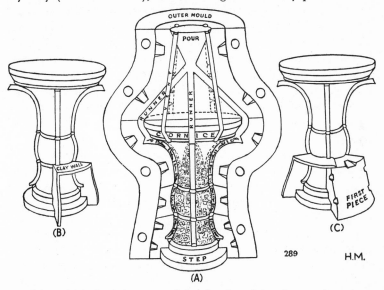

moulds, which had been used in the foundries for casting these vessels, have been found. The central illustration *A* shows the further half of such a mould with the wax model of the vase, complete with runners and vents, within it. Fig. 289 *B* shows the model of the vase in wax, with core, " step " and " cornice," and a clay band in position ready for the formation of the first piece. (Note that in drawings *B* and *C* the modelled ornament has been omitted, as its presence tended to confuse the appearance of the work). The Step and Cornice are projecting parts of the core intended to support some of the pieces of the mould. They are not parts of the vase itself.

We may follow the course of the work thus. The material for the core was prepared first. A mass of clay, mixed with sand, powdered brick, and sawdust or bonedust (this last to make it porous on firing) was the material chosen for the core. Each moulder has his own preferences, for moulds and cores are made from many materials:— of loam; sand with some binding material; plaster-of-Paris mixed with brick-dust, pumice powder, fireclay or soapstone; or of one of the other modern mixtures, which may be purchased ready for use. Let us suppose that you are to use " compo ": a mixture of half plaster-of-Paris, some sawdust or bonedust, the remainder being one of the infusible materials already referred to. The plaster should be such as will set hard in five minutes if mixed as described on page 21. Try a spoonful first. Cellini sometimes used a compo made from 2 parts of plaster, 1 part powdered brick and 1 part powdered bone. The compo will set hard in five minutes, so do not mix more than you need. You can always fill a spoon with the compo and put the bowl of the spoon right under water. When the bubbles stop rising, tip all the free water away, and stir the compo till it is quite smooth, like cream. Then you can use it.

It should be remembered that the bronze will shrink a little when cooling. And if the core is of a very hard consistency and the metal thin, you may get a crack in your casting. So the sawdust or powdered bone are added to the other ingredients of a core in order to make it a less rigid structure.

A potter's wheel was employed, and the lower portion of the core, with the projecting part below, marked " step " in the larger drawing, was thrown. The lower part of the core reached as high as the top of the first piece of the mould, *C*, that being the level of the actual bottom, or septum of this vessel. Above the septum the remainder of the core (a separate much larger piece than the first) filled the upper part of the work, with an overhanging portion, here called the " cornice, " completing the potter's task.

The lower part of the core was dried, and covered with a layer of wax of the thickness desired for the bronze. The septum or bottom of the vase was represented by a flat sheet of wax laid over the top of the first part of the core. And its edge was joined to the almost vertical sides of the vase by melting them together with a hot tool. The wax, representing the side of the vase, would extend downwards as far as the top of the step.

The core for the upper part of the vase having been prepared by throwing on the wheel, and drying, was then covered with wax, from its lower edge to the underside of the cornice. Then it was placed on top of the wax septum which covered the lower part of the vase, and the two parts were joined together by melting the wax along the joint between them. The fins and the whole of the ornament was now modelled from the wax which formed the body of the vase, together with any additional material which might be required.

It is probable that the four vertical projecting " fins " to be seen on the drawings would be recognised at once as being conveniently placed as runners for the entry of the molten metal into the mould. (The usual small breaks in their length, opposite the traverse bands in the ornament, could be filled in temporarily by small pads of wax). The model for the pour was a funnel-shaped mass of wax, supported on four rods or runners of wax which extended to the tops of the fins, and, when the wax was removed, provided passages for the molten metal. A further series of wax rods, leading upwards from the rim of the vessel, formed vents for the escape of the air when the metal entered the mould.

The piece-mould was constructed as follows. A strip of clay about about ¾ inch wide and ¼ inch thick was fitted against each of the two vertical fins which partly framed one quarter of the lowest section of the vessel, Fig. 289 B. A third, horizontal strip, placed in line with the septum joined them. The stepped-out part of the core formed part of the fourth side of the cell in which the first piece of the mould was to be made. The surface of the clay bands and of the step was oiled to prevent adhesion. Some of the prepared compo was ground finely, and painted over the wax and against the adjacent clay bands and step. Care was taken to ensure that every part of the ornament was completely covered and that there were no air-bubbles. When this layer had dried, several additional layers of the compo were painted over the first, the later layers containing more of the roughage employed to produce porosity.

When the piece had been built up to about an inch thick, and had dried sufficiently, the clay bands were removed and the piece carefully lifted from the model. It was trimmed up and replaced after a series of wedge-shaped mortises had been cut along its edges so that the adjoining pieces, about to be made, might register accurately. Temporary walls of clay were now fitted to outline the next piece, one edge of the first-made piece and part of the stepped-out core forming parts of the second cell, C in Fig. 289. The walls were oiled, and the second piece of the mould was built up in the same way as the first. When sufficiently dry the second piece was lifted away, trimmed, and its mortises cut. The remaining pieces of all three tiers were formed in a similar manner. The original wax of the " Tsun " had now been invested inside and out by the core and the mould. Then a fourth tier of pieces was constructed, embracing the pour, the runners and the vents. When the last piece was dry enough to be handled an outer mould in two halves, was made to cover all the pieces. But at the top it left exposed the pour and the exits from the vents, Fig. 289 A. It might be strengthened by suitably placed iron rods. The whole mould was now laid on its back, and one half of the outer mould lifted away. Each piece, beginning at that one last constructed, was lifted away from the model and laid in its place within the outer mould.

Every part of the wax was removed. The purpose of the step and the cornice will now be clear. They help to ensure the correct registration of the many pieces, which might become displaced when the wax septum and the other wax portions of the model were no longer present.

Occasionally a Chinese founder would ensure the separation of the upper and lower parts of the core by leaving between them a few irregularly shaped flakes of bronze, perhaps $\frac{1}{8}$ inch thick and $\frac{1}{4}$ inch across. These kept the two parts of the core apart, and, when the molten bronze was poured, themselves became incorporated with the rest of the bronze forming the bottom or septum of the vessel.

Any defect in the face of the mould could now be made good, for accessibility to the modelled surface of the mould is one of the virtues of a piece-mould. The whole mould was tied firmly together, allowed to dry slowly, then baked to terracotta hardness, and filled with metal while hot.

208

The statuette shown in Fig. 289a is that of an athlete, seated, with a moulded base. Both figure and base are to be cast in bronze in one piece by the waste wax or, as it is often called, the cire perdue, process. The figure and its base are already in wax, and the core, properly ventilated is within them.

It will be well to consider first how that wax model was made, and how its core came to be within it. The original model for the figure may have been made in clay, or in plasticine, and then it would have been cast in plaster in a plaster " waste " mould. That would be a plaster mould in perhaps only two pieces, which would have to be chipped to fragments to expose the plaster cast within it. Then a new plaster mould of 20 or 30 pieces would be made from it. Plaster casts of antique statues are often sold with the seams, which mark the position of the joints in the mould, still visible. An examination of one or two of these casts will teach you a good deal about the planning out of the different pieces which are necessary for the moulding of a complete figure in the round.

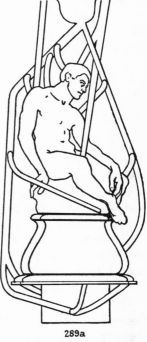

289a

When a mould is in many pieces an outer or " mother " mould, in two or more pieces, is necessary in order to keep all the others in their true positions.

You should look carefully over the model and decide where the joints in the mould must come. Each piece of the mould must be of such a shape that it is possible to remove it from the model without any undercut portion catching and holding. You must be able to withdraw each piece in turn, yet when all are in place the model and the jets and vents are entirely enclosed in the mould. For the statuette a " piece " mould was made in plaster, in which the whole work, including its undercut portions, could be cast at one time; and the undercut parts, from which a mould in one piece could not have been removed, were provided for by the construction of a number of loose pieces which could be removed separately.

Sometimes, instead of a piece-mould, a mould is made of some flexible material from which a cast in plaster or in casting-wax may be obtained. Such a wax cast will need a core, with its supporting irons, and the complete system in wax of a pour, runners and vents required for the later stages of the work. Then over all will be made the final mould of some infusible material in which the bronze will be cast.

To return to the piece-mould. As this plaster mould had been made in a number of pieces, naturally these would be provided with an outer mould in several parts to keep them in place. For this figure (Fig. 289a), the outer mould might be in three or four parts, each part retaining within its boundaries a number of the small pieces.

Now for a standing figure or one with outstretched arms, flying draperies or other loosely-connected parts, it may be necessary to provide the bronze cast with iron rods or wires where additional strength is required, or where the core may need support when the wax which intervened between it and the mould is absent. These " irons " as they are called, whose extremities may rest in recesses cut in the mould, should be so arranged that they do not disfigure any important parts of the modelling. After the bronze has been poured their extremities may be sawn off and drilled out, and plugs of bronze screwed into their place.

The thickness of a bronze cast varies, of course, with the size of the work and with its form. Thus, for a statue standing on one foot the metal in the standing leg and ankle would be made thicker than if the weight came on both. Three-eighths of an inch is about the general thickness that a life-sized figure would be cast, though for such a work in the pose mentioned above, the thickness at the ankle might be considerably greater, and a strong iron support would be provided. Do not forget that the core of a figure will be surrounded by molten metal when the bronze is being poured. Therefore it should be provided with efficient vents. In this figure some waxed strings leading from the bottom of the base to the air-vent at the top of the head should be provided to vent the core. They will be burnt away when the mould is fired, leaving clear ventilating channels.

Those parts of the surface of the plaster piece-mould which will come into direct contact with the casting-wax must be treated in such a way that the liquid wax, which is to be painted or poured against them, will take a good impression of their forms and yet will not adhere too tightly to them. It is well therefore first to treat the plaster surfaces with a coat of shellac, which will harden them and make them less absorbent: and then to give them a coat of oil.

The surfaces of the plaster " pieces " having been thus prepared, the required wax cast can be made in the following way. You take each group of pieces as they lie within the different parts of the outer plaster mould and paint some of the melted casting-wax on to their modelled surfaces. You do this for each group of pieces as they lie in their own parts of the outer mould, and you build up the wax till it is everywhere about the thickness you wish the bronze to be. If you now put together two adjoining parts of the outer mould, each with its own group of pieces within it, there will probably remain a strip along the joints where the wax layer is thin, incomplete or absent. You may fill up these gaps as far as possible by further painting with wax. But to ensure that a good thickness of wax shall completely fill the gaps, when you have put the whole mould together you should pour a good supply of melted wax into the hollow mould, and turn the mould about so that the molten wax lies for a minute or so in turn over each of the doubtful joints. When you consider that a sufficient depth of wax has been deposited along each joint the remaining wax may be allowed to drain out of the mould. Then see that the irons are in place, and the mould is ready for the core.

An alternative plan is that in which the core is prepared first. You roll out sheets of wax, or plasticine, using a roller, as in making pastry. The sheets should be rolled to the thickness required for the bronze. Then cutting the sheets to convenient shapes you line every part of the interior of the mould with them, pressing the sheet into the various parts without thinning the pieces. You try to produce a layer of wax of an even thickness. You are settling now the thickness of the metal and the shape of the core, so any parts you wish to thicken or to make solid you may fill up with the wax. But you should keep to one general thickness. If you leave a fold of drapery say half an inch thick near a part only an eighth of an inch you will probably get a cracked cast. Put the irons in place. Bring all the parts of the mould together and as far as possible make the wax lining continuous. Tie the parts of the mould firmly together and see that there are no leaks. You can now mix and pour the material for the core. When that has set take off the outer mould and remove each of the pieces, in order, putting each one into its proper place in the outer mould. Then remove every fragment of the wax or plasticine. Tidy up the core, there may be projections on it where the wax lining of the mould was incomplete. Test the position of the core in its relation to each part of the mould, to see that it has the necessary room round it everywhere for the layer of wax, and later for the bronze. Make sure that the core cannot slip aside and come too close to the mould anywhere. Cut a half-inch hole at the top of the head and form round it in plaster a good-sized cup into which the wax may be poured. There are so many joints in the mould which will act as vents that it is not necessary to provide the elaborate system of vents for the wax such as will be required for the bronze. For, for that there will be a single mould in one piece over its whole surface. Should you find in the mould any part of the figure from which the air could not escape when the wax is poured in, you may drill a hole of suitable size, pointing upwards, from the top of it into the gap between the outer mould and the piece concerned, through which the air may escape.

With a model of convenient shape it is sometimes possible to form the pour and the vents out of the thickness of the mould, by cutting suitably-placed passages between the mother mould and the pieces which lie within it. The hollow for the pour should commence at that side or end which will be uppermost when the wax is poured. It should reach to that part of the mould which will be the lowest part, and enter the cavity there. Branches may run from the main passage to other parts of the cavity when it is necessary to lead the molten wax to those spots. Vents may be cut or scraped from any place in the cavity where air might be trapped. Of course the series of vents must be kept quite separate from the pour and runners. Any gaps between the pieces which might allow the wax to stray, may be blocked by inserting little pads of clay between the inner and the outer mould, before pouring in of the wax.

Clean and oil each section of the piece-mould as it lies in the outer mould. Give the core a coat of shellac, and when that is hard, brush it over with oil. Then place it within the mould. Tie the whole mould together tightly, and fasten up with plaster any gaps there may be below the bottom of the base. Then put the mould in a warm oven. Keep it there for several hours, as you wish both the mould and the core to be hot enough to prevent any chilling of the wax. It should flow into every part of the mould, and may even find its way between the loose pieces here and there into the space behind them. But it should do no harm there. Pour the wax in a steady stream, trying to avoid the carrying of air within it into the mould. Keep the cup full till the flow stops entirely. Leave it until it is quite cold and the wax has set hard. You may now remove the mould and clean off the little ridges left by the joints in the mould.

In Fig. 289a the main pour, the jets or gates, and the vents, also in wax, have been fixed in position. Let us examine the sketch and ask ourselves how and why they have been so arranged, and if there is anything else to be done before we begin to construct the mould over the whole work.

Now there are two principles on which the metal may be poured—the descending, and the ascending. In the former case the molten metal enters the mould at its highest point and runs between the core and the face of the mould to the bottom, then gradually, after filling up all the spaces provided for it there, it finally reaches the top again. On the other principle the molten metal flows down passages provided for it in the body of the mould and enters the cavity which it is to fill from below, instead of from above, and gradually rises to the top.

If you think as to what happens inside a mould when the metal is poured you will realise at once that the ascending principle is likely to be the better of the two. When the molten metal enters the mould the air is driven before it, and must get out somewhere. So the vents have been placed so that it may escape easily. But if the work is arranged on the descending principle, on its way to the vents the air must meet the stream of molten metal, which comes trickling over the core and the face of the mould. Some of the air may be caught by the molten metal and be carried along with it. Expanding violently, it may bubble out through the liquid, causing a great disturbance and perhaps injuring the surface of the mould. If, however, the metal enters the mould from the bottom, all the air and the vents are above it. The air can then get out as fast as it likes, without any danger of trapping or other disturbance. Also any scum or dross will float on the surface of the metal and be carried to the vents instead of being caught by the descending metal and being carried perhaps to the face of the mould. Metal poured on the descending principle passes twice over the face of the mould, and has more opportunity of damaging it. But on the other plan it enters the cavity from the bottom and flows smoothly upwards. The pour, or runner, is very frequently branched, so that the metal may reach all the more distant parts of the mould simultaneously. Here there are two primary channels, one dividing into four in order to feed the four lowest corners of the base. The intention being that the lowest part of the mould should be filled evenly and quickly, so that the molten metal should be able to rise upwards smoothly, without any check. The branches from the large jets are intended to help to fill those parts of the cavity to which they lead, when the lower parts of the mould are completely filled.

The core has been ventilated by means of a small bundle of waxed strings, running from the head right through the figure and its base. The strings, of course, burn away when the mould is fired, leaving clear passages for the escape of the air.

Before the wax model is covered by the mould there is yet one more operation to be performed. Some means must be provided to ensure that when the wax is removed from the mould the core will remain exactly in its place within it. For should it move at all, and some part of it approach the inner surface of the mould at any point, then there would not be enough room for the proper thickness of metal there, and a hole in the casting might be the result. It is usual therefore to drive a number of iron nails or bronze rods through the wax, well into the core, leaving half an inch or more of the nail projecting from the wax surface. These connecting links between core and mould are called chaplets. When the final mould, that in which the bronze is to be cast, is formed over the whole model and its pour, runners and vents, then the projecting parts of the chaplets will become firmly enclosed within the material of the mould, and the core be held firmly in place. The mould may be made from one of the mixtures described on pages 204, 206 and 220–5. The mixture is painted all over the work, leaving exposed only the vents and the top of the cup at the head of the pour. You gradually build up the mould until it is perhaps an inch or an inch and a half in thickness, using the finest-ground material first, so that you obtain a good surface to the mould, and coarser-ground material for the later coats. To strengthen the mould you may wind iron wire round it, or fix iron rods, bent to shape.

The wax model, enclosed within its mould, is placed head downwards in an oven or furnace and the wax melted out of it. If you employ the former, you may save the wax for future use. But the mould must be thoroughly baked in a furnace in order to harden it and to burn away any remaining wax, string, sawdust and other fusible material that may have been used in the investment material. The temperature must rise to red heat and the mould burnt hard. When hot enough to ignite a piece of string let down into the pour, the metal is poured.

When the metal has set and the mould has been broken away, all the jets and vents, originally in wax, will now be represented by bronze bars projecting from the cast. And the chaplets inserted in order to keep the core in place will still project from the surface. All these projections are now sawn off and the scars left on the bronze are chased up. The remains of the nails are drilled out, the holes tapped, plugs of bronze screwed in, and the surface tidied up as before.

CHAPTER XXIX

METAL CASTING (*continued*)

Casting in sand. History. Preparation of the sand or loam. Casting flasks.
The piece-mould.

SANDCASTING. This is a method of casting metal in which the mould is composed of sand. It is rammed tightly against the model, or " pattern," while it lies within a pair of " casting flasks." These are iron frames, or " boxes," without tops or bottoms. They are made in pairs, and " register pins " on the rim of one box fit into " eyes " on the other. The boxes may be separated to remove the pattern. The process of casting in sand is widely employed to-day for iron, steel and bronze castings. It seems to have been invented in the fourteenth or fifteenth centuries A.D. when there were great developments in the smelting and casting of iron in Germany, France and England. Writing in the eleventh century, Theophilus makes no mention of it, and diligent search has revealed no earlier reference to it, nor evidence of its employment. But it had come into general use in the sixteenth century, when Biringuccio in his *De la pirotechnia* (1540) gives a detailed account of the process.

Castings from early times in Egypt, China and other lands reveal cores of sand mixed with some binding materials, and sand cores seem to have been in constant use down the ages. But the use of sand, packed into flasks, as a moulding material, was a late discovery.

Piece moulds may be made in casting sand or in loam. The pattern or model which is to be moulded in sand is generally of wood or some other hard material, for naturally one could not use sand for moulding models in wax, clay or other damageable material. The methods employed for sand casting differ considerably from those already described.

To prepare the sand it is well to take a large wooden tray on which to work. On this place the sand or loam which you are to use. Mix a little water with it; not too much, and work it about with a piece of wood measuring, say, 8 inches by $3\frac{1}{2}$ inches and

⅜ inch thick. Put the heap of loam at the far side of the tray, and with the board scrape it towards you a little at a time. The loam when mixed, should just hold together when it has been gripped tightly in the hand. It will hold together if made too wet, but you require it as dry as possible—if only it will bind. Next take a pair of flasks or casting boxes (Fig. 290). Lay one flask with its register

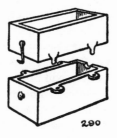

290

marks upwards on a piece of board or a small tray. Set both down in the large tray, and with a thin piece of board used as a shovel, fill the flask, scraping off any excess with the board. Press the loam together tightly, and then lay your model or " pattern," which has previously been brushed over with French chalk, in a space you scrape for it. About half of the model should project above the top of the flask. Press the sand against the lower half of the model and level it off neatly all round, leaving the surface of the loam smooth and firm. Now dust over the model and the loam in the flask with parting dust. This is to prevent the loam which is afterwards put on from adhering to the other part of the mould. Pea-flour or lycopodium is used for this purpose. You have now to make of loam a mould for the upper side of the pattern. If there are under-cuts, make a number of pieces to cover the undercut parts of the work, each piece being of such a form that it may be withdrawn without binding in any undercut place. Strengthen any fragile pieces by painting them with gum water.

Take a pinch or a handful, as the case may be, of the loam and press it against the model, building it into a neat little mass of the shape required. Make key-holes in its edges so that when you make the adjacent pieces they will register neatly. Each piece of the mould is to be dusted over, when completed, with the parting dust. A fork made from a couple of stout needles stuck in a piece of wood is a convenient tool for lifting pieces of the mould without doing them any damage. See that the back of each piece is smooth before you finish with it. When the upper half of the model has now no exposed undercuts, you must make the cope, or case, or mother mould, which is to keep all the pieces in position. Put parting dust over all the pieces as they lie, and then put the second flask in position on the first. Fill it up to the top with loam, pressing it round the pieces and against the sides of the flask. When it is quite tightly packed and full, level off the top of the loam with the edge of a board. Now turn the flasks over, and lift off the one first filled. Knock out the loam from it, for the impression of that which was at first the underside of the pattern will probably be incomplete. The parting dust will have made a clear line of separation between the loam in the two flasks. Put fresh parting dust over the work, and if there are undercuts on this side, proceed to cover them with pieces as you did on the other side. When these are finished, replace the empty flask and make the cope or case for this side also. You may now separate the two flasks. The top flask and half the mother mould will come away together, leaving the small pieces in their places on the pattern. Lift out the pieces one by one and carefully put them in their places in the cope or mother mould. Next bend and fix the irons which are to support the core. Dust over the inside of the mould with parting dust, and fill the cavity with loam, pressing it well against the irons. You will have now a replica of the figure which is to be cast. Pare it down so that a space may be left between it and the surface of the mould the exact thickness you wish the metal to be. The pour and vents should now be made as already described.

A wooden pattern is generally well varnished to keep the damp from getting at it. In casting from such a pattern dust it over with French chalk to keep the loam or sand from sticking. To remove a wooden pattern from the mould, stick a point firmly into it and give it a few taps sidewise with a pillar-file. This will free it from the mould, and you will be able to lift it out. Use French chalk and charcoal to face up. If necessary, strengthen with gum water. To ensure a good surface some founders smoke the mould with a pitch torch and then replace the pattern for a moment.

CHAPTER XXX

METAL CASTING (*continued*)

Cire perdue work. Definition. The wax. Preparation of wax cast. Lining mould with wax. Preparation of core. Fixing pour and gates. Casting a standing figure. Material for mould. Making the mould. Cellini's method. Firing the mould. Pouring the metal. Cire perdue in Central America, Ashanti, Scandinavia.

CASTING by the cire perdue, "cera perduta" or "waste wax" process has been practised in many lands from early times. The method, shortly, is this. The model which is to be cast in metal is made first in wax. Then a complete mould of the work is made in one piece, leaving a passage through which the wax may be melted out and the metal poured in. The mould is heated and the wax melted or burnt out, and replaced by molten metal. The mould is broken up, and the metal cast exposed. For all except quite small works, which are cast solid, a core is prepared as described in Chapter XXVIII.

Among careless writers it is the fashion to attribute every intricate metal casting to cire perdue work, but it cannot be too strongly emphasized that unless the outer mould was in a single piece from which the wax could be removed only by melting, the method employed was not that of cire perdue casting. It follows that if a mould in more than one piece is employed, which could be opened to remove the model, even in fragments, the casting is not cire perdue work.

In preparing the work the first thing to consider is the wax. This must be suitable for modelling in, and its composition must be such that it can be melted or burnt out from the mould without leaving any residue. Plasticine therefore cannot be used. A mixture of beeswax and Venice turpentine may be employed, though many founders add resin, pitch, tallow, or other ingredients. Beeswax, paraffin wax as used for candles, or Japan wax are quite good, but resin should be added to toughen them. Almost any mixture which will fulfil the two conditions mentioned above may be employed. Wax being semi-transparent, however, it is well to add some colouring matter to make it easier to see the modelling. Any dye may be used which will entirely burn away when the mould is fired. You should try a piece of the coloured wax before you employ it for any work. Put it in a clean, covered crucible and burn it all away; if it leaves no residue it is safe to use. It should, of course, be made harder in warm weather, for a very sticky surface is difficult to work on; and however you prepare the wax model you are bound to work on it to some extent.

The wax being ready, the next thing to do is to prepare from it a cast from your model. For a large work this would be made in several pieces. Even in a small one, say of a man on horseback, it might be prepared in several parts which would be afterwards joined together. For this wax cast you will require a piece mould, made in plaster as described in Chapter XXVIII, or in gelatine or some other plastic material. A quite small work may be cast solid, so you have but to fill the mould with wax and wait for it to set and then to prepare the mould for the metal casting. For cored work, however, you must proceed on a different plan. Inside the mould you have to spread an even layer of wax of the exact thickness you wish the metal cast to be. You may wish the wax, and therefore the metal, to be thicker in some parts than in others (see pp. 210–11). You must therefore spread a thicker layer of wax in those places.

There are several different ways in which you may prepare the wax model, much depending on the shape of the work. One plan is that in which the wax is poured into the mould round the core. Cellini used to work in this way sometimes, and he greased the inside of the mould with bacon fat. It is possible, however, that the wax might not penetrate to every part of the mould. For the complete system of vents, which will be arranged later, is not provided for in the plaster mould; and the wax may be chilled by contact with the mould before it has penetrated everywhere; or the air may be trapped in places and make the wax faulty. Another plan is therefore generally adopted. In this, molten wax is painted into the two halves of the mould to make sure that the whole surface is properly covered. Then the two halves are put together and the whole mould filled with melted wax. After a few seconds this is emptied out, leaving another layer of wax over that first painted in. This operation is repeated again and again until there is a sufficiently thick layer of wax inside the mould. The mould should then be put into a cool place, so that the wax may be properly set before the mould is removed. The wax cast may then be kept cool in a bowl of water. If the work measures but a few inches in height and is not an awkward shape, it will be safe to handle without a core. But for larger work it is well to make the core before the wax is removed from the mould. Holes may be cut through mould and wax to take the iron wires which are to keep the core in position when, later on, the wax itself is removed. If the wires had been fixed before the wax cast was made they would have been coated with wax and would not have held the core firmly. Sometimes the wires may be arranged to end in a line with the seams of the mould. A sufficient number should always be provided to hold the core safely in whichever direction the mould may be turned.

Mix up the material for the core as directed on p. 206, and pour it inside the wax in the mould. When the core has set remove the mould. If you had removed the wax from the mould first, it might have been distorted by its own weight; and the pressure of the core might distort the wax if the latter had not the support of the mould when the former was setting. The irons which penetrate the core will be seen projecting from the wax in all directions. You must now remove all the seam marks on the wax and give the final touches to the modelling. Another plan is that in which the irons to hold the core are fixed after the final touching up of the wax, holes being drilled through the wax into the core, and the wires or nails pressed into them. The outer extremities of the wires will be gripped later by the new mould which is to be formed round the work. But, of course, if the work is large, irons may be necessary from the first to support the weight of the core.

When you have finished tidying up the modelling you must make in wax the pour, the gates, the vents, and any lugs required underneath the work by which it may be fastened to its base when completed. In the metal casting these lugs will be just lumps of metal into which screws may fasten. They are all to be made from the same wax as the model. Make a number of rods or threads of wax ready for use. Then decide where you will have the pour and gates. Remember that each gate or vent which you make will be replaced later on by a rod of metal growing out of the cast, and these rods will have to be sawn off and the surface of the metal chased up again. So do not fix them in places where they will damage the modelling much. At the same time you must have a sufficient number of gates to allow the metal to get to every part of the mould as quickly as possible.

Let us suppose that you are casting a small standing figure with wings, the tips of which point downwards, clear of the legs; the figure resting on a small wax base; the metal to be poured on the ascending principle. For convenience in working it will be well to prepare the wax cast with the figure standing on its feet, and afterwards to turn it upside down to pour the metal in. The three highest points of the figure as it stands are the head and the tops of the wings. It will be well to let the metal enter the mould at these three places; so take thickish rods of wax, warm their ends and stick them on. Take care to put them in places where they will not injure the modelling much. Bend the rods of wax well clear of the figure and unite the three into one. This rod must extend to below the wax base of the figure as it stands; it is the main pour. It will be well to add a few additional gates through which the molten metal may flow to any point which might not be easily filled. Now you must fix the vents. One will be required at the tip of each wing, others at the hands, and at the lowest parts of the wax base. If you follow in imagination the course of the metal from the head and the top of the wings towards the feet, you will be able to see where the air might get trapped. To every such place attach a thread of wax of suitable thickness. The mould will be turned upside down for the metal to be poured in, so that the pour and vents, which now come down below the feet of the figure, will be uppermost then. There will be a great deal of heated air to escape, so put plenty of vents. All these rods and threads of wax, which represent the vents, should be bent well clear of the figure and reach lower than the wax base. They may combine here to form one or more large vents. The vents must be kept quite separate from the pour and gates. When all these have been fixed you are ready for the final mould.

Every founder has his own special material for moulds. Some use loam, which is a specially strong sand mixture often containing a proportion of refractory clay together with horse hair, chopped straw or dung. There is no reason, however, why the plaster and brickdust compo given in the last chapter should not be employed. However, for a loam mould, take some loam and grind it extremely fine in a mortar with paraffin. Grind also as finely as possible some burnt fireclay (old crucibles, if you have any), ganister, emery or almost any other fire-resisting substance. Mix these two powders together and, using them as a paint, go carefully over the wax model with a brush. Many founders add some binding substance to this loam mixture—white of egg or a solution of cow or horse dung. For the second coating add fine sawdust and finely shredded asbestos to the mixture. The use of sawdust as an ingredient in furnace casings, moulds, etc., is largely due to the work of Mr. Thomas Fletcher of Warrington, the well-known maker of gas-heating appliances. The sawdust is, of course, burnt out later on, leaving a very strong, light and porous mould. The fibres of asbestos tie the other materials together. The Japanese use boiled paper instead of asbestos fibre. Their paper is made from the inner bark of the mulberry tree. It is the best long-fibred paper known—that made from rags is much shorter in the grain. The outer surface of each coat should be left rough, so that the next may hold well to it. Each coating should go over all the surface of the model except the vents, the gates and the pour. The materials for the outer coatings need not be so finely ground. Let each coating get fairly dry before the next is painted on.

When the spaces between the model and the vents and pour have been filled up, and the mould has grown strong enough to allow it, wind binding wire round and round the whole mould. This will do much to strengthen it against the weight of the metal. Then add a few more coats to the mould. The thickness for the mould may be $\frac{3}{4}$ inch to $1\frac{1}{2}$ inches for a mould a foot high, and thicker in proportion for larger work. Before the metal is poured in, the mould will be packed round with sand, as described later.

Cellini, describing how he cast the Nymph of Fontainebleau, says: " I pounded up some ox bone or rather the burnt core of ox horns. It is like a sponge, ignites easily, and is the best bone you can get anywhere. With this I beat up half a similar quantity of gesso of tripoli " (we should use plaster of Paris), " and a fourth part of iron filings, and mixed the three things well together with a moist solution of dung of horses or kine, which I first passed through a sieve with fresh water, till the latter took the colour of the dung." He gave the wax model three coatings, each of the thickness of the back of a table knife, letting the mould dry between each coating.

Then he gave it several coatings of clay, or loam, in which rags had been left to rot for some months. Another mould he made of loam well dried and sifted, mixed with rotten rags and a little cow's dung. These he beat well together. Then he took " tripoli such as jewellers use to polish their gems with," powdered it up very finely and painted it over the model. After this he used the loam.

To cast a figure Cellini proceeded in the following manner. He first made a piece mould from his model in plaster. Inside this he spread a layer of wax of the exact thickness he wished the metal to be. (It might be thicker in parts, where required for strength.) When he had covered the inside of the mould in this manner, he made an iron framework to support the core. The extremities of this framework rested in recesses cut in the piece mould. The core was then built up round the irons. The material used was clay, or loam, in which rags had been left to rot for some months. Two-thirds clay to one-third rags was the proportion employed. When the core filled the entire space within the wax, Cellini wound thin iron wire round it from head to foot. He then took it out from its place within the wax and baked it. The core was given a final coating with a mixture of powdered bone, brickdust and loam. It was then fired again. The layer of wax was now removed, and the surface of the mould greased with bacon fat. An opening was made for the pour, and a number of vents—to prevent any trapping of the air. The core was placed inside the mould and well melted wax poured in. The mould was opened after a day or two, and the final touches given to the modelling of the wax figure. The figure, the pour, the gates and the vents were now all in wax. He then made the final external mould, for the bronze.

When casting his figure of Perseus, Cellini arranged the pour so that it ran down at the back of the figure to both heels, with many gates. He kept the figure in the vertical position all the while. In fixing his vents, therefore, he was careful to lead them all downwards at first, clear of the figure; he was thus able to melt the wax out without reversing the mould. The ends of the vents were afterwards connected to vertical pipes, which rose to the level of the top of the pour. In the case of his Perseus, to make sure that the core should not shift in the mould, and to provide spaces through which the core might be afterwards removed, Cellini cut away the wax at a number of places in the flanks, shoulders and legs. At these points, therefore, the outer mould would be in contact with the core, and support it firmly. The outer mould was made as described above, and bound round with hoop iron. The wax was melted out in a gentle fire. The whole mould was then thoroughly fired. It was afterwards put into the casting pit—a deep hole dug in the floor, opposite the mouth of the furnace. The vents were carried up to the floor level by earthenware pipes, and the pit filled up with tightly rammed earth. A walled channel was built from the furnace to the pour, and a fire kept alight in the channel till it was baked thoroughly dry.

Cellini made both core and mould sometimes from a mixture of plaster, burnt bone and pounded brick. This, he points out, is a much quicker method of making a core than that above described. But unless you are sure of the plaster it is an uncertain one. For poor plaster, or plaster which has been kept too long, will not set firmly. He very properly advises you to try your materials first. He used one part of plaster to an equal portion of pounded bone and brick. The core was made by pouring compo (round the irons) inside the wax lining of the piece mould; the core was then bound round with iron wire and given a final coat of the compo. Then it was fired. The final wax cast was next made as described above, and the compo mould formed round it. When this had reached a thickness of about $1\frac{1}{2}$ inches it was strengthened with iron bands given a final coat of compo and fired.

The mould having been formed round the wax model in one of the ways above described, the wax must be melted out. If the work is small and the pour and vents point that way the mould may be turned upside down, and heated in an oven until all the wax has run out. For a larger work a rough kiln must be built round the mould and a fire kept up till all the wax has been removed. The mould is then allowed to cool, and any drain holes made for the escape of the wax, which will not be required afterwards for vents, are carefully stopped up with the same material as that of which the mould is made. The fire is then lighted again. And, in any case, whether the mould be large or small, of loam or compo, the firing must be continued till the whole mould is a good cherry-red colour. In this manner the mould is hardened, fusible materials are burnt out of it, and every trace of moisture expelled. It should be hot enough to set fire to a piece of paper or tarred string let down into the pour. For small castings the metal may be poured while the mould is red hot. But in large ones it is first allowed to cool down a little, for when there is so much metal there is no likelihood that it will get chilled; and there would be danger of overheating the face of the mould if that were red-hot when the metal entered.

The mould having been fired, it is usual to bury it in a box or pit, and to tightly pack it round with earth—which should not be very damp. If the vents are not entirely within the mass of the mould they must be carried up to the top of the box, or to the ground level, as the case may be. Remember that the molten metal will follow the air through them and it may rise as high as the level of the metal in the pour, so the pipes used should be quite dry, and any joints carefully looked to. A hollow or basin should have been formed at the head of the pour for convenience in getting the metal into it. Some founders make a large enough hollow to hold all the metal required for the work. They fix a fireclay or plumbago plug to the pour, and withdraw it when the basin has been filled. The molten metal then cannot carry any air bubbles down with it; nor can any dross enter the mould, for it will naturally float on the top of the molten metal. The plug must be tall enough to project above the top of the hollow, to enable it to be lifted out with the tongs when the basin is full.

In several widely separated parts of the world native craftsmen employ the cire perdue process for casting their utensils and ornaments in gold or in brass. The craftsmen of Mexico, Central America and Ecuador prepare thin slabs of wax which they decorate with modelled ornament or patterns formed from wax threads. The mould is made with a fine clay surface. It is painted on in thin layers in order to obtain a perfect reproduction of the pattern. The wax is melted or burnt out in the usual way. In Ashanti, Benin and other places in West Africa the native brass-founders skilfully employ the cire perdue method for the production of their figure work, ornaments, weights, etc. They have developed a number of interesting variations from the methods practised elsewhere. One is their practice of luting the mould and the crucible together. They fill the latter with a sufficient quantity of brass—small pieces of trade brass rod. Their furnace may be an old pail filled with charcoal, the fire being excited by a pair of European-pattern domestic bellows. When the mould is bright red-hot, and

226

the founder considers that the metal is ready, he removes the combined crucible and mould from the furnace and turns it so that the metal may flow into the mould. When cooled, the mould is broken open and the casting cleaned up. Other interesting examples of this native work are to be found in their animal casts. For instance, if a model of a hedgehog is to be cast in brass, the core is formed first. It is made in clay and dried. Then many rods or strips of wax are laid over it, side by side, in order to cover it with an even layer of wax. Then the quills are formed from thick threads of wax, and the modelling completed. Fine liquid clay is painted in thin layers over and between the quills and other details of the modelling, and the completed mould is thus gradually built up. The wax is melted or burnt out.

Moulds for pieces of jewellery or other small works can be made by painting clay or one of the other compositions discussed above over a wax model. Some of the Scandinavian craftsmen of the ninth century A.D. made models in wax of brooches which had the general form of a tortoise, with a design of interlaced dragons or strapwork covering the surface. The craftsman painted liquid clay over the wax, filling up all the hollows in the design and gradually building up a complete mould of the external form of the brooch. He would lift the mould and remove as much as possible of the wax within it. Then he took a piece of thick, rough cloth, cut it to shape, and pressed a single layer of it as far as possible into the hollow of the mould. It covered the back of all the modelled pattern and the rim. He then filled up the remainder of the hollow with clay. He made suitable holes for the pour and gates and a few small holes round the rim for vents. When dry, he put the whole mould in the fire and burnt it to a brick-like consistency. The piece of cloth and any wax left in the hollows were burnt away, leaving a complete mould ready to be filled with metal. In the completed work the texture of the cloth may yet be seen on the bronze surface within the brooch.

CHAPTER XXXI

METAL CASTING (*continued*)

Cire perdue. Recent developments. Rubber moulds. Materials for investment.
Centrifugal casting.

CERTAIN RECENT DEVELOPMENTS in the technique of waste-wax (cire perdue) casting, sponsored by the Development and Research Department of the Mond Nickel Company Ltd., and the Design and Research Centre for the Gold, Silver and Jewellery Industries, Goldsmiths' Hall, London, have made it possible to produce very quickly and cheaply many accurate casts from an original model. For example, it is desired to reproduce in quantity a three-stone finger-ring in gold or platinum. By the method described here twenty such rings, ready for their final finishing, may be produced at a single pouring of the metal.

Each ring passes through two casting processes, the first cast being in wax, formed in a mould of rubber, the second in metal, poured into a mould made in some infusible material. Let us consider the three materials, the wax, the rubber, and the material for the final mould. The wax should have a fairly low melting range, say 55° to 75° C.; when molten it should be fluid and easily cast; it should not shrink, nor adhere to the mould on setting; it should be tough when warm, and set with a hard, smooth surface; it should leave no residue when burnt, and its properties should remain unchanged however long it may be kept molten. Waxes which fulfil these conditions may be obtained commercially. The rubber for moulding is a specially compounded natural rubber, which is vulcanized by heat and pressure. It may be purchased in sheets of a convenient thickness—generally a little more than ⅛ inch. This material has been found to be quite satisfactory even for very complicated, delicate forms. The investment powder, the refractory material from which the final mould is formed, consists in 25 to 50 per cent. of silica (a fine sand), and burnt gypsum (a form of plaster of Paris). The variety of investment powder known as Hydrocal is widely employed for this purpose.

The original pattern should be carefully made by hand, for time and trouble spent upon it are repaid many times over by the practically finished condition of the casts. The original ring should be complete, with its coronets ready for the stones. In order to prevent any possible reaction between the model and the rubber mould during its vulcanization, it is well to give the former a thin plating of rhodium or nickel. To the middle of the shank a short length of wire is soldered. This wire forms the model for the " sprue " or pour, through which the molten wax will enter the mould. The wire may be about 0·1 inch (2·5 mm.) in diameter and 0·75 inch long. In order to provide a little reservoir of wax, from which, while the wax cast is solidifying, it may draw a further supply to make up for shrinkage, it is well to add a little lump, or flattened collar, to the wire where it joins the ring. This is shown in Plate 26. The end of the sprue is bound with a single layer of wire about 0·022 inch (or 0·56 mm.) thick over the last $\frac{1}{2}$ inch of its length. The purpose of this binding is to provide the moulding frame, or flask, with a good grip on the sprue. The sprue channel in the rubber mould should end in a cylindrical or conical cavity, measuring rather less than $\frac{3}{16}$ inch each way. So the sprue channel in the moulding frame should be shaped accordingly.

The next consideration is the preparation of a mould in which the wax model may be cast.

A moulding frame of suitable size is chosen. This is a two-tiered metal frame about $\frac{3}{4}$ inch deep, with an opening measuring $2\frac{1}{2}$ by 2 inches through both halves, and registration pins to ensure the correct replacement of one half upon the other. A sufficient number of pieces of rubber to completely fill the opening in the frame are cut with shears from the raw rubber sheet, and some of them are packed within the lower half of the frame, filling it to the parting line. The pattern ring with its wire-wound sprue is fitted above them with the bound portion of the sprue resting in the recessed part of the frame provided for it. When the upper frame is put in position, the wire-bound sprue is gripped securely in place, and the pattern cannot wander away from the central line of the frame. The upper half of the frame is itself filled with some of the rubber sheets; the whole thickness of rubber being now about 1 inch. The upper and lower exposed surfaces of rubber are dusted with French chalk and the complete frame enclosing the rubber-surrounded pattern is placed between the heated plattens of a press. Pressure is applied after the rubber has become hot. For most work a pressure of 1200 to 2000 pounds per square inch is required, the time of curing being fifteen to forty minutes and the temperature 145° C. The frame and rubber mould may be cooled in water. The frame is then prised apart, and the solid block of vulcanized rubber, with the end of the sprue projecting from it, removed. The rubber is tough and elastic, and must be cut apart to remove the pattern. The cutting may be done conveniently with a surgical scalpel, or a sharp penknife. In practice it is found well to cut the block into two approximately equal parts, but to allow a small registration key to project at each corner of one half: the projections naturally fitting into corresponding recesses in the other half. These keys ensure the correct replacement of one part of the mould upon the other. It is convenient to hold open with a claw grip the end of the rubber block while it is being cut. Cutting commences against the sprue, and is intended to split the block into halves, though the registration keys must be left at each corner on one side. This initial cut along the central line is continued right round the block. Then, with sprue uppermost, the rubber block is held open with one hand while the cutting proceeds along the circumference of the ring, and across its inner diameter. In order to free the mould where it grips the coronets, the base of their cores at their narrowest part is cut right through. The whole of the coronet cores are left adhering to one half of the mould, but the little rubber threads which pass through the " lights " or perforations in the coronets must be severed at their narrowest part when stretched. It has been found convenient to leave on one half all cores which do not project at right angles to the cut face of the mould, so that the other half mould may be lifted off before the more difficult withdrawal of the internal cores from the metal pattern, or the wax cast, is undertaken. The mould is now ready for the wax.

Experience has shown that the most convenient and certain method of filling the mould is by injecting the molten wax under air pressure. A convenient injector has been devised at the Research Centre. It consists in an electrically heated, thermostatically controlled, pressure-tight container for the wax. The pressure in the container is derived from a cylinder of compressed air which is fitted with a reducing valve. A pressure of 8 to 10 pounds per square inch has been found satisfactory. A nozzle on the side of the container opens when the mouth of the mould is pressed against it, and a fine stream of molten wax is emitted, being driven forward by the air pressure in the container. The wax is thus forced into the mould, filling it completely in a few seconds. The nozzle closes automatically as the mould is withdrawn. When, in about a minute, the wax in the mould has set, the cast wax ring may be removed, and further casts made. In practice it is found convenient to hold the mould firmly in the hand between two rectangular metal plates, one on each side. After running four or five wax casts, the faces of the mould should be lightly dusted with French chalk or talc, any excess powder being blown away.

The wax replicas may be arranged in a close group for casting a number of them in metal simultaneously. They may be placed in two concentric rows on a disc of wax which stands on a short wax stem (the pour). The rings should not be allowed to approach each other anywhere closer than about $\frac{3}{32}$ inch; otherwise they should be in as compact a group as possible. Additional gates or sprues may be employed where the shape of any work to be cast requires them. The wax stem stands on a circular metal plate. The wax casts should be washed or wiped free from any trace of the French chalk or other die-dressing before the investment, or mould, is poured round them. A metal tube or " flask," preferably of stainless steel, $\frac{1}{2}$ inch taller and wider than the assembled wax casts, is placed round them. It rests upon the metal base plate and is sealed to it with wax, plasticine or clay. It should be provided with a liner of asbestos paper, which facilitates both the escape of air from the mould, the expansion of the investment on setting, and its removal from the flask. The investment powder is mixed with water just as plaster is mixed (see p. 21), and poured over the wax casts within the flask. By careful pouring and by shaking the mould every effort should be made to prevent the formation of air bubbles. The flask may be subjected to vacuum treatment to assist in the removal of any entrapped air. The investment expands slightly on setting, which may take some ten to thirty minutes. When quite hard the mould is removed from the flask, the asbestos paper making this operation an easy one. The mould is now heated to between 100° and 300° C. to eliminate the wax and to drive off the free water. The temperature is then raised to some 800° C., and allowed to cool to the desired casting temperature, which may be between 500° and 800° C.

The aim of the casting process is to force the molten metal by pressure into the cavity in the mould left by the elimination of the wax, and to ensure that the cast is adequately fed during solidification. Pressure-casting by steam has long been practised by the dentist, and casting by compressed air has proved its value. But recent developments in centrifugal casting provide a method whereby the molten metal is thrown into the mould by centrifugal force, and seem to provide the most complete and satisfactory solution to the jeweller's problem. The crucible and mould are linked together and attached to one end of a pivoted arm, with a balancing weight at the other. The arm is rotated by a spring or an electric motor, set in motion when the metal has been melted. This may be done with the blowpipe while the crucible is clamped against the mould on the pivoted arm. The centrifugal force set up by the rotation of the arm drives the metal under pressure into the mould, and retains the pressure until the rotation is stopped. When cold, the mould is broken up and the castings finished in the usual way

CHAPTER XXXII

METAL CASTING (*continued*)

Furnaces. Metals. Melting and pouring. Low melting alloys. Breaking down the mould. Finishing the casting.

FOR SMALL CASTINGS, weighing anything up to 12 lb., one of Fletcher's injector furnaces is the most convenient. A gas supply pipe of about ¾ inch internal diameter and a No. 5 foot blower are necessary. These furnaces are simple cylindrical casings of specially prepared fireclay, in which the crucible stands. The jet enters the furnace through an opening near the bottom and the products of combustion escape through a small hole in the lid. For larger work than this, a natural draught furnace of the ordinary foundry pattern is generally employed; although gas furnaces of much larger size are sometimes to be met with. The foundry furnace is arranged like Fig. 291. It has at the bottom an iron grating through which the air comes, and the ashes fall.

291

The crucible is supported on a stand which rests on this grating, a handful of ashes having been previously thrown on it to keep the crucible from sticking. The entrance to the chimney is at the side or back of the furnace, a couple of inches above the top of the crucible. It is provided with a damper, which can entirely close it. A lid covers the top of the furnace. The crucible, ready filled, and covered by its lid, is placed on the stand inside the furnace. A few shovelfuls of red-hot coke are thrown round it, and the remainder of the space inside the furnace, up to the top of the crucible, is filled up with broken coke. The lid of the furnace is replaced and the damper drawn. A series of these furnaces is built along a wall of the foundry, several being heated at once when a considerable amount of metal is required for one cast.

Of much greater power is the reverberatory furnace (Fig. 292), which is used when a very large amount of metal is required—in casting a statue, for example. No crucibles are employed in this furnace, the metal resting on the floor of the furnace itself. The floor slopes down to the outlet hole, which is closed with a plug till the metal is required. The fireplace is at one end of the furnace and the chimney at the other. The flames pass from the fireplace over a low wall and strike against the roof of the furnace. This, which has a flattened dome shape, drives them down on to the metal before they reach the chimney. A bricked channel, thoroughly dried, runs from the mouth of the furnace to the pour in the mould, where it rests in the casting pit.

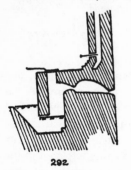
292

The metal must be our next consideration. Platinum cannot be melted with the ordinary gas blowpipe or in the furnace; a supply of pure oxygen, as in the oxyhydrogen blowpipe, being necessary to fuse it. Gold and its alloys cast well, as do fine and standard silver (see Chapter II). The metal or alloy is generally put in a fireclay crucible with a little powdered borax on top. Pieces of charcoal should be put in it also, but powdered charcoal if used would be likely to get into the cast and injure it. More metal can be added when that put in first settles down in the crucible. Add a tiny piece of zinc to the gold or silver before pouring. Copper does not cast very easily, so it is generally alloyed. The addition of a little tin, zinc or lead to the copper produces an excellent compound. When copper is alloyed with a small proportion of tin, the result is known as bronze, if alloyed with zinc it is known as brass. But there are so many alloys in which copper predominates that many people call them all brasses. The ingredients of a few well-known alloys are to be found on p. 304. Bronze, composed of copper with a small percentage of tin, is not as good as a similar alloy to which a little zinc or lead has been added; so the bronze used by founders frequently has 3 or 6 per cent. of both tin and zinc and perhaps 1 per cent. of lead. In making these alloys the copper should be melted in a crucible under a layer of charcoal. Pearlash, cream of tartar or even common salt is used as a flux. They are all better than borax. The tin, or tin and zinc, should be warmed to near their melting point and then added to the copper. The mixture

234

should be thoroughly stirred. If lead is an ingredient it does not actually alloy itself with the bronze. It remains as separate globules spread throughout the mass, unless it is allowed to sink to the bottom. The mixture should be well stirred before pouring. Many founders stir a molten alloy with a stick of green wood, for the gas-bubbles rising from it help to bring to the surface any impurities in the alloy. Casts are frequently made in lead, zinc or in one of the fusible alloys, and these casts are afterwards chased up and used as patterns for casting replicas. Plaster of Paris, employed alone, is not a good material in which to cast molten metal. It seems to be of so compact a nature that air bubbles which form in it on contact with hot metal are unable to escape through the plaster, so they come bubbling through the metal instead, with unpleasant results. It should be mixed with other more porous materials.

Thirteen parts lead, 3 parts zinc and 6 parts bismuth make a useful alloy for small castings. Very sharp casts may be obtained with it, as there is considerable expansion of the mass on cooling. Type-metal acts in a similar manner and gives good casts.

Easily Fusible Alloys

A number of very fusible alloys are known. The following are some of the most useful:

Melting range			Lead	Tin	Bismuth	Cadmium
60°–68° C.	.	.	26·7	13·3	50	10
72°–72° C.	.	.	27·80	12·40	50·5	9·3
70°–80° C.	.	.	34·5	9·3	50	6·2
70°–84° C.	.	.	30·91	14·97	50·72	3·4
94°–104° C.	.	.	22·0	22·0	56·0	
94°–143° C.	.	.	33·34	33·33	33·33	
94°–149° C.	.	.	16·0	17·0	67·0	
143°–163° C.	.	.	43·0	43·0	14·0	

N.B. All alloys containing cadmium are liable to undergo rapid oxidization in contact with water.

Although lead and tin alloys are very generally melted in an open iron ladle it is wasteful to do so unless the surface of the molten metal is covered by some substance which will exclude the air. Linseed or olive oil will do quite well. Otherwise it is better to use a deep, narrow vessel, for molten lead oxidizes very rapidly in contact with air, so the less surface exposed the better. The dross which forms on the surface should be removed with an iron spoon and the metal poured immediately afterwards.

Copper alloys should be stirred well before the crucible is removed from the furnace. Some founders do this with a piece of charcoal gripped in the tongs, others stir with a green stick, as noted above. The crucible tongs have curved jaws which securely grip the crucible so that it may be lifted safely. The molten metal is skimmed to remove any dross or floating charcoal and tipped into the basin-shaped hollow at the head of the pour. If there is no such hollow provided, it is well to keep back with a strip of iron any dross, flux or charcoal which may yet float on the metal. The metal should be poured in very steadily, that is to say, in a continuous stream without any stoppages. The metal should run in quietly, without bubbling or welling up, and gradually rise in the vents. Continue to pour steadily until the metal ceases to run down. Leave a good mass, or "head," of metal in the pour. Its weight will force the metal below it into all the hollows of the mould if the vents are working properly. If all has gone quietly, the head of metal will go a little hollow in the centre as the metal cools. If, however, the metal bubbles and splutters when you pour, either the gates and vents have not been properly constructed or the mould is damp. In either case the cast will probably be damaged.

The mould should be broken down as soon as possible after the metal has set. But it must be done carefully, for the heated metal is easily injured. With a hack saw cut off all the gates and vents, for they are now represented by rods and threads of metal attached to the cast. Saw them off as close to the work as possible. If the core is to be removed, rake it out through any available opening. In casting large bells it is usual to rake out the core before the metal has had time to cool down, for the shrinkage of the bell on the core might otherwise cause cracks in the casting.

The irons which supported the core should be cut out. The whole work is now scrubbed clean; and afterwards, if small, boiled out in pickle. Casts made in some of the fusible alloys above mentioned cannot, however, be pickled in boiling solutions. The holes made by the irons are now to be plugged up. They should be tapped, and pieces of metal screwed into them. All rough parts are now gone over with files and riffles, and finally with chasing tools. After tapping the lugs for the screws which are to hold the cast on to its base, if required, the work is ready for colouring.

236

CHAPTER XXXIII

CONSTRUCTION

Hollow handles. Compound mouldings. Fitting moulding to a tapering vessel. The folding iron. Square and round trays. Buckling in sheet metal. Fixing a tablet to a wall. Inkpot tops.

A NUMBER OF POINTS of construction are dealt with in this chapter. The building up of the hollow handle for a flagon (Fig. 293) is effected in the following manner. Cut a strip of metal the full length of the handle—measured round the curve, and wide enough to make the inside part, *DEF*. The handle is, of course, rounded at the inside, flat outside, and tapering towards each end. The strip tapers in a corresponding manner. The

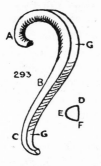

outside, *DF*, is made from a separate piece. Bend the strip to the proper curve, *ABC*, and solder a piece of thick brass wire between *A* and *C*. You must use hard solder. The soldering will anneal the strip. Now find a stake the end of which will fit into the curve *DEF*. A mandrel may do, or the pointed bickiron; or perhaps the rounded side of the head of the raising hammer. Held in the vice, a hammer-head makes a very efficient stake. On whichever tool is most convenient drive the edges of the strip round into the curve. It is necessary to stretch the edges to get them round, so you may have to anneal the work before it will go far enough. Watch carefully that you keep the axis of the work straight. Planish the handle all over before you remove the brass stay. Then mark carefully the profile of the edges *G* from both sides. Cut and file the edges true. And, holding a straight-edge across them, see that it is at right angles to the handle at every part of the curve *G* when looked at from either top or bottom. When you are quite satisfied with this and with the curve of the handle from every point of view, bevel off the inside corner of the metal all along the edges *G*. Now take another strip of metal, *DF*, as long as the handle, and a little wider than the gap between the edges *G*. Lay it flat on the bench and run the burnisher or a round-faced hammer up and down the middle of it several times. This will give it a very slight curve from side to side. Anneal the strip, and bend it round the handle, the convex side of the strip to be outside. With a steel point scratch a line on the strip against the edge *G*. Cut and file the strip to the exact width required (*DF*). Then bevel away the inner corners of its long edges. When the strip is put into position against the curved piece *DEF*, it should fit exactly, and the joins come neatly at the corners *D* and *F*. Of course, you may, if you like, omit all the bevelling. The join in that case will not come quite at the corner. Borax the two long joins and tie the pieces together. To make sure that the two pieces are properly joined all along, it is well to solder only 2 or 3 inches at a time, allowing the unsoldered portion to spring open a little way occasionally in order to allow room to place the pieces of solder inside. Take care not to buckle the piece *DF* in so doing; nor must you allow the solder to flow along any part of the joint which is sprung or bent open at all. To make sure of this, do not allow the metal to get red-hot except in that part of the joint in which the two parts are in close contact. You can in this way gradually solder the handle from end to end. The thumb-piece, if there is one, can now be made and soldered on, as can the little pieces which close the ends of the handle. Do not omit to drill a little hole in the handle somewhere where it will not be seen, to allow any confined air to escape.

To build up a compound moulding, say, for the base of a chalice, of which Fig. 294 is the plan and Fig. 295 the enlarged profile. The principal difficulty will be to keep everything concentric and true in the fitting and soldering, so too much care cannot be taken in making each individual piece true in itself. The plan shows four curved pieces and four projecting corners. You will require a straight piece, long enough to produce the eight little pieces for the corners; and four rings for the curved parts. Rather more than half of each ring will be required, so in this case the segments cut away will be useless. Suppose you make the rings first. The lowest

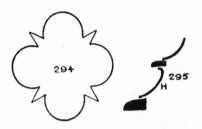

part of the moulding is formed from a thick strip bent flatwise into a circle. Do this as described on p. 132. Cut each ring from the strip when it has been bent to the curve and trued up on the T-stake. When the rings are soldered you can turn them true on the lathe. If you have no lathe, file them. Take strips of metal for the next part of the moulding *H* (Fig. 295). Join their ends and on a suitable stake shape the rings thus made. Collet hammers (Figs. 133, 134) will be found very useful for this part of the work. You will notice that you may save yourself a good deal of hammering if, instead of using a straight strip of metal to turn round into the ring *H*, you use a curved piece, set out as described on p. 251. A curved piece of metal so set out can be made—it forms part of a cone —as shown in *J* (Fig. 296). It is obviously easier to make *H* from a ring shaped like *J* than from a straight one like Fig. 297. You may find that a small hammer held in the vice will make a suitable stake for doing some of the shaping on. When the rings are correct in

shape, wire them on to the moulding already made and solder them there. Take care to keep the joins in each ring and band in that part of the circumference of the circle which will be cut away when you are fitting the various pieces together to form the foot of the cup. But though you keep the joins near together, do not let them come exactly one over the other, as they might slip and give trouble.

When you have completed the rings try them in the lathe, and true them up if necessary. Each ring should stand exactly the same height.

Now you must take in hand the straight pieces for the foot. The thick strips may be filed to shape, or bent round into rings edgewise —not flatwise as for the circles—soldered and turned to the proper section on a big chuck. Afterwards you must cut through the join in the ring and straighten the metal out. It will be a long, straight strip of the correct shape for the lowest member of the moulding. Build up the straight moulding as you did the rings, and take care that when finished it stands just the same height as they do. Cut the corners in a suitable mitre block, but see that the moulding stands level when you are cutting it. Fit the joints carefully, standing the pieces of moulding upon the tracing, on a surface plate or sheet of plate glass, to make sure that everything is level. Solder each corner separately, then stand it on the tracing again as before, and mark where it is to join the circles. Take the circles also, and cut out from each the part that is not required. Fit corners and circle together carefully. Finally solder each circle to its right-or left-hand corner, and the four pieces together. Rest the work, when soldering it, on a very level surface; but put broken pieces of piercing saws between the work and the slab, otherwise you might have some difficulty in getting its lowest member hot enough. The complete bottom moulding is now ready to be fixed to the foot of the chalice. Remember that if you boil the work out after each soldering and put rouge, loam or whiting on the joints which have been already soldered, there will be little likelihood of their coming apart at subsequent firings.

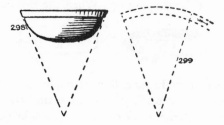

When a strip of moulding has to be applied to a tapering shape like Fig. 298, you will have considerable difficulty in getting it to lie flat against the work all round unless you bend the moulding to a suitable curve first. If, however, you draw the elevation of that part of the work against which the moulding is to fit, and set out the curve as described on p. 251, then a moulding bent to that curve, as in Fig. 299, will, when bent into a circle, fit closely against the form shown in Fig. 298.

A tool which will be found extremely useful is that known as the folding iron (Fig. 301). It is made from a strip of iron or steel measuring, say, 3 feet by $1\frac{1}{2}$ inches by $\frac{1}{2}$ inch. This is folded in two, being forged thinner at the fold, so that its two halves may be easily sprung apart sufficiently to allow a piece of sheet metal to be slipped between. Suppose you have to turn up the edge of a rectangular tray, or to bend a piece of metal round to make the four sides of a box. Mark with pencil where the bend is to come. Then slip the sheet between the two halves of the folding iron and bring the pencil line level with the top of the iron. Grip the latter in the vice. If the ends of the iron gape apart, grip them also in the jaws of a hand-vice. You may now bend that part of the tray which projects above the folding iron right down on to its top surface, and tap the corner or edge down smoothly with mallet or hammer. The two long sides of a tray may be bent thus. The two shorter sides must be bent down over a flat, square-edged stake if you have no short folding irons which are available for the work.

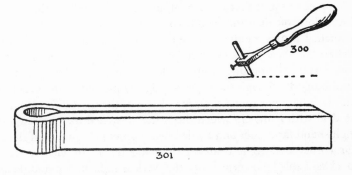

When a rectangular box is made from sheet metal the latter is sometimes scored deeply at the places where the bends or corners are to come. For this, the tool shown in Fig. 300 will be found convenient. It consists of a handle, a shank, and a small steel cutter which passes through a hole in the shank and is kept in position by a set screw. A similar tool may be made from an old file. Its tang is bent down and then ground to a suitable cutting edge. It should be hardened and tempered.

The repoussé ornament on a circular tray is often worked before the centre of the tray is sunk. The repoussé work stretches the metal a little, with the result that it may be warped and buckled. It must be made true again before the other work can proceed. To remove a buckle in a piece of metal: lay it upon a flat bench and take a mallet, the head of which is in section like Fig. 198, that is to say, flat, with the corners rounded off. Now a buckle in a sheet of metal means that some part or parts are stretched more than the rest. It is very difficult, almost impossible, to contract the part that has been stretched, but it is possible to so expand the parts near it that the sheet of metal may lie flat again. The metal may have been stretched either at the edge or nearer the middle of the sheet. If the edge is stretched you will notice that some part of it will not lie flat however many other parts you hold down. Notice where the sheet looks tight and does not move about when you press other parts down. You must work with a good deal of judgment, but you must give that tight place a few good blows, a dozen perhaps, to stretch it. As it stretches it will relieve the edge and allow it to go down.

Remember that if an edge is stretched you must on no account hammer it any more, as you would only stretch it still further. Hammer the part that looks tight, and that will relieve the stretching. Now, on the other hand, your piece of metal may have been stretched in the middle. Its edge is tight, and must be expanded. Where the sheet is stretched in the middle it will rock on the bossed out part, or, if you turn it upside down and press it hard, stand up in the middle though the edges are tightly pressed to the bench. In this case hammer round the edge. Perhaps the most difficult buckle to deal with is that in which the metal is twisted like a screw—the right-hand far corner and the left near corner going up, and the left far corner and right near corner going down, or vice versa. A buckle of this kind means that the work is tight in the middle and must be stretched from the centre and in lines parallel to the diagonals. When nearly correct don't give a blow too many, but see the effect of each one. It may be necessary to anneal the work.

To return to the round tray. When you have got it flat, see that the edge is truly circular. If it is to have a wired edge, do that work now. Then with the compasses mark the line within which the sunken part of the tray is to come. To sink the hollow in the tray use a hammer like that shown in Fig. 137: its face measures about $1\frac{1}{4}$ inches by $\frac{7}{8}$ inch. You may sink the tray by holding it on a flat stake and hammering the metal so as to stretch and sink it all round, just within the compass line. While hammering so you tilt the far edge of the tray upwards and hold the compass line just over the nearer edge of the flat stake. Hammer all round quite evenly and go on until a sufficient depth has been attained. You finish this sinking by planishing the hammer-marks smooth, using a flat block of hard wood as a stake. The sunken part of the tray should turn downwards quite suddenly from the rim, so to hammer this part the tray has to stand almost vertically on the stake. If the weight of the tray is too great to manage easily with the left hand, have a pulley fixed above the bench. At one end of the cord put a weight, at the other tie a hand-vice. With this you may grip the far edge of the tray and so relieve the strain on your wrist. A small tray may be sunk in a hollow hammered in a large block of lead, the shape of the hollow being such that part of the finished tray could lie in it, if necessary. Planish the tray on the wood block as above.

There are several ways in which it is possible to fix a tablet to a wall. If the work is light and you may screw through from the front of it, it is usual to let into the walls plugs into which the screws may go. To drill a hole in a stone wall, take a well-tempered chisel, 9 or more inches long, and after carefully marking the place, give the chisel a series of smart blows with a hammer or mallet. Rotate the chisel a little after each blow, and you will find that the chisel point gradually splinters a circular depression in the stone. Go on till the hollow is deep enough, and enlarge it a little at the bottom—dove-tail fashion. Then take an oak peg, thoroughly dried in an oven, and drive it into the hole. Saw its head off afterwards, flush with the wall.

With a heavy memorial it is usual to provide metal rods projecting several inches from the back of the work. These rods are roughened all along and slightly expanded at the extremity. Holes are bored in the wall as described above: the memorial tried in its place, and afterwards removed. The holes are then all filled with Portland cement. The memorial is again put into position, the rods pushing their way through the cement. The work is shored up till the cement is dry. It grips the rods very strongly, making the work quite secure.

The metal tops to glass inkpots are fixed on with plaster of Paris. They may be removed by soaking the tops in a strong solution of lump sugar and water.

CHAPTER XXXIV

SETTING OUT

Tools. Transferring drawings to metal. Measurements. Various geometrical problems. Inscriptions. Rectangular ring for small work.

IN THIS CHAPTER are given a number of hints and rules which may be useful in the setting out of work.

The tools required for work on paper are:

1. *A drawing board.* This should be square at the corners, the sides should be absolutely straight and the surface level. The size must depend on the kind of work you are doing.

2. *A T-square.* The head and blade of this tool are usually fastened together at right angles with screws. The angle between the two parts is liable to variation, so its accuracy should be tested occasionally. The working edge of the blade should be bevelled, so as not to throw a shadow on the work. The T-square should always be held firmly against the left-hand side of the drawing board when in use. Any number of horizontal, parallel lines can be drawn thus.

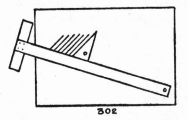

302

Lines at right angles to these can be drawn either by the aid of a set square, which is held firmly against the T-square, itself held against the side of the drawing board; or the T-square itself may be gently slid down the board while the fingers rest upon it and hold the pencil which rules the line. With a little practice lines can be ruled in this way quite as accurately as by the aid of the set square. The T-square should not be turned so as to work from another edge of the drawing board.

3. *Two set squares.* These are triangular pieces of wood, vulcanite

245

or xylonite. Those having the angles of 60 degrees and 45 degrees are most generally useful. By sliding these tools along the T-square to other positions any number of perpendicular or diagonal lines may be drawn. For sets of lines required at other angles, place one of the squares on the paper so that its side points in the required direction; then put the T-square against it. Hold the T-square down and slide the other along it to the positions required for ruling the lines. If, however, much work has to be done at such an angle, the paper may be slewed round on the board and pinned in a fresh position, so that the lines may be ruled by the aid of the T-square alone.

4. *A set of mathematical instruments.*

5. *A protractor, for setting out angles.*

6. *Drawing pins.* These should be driven in not quite at right angles to the board, so that some part of the heads touch the paper. They hold it better so.

7. *Paper, pencils and charcoal.* The latter is very useful for roughing in large work.

To transfer a drawing to metal. Put a sheet of carbon paper between the drawing and the metal and go over the outlines with a pointed tool. A knitting needle set in a handle, as the lead is set in a pencil, makes a useful tracing needle. Its point should be rubbed smooth. Another way is to use a mixture of wax and whiting. Warm the metal and smear a very thin layer of the composition over it. Make a tracing of the drawing and turn it face downwards on to the white film left on the metal. Lay a piece of notepaper above and rub hard all over with the handle of a knife. The drawing will be reversed.

To draw on metal, first roughen the surface with fine emery paper or pumice-stone and water, taking circular strokes. Pencil lines made in any direction will show on this surface. Erasions may be made with fine emery paper used as before. A pen and ink may be used, and faulty ink lines trued up with a knife point.

The tools required in setting out work on metal are: A rule, preferably of steel. An accurate straight-edge, also of steel. A square—this is made of two pieces of steel firmly fixed at right angles to each other. A pair of dividers or compasses, with quadrant. A marking tool made from a length of $\frac{1}{8}$ inch steel wire, ground to a sharp point.

It is a good rule to take all measurements and angles from one central or base line. In careful work, measurements should be transferred from the rule to the work by means of the dividers. In doing so it is well to avoid the last inch on the rule. A measurement of an inch, say, taken from the extremity of the rule is likely to differ a little from one taken at another part. Not necessarily because the rule has become worn and rounded at the end, but because one point of the dividers rests on the end of the rule—somewhere, rather than in an accurately placed cut on the surface.

In marking off successive measurements always add the length of the new section to the total of those which have gone before, and measure from the base to that total length. Greater accuracy is attained in this way than by that in which each successive measurement is carried on from the mark made for the last.

To find the centre of a straight line with the compasses (Figs. 303, 304). Open them to a span of about half the length of the line.

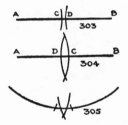

Place one leg at *A* and make a mark *C* on or across the line. Lift the compasses and place one leg at *B*. Make another mark *D* on the line. The centre is exactly half-way between *C* and *D*. It may be guessed, or the span of the compasses adjusted until marks made from either end of the line, as above described, are found to agree. It does not matter if the dividers are set to too great or to too small a span in the first instance. The method to be followed is the same in either case.

The centre of any regular curve may be found in the same way (Fig. 305).

To divide a given straight line *EF* into any number of equal parts (Fig. 306). If you cannot do so by measurement with the rule, proceed as follows. From one end of the line *EF*, draw another line, *EG*, of any length and at any angle. From *E* along the line *EG*, set off the required number of equal parts, say nine, taking any convenient unit—inches on a foot rule, for example. Join 9 and *F*.

Then draw lines parallel to 9F through each of the divisions, 8, 7, 6, etc., cutting the line EF. The line EF is now divided as required.

To find the centre of any square (Fig. 307). Draw diagonals HK and IJ. They will cross in the centre of the square.

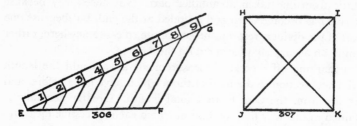

To find the centre of any circle (Figs. 308, 309). From any point in its circumference L, with a distance equal to about half the diameter of the circle for radius, describe a small arc, M. With the same radius from two other widely separated points in the circumference describe small arcs N and O. The centre of the circle lies between the arcs M, N and O and may be guessed. Or, adjust the dividers until arcs struck from any point in the circumference all pass through one point. This will be the centre of the circle. It does not matter if the dividers are set to too great or to too small a span at first.

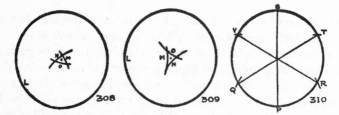

To divide a circle into three or six parts (Fig. 310). Find the radius of the circle. This is the distance from the centre to the edge. From any point, P, in the circumference strike an arc of the same radius, cutting the circle in two places, Q and R. Either with Q as centre and QR as radius describe an arc, cutting the circle in S; or draw a diameter passing through P and the centre to S. The circle is now divided into three equal parts in Q, R and S. To divide it into six, draw lines from Q and R through the centre, cutting the circle in T and V. Or, with PQ as radius and S as centre describe an arc, cutting the circle in T and V. Or, step the distance PQ round the circumference.

To divide a circle into any number of equal parts (Fig. 311). Draw a diameter AB to the circle. With A as centre and AB as radius describe an arc. With B as centre and the same radius describe another arc, cutting the first in C. Divide AB into as many parts, say five, as you wish the circle divided into. Draw a line from C through the second division in all cases, whatever the number of

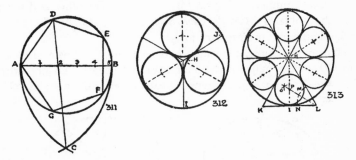

parts may be, cutting the circle in D. Step the distance AD round the circle EFG. If AD, DE, EF, FG and GA are joined, a regular pentagon has been described in the circle. In the same way any regular polygon may be constructed. The pentagon has five sides. The hexagon six. The heptagon seven. The octagon eight. The nonagon nine. The decagon ten. The undecagon eleven. The duodecagon twelve.

To draw the given geometrical figures in the circles (Figs. 312, 313). Divide each circle into twice as many parts as there are foils. Let H be the centre of the circle. Find by trial the largest circle which can be inscribed in the space HIJ. Set out the distance from H to its centre on alternate radii and describe the other circles.

To work this problem geometrically (Fig. 313). After dividing the circle into twelve parts, draw KL at right angles to HI, and complete the triangle HKL. Bisect the angle KLH. You do this by taking L as centre and striking the arc NM at any distance. From N and M with any radius strike two other arcs crossing each other in O. Join OL, cutting HI in P. With P as centre and PI as radius inscribe a circle. It will fit exactly into the triangle HKL. With H

as centre and *HP* as radius mark the centres of the other circles and complete the figure.

Problems similar to those given above are often met with in setting out the bases of cups, chalices, bowls, etc. They may be dealt with in yet another way—by the use of a protractor. If you remember that the circumference of a circle is divided into 360 degrees, you have a very small sum to do to find out how many degrees must be allowed for each part of, say, a nine, ten, twelve or fifteen sided figure. You have then but to set out with the protractor the correct number of degrees for each part. For other and more difficult problems Morris's *Geometrical Drawing for Art Students* is probably the best book to turn to.

To draw an ellipse, the length and breadth being given. Let *AB* and *CD* be the major and minor axes (the length and breadth). They are drawn in Fig. 314 crossing each other at right angles. *O* is

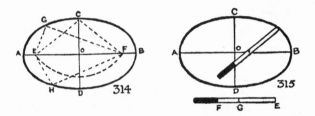

the centre both of *AB* and *CD*. With radius *AO*, and centre *C*, describe an arc cutting *AB* in *E* and *F*. These two points are called the foci. Take three pins and stick them firmly in at the points *C*, *E* and *F*. Tie a piece of string round these three pins running from *C* to *E* to *F*, and back to *C* again. Remove pin at *C* and replace it with a pencil. Move the point of the pencil round, keeping the string tightly stretched. The curve traced by the pencil point will be an ellipse. *G* and *H* show the position of the pencil at three different times on its journey. The dotted lines proceeding from *G* and *H* to *E* and *F* show the position of parts of the string at those times.

Second method (Fig. 315). Set up the axes *AB* and *CD* as before. Take a piece of paper, or a long, flat ruler and make *EF* equal to *AO* and *EG* equal to *CO*. Place it so that *G* may be on the major (longer) axis and *F* on the minor (shorter) axis. Then *E* will be a point on the curve. By shifting the paper, and always keeping *G* on the major and *F* on the minor axis any number of points on the curve may be obtained. Draw the curve through these points.

In constructing narrow, deep vessels or those figures whose shape approaches that of a truncated cone, a considerable saving in time may be effected if a seam up the side be permitted, for in raising a deep shape without a join a good deal of time is required. Almost any vessel of the types shown in Figs. 316 to 318 may be constructed

by cutting a suitably shaped piece to form its sides, and another flat piece for the bottom. But the exact shape shown in the figures could not be obtained from any flat piece of metal. The nearest one can approach to it is shown by the dotted lines inside each figure. They represent part of a cone—a tapering tube. If a piece of metal were cut to such a shape it could be altered into the form required by snarling and shaping. But remember that it is easier to expand parts of a shape to the correct size than to reduce them. So as a rule, draw the dotted lines just within the narrowest parts of the outline of the vessel. Experience only can guide you to choose the best position to place them. First draw the elevation of the vessel. Then, if its sides are not straight, mark in the dotted lines as indicated. Let *ABCD* (Fig. 319) be the elevation of the shape required. It would do, upside down, for a bowl of the shape shown in Fig. 317. Produce the sides *BA*, *CD* till they meet in *E*. With *E* as centre and *EA* as radius describe an arc. With *E* as centre and *EB* as radius, another arc. Along the larger arc mark off *F* and *G*, making *BF* and *CG* each equal to *BC*. Beyond *G*, mark off *H*, making *GH* equal to one-seventh of *BC* or of *CG*. This distance can easily be guessed. The total distance *FH* is, therefore, $3\frac{1}{7}$ times *BC* (see p. 301). From *F* and *H* draw straight lines towards *E*, cutting the smaller arc in *I* and *J*. Then *IFHJ* is the shape required.

251

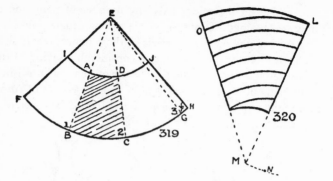

A piece of metal cut to that shape will curl up to form the sides of the vessel *ABCD*. The join up the side must be soldered and the metal snarled and hammered to the curved shape required.

In setting out ornament on the four sides of an oblong box, usually made from one long strip of metal, do not forget that the long and short sides come alternately. Thus: long, short, long, short.

The stems of candlesticks and other objects are often made with a spiral twist or flute (Fig. 323). This twisting or fluting can be worked upon the piece of sheet metal which is to form the stem before it is bent round into cylindrical form and soldered. Suppose that the twisted stem is to be 6 inches high by 1 inch in diameter. Take a piece of sheet metal measuring 6 inches by $3\frac{1}{7}$ inches (Fig. 322). On the back of the metal you have now to set out the lines of the ridges which form the twist. They will afterwards be driven

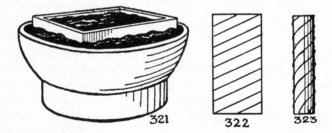

up by repoussé work. Let us suppose that the ridges are to cross the stem as shown in Fig. 323. Divide the two long sides of the metal into nine equal parts. Draw a straight line from the top right-hand corner to the third mark down on the left-hand side. Now draw other lines parallel to the first through all the marks previously made. Put the work on pitch and drive up each line as a ridge on the other side of the metal. When this is done clean off the pitch and bend the sheet of metal round in cylindrical form, with the ridges to the outside. They will follow on at each side of the join quite accurately; some little care is necessary, however, in getting the edges to fit well enough before soldering. After this you may fill the tube with pitch; or if it is of brass or copper, with lead, and complete the modelling. It is dangerous to put molten lead into contact with silver—there is so much danger that it may " burn " its way into the silver (see p. 39). The turn in this case will be a left-hand twist. To obtain a right-hand twist you have only to join the top left-hand corner to the third mark down on the right when you are marking the metal, and then to put the other lines parallel. To make a quicker twist you must join the top corner to the second or first mark down on the opposite edge, instead of to the third. The ridges will, however, be wider apart unless you reduce the space between the marks. For a slower twist join the top corner to the fourth, fifth or sixth mark opposite. The ridges will be closer together unless you make the marks further part in this case.

To produce a similar twist on a tapering stem you must make the marks at each side of the curved shape (Fig. 320). This shape you set out just as you did that shown in Fig. 319 above. Then with the compasses set to the distance LM, you make an arc, MN. From the point N, which you find by trial, and without altering the span of the compasses, you may reach one of the marks, O, at the left-hand side of diagram. From N as centre you make a series of arcs cutting each one of the marks at the side of the diagram, reducing the span of the compasses each time, but always keeping N as the centre. If you had wished to produce a slower twist you could have joined L to the second, third, fourth or fifth mark down. The point N in this case would have been found much further to the right on the drawing. Set out in this way the spiral will be found accurate enough for practical purposes, though it is not geometrically correct.

In setting out an inscription the first thing to do is to count the total number of letters in all the words, reckoning the spaces between words as letters—for the space between two words may take up about the room of one extra letter. Then consider the space available in your design. It may be long enough for the inscription to go into a few lines of large letters, or so narrow as to require numerous lines of lettering. Reckon out roughly how many letters will go into a line. To do this, lightly rule two parallel lines across the paper at a distance apart equal to the height of the letters you would like to use. You are trying to find out if there is room for letters of that size. Having ruled the lines, lightly sketch in part of the inscription to try how many letters are required to fill the line. It is only necessary to sketch in part of each letter very lightly before going on to the next. When the line is complete count up the number of letters you have worked into it, reckoning spaces between two words as letters, as before. Having found how many letters will go into one line, a simple calculation will show how many lines are required for the whole inscription. Measure up the available space to see if there is room for that number of lines with the necessary intervals between them. It may be that there is not room, and you must either use smaller letters, drawing the parallel lines above mentioned closer together; or you must compress the letters laterally, so as to get more of them into a line. On the other hand, you may have room to spare, and can therefore enlarge the letters or spread them out more. One or two trials may be necessary before a suitably sized letter can be settled upon. In finding out how many letters a line will hold, it is not always necessary to draw a complete line of the inscription. A half or a quarter of a line may be all that it is necessary to fill, and the number of lines required reckoned from that.

Proper names or dates should never be spaced so as to come partly on one and partly on a second line if it can be possibly avoided, nor should any unusual division of a word be made. The number of letters which can go into certain lines of the inscription may be thus affected, and any variation must be reckoned with in finally deciding on the size of letter to be used. In the chapter on repoussé work (p. 123) there are given some further hints as to the spacing of lettering for execution by that process.

In setting out small work—an engraved pattern or inscription, for example—some difficulty may be met with in firmly holding the work in such a manner that a set square can be used on it. It is a good plan to make a rectangular ring of iron or brass (Fig. 321), the top and edges of which are quite true and square. Fix this on the pitch bowl with its upper part projecting a little above the surface. Work can now be fastened down on the pitch within the rectangle in the usual way, and the square held against the ring while lines are being ruled. It is, of course, necessary to keep the working edges of the ring quite free from pitch.

CHAPTER XXXV

POLISHING AND COLOURING

Polishing. Firestain. Avoidance of firestain. " Firefree " silver. Metal colouring. General rules. The colouring of gold. The gilding of silver. The colouring of silver. The colouring of copper and brass.

THERE IS A WIDE CHOICE open as to the manner in which a piece of work may be finished. After its structure is complete, it may be coloured, oxidized, left with a dull (matt) surface, polished brightly or plated. Let us take the finishing of a plain, silver box as an example. After the final soldering the work is boiled out in sulphuric acid pickle to remove the borax and any oxides which may be adhering to it. From the pickle the silver emerges with a dull, matt, but perfectly white surface. All superfluous solder and other unevennesses are now removed with a file, and the work may be gone over with a scraper. Particular attention is given to scratches. To remove a scratch. Scrape in the direction of its length, or diagonally, until the metal round about is scraped down to the level of the bottom of the hollow. Do not scrape across and into a scratch. Work in this direction will only deepen and widen the groove. The box may now be gone over with water-of-Ayr stone, pumice and water, or glass paper. The water-of-Ayr stone is a grey slaty stone. When wetted it should look light in colour with dark spots: not even-coloured. It is always used wet. The pumice may be in lump form or in powder. In the latter case it is applied with a flat stick or brush. Glass paper is used rather than emery, for if any emery gets into the lemel it is difficult to remove, while the glass comes away with the flux when the lemel is melted.

Curved rather than straight strokes are the rule in polishing: the work goes truer so. The various materials for polishing are used in the order of their fineness, the finest ones coming last. Care must be taken to remove every particle of the coarser polishing materials before the finer kinds are applied. The sticks or mops used for each material are therefore kept in separate boxes or tins.

After one of the three materials mentioned above, a softer cutting material is used. This is blue stone; it is followed by either tripoli or crocus. The whole work is gone over each time, to get it to an equal smoothness. After this, jewellers' rouge is applied. It is mixed with water and just a little grease. The latter keeps the rouge from working into the surface and producing a reddish film which is difficult to get rid of. This discoloration is known as " foxing." A final polish is given with the hand alone. The work is then washed in warm water and dried in hot sawdust.

When using the polishing lathe take oil and crocus or tripoli on a brush, after the blue stone. Then with the same polishing material use a swansdown mop, centred truly. This will remove the brush-marks. Finish with rouge on another swansdown mop.

Copper or brass work is filed or scraped smooth. It is then gone over with coarse emery cloth, No. 2, and afterwards with fine, F.F. Or the work may be done on the polishing lathe with suitable bobs and mops.

The colour of silver when it has undergone the treatment described above will be very much like that of an ordinary mirror. Its surface will be quite smooth—all hammer-marks, scratches and other evidences of its method of manufacture having been removed. Now this high (black) polish is only possible if the whole of the original surface of the silver has been removed in the process of polishing. Sterling silver, as a rule, consists of 92·5 per cent. silver and 7·5 per cent. copper. The customary temperature employed in annealing it is 600° to 700° C. In the workshop the annealing is often done on the open hearth with gas blowpipe, even though certain difficulties arise from their use. For one effect of heating the silver in air is that some of the copper alloy near the surface is attacked by the oxygen in the flame, and the two substances combine to form a coating of copper oxide on the surface of the work. As this discoloration would penetrate further and further into the metal at subsequent annealings, it was found convenient to add 5 per cent. to 10 per cent. of sulphuric acid to the water in which the metal was quenched. The effect of this quenching in " pickle," as this dilute sulphuric acid bath is called, is the removal of nearly all the copper oxide from the surface, leaving a thin layer, perhaps a thousandth of an inch in thickness, of pure silver there. On account of this change in the quality and structure of the silver near the surface there results a difference in the colour of the surface if polished.

This changed colour is called " firestain " or " fire." As a rule it extends only one or two thousandths of an inch beneath the surface, and it may be removed by scraping or grinding. But unless the whole surface of the work is thus treated it will not have an even colour when polished. It will show a " black " mirror-like polish on those parts which have been scraped or ground since the last annealing, and a cloudy grey or yellowish tone in the parts which have been affected by oxidation. It was to overcome this difficulty that the custom of grinding or scraping the whole surface arose. For this operation removes all the material affected by the fire, leaving silver of " standard " quality exposed everywhere. However, many people feel that the " black " polish thus attained is obtained at too great a cost. For in the grinding and scraping necessary for its production all those touches which give a human interest to the work—" tricks of the tool's true play "—tend to disappear, and the surface becomes machine-like, " faultily faultless, icily perfect, splendidly null."

Naturally, efforts have been made to overcome the difficulties arising from this change of colour, and to avoid the extra work which it imposes. Sometimes the annealing has been done in a muffle furnace, filled with hydrogen or nitrogen, or some other inert gas, to prevent oxidation. Or the surface during the annealing was covered with a layer impervious to oxygen—borax flux or boracic acid, mixed with yellow or brown ochre, applied as a paste with water or spirit. Or the annealing has been effected in a vacuum chamber, or in a salt bath, held at a suitable temperature, by which means the oxygen in the air has been prevented from attacking the alloy. Or the whole surface has been removed by " stripping." That is to say, that the silver article has been used for a very short time as the anode in an electro-plating bath, and some of its surface has been dissolved in the plating solution. Or it has been dipped in a 50 per cent. cold solution of nitric acid, all joints having been protected by rouge, whiting or ochre. The dip is repeated if necessary. But the acid should be washed off without delay. Or the work has been electro-plated over the " fire " with either silver, chromium or rhodium. Some of these remedies give rise to other difficulties. For example, the coating of borax or boracic acid may cause trouble with soldered joints by encouraging the solder to flow once more. Therefore care must be taken to cover all solder with a layer of rouge, whiting or ochre. But all these processes involve extra work. So efforts were made to discover a " fire-free " silver. And it was found that a " standard " silver, composed of:

Silver	.	.	.	.	.	92·5 per cent.
Copper	.	.	.	.	.	6·5 ,,
Aluminium	.	.	.	.	.	1·0 ,,

was free from the effects of fire. But it was not quite so easy to solder when using the ordinary borax as a flux. However, the addition of a little lithium fluoride to the borax overcame that difficulty. Lithium fluoride is expensive, but as little as 5 per cent. may be employed.

Work can be made quite bright by means of the burnisher alone. This tool is made in a number of different shapes, two of which are shown in Figs. 44, 45. The point is of steel, haematite (iron) or agate, and the handle about 9 inches long. In making a burnisher use the best tool steel. Shape it and get it as much polished as possible when soft. Then harden, and temper to a pale straw colour (see Chapter XXXVI). Polish it again with crocus powder. Finish with Sheffield lime on a buff. Keep the burnisher in order by giving it an occasional rub on a buff with putty powder and rouge. In using the burnisher, hold the blade towards you—at the little finger side of the hand. Lubricate the work with soft soap and water, mixed rather thin and cloudy; or with saliva instead. Turn the work about, and alter the direction of the strokes till the surface is burnished quite smoothly. Then go over it with cotton wool on which is a drop of oil and rouge—finally with clean cotton wool and dry rouge. Wash it in warm water with soap, and dry out in hot boxwood sawdust.

A prong from a tortoise-shell comb is very useful for getting the polishing materials into narrow spaces—the tortoise-shell being of just the right hardness to hold them efficiently. Quills or sticks of boxwood also are used for this purpose. To polish small openings—pierced right through the work—a jeweller has a bundle of threads fastened under one of the arms of the bench. One or more of these is put through the hole and the work slid up and down the thread till the polishing material—crocus and oil—with which it is coated has done its work. On other threads is rouge for the final brightening.

When all the scratches have been removed and the surface of the work is quite true, say, after the water-of-Aye stoning, or better, after the tripoli, a dull ("matt" or "frosted") surface can be obtained on silverwork as follows. Make the work red hot—to oxidize the copper alloy at the surface—then boil the work in dilute sulphuric acid. This solution removes the copper oxides from the surface and leaves a thin film of pure silver all over. The colour of the silver is now a dead white. A rougher unpolished surface can be obtained by sand-blasting. In this process fine sand is blown by compressed air against the work. It makes quite a dull surface, like that on ground glass. Yet another very fine dull surface is obtained by the use of a wire brush on the lathe. In all these methods of finishing work the scratches must be removed first, otherwise they will show.

The colouring of metals: General preparation

After a piece of work has been polished a further course of treatment may be given it. Its surface may be "coloured." To do this successfully it is absolutely essential that the metal shall be perfectly clean. Any dirt, grease or oxides on its surface will prevent the solutions from acting evenly. When the work has been cleaned it should not be touched by the hand or even exposed to the air for longer than necessary. All borax should have been removed and all filing and polishing of the surface completed before the colouring is undertaken. A silver or copper wire may be fastened to the object for suspension to save it from contact with the hands. The work may then be boiled in a solution of soda or potash to get rid of any grease. One pound of potash to one gallon of water is a good proportion. The work is then well rinsed in clean water before it is put into the colouring solution. Small work, a brooch or a necklace which has been in use, may be cleaned with benzine before colouring. Larger work, if unpolished, may be cleaned by sandblasting or with fine sand and water, applied with a brush. Bath brick or pumice powder may be used instead. This material will not roughen the surface of the work so much. Care must be taken to prevent any of the colouring solutions from entering the settings of translucent stones, for the solution would dull the foil or other backing.

It is a good plan to remove the work from the colouring solution as soon as it has begun to take effect, and to give it a good scratch-brushing. Then, after a rinse in clean water, it may be replaced in the solution. A more even colouring is generally attained in this way than when the scratch-brushing is omitted. The action of the solutions given below may be stopped at once by removing the work and rinsing it well in clean water. The work will come a little lighter in colour during the subsequent brushing and brightening up, so the colouring should be allowed to proceed till the work is of a darker shade than that finally required.

The colouring of gold

We have seen that the colour of alloyed gold, 22, 18, 14 or 9 carat, and that of the solders employed in its manufacture, is different from that of " fine " gold. Therefore in order to give a good colour to the finished work, in fact, to give it a surface of pure or nearly pure gold, the work is treated in one of the following ways:

(a) By boiling it for a few minutes in a solution which will dissolve the alloy near the surface, leaving there pure gold only. For the poorer qualities of goldwork this process can hardly be applied, for in alloys, say, of 12 carat or lower quality, half or more of the mass of the work is composed of alloy, and the solution would remove so much of this material as to leave the surface of the work rough. But for gold of 14 carat or better quality no serious roughening results. The following solution may be employed:

Potassium nitrate (KNO_3)	.	.	4 parts.
Sodium chloride (NaCl)	.	.	2 ,,
Hydrochloric acid (HCl)	.	.	1 part.

The nitrate and salt are ground together into a fine powder and placed in a deep plumbago crucible which has been made hot over a Bunsen burner. They are stirred with a wooden spoon till heated throughout. A little boiling water and the acid are added and the stirring continued till the mixture boils up to the top of the crucible. The gold work, previously cleansed in a hot potash or soda solution, and rinsed in boiling water, is suspended in the solution by a platinum or silver wire for about a minute and then well washed in boiling water. A little more water is added to the colouring solution and when it boils the work is dipped for another minute, and again washed in boiling water. The operations are repeated till the work has attained the desired colour. After a good boiling in clean water it is dried in boxwood sawdust. The work is then scratch-brushed with a fine brass wire brush, or otherwise finished.

(b) Another method is sometimes employed. Take:

Potassium nitrate (KNO$_3$)	2 parts.
Sodium chloride (NaCl), i.e. common salt	1 part.
Alum	1 „

These substances are ground to a fine powder and placed in a tall, previously heated plumbago crucible over a Bunsen burner, and stirred with an iron rod. As the temperature rises the mixture boils up, becoming eventually a yellow-brown fluid. The work, suspended on a silver or platinum wire, is dipped in dilute nitric acid, rinsed in boiling water and then swung about in the solution for a minute or two. It is then immersed in boiling water to which a little nitric acid has been added, and again put into the solution. The operations are repeated till the work takes the desired colour. It is then washed in hot water and dried in warm boxwood sawdust.

(c) The methods of colouring gold, above described, have been largely superseded by electro-gilding, or " flushing." By the electro-plating process, operating at various temperatures and conditions, to attain the desired colour, a thin film of gold is deposited over the whole surface of the work. Whatever its actual quality may be, its surface is covered with a layer of high quality gold. As a result, a 9-carat work can have the same finished colour as an 18-carat one.

The gilding of silver

Until modern times the gilding of silver was effected by the use of an amalgam of mercury and gold. A layer of the amalgam was spread over the metal, and the mercury was driven off by heat. Using such an amalgam, applied with a cork, it is possible to cover a silver surface with a good layer of gold. The mercury is driven off by heating the work till the gold colour appears. It is dangerous to breathe the mercury vapour, so the operation should be performed in a fume cupboard, or in a fireplace where there is a good draught. The Romans, and all nations to whom a knowledge of their craftsmanship descended, used this method of gold plating, freely.

Electro-gilding is the more usual method employed in modern times. Any portions of the work which are not to be gilt are protected by painting them with a " stopping-out varnish."

The colouring of silver

The popular term " oxidized silver " is misleading. " Sulphur-ized silver " would be more correct. The discoloration of its surface, which gives so much trouble to all who have the care of silverware, is not due to the action of oxygen. Unless produced intentionally, it is due to the action of minute traces of sulphurous gases in the atmosphere, particularly in towns. To a similar cause is due the decay of our leather bookbindings. With silverware the sulphur combines with some of the silver, forming silver sulphide, which appears as a dark tarnish on the metal surface. If allowed to remain untouched for many years it forms a thick black covering to the metal, similar to niello, which indeed, in many cases, is identical in composition.

The Japanese, who are masters in the art of colouring metals, employ an alloy of silver and copper, with a trace of gold, which, when coloured, becomes a very beautiful silver-grey. An examina-tion of any collection of Japanese sword guards, such as those in the British or the South Kensington Museums, will demonstrate the versatility and the technical skill displayed in the chasing, the inlaying, and the metal colouring of these magnificent craftsmen.

Gold colour on silver

Take:

A cold solution of

| Barium sulphide (BaS) | . | . | . | 1 gm. |
| Water . | . | . | . | . | 7 oz. |

Or a hot solution of

| Ammonium sulphide $(NH_4)_2S)$. | . | 1 gm. |
| Water . | . | . | . | . | 7 oz. |

If the work is allowed to remain long in either of these solutions its colour will gradually change to crimson and brown. It is there-fore convenient to work with a cold solution and to stop the action when the colour has become strong enough.

Brown. If the work is dipped in either of the above solutions when warm or boiling, the colours change rapidly from gold, through various shades of purple to brown. It should be removed as soon as the colour has become sufficiently strong. If it is allowed to remain longer, the brown will become colder in tone.

Greyish-brown. Ammonium sulphide ($(NH_4)_2S$) in alcohol. This should be painted on with a brush.

Grey. Use platinum chloride ($PtCl_4$) in alcohol. This may be painted on with a brush. When dry its colour may be lightened by brushing it with pumice or by scratch-brushing.

Blue. This colour may be obtained by exposing the work to the fumes of sulphur (S) heated in a closed box.

Blue-black. A hot solution of:

Barium sulphide (BaS) . . .	1 gm.
Water	7 oz.

or Potassium sulphide (K_2S) . . .	1 gm.
Ammonium carbonate $(NH_4)_2CO_3$.	2 gm.
Water	7 oz.

The metal assumes a plumbago tint on scratch-brushing.

Black. Employ a hot concentrated solution of:

Ammonium sulphide in water.

The colouring of copper and brass

The composition of the many alloys of copper which pass under the generic name of " brasses " is so varied that their reaction to a colouring solution can hardly be foretold with certainty. It is well, therefore, to test a spare piece of the metal in the solution before treating the work itself. In general, the solutions work quicker and more efficiently when hot. And, as a rule, a more even colouring is produced if the work is withdrawn from the solution after a short period, washed, and given an all-over, even brushing with a brass-wire brush before returning it to the solution.

Light brown. A hot solution of:

Copper sulphate	1 part.
in Water	2 parts.

A much darker shade is produced by prolonging the period of immersion.

Brown. A number of shades of brown may be produced by dipping the work for shorter or longer periods in a hot solution of

Barium sulphide.

Brown. The following solution should be applied with a brush.

When the colour is satisfactory, stop the action by washing in plenty of water. A little olive oil may be rubbed into the surface.

Hydrochloric acid	12 parts.
Arsenic	1 part.
Iron oxide	1 „

Brown. Take:

Ammonium sulphide. . . .	1 gm.
Water	7 oz.

In the hot solution the colour will change rapidly from gold through various shades of crimson to brown.

Dark brown

Potassium sulphide	1 gm.
Water	7 oz.

Use as above.

Sage green. Use a hot solution of

Copper nitrate . . .	1·5 gm.
Water	6 oz.

Olive green. Use

Iron perchloride . . .	1 part.
Water	2 parts.
or Ammonium chloride . .	1 part.
Water	2 parts.

Dark green. A mixture of

Copper sulphate . . .	1 part.
Zinc chloride	1 „

is mixed with 1 part of water. The paste is applied to the work and allowed to dry on it. It is then washed off. The work is then exposed to the light, and the discoloration at first present changes to a dark green, almost black.

Dark green. Bronze work exposed to the atmosphere of a large town gradually acquires a dark patina. If it is treated monthly with a very thin coating of olive or bone oil it will acquire a fine dark green patina. The work should be rubbed as clean as possible at each treatment.

Antique bronze.,   Take:

Copper nitrate ($Cu(NO_3)_2$)	.	. 1 gm.
Ammonium chloride (NH_4Cl)	.	. 1 ,,
Calcium chloride ($CaCl_2$)	.	. 1 ,,
Water		. 20 ,,

The solution may be painted on the work.

Black.   Use a hot concentrated solution of barium sulphide or of ammonium sulphide.

Black.   Take:

Copper nitrate	. 1 part.
and Water	. 2 parts.

Add ammonia cautiously till the precipitate which first forms is just re-dissolved.

Black.   Take:

Copper sulphate . . .	. 60 gm.
and Water sufficient to dissolve it.	

Add sufficient ammonia to re-dissolve the precipitate which first forms.

CHAPTER XXXVI

THE MAKING AND SHARPENING OF TOOLS

*Carbon steels. Alloy steels. Forging. Hardening. Tempering. Grinding
Sharpening. Stropping.*

ALTHOUGH you may buy ready made, or have made to your
order, tools of any shape, yet some experience in the making
of the simpler kinds is very desirable. A repoussé tool of
some special shape is required, a small chisel, a mandrel for winding
wire upon. Days or weeks might pass before the right tool could be
obtained. Yet it could be made in a few minutes, in half an hour.
Let us try. But first a word or two about the material of which it is
to be made. Knives, chisels, files, drills, cutting tools generally, and
many other types of tools are made from steel. This material is iron,
made stronger and tougher by the addition of small percentages of
carbon, tungsten, nickel, chromium, vanadium, etc. Tool steels
may be roughly divided into two great groups: " Carbon steels,"
and what are known as " alloy or high speed steels." The former
contains from 1·5 to 0·75 per cent. of carbon. They were in
general use up to 1894, and are still very widely used for general
purposes. Carbon steels, however, begin to lose their hardness
at a temperature of 260° C., so, though quite suited for all the
ordinary tools used by metalworkers, they cannot be used for
high speed work on lathes and milling machines. There is no
convenient way known in which they may be kept cool enough to
retain their hardness. Alloy or high speed steels are those in which
the iron is mixed with a small percentage of tungsten, or one or
more of the other metals mentioned above. These steels will keep
their hardness even when red-hot, for they may become heated up
to about 650° C., a dull red heat, without their cutting capacity
being seriously impaired. However, carbon steels are those which
one is most likely to meet with. They are made in different brands
for various kinds of tools. None should be heated more often than
absolutely necessary, for with repeated heatings part of the carbon
is burnt out and the quality of the steel impaired.

267

Tools made from tool steel may be hardened and tempered as described below, but those made from mild steel cannot be hardened to the same degree. But there is a process, known as case-hardening, by which the metal at the surface of the tool may be turned into a steel which may be hardened and tempered. By this process additional carbon is absorbed by the surface of the tool, transforming it locally into a hardenable steel. There are a number of materials which may be employed in this carburizing process. Such a one is sodium cyanide. The work is heated for a period of a few minutes to several hours in contact with the case-hardening compound. It is then quenched in water or oil. It may have further heat treatment if necessary.

Brass is too soft for cutting tools. It is sometimes used for repoussé tools, but those made from this material should be avoided. They are liable to get bent or otherwise damaged. Let us therefore take tool steel for the work we have in hand—a small chisel, shall we say. Tool steel may be bought in rods, round, square, hexagonal or octagonal, of almost any size. Take a $\frac{5}{16}$ inch octagonal rod and cut off $3\frac{1}{2}$ inches. To file it to shape would take too long and would wear out the file unnecessarily. To hammer it to shape when cold would be almost impossible, for it is so hard that it would probably crack in the process. It must be forged when hot. Any good fire will supply sufficient heat, but the work can be done in a furnace or with a blowpipe. Take a pair of strong pliers or tongs with which to hold the tool you are making, and put the end of the piece of steel rod in a clear part of the fire. Now tool steel can be forged when red hot, but it should not be brought to a pale yellow or white heat, such as the brightest part of a good fire, more than a few times. Nor must hammering proceed when it has cooled down to a dull red heat. In the former case it will become technically " burnt," and in the latter it is liable to be cracked. When the steel is at the right temperature hold it with the tongs, and hammer it to shape on an anvil or some heavy stake, using any suitable hammer. If it gets cool before you have finished, heat it again. It may be finished with a file where necessary. Then reheat it to a cherry red and allow it to cool down quite slowly before hardening and tempering.

To harden a steel tool. Prepare a vessel or bath of water in which to cool the tool. It should be large enough for this to be done without any appreciable heating of the water. Add some salt to the latter. Salt water or brine gives greater hardness than pure water. The temperature of the bath should not be below 60° F. (16° C.). Heat the tool to a bright red colour. Stir the water so that it is going fast round and round in the pail or whatever vessel you are using. Then plunge the tool straight down into the swirl, holding it in the tongs and moving it about until cold—the object being to get the tool cooled as quickly and evenly as possible. Moving water does this quicker than still water. Tools are sometimes quenched in oil, mercury or other liquids; small ones by sticking the point into a tallow candle. The use of oil or tallow for this purpose makes for toughness in the tool rather than for great hardness. Tools made from alloy steel are usually hardened in oil, though for some brands a blast of cold air is used instead. To return to our work. The tool is now hardened, but it is extremely brittle. If used in its present condition its edge would break almost at once. Before it can be safely used it must be tempered.

To temper. First clean up one side of the tool by grinding it on a stone or on emery paper. It is too hard to use a file upon—you would only spoil the file. The last inch or two of the tool should be bright and clean. Next apply heat to one end or the middle of the tool, but not to the point. This may be done with a blowpipe, or by laying the shank of the tool on a piece of red-hot iron, but in no case must the point be heated directly. It should get gradually heated as the warmth creeps up the tool. As the tool becomes hot the colour of the polished side changes. Bands of different colours appear close to where the heat is applied and creep down the tool towards the point. First pale yellow, then straw colour, then brown and finally blue like that on a clock spring. These colours indicate different degrees of hardness. Steel, tempered pale yellow, is very hard but very brittle. It is useful for razors and fine cutting tools, but it is too brittle to stand much hammering. Chisels are tempered to a brownish-yellow or dark straw colour at the point, the shank of the tool being not quite so hard. For, the tempering being done as above described, the shank of the tool gets hotter, and softer, in the process than the point does. Saws are tempered blue, as they must be flexible and not brittle. When the colour at the point of the chisel indicates that the temper has been " let down " sufficiently any further softening is stopped by putting the tool in cold water again. The chisel has now been hardened and tempered. It must yet be ground and sharpened for use.

To temper a small drill. With the pliers hold a piece of sheet copper, measuring about 3 inches by 1 inch, over a Bunsen burner or small gas jet. With another pair of pliers hold the drill by the shank over the copper. Let part of the shank of the drill touch the edge of the copper. The copper will protect the drill from direct contact with the flame, yet sufficient heat to temper it properly will reach the drill through its place of contact with the copper. Proceed as described above.

To temper a spring. Cover the spring with two layers of iron binding wire, about 26 Standard Wire Gauge, coiled quite closely. Dip it into olive oil or linseed oil—whichever you have by you. Hold it over a flame until it catches alight. Let it burn itself out. At once uncoil the wire, and the spring will be found to be properly tempered. It is not necessary in this case to dip the work in water to stay the tempering. If two or three strands of the wire are coiled on the spring at once the work is done quicker. A Japanese sword-smith when about to harden a blade, entirely covers it with a thick layer of clay. This he removes from a narrow band on each side of the cutting edge. He heats and quenches the blade. Its cutting edge is hardened by the sudden cooling. And the back, protected by the clay, remains comparatively soft and tough.

The colours to which steel tools are tempered for various purposes are given below with temperatures:

	Cent.	Fahr.	
Light straw colour	221°	430°	Razors.
Dark straw . .	243°	470°	For wood, ivory and vulcanite tools.
Brown-yellow .	260°	500°	For gravers and tools for metal-cutting.
Bright blue. .	288°	550°	For springs and saws.

A method by which the temperature—and hardness—of the steel may be accurately regulated is that by which the tempering is done in a bath of molten metal. Different alloys of lead and tin can be made, the melting points of which correspond with the various degrees of temper required in the steel.

Composition of Bath		Melting-point		Colour of steel at temperature given
Lead	Tin	Cent.	Fahr.	
14	8	215°	420°	Very faint yellow.
15	8	221°	430°	Faint yellow.
16	8	227°	440°	Light straw.
17	8	232°	450°	Straw.
18·5	8	238°	460°	Full straw.
20	8	243°	470°	Dark straw.
24	8	249°	480°	Old gold.
28	8	254°	490°	Brown.
38·8	8	266°	510°	Brown with purple spots.
60·8	8	277°	530°	Purple.
96	8	288°	550°	Deep purple.
200	8	293°	560°	Blue.
Boiling linseed oil	.	316°	600°	Dark blue.
Melted lead	. .	327°	620°	Greyish-blue.

To grind a chisel. The angle between the two faces at the cutting edge of a chisel varies with the material which is to be cut. The harder the material, the greater the angle between the two faces. Thus for paring soft wood an angle of 15 degrees or less may be used, but it would not be safe to use the mallet with so slight an edge. Much depends upon the thickness of the tool a little way behind the edge. The edge of a good hollow-ground razor in working order may have an angle of 16 degrees, for in setting a razor the thickness of the back regulates the angle at which the edge is ground. An angle of about 25 degrees is safe to use with a mallet in hard wood, if the tool is tempered rightly. For metal the angle at which the chisel point is ground must be blunter still. For work on thick metal the thickness of the point a little way from the edge is perhaps as important as the actual angle of the cutting edge. For the blows given are fairly heavy, and they drive a narrow chisel deep, whatever the form of its edge may be.

Grinding is done on a grindstone or an emery or corundum wheel. So great is the amount of heat produced in this process that, unless the stone is kept wet, in the course of a few seconds the tool will get so hot that its temper will be spoilt. In that case it must be hardened and tempered afresh. Tools may be ground with the grindstone running either towards or from you. The stone " running towards you " means that when you are in the position for grinding a tool, that part of the grindstone between the top of the stone and your hands is travelling towards your hands. It is a little more difficult to hold a tool when the stone is running towards you, but the work is done quicker. Each of the two sides of the chisel which meet at the cutting edge should be left quite flat, or even slightly concave (following the curve of the grindstone), but not convex. The tool is held in the right hand, and its further end is pressed against the stone by the first two or three fingers of the left hand. The angle at which the tool meets the stone can be adjusted by raising or lowering the hands. It is usual to move the tool from side to side of the grindstone as the work proceeds. This is done to avoid wearing grooves in the stone. It sometimes happens, in grinding with the stone running from you, that an edge of metal, as thin as a sheet of paper and quite flexible, is left at the extreme edge of the tool. This is known as the " wire edge " or " arris." It will generally break off in the course of sharpening and leave the tool quite keen. When the grinding has proceeded far enough the chisel may be sharpened on an oilstone.

Sharpening is but a continuation of the process of grinding. It is done on smoother stones—slower in cutting. But a finer edge is produced than it would be possible to obtain with grindstone alone. Lay the oilstone on the bench with its end to the front edge of the bench. Hold the tool as before, and rub from end to end of the stone. The middle part of a stone generally has more wear than the edges, and so gets worn hollow. Try to avoid this. Proceed with the sharpening until the rough scratches left by the grinding have been smoothed out, and the tool has a true, dull-polished surface at the extremity. The wire edge may still be present, but it will be rubbed off later on the strop.

Stropping produces an extremely fine polished or burnished edge of the tool. The strop, unlike the grindstone and oilstone, does not remove any metal. The cutting edge of the tool on leaving the oilstone has a comparatively rough surface, the little ridges or grooves or fibres at the edge running in all directions. The purpose of the stropping is to stroke or burnish them so that they point in one direction only—from the back or handle towards the cutting edge to the tool. A mixture of tripoli, rouge and tallow may be used on the strop. It is well to remember that in the case of any cutting tool whatsoever, whether it be a pocket-knife for peeling an apple, a drill, or a lathe for an 18-inch gun, the efficiency of the tool ultimately depends on the keenness and truth of the last hundredth, or twenty-fifth, or sixteenth of an inch, whichever you like, of that tool's cutting edge. All the rest of the tool is but handle, with various labour-saving devices, for applying that cutting edge to its work. It is well, therefore, to see to it that the cutting edge of your tool is correct in form and properly applied.

CHAPTER XXXVII

DESIGN

*The craftsman, ancient and modern. His training and opportunities.
Design. Unity. Growth. Line. Modelling a design. Mouldings. Importance
of the " jewel."*

IN THE NATIONAL MUSEUMS we have vast collections of work
of all ages and countries. This work is valuable to us in many
ways, but not least in showing how the old craftsman thought
out the problems which were set him—problems in many cases new.
We gain a useful experience if we try to put ourselves in the old
worker's place, and think out the problem from his point of view.
He generally had to work with less efficient tools than those available
to us. He had no gas to solder with, for example. He often had to
make his own files and solder. He had to melt his own silver or gold
and cast it into an ingot of suitable shape for the work. He often
carried the whole work through alone. For he was capable of doing
the raising, the repoussé work and chasing, the fitting and the soldering, the enamelling or niello work and the gilding. All these things
reacted on the design. For he had his say in that also, and we can
see how his personal equation asserted itself in this. One craftsman
was fond of trying twisted wire patterns, another of enamelling,
another of niello or repoussé; and he makes you see that he is
interested in it. The modern practice whereby the gold- or silversmith confines himself to a single branch of the craft does un-
doubtedly result in wonderful technical skilfulness, and in cheapness
of production. But its influence is definitely against the production
of work which " holds together " æsthetically. For that quality is
hardly to be obtained when the work passes through so many hands,
and each craftsman, perhaps naturally, endeavours to make his
part of the work " tell " most. The subordination of some parts is
essential in a work of art. So it comes to this. The great bulk of
the work turned out in future will continue to come from workshops
carried on as at present—one job passing through many hands.
For the majority of the people who buy do not worry about the

274

æsthetic quality of the work at all. But there will always be a demand for work executed throughout by one man—a man who can both design and carry the work through.

We in our day, like the old craftsman in his, must think out the problems in our own way. We know, far better than he, what has already been done. Our books and museums tell us that. But to copy an old work, or to collect details from this and that and to put them together as a new design is not enough. For we must remember that if the people who care for artistic work and good craftsmanship are to be interested in our work, it can only be if they can see in it that we were really interested in it ourselves. If we think the thing out for ourselves, if we suppress, strengthen or modify details of our design because we feel that it will be " pulled together " by our so doing, we are putting into it thoughts which will interest those who care for artistic work. If we have a care for fine craftsmanship, others also will appreciate our work. But to hold the balance between fine design and fine craftsmanship, so that the latter, though present, shall not take precedence over the former—that is the true aim; and we are happy when we strive for it. Eccentricity in design certainly catches the eye: but it is almost impossible to live with it. Over-insistence on technique, aggressive craftsmanship, over-acting, quite naturally elbow out æsthetic feeling. One idea must take precedence, and if that happens to be technique, the other goes.

If we look at Nature she will give us many hints as to design. We must look not only at plant forms, but also at butterflies. beetles, lobsters and crabs. At bones also—the forms at the underside of a human skull, for example. We should model the forms to really understand how they go. We should consider all the modelled or carved work that we meet with; and try to understand why the sculptor or carver turned this form so, and that in the other direction. The study of the work of a sculptor like Alfred Gilbert is a true education. The details of his Piccadilly fountain, for example, will well repay a thorough consideration. They have a wonderful flow of form and line.

The objects which we design may be broadly divided into two classes. (1) Objects intended primarily to look beautiful, their usefulness being but a secondary consideration, or no consideration at all. In this class come the mediæval nef and standing cup, and the modern table-centre. And (2) objects intended for use. These may be as beautiful as the others, but certain limitations must be observed in their design and construction. They are intended primarily for use, so nothing must be allowed to interfere with that. The lip of a cup which is to be used must be of such a form as to allow of it. The spout of a jug must be a practical one, and the handle of a form which would allow you to lift and empty the vessel. The base of a lampstand must be sufficiently wide and heavy to ensure the safety of the lamp. A door-knocker should be so designed that it would be possible to grasp the knocker—and that it should be heavy enough.

The first point, then, to remember in designing anything whatever is that the object made shall efficiently fulfil its purpose. If it is primarily intended for decorative purposes and its practicability as a usable object is of minor importance—then you are free from the limitations of usefulness—its principal purpose is that of looking beautiful. But if the object is primarily intended for use, no beautiful proportion, no amount of decoration will compensate for any omission in that respect. The prize cup (Fig. 324) is an example of

a design which is a failure. For though a prize cup may be used a few times for drinking from, that is not its principal purpose. It is primarily intended as a thing to be looked at, as a pleasant souvenir of a successful effort. But this cup is not pleasant to look at—it is so bad in proportion. Its height is divided into two equal portions: a mistake. And its forms are not good. Like so many current designs, its shape was primarily determined by the ease by which it might be spun. It is certainly a usable cup, but its more important purpose has been overlooked; it is unpleasant to look at. Fig. 325 shows an unusable lip.

Having then settled the purpose which your design is intended to fulfil, the next things to consider are proportion and mass. Until these are settled it is of little use to go into details. You must consider the proportion between part and part. It is not well to divide a design horizontally or vertically into two or three apparently equal parts. One part should take precedence. It should be greater in height or width or bulk than the other part or parts. The fact that they are so subordinated to the principal mass very greatly assists in giving that feeling of unity which is so necessary to any work of art. It is true that the principal mass need not be very much greater than its subordinates, but in some way it must be more important—either in form or colour.

The feeling of unity just mentioned as being an essential feature in a work of art may be explained in the following manner. If a number of lines or other forms (Figs. 326, 327) are strewn about in

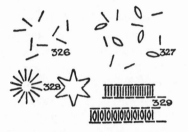

an irregular manner the impression given is that of a number of objects. If, however, the lines or forms are arranged in some regular order—to make some pattern (as in Figs. 328, 329)—the mind is able to grasp them all at once as a unity—a star, a border. The forms need not be all alike for this purpose. What is necessary is just that there shall be some formal order in the grouping. An untidy room worries one not just because various articles are out of place, but rather because, in the æsthetic sense, there is no unity in it. Books are strewn about at various angles on tables and chairs, the table-cloth is awry, letters and papers are here, there and everywhere, the furniture is moved into awkward places, and so on. You have but to put the books, furniture and the other things into some formal order (not necessarily into their proper places), and the sense of untidiness will vanish. You have obtained order and unity once more. You will find that this sense of unity is essential in a work of art. Your attention must not be distracted by lines, forms or colours which do not help towards its attainment.

It is difficult to say why this sense of unity gives so much satisfaction. Without doubt it is a lesser intellectual strain to think of the work as a unity than to remember a number of different parts. Just so it requires more effort to describe the various characteristics of some flower, the name of which is unknown to us, than to point to it. The concept of the work as a unity of definitely recognizable form is less difficult to us than an attempt to grip mentally a number of different facts about it—so we prefer the former.

A number of more or less naturalistic details put together will not make a design. The details must be bound together in some formal manner. You feel the need for some architectural feeling—principal and secondary masses; a feeling for symmetry; horizontal and vertical lines to give steadiness to the composition, and to afford a contrast to the more playful curved parts.

The details of the ornament should be kept to about the same scale throughout the work, no part looking as though it really belonged to a larger (or smaller) work. No feature in the ornament should be allowed to overpower all the others. Geometrical forms have an unpleasant habit of doing this sometimes. Thus, a diamond or oval shape in a panel may easily become too prominent; or a long line of simple curvature may show up more than you wish. To quiet curved lines you may cross them by others; or you may employ straight lines to contrast with and steady them.

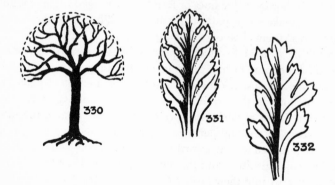

A feeling for growth is most valuable. It helps you to trace long lines through the composition, tying up the various parts of the design by leading the eye on from one to the other, just as your eye may travel from the ground, up the roots of a tree (Fig. 330), up the stem, up the branches and right round the outline without any very sudden break. And in the leaf (Fig. 331) it is easy for the eye to travel in the direction of the dotted line, jumping across the notches without a check. So in a design it is restful, it gives a feeling of satisfaction, a sense of unity, if your eye may travel from part to part of the work without any very sudden jerk. The working of this rule may be traced in objects of art of quite another kind. If you look at a picture by an artist who had a feeling for line—Raphael, or our own Burne-Jones—you will see how no part could be taken away from the composition without injuring it, for the lines which bind all the picture together, making a unity of it, would be broken. If you should be able to remove a portion of any design without injuring it, you may be sure that the design is not sufficiently thought out and bound together. The leaf (Fig. 332) may be compared with the other. It shows lines which do not " follow on " or " compose " well.

No part of the design should be entirely cut off from the remainder by a very strong line. The lines of composition should be so arranged that the eye is led past the dividing line, that the different parts overlap a little, as it were, tying themselves up with the lines on the other side of the division. In the illustration (Fig. 333) the

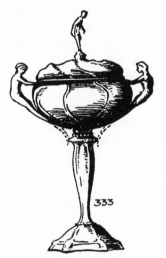

333

tails of the mermaids are carried down below the base of the bowl to pick up the line of the stem. If they had finished against the bowl all the upper part of the design would have been apparently cut off from the stem.

279

Constructional lines should always be acknowledged. Thus, ornament from the panels should not overflow any of the edges or corners of a box, ignoring the constructional value of these features. The ornament should either decorate the panels of the box, or the edges, or go in bands round it. The same pattern should not sprawl over parts of a side and an end, say, in an informal manner, leaving other parts plain.

Straight horizontal or vertical lines have a wonderfully steadying effect on a design. It does not seem to matter how playful and curved the other lines may be if you have a number of these steadying lines. They must be repeated with sufficient strength to pull the whole work together. The instability and want of restfulness of much continental art and of works designed in the style of " l'art nouveau " were due very largely to the absence from the work of these strong horizontal and vertical lines. If a design looks fussy or flippant it is a fairly safe rule to try the effect of some of these steadying lines upon it.

It is an excellent plan to model a design to full size in clay, wax or plasticine. You can then see exactly how things will come, and you can try experiments. See if it will help to make any of the shadows deeper, or the mouldings stronger. See that the whole work does not look too flat or shadowless. See that the lines flow gracefully, that the ornament is right in scale, that each part has sufficient room. If you work thus you may make a work of art. Do not settle everything on paper first.

Let your ornament be appropriate. Fishes on a fire-screen look out of place—in the drawing-room at any rate.

Do not cover the whole work with ornament. Leave plenty of plain spaces to contrast with it. You may then make the ornament as rich as you please.

A moulding is a device by means of which a line of light and shadow may be drawn across the work, or an angle filled with interesting light and shade. Thus the angle *ABC* (Fig. 334) has to be dealt with. You may choose to fill it with the straight line *AC*, and the effect in front will be that of a flat, grey shadow. This shadow will be made darker at the top and lighter below if you curve the surface in as in the dotted line. But you may wish to have a line of light instead of shade at the top. To obtain this you bulge the moulding out as in Fig. 335; and if you also like a little streak

280

of light at the bottom you tilt the surface out again there. Or you may prefer to reverse the order and have the light at the bottom, as in Fig. 336. You may, if you will, break the mouldings up into many parts, large or small. The various members look better if they are varied in size and curvature. The light and shadows on curves which are sections of ellipses (Fig. 337) look much more graceful than those on curves whose sections are based on the circle (Fig. 338).

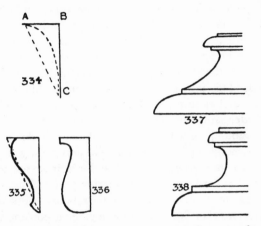

Perhaps it is hardly necessary to point out that you should never design anything without taking into account the amount of money available for the work. The cost must enter into your calculations as an essential factor in the majority of cases.

The importance of precious stones and enamels can hardly be over-estimated. Let us try to think what their purpose may be æsthetically. We will first glance at the materials we have to use—their colours and textures. On our richest garments we place metals of various colours. White or grey—platinum, silver, steel, etc. Yellow—gold, brass, etc. Black—niello. Red—copper. Various browns and greys obtained by oxidization. Textures vary from a dull matt to a highly polished surface. And surfaces are of any form, tilted to or from the light. We have also ivory, coral, pearls, opaque and translucent enamels and stones. Apart from expense and other considerations, these materials differ in æsthetic " quality " and " preciousness." A highly polished piece of metal looks more precious than a similar piece of metal with a matt surface. A coloured, brilliant stone, is more important than a dull-coloured or a dull-surfaced one; just as a piece of brick has less of this quality of preciousness than a polished flint, so the hardness, brilliance and smooth surface of the diamond set it above them all.

We are now in a position to ask: What is the essential purpose of, the real reason for, the use of jewels as such—of enamels as such? They represent the most precious looking, the richest in colour, the brightest and clearest in texture of all the materials with which we have to deal—something to which all other work and material may lead up. It is not because they are costly; it is not so much, at bottom, because they are rare; but because they form the culminating point in the scale which leads from the duller and poorer materials up to the richest and most precious looking things that we can find. This may seem obvious, I know. But it is at times necessary to remind ourselves of first principles. We may not, as a rule, embroider satin curtains with wool, a poorer-looking material on a richer ground; but I have seen it done. We don't, as a rule, set uncut diamonds or rubies in our jewellery, costly though they may be: but I have seen it done. We don't, if we are wise, use a coloured marble border to a white marble tablet. But it has been done. Just as metal is richer than cloth, repoussé work than plain metal, so an enamel or fine stone is more precious-looking than them all. We know how lonely an unset jewel looks, how hopeless an enamel panel looks without a frame. They are both superlatives without a context, and—unhappy are they.

If we try the effect of placing a row of coloured stones round a large diamond, and again a row of diamonds round a large emerald or sapphire, we shall see how in the latter case there is a much greater feeling of unity than in the former. The coloured stones in the former distract the attention from the diamond—which, though it may hold its own by right of place, yet has to fight for precedence against their colour. The emerald or sapphire, on the other hand, takes precedence both by colour, size and position, as it should do.

The whole work should be kept in tone, and lead up to the principal jewel, the latter taking precedence both in colour and in brilliance, while the whole of its surroundings are kept without discordant notes. This principal was clearly grasped by those mediæval craftsmen who decorated the Cathedral of St. Mark at Venice. In this great church there is neither stained glass nor picture, white marble nor black. But the floor and the walls are everywhere covered with slabs of coloured marble, arranged in patterns, and glowing with colour; while over all is a roof of dull gold mosaic, with splashes of colour all about, so that the whole church glows with gold and colour. You look towards the altar and see priests in bright raiment, brighter than the walls, one step higher in our scale. And you see there " the fair linen cloth "—the one touch of white, with bright golden vessels upon it. And high over the altar, the centre and culminating point of that which has spread the fame of this great cathedral far and wide throughout the world, is the great Pala d'Oro, the golden altar-back with its million's worth of gold and jewels. Everything leads up to it. And you feel the glow of colour in your eyes, the scent of incense in your nostrils, of music in your ears, and through it all ring the clear tones of little boys' voices. And that is St. Mark's. Its fame is not due to the mosaics or the marble, but to the artists who kept the whole work in tone, and let all the decoration lead up to the one central point of interest, and through that to the song of praise. There is hardly a discordant note. You would like to see mediæval dresses and armour worn there, for modern garb is dull in comparison. But the church is great enough to hold its own, and to teach to those who would learn, the great principles of colour and of unity.

The Cathedral of St. Mark at Venice is perhaps the finest example in existence of an æsthetic arrangement of material on the grand scale, which passes by regular degrees from the lower qualities of marble, mosaic and metal to the supreme glory of its central jewel—the Pala d'Oro. But there are also in Italy a few buildings of the highest order in which there seems to be no gradual building-up of the music towards its climax, such as we have in St. Mark's. But rather do we find a building which, seen in its urban setting, is of such a quality that we must judge it not as a setting for the principal jewel, but as being the actual jewel itself. Such a work is the sixth-century Byzantine Church of San Vitale at Ravenna. It has what is probably the most beautiful interior in Europe. It seems to have innumerable arches and columns, all glowing with delicately-graded colours, passing from the light warm-toned brickwork of which the church is built, and the unpolished marble floor, with its many-tinted natural patterns, by the shining marble of the columns and walls, which glow with waving bands of white, green and blue; warmed by the subdued light which filters through

283

windows of translucent onyx and alabaster: passing up the colour-scale to the mosaics on the walls and roof with their balanced masses of colour and of gold. There is a unity in the whole scheme, one in which every touch of colour—misty white, green, blue, orange or violet—combines with its neighbours to form a delicate, glowing harmony, as in a fine opal. And one feels that the unknown artists who built and decorated the church have to their credit an achievement which is second to none in the whole world.

If you turn to almost any other church—to some of the French cathedrals, for example—you find large masses of quite inharmonious colour thrown about anywhere and everywhere. Large pieces of white marble, with black marble for contrast, which are sufficient to destroy any attempt at tone or colour. If colour is wanted, they must go.

Now principles which you have learnt in large things you may apply in small. And in jewellery or metalwork so arrange your colours and ornament that they may lead up to the principal feature, and remain in subordination to it. Our scale then runs from plain metal, through repoussé work (with its lights and darks), up to enamels and stones with their hardness, brilliance and colour.

In England we have the unfortunate habit of thinking of work as weighing so many ounces of silver or of gold. We do not think enough of its æsthetic quality. In many cases it would be well if more than one metal were employed on a single piece of work, but this is impossible if it is to be hall-marked. The inlays, stratified fabrics, and niello discussed above give to the craftsman methods of decorating plain surfaces at present practically unknown here, but they may be pressed into service by anyone who values colour and harmony more than a hall-mark.

CHAPTER XXXVIII

BENVENUTO CELLINI

THERE IS ONE CONSIDERATION which, more than any other, the designer must bear in mind in judging the work and the craftsmen of the past. It is that a man's work must be judged on its own merit, and on that alone. Reputation is hardly a safe guide. Great reputations may be based on divers grounds; but they do not all stand quite safely on the bases generally attributed to them. Cellini's is a case in point. You have but to look into almost any book dealing with goldsmiths' work to find the name of Benvenuto Cellini tacitly accepted as that of the greatest goldsmith the world has seen. But should you endeavour to turn to his works in the craft to see upon what ground this great reputation may be based, you will meet with the initial difficulty that few examples of it have come down to us, and those which have are not specially good. Upon what Cellini's reputation is truly based it will be my endeavour to show.

First, then, let us look at the materials. Works attributed to Cellini may be seen in many of the national museums of Europe. The great salt-cellar, made for Francis I of France, is at Vienna; other pieces are at Florence and elsewhere. M. Eugène Plon, in his great work on Cellini, illustrates all the important work by, or attributed to, the master. A copy of this book is to be found in the National Art Library at South Kensington. From it, and from an inspection of some of the works themselves, a pretty fair idea as to his attainments may be gained. Cellini also wrote two books about himself—his autobiography and his treatises on Metalwork and Sculpture. From them we may learn much of the man himself, his life and character.

Cellini was born in 1500; he placed himself with a goldsmith at the age of fifteen, against the desire of his father, who wished him to become a musician. As a goldsmith he worked throughout his life. But in Cellini's time the goldsmiths' craft and the goldsmiths' guild embraced workers in many different materials. There was no strict dividing line between goldsmith and sculptor. Luca della Robbia and Ghiberti, to mention only two famous names, began life as goldsmiths. It is not to be wondered at that Cellini also should try his hand at clay and bronze and marble. Of all the work which came from his hand Cellini was proudest of his sculptures. He described himself as sculptor, goldsmith and die-sinker.

He worked for many masters—Popes, Dukes, Cardinals, and for the King of France, producing jewels, silverware, coins, busts, statues, base-reliefs, a figure 54 feet high, plans for fortifications— nothing came amiss to this most versatile man. Yet he was not a great artist in the true sense of the word. His taste was in many ways deplorable. Nearly always the craftsman overpowers the artist. He had a lack of feeling for proportion; the figures on his great salt-cellar, for instance, are too large for the rest of the work. His figures are stiff and wooden, and lack proportion, though they are often well thrown about. His work is overcrowded with detail— and this is frequently far too great in scale. The placing of the head in the coins and medals is sometimes very poor indeed. In silver-work and jewellery his work stands technically on a level with that of many of his contemporaries—neither better nor worse. In it Cellini shows no sign of transcendent genius—but rather the joy of a keen workman delighting in the overcoming of technical difficulties. But there is one sin at least which he never committed—that of thinking too little of himself and his work. By force of character he held his own among his contemporaries: for the future he provided by his writings. But for them his name would stand far lower. He was one of the very greatest craftsmen of the sixteenth century, but he was a poor artist. His true claims to fame are his versatile craftsmanship and literary power. Other goldsmiths have done finer work, but Benvenuto Cellini is the author of the most delightful autobiography ever written.

CHAPTER XXXIX

ASSAYING AND HALLMARKING

Gold. Preliminary assay. Final assay. Silver. Hallmarking. Maker's, standard, city and year marks. Irish hallmarks. Foreign plate.

GOLD, WHEN DISCOVERED, is never quite pure and, as pure or " fine " gold is too soft to wear well, for general use it is alloyed with some other metal or metals. The metals usually employed for this purpose are silver and copper. The quality of a piece of goldwork may be estimated by means of the " touch-stone " and " touch-needles." A touchstone is a hard black stone or piece of black pottery, and the needles are small sticks of gold of known quality. With a firm stroke the part of the work to be tested is rubbed on the stone, leaving a streak. Alongside it another streak is made with a touch needle. A drop of dilute nitric acid (water 1 part, acid 1 part) or aqua regia is put on both streaks and its reaction noted. The lower the quality of the gold the greater is the attack. Pure gold is insoluble in nitric acid, but any alloy present is attacked. If the gold is of higher quality than 9 carat nitric acid acts too slowly, so aqua regia (a mixture of nitric and hydrochloric acids) is used instead. The amount of attack is indicated by the darkening of the surface. To discover the quality of a piece of gold with accuracy it must be assayed. As in the process of manufacture the alloy may have been removed from the surface layers of the work, it is usual to scrape them away locally to expose part of the solid body of metal, and from those deeper layers to take the sample for assay. The method followed is this. A weighed quantity of the gold is melted, with some lead, in a cupel (a small porous cup, made from bone-ash or magnesia). The lead and copper are oxidized by the heat, the oxides fuse and are absorbed by the cupel, and the gold and silver are left behind as a metallic " button." This is weighed, and rolled out into a thin ribbon. The silver is dissolved or " separated " from the gold by boiling the ribbon in nitric acid, which attacks the silver and leaves the gold as a brownish scale or powder. This is washed, dried, weighed and melted.

Experience has shown that to obtain a complete separation of the metals there must be present 3 or more parts of silver to 1 of gold. So, if less than that amount of silver is present at first, it is necessary to add more silver to make up the required proportion. This operation is called " quartation." Accurate results can be obtained only when the correct amount of lead is used, and the proper proportions of gold and of silver—one and three—are present. It is usual to make a preliminary assay.

PRELIMINARY ASSAY

A sample of the alloy to be tested, weighing 0·25 gram, is wrapped up in a small piece of lead foil. In a muffle heated to cherry-red (c 900° C.) a cupel weighing 6 to 7 grams is placed, and allowed to get as hot as the furnace. Then 5 grams of lead are dropped into it. When the lead is liquid, the little packet of alloy in its lead-foil covering is taken in the tongs and dropped into the molten lead. The muffle door is closed until the alloy has melted and the liquid shows a bright upper surface. The cupel is now moved to the middle of the muffle and the furnace-door left open so that the air has easy access to it. After about twenty minutes all the lead will have been absorbed, as shown by the appearance of the " blick." This is a distinct brightening of the metal when the outer layer of lead oxide becomes thin enough, and the bright alloy suddenly shines through. The cupel is removed at once and allowed to cool down. The " button " of alloy is removed from the cupel and scrubbed with a brush to remove as much as possible of the bone-ash adhering to it, and to clean its surface. Its colour is then considered.

FINAL ASSAY

If the colour of the button is:

(a) *A good or reddish-yellow.* Then it will contain 90 to 70 per cent. of gold and 10 to 30 per cent. of silver. Say, 0·20 gram gold and 0·05 gram silver. To make up the proportion of 3 parts or more silver to 1 part gold, it is necessary to add 0·625 gram, or 2½ parts of silver, together with 5 grams of lead.

(b) *A greenish-yellow, or rather darker.* It will contain 75 to 55 per cent. of gold, and 25 to 45 per cent. of silver. Say, 0·16 gram gold and 0·09 gram silver. To this should be added 0·50 gram, or 2 parts silver, and 5 grams of lead.

(c) *A scarcely perceptible yellow tint.* It will contain 50 to 40 per cent. gold and 50 to 60 per cent. silver. Say, 0·12 gram gold and 0·13 silver. To this add 0·25 gram or 1 part silver, and 5 grams of lead.

(d) *Silver white.* It has 45 per cent. or less of gold and 55 per cent. or more of silver. Say, 0·11 gram of gold and 0·14 of silver. To this add 0·25 gram of silver, and 5 grams of lead.

If the gold alloy happens to be one with copper only as an alloying material, then a sample of the usual weight, 0·25 gram, is taken, with 8 grams of lead. This is thirty-two times the weight of the sample, against 5 grams, or twenty times the weight for the gold-silver-copper alloy.

To proceed with the assay. The cupel is heated, and the sample of alloy, together with the silver for quartation and two-thirds of the lead dropped into it. The last third of the lead is added when the first part has been absorbed. When the " blick " appears, the cupel is removed from the furnace. When cold the button is lifted from the cupel, and, after being scrubbed clean, it is flattened with a clean-faced hammer on a smooth stake. It is annealed, and rolled down in the flatting mills to about 0·01 inch (size 3, B. Metal Gauge) in thickness. It is then coiled into a tight roll, known as a " cornet." In some dilute nitric acid (water 1 part, acid 1 part) the cornet is boiled for ten to fifteen minutes. It is then removed and washed in boiling water, before being put into a fresh solution of acid. This is made of water, 1 part, and nitric acid, 2 parts. After boiling for some twenty minutes the cornet is removed, for by this time all the silver will have been dissolved. The gold will remain as a brown scale or powder. It is carefully washed to remove the acid, and heated in an oven to dry it. It contracts considerably on drying. The gold is carefully weighed, and the difference from its former weight noted. This represents the amount of alloying material. A certain, quite small, quantity of copper may yet remain in the gold, and it cannot be eliminated even by a second cupellation with a fresh quantity of lead.

For the cupellation of English Standard silver, six times its weight in lead is usually employed.

HALLMARKING

By British law the quality of all gold or silver articles (with some exceptions, including some jewellery) must be determined by assay at certain " Offices " or " Halls," and if found to be up to the required standard, they are stamped with a series of marks. These marks, collectively, are known as the " Hallmark." They are: The " maker's " or " private " mark of the manufacturer (or, in a few cases, that of the dealer). This, nearly always, consists of the initials of the individual or firm. The mark is stamped on the article, whether of gold or silver, by the maker himself before the work goes to the " Hall " for assaying and stamping.

Then three official marks, stamped by the " Hall " after the assay has proved satisfactory. They are:

1. The " standard marks," which indicate the quality of the gold or silver article.

2. The " city mark," of the town in which the Hall or Office is situated.

3. The " year mark," the year in which the work was assayed and stamped.

Also, formerly, (4) A " duty mark." This mark was discontinued in 1890 after being in use for rather more than a century. It indicated that a tax on the article had been paid.

1. *The " standard marks," for gold*

For London, Birmingham, Sheffield and Chester it is a Crown, with the additional mark 22, or 18, for 22-carat or 18-carat work respectively. Between 1576 and 1844 a Lion passant was used instead of a crown on 22-carat work. Edinburgh and Glasgow have the Thistle with the mark 22, or 18, for 22-carat or 18-carat work respectively. Glasgow has also a Lion rampant on both 22-carat and 18-carat work. In 1854 three standards lower than 18-carat were instituted. They were 15, 12 and 9-carat. Since 1932 only two lower standards are recognized. They are " 14 " and " ·585," used together, for 14-carat work, and " 9 " and " ·375," used together, for 9-carat work. All the Assay Offices in the United Kingdom follow this ruling. In the same year the standards " 15 " and " ·625," used together, for 15-carat work, and " 12 " and " ·5," used together, for 12-carat work, were discontinued.

The standard marks for silver

STERLING SILVER (925 parts of fine silver per 1000).

London and Birmingham. A Lion passant.

Sheffield and Chester. A Lion passant guardant.

Edinburgh. A Thistle.

Glasgow. A Thistle and a Lion rampant.

BRITANNIA STANDARD (958·4 parts of fine silver per 1000). This standard was instituted in 1697, but as the metal is rather soft it does not wear so well as standard silver. It is but little used.

London and Chester. A Lion's head erased, and a seated figure of Britannia.

Birmingham and Sheffield. A figure of Britannia.

Edinburgh and Glasgow. A Thistle and a figure of Britannia.

2. *The " city " or " assay office " mark, for gold and silver*

London. The office mark is the Leopard's Head (the arms of the Goldsmiths' Company).

Birmingham. An anchor. This mark is not found on gold until the year 1824, for at the foundation of the Birmingham Office in 1773, until 1824, it was authorized to hallmark silver only.

Chester. A sword between three garbs. For gold and silver.

Sheffield. For gold, a York Rose. For silver, a Crown.

Edinburgh. A Castle. For gold and silver.

Glasgow. The city arms. These are a tree with a bell hanging from its branches, and a robin seated at the top, while across the trunk is a salmon with a ring in its mouth. All these objects are derived from legends concerning the life of St. Mungo, the patron saint of the city.

The following towns had assay offices which are now closed:

Exeter. A castle. The shield which bears it is divided into two parts by a verticle line. This office was working from mid-sixteenth century to 1882.

Newcastle. Three separate castles. Working from mid-seventeenth century to 1883.

Norwich. A castle above a lion passant guardant. From sixteenth century to 1701.

York. On a cross, five lions passant guardant. From mid-sixteenth century to 1856.

For Irish hallmarks see below.

3. *The year mark, or date letter, for gold and silver.*

To indicate its year of manufacture or, more exactly, the year of its hallmarking, each office stamps a work submitted to it with a letter of the alphabet. The letter employed is altered year by year;

and when one series of letters has been used up, a new series is commenced composed of letters of a different type, perhaps on a shield of a different shape. This series runs its course, to be supplanted in due time by new series and new shields. From 1478 onwards London has employed a cycle of twenty letters (A to U, omitting J). The other offices have adopted series of twenty, twenty-five or twenty-six years. The series employed by different offices do not run concurrently, nor do they begin on the same day, and in no case does the year begin on January 1st. As a result each year mark is used for parts of two consecutive years, say, May 29th, 1874, to May 28th, 1875. Tables showing the date letters of the different assay offices with the year in which each was employed may be found in the usual books of reference.

4. *The duty mark, now discontinued.* A tax was levied on gold and silver ware between the years 1784 and 1890. As evidence that it had been paid, a stamp was placed upon each piece of work. The mark represented the head of the reigning sovereign, George III or IV, William IV or Victoria.

Irish Hallmarks

The Dublin Assay Office received its charter from King Charles I in the year 1637, and in general it followed the practice of the other Assay Offices. At the establishment of the Irish Free State in 1922, the Dublin Office (the only one in Eire) came under Irish law, and its regulations differ somewhat from those current in the United Kingdom.

The marks recognized now are the Maker's Mark—this consists of initials only—and three official marks, affixed by the Dublin Assay Office.

1. *The standard marks for gold*
   For 22 carat quality the mark is a harp, crowned.
   ,, 20 ,,   ,,   ,,   ,,   a plume of three feathers.
   ,, 18 ,,   ,,   ,,   ,,   a unicorn's head, erased.
   ,, 14 ,,   ,,   ,,   marks are the figures 14 and ·585.
   ,, 9 ,,   ,,   ,,   ,,   ,,   9 and ·375.

   The standard mark for silver
   Only one quality is recognized. The mark is for Sterling silver, and is a harp, crowned, as on 22-carat gold.

2. *The official mark*, covering the whole of the Irish Free State, is a figure of Hibernia seated by a harp, and holding in her right hand a spray of palm or olive.

3. *The year mark, or date letter*

The Dublin office adopted the usual practice of using a letter of the alphabet to indicate the year in which the work was marked. The type of letter and the shape of the shield are changed periodically. From January 1st, 1932 onwards, the twelve-month period for each date letter commences on January 1st.

4. *A duty mark, now discontinued*

From 1730 to 1807 this was a figure of Hibernia. After that date the head of the reigning sovereign was used. The plate tax, and the mark, were discontinued in 1890.

Foreign plate

Gold and silver ware manufactured in Eire or in any other " foreign " country, on importation into the United Kingdom, must be submitted for assay and hallmarking. For such wares different marks are employed by each of the six assay offices in the United Kingdom. Eire has a similar rule concerning wares manufactured in the United Kingdom or any other " foreign " country. Foreign wares exposed for sale are liable to confiscation if not so marked.

CHAPTER XL

VARIOUS TABLES AND STANDARDS

MEASURES OF LENGTH

THE YARD is the distance, at 60° Fahrenheit, between two marks on a bronze bar deposited with the Board of Trade, London. Gauges for the inch, foot and yard may be found on the north side of Trafalgar Square, and in the Guildhall, London.

The metre is the length, at 0° Centigrade, of a platinum bar preserved at Sèvres, near Paris, and known as the Mètre des Archives.

1 inch (in.) = 25·39977 millimetres (mm.).

12 inches = 1 foot (ft.) = 30·479 cm.

63,360 inches = 5280 feet = 1760 yards = 1 statute mile = 1·6094 kilometres.

1 millimetre = 0·039370113 inch = about $\frac{1}{25}$ inch.

10 mm. = 1 centimetre (cm.) = 0·3937 inch.

100 mm. = 10 cm. = 1 decimetre (dm).

1000 mm. = 100 cm. = 10 dm. = 1 metre (m.) = 39·370113 ins. = 3·2808 ft. = 1·0936 yard.

1 kilometre (km.) = 1000 m. = 0·62137 mile.

A kilometre is approximately five-eighths of a mile: so that 8 kilometres (4·97082 miles) may be regarded as 5 miles.

1 acre = 208·7103 feet square.

CONVERSION TABLE

To convert

Inches into millimetres multiply by 25·39977

Millimetres into inches multiply by 0·03937

SURFACE MEASURES

1 square inch (sq. in.) = 645·16 sq. mm.

144 square inches (sq. in.) = 1 square foot (sq. ft.).

9 square feet (sq. ft.) = 1 square yard (sq. yd.)

1 square centimetre (sq. cm.) = 0·15498 square inches.

1 square metre (sq. m.) = 10·763 sq. ft. = 1·19596 sq. yd.

1 square kilometre (sq. km.) = 0·38611 sq. mile.

MEASURES OF WEIGHT

A pound (avoirdupois) is the weight of a certain piece of platinum deposited with the Board of Trade, London.

A kilogram is the weight of a piece of platinum at Paris known as the Kilogram des Archives.

Troy weight is used in Great Britain for precious metals : platinum, gold, silver, etc. But the decimal system is now generally employed when dealing with fractions of an ounce. Thus $17\frac{1}{2}$ ounces of silver are written 17·5 oz., rather than 17 oz. 10 dwt. There is no Troy pound.

Avoirdupois weight is in general use for other materials.

1 grain troy = 0·00208 oz. troy = 0·0648 gram = 1 grain av.

24 grains troy = 1 pennyweight (dwt.) = 0·05 oz. troy = 1·5552 grams.

1 ounce troy = 31·1035 grams = 480 grains = 1·0971 oz av.

16 drams avoirdupois (dr.) = 1 oz. av.

1 ounce avoirdupois = 437·5 grains – 28·3495 gram = 0·9114 oz. troy.

1 pound avoirdupois = 7000 grains = 16 oz. av. = 14 oz. 11 dwt. 16 gr. troy = 453·5924 gram.

1 hundredweight (cwt.) = 50·8 kilograms = 112 pounds (lb.).

1 ton, British = 1016 kilograms = 2240 lb. = 20 cwt.

1 ton, American = 908 kilograms = 2000 lb.

1 milligram (mgm.) = 0·015 grains.

1 gram (grm.) = 15·43235 grains = 0·032151 oz. troy = 0·352736 oz. av. = 0·0022046 lb. av.

1 kilogram (kg.) = 2·2046223 lb. av. = 35·2734 oz. av. = 32·1507 oz. troy = 1000 gram.

1000 kilos (1 tonne) = ·098421 British ton.

1 cubic centimetre of water = 1 gram = 15·432 grains = 0·03527 oz. av. = 0·03215 oz. troy.

1 cubic inch of water, distilled = 252·458 grains.

1 gallon water, distilled (277·274 cub. in.) = 10 lb.

1 cubic foot of water = 62·321 lb. (legal standard).

35·943 cubic feet of water = 224 gallons = 1 ton.

= CONVERSION TABLES

Grams	into grains	multiply by	15·43235
Grams	,, ounces av.	,,	0·03527
Grams	,, ounces troy	,,	0·03215
Centigrams	,, grains	,,	0·15432
Kilograms	,, ounces av.	,,	35·2739
Kilograms	,, pounds av.	,,	2·2046
Kilograms	,, ounces troy	,,	32·1507
Ounces av.	,, grams	,,	28·3495
Ounces av.	,, kilograms	,,	0·2835
Pounds av.	,, kilograms	,,	0·4536
Ounces troy	,, grams	,,	31·1035
Ounces troy	,, kilograms	,,	0·0311
Gallons	,, litres	,,	4·54102
Litres	,, gallons	,,	0·220215

WEIGHT OF PRECIOUS STONES

The British legal standard for the weighing of precious stones and pearls, from the year 1913 onwards, has been the Metric Carat of 200 milligrams. This standard corresponds with that in use in the Continental diamond markets, in South Africa, and in the United States. Before 1913 a carat of 205 milligrams was most generally employed.

The weight of a diamond is reckoned in carats and in one-hundredths of a carat (in decimals), though very often the fractions of a carat such as ½ or ¼ are used in conversation. But for pearls the carat may be reckoned as being composed of 4 grains. So a pearl may be spoken of as a 2-grainer or 3-grainer. Small diamonds are referred to by the number that would go to a carat: 40, 50, 100, 300 and so on.

Approximately 141¾ metric carats = 1 ounce avoirdupois.

MEASURES OF CAPACITY

The gallon is the volume occupied by 10 pounds of distilled water weighed in air at the temperature of 62° Fahrenheit. The litre is the volume of 1 kilogram of water *in vacuo* at 4° Centigrade.

1 fluid ounce (water) = 1 ounce avoirdupois = 28·417 cu. cm. = 0·0284123 litre.

1 pint (water) = 0·56824 litre = 568·245 cu. cm.

2 pints = 1 quart (Imperial).

4 quarts = 1 gallon (Imperial) = 4·545963 litre.

1 gallon U.S.A. = 0·83254 gallon (Imp.) = 3·785 litre = 231 cu. inch.

1 gallon (Imp.) = 1·2 gallon (U.S.A.) = 4·545 litre.

1 cubic centimetre (water) = 1 gram = 0·061 cubic inch.

1000 cu. cm. (water) = 1 litre = 1 kilogram.

1 litre=1·7598 pint (Imp.)=0·2201 gallon (Imp.)=61·0363 cu. in. = 0·035322 cu. ft. = 0·26417 (U.S.A.) gallon.

1 cubic metre (water) = 1000 litres = 1000 kilograms = 1 metric ton.

1 cubic metre = 35·31338 cu. ft. = 1·3079 cu yd.

1 cubic inch = 16·386 cu. cm.

1 cubic foot = 28·311 litre.

1 cubic yard = 764·4 litre.

MEASURES OF TEMPERATURE

There are two different scales to which thermometers are divided. They are known as Fahrenheit and Centigrade, the first being named after its author. The Fahrenheit scale is in general use in this country. The Centigrade is in regular use among scientists, and in countries which use the decimal standards.

The two scales are divided thus:

	Fahrenheit	Centigrade
Water boils	212° F.	100° C.
Freezing point (melting ice) .	32° F.	0° C.
Zero	0° F.	0° C.

CONVERSION TABLES

Fahrenheit to Centigrade

From the number of degrees Fahrenheit subtract 32. Multiply the result by 5, and divide by 9.

Examples. (a) What temperature on the Centigrade scale corresponds with 86° F.? Answer. Subtract 32° from 86° This makes 54°. Multiply by 5 = 270°. Divide by 9 = 30°. Result, 30° C.

(b) To what temperature on the Centigrade scale does — 13° F. correspond? Answer. Subtract 32° from — 13. This makes — 45°. Multiply — 45° by 5, and divide by 9. Result, — 25° C.

Centigrade to Fahrenheit

Multiply the number of degrees Centigrade by 9, divide by 5 and add 32.

Examples. (c) Find on the Fahrenheit scale the temperature corresponding with 45° C. Answer. 9 times 45 are 405. Divide 405 by 5. Result, 81. Add 32 to 81. Result, 113° F.

(d) What temperature Fahrenheit corresponds with —40° C.

Answer. The temperature is $40 \times \dfrac{9}{5} = 72°$ F. below the

freezing point (32° F.). Or 40° F. below the zero of Fahrenheit Therefore — 40° C. = — 40° F.

A Rough Method of Estimating High Temperatures

Degrees centigrade

232 . . .	Tin melts.
419 . . .	Zinc melts.
500–600 . . .	Faint red glow.
650–700 . . .	Dull red.
800 . . .	Cherry red.
893 . . .	Standard silver melts.
900 . . .	Bright red.
961 . . .	Fine silver melts.
1000 . . .	Very bright red, verging into yellow.
1063 . . .	Fine gold melts.
1083 . . .	Fine copper melts.
1280 . . .	White heat.
1350 . . .	Steel melts? varies.
1480 . . .	Nickel melts. Blinding white.
1500 . . .	Iron melts? varies.
1773 . . .	Platinum melts.

Temperatures obtainable in:—

	Degrees Centigrade
Bunsen burner flame	1100–1350
Méker burner flame	1450–1500
Petrol blowlamp flame	1500–1600
Oxy-hydrogen flame	about 2000
Oxy-acetylene flame	,, 2400
Electric arc	,, 3500
Electric arc (under pressure) . . .	,, 3600
Sun	,, 5500

Decimal Fractions of an Inch in Millimetres

in.	mm.	in.	mm.	in.	mm.
·01	·254	·35	8·890	·68	17·272
·02	·508	·36	9·114	·69	17·526
·03	·762	·37	9·398	·70	17·780
·04	1·016	·38	9·652	·71	18·034
·05	1·270	·39	9·906	·72	18·288
·06	1·524	·40	10·160	·73	18·542
·07	1·778	·41	10·414	·74	18·796
·08	2·032	·42	10·668	·75	19·050
·09	2·286	·43	10·922	·76	19·304
·10	2·540	·44	11·176	·77	19·558
·11	2·794	·45	11·430	·78	19·812
·12	3·048	·46	11·684	·79	20·066
·13	3·302	·47	11·938	·80	20·320
·14	3·556	·48	12·192	·81	20·574
·15	3·810	·49	12·446	·82	20·828
·16	4·064	·50	12·700	·83	21·082
·17	4·318	·51	12·954	·84	21·336
·18	4·572	·52	13·208	·85	21·590
·19	4·826	·53	13·462	·86	21·844
·20	5·080	·54	13·716	·87	22·098
·21	5·334	·55	13·970	·88	22·352
·22	5·588	·56	14·224	·89	22·606
·23	5·842	·57	14·478	·90	22·860
·24	6·096	·58	14·732	·91	23·114
·25	6·350	·59	14·986	·92	23·368
·26	6·604	·60	15·240	·93	23·622
·27	6·858	·61	15·494	·94	23·876
·28	7·112	·62	15·748	·95	24·130
·29	7·366	·63	16·002	·96	24·384
·30	7·620	·64	16·256	·97	24·638
·31	7·874	·65	16·510	·98	24·892
·32	8·128	·66	16·764	·99	25·146
·33	8·382	·67	17·018	1·00	25·400
·34	8·636				

Equivalent Values of Millimetres and Inches

Millimetres	Inches	Millimetres	Inches	Millimetres	Inches
1	·0394	10	·3937	19	·7480
2	·0787	11	·4331	20	·7874
3	·1181	12	·4724	21	·8268
4	·1575	13	·5118	22	·8661
5	·1968	14	·5512	23	·9055
6	·2362	15	·5906	24	·9449
7	·2756	16	·6299	25	·9843
8	·3150	17	·6693	26	1·0236
9	·3543	18	·7087		

MEASURES OF LENGTH

Inches	Millimetres	Decimals of an inch	Inches	Millimetres	Decimals of an inch
1/64	·39687	·01563	17/32	13·49362	·53125
1/32	·79374	·03125	9/16	14·28737	·5625
1/16	1·58748	·0625	19/32	15·08111	·59375
3/32	2·38123	·09375	5/8	15·87485	·625
1/8	3·17497	·125	21/32	16·66859	·65625
5/32	3·96871	·15625	11/16	17·46234	·6875
3/16	4·76245	·1875	23/32	18·25608	·71875
7/32	5·55620	·21875	3/4	19·04982	·750
1/4	6·34994	·250	25/32	19·84356	·78125
9/32	7·14368	·28125	13/16	20·63731	·8125
5/16	7·93743	·3125	27/32	21·43105	·84375
11/32	8·73117	·34375	7/8	22·22479	·875
3/8	9·52491	·375	29/32	23·01853	·90625
13/32	10·31865	·40625	15/16	23·81228	·9375
7/16	11·11240	·4375	31/32	24·60602	·96875
15/32	11·90614	·46875	1	25·39977	1·000
1/2	12·69988	·50			

PENNYWEIGHTS AND GRAINS WITH DECIMALS OF OZ. TROY
TROY WEIGHT WITH MILLIGRAMS

Dwts.	Decimals	Grains	Decimals	Oz.	Milligrams
20	1·000	24	·050	·001	31·1035
19	·950	23	·047916	·002	62·2070
18	·900	22	·045833	·003	93·3105
17	·850	21	·04375	·004	124·4140
16	·800	20	·041083	·005	155·5175
15	·750	19	·039	·010	311·0350
14	·700	18	·0375	·020	622·070
13	·650	17	·035416	·030	933·1050
12	·600	16	·033	·040	1244·140
11	·550	15	·03125	·050	1555·1750
10	·500	14	·02966	·10	3110·350
9	·450	13	·027083	·20	6220·700
8	·400	12	·025	·30	9331·050
7	·350	11	·022916	·40	12441·40
6	·300	10	·020833	·50	15551·750
5	·250	9	·01875	·75	23327·625
4	·200	8	·01666	1·0	31103·50
3	·150	7	·014583		
2	·100	6	·0125	1·0 oz. = 31·1035 grams.	
1	·050	5	·010416		
		4	·00833		
		3	·00625		
		2	·004166		
		1	·002083		

Properties of Circles

1. Diameter $\times$ 3·14159 = circumference.

To find the circumference, i.e. the distance round the edge of a circle, multiply its diameter by $3\frac{1}{7}$. Thus, if the top of a bowl measures 7 inches across it will measure 22 inches round the edge. This rule is a very important one, as it is used so frequently. Three and one-seventh is the nearest easy fraction to 3·14159, and it gives results correctly enough for practical purposes.

2. Diameter squared $\times$ ·7854 = area of circle.

To find the area of a circle. Multiply its diameter by itself and the result by ·7854. Thus for a circle 10 inches in diameter. Multiply 10 by itself, $10 \times 10 = 100$ square inches. Multiply 100 square inches by ·7854. The result is 78·54 inches—a little over $78\frac{1}{2}$ square inches, which is the area of a circle measuring 10 inches across the middle.

The table printed below, " Areas of Circles," may be employed in conjunction with a table printed overleaf entitled " Approximate weight of 1 square inch of silver," etc., thus. To find the weight of a disc of silver 8 inches in diameter, size 12 on the metal gauge.

Areas of Circles

Diameter	Area	Diameter	Area	Diameter	Area
1 in.	·7854	$4\frac{1}{2}$ ins.	15·9043	$12\frac{1}{2}$ ins.	122·718
$1\frac{1}{8}$,,	·9940	$4\frac{3}{4}$,,	17·7205	13 ,,	132·732
$1\frac{1}{4}$,,	1·2271	5 ,,	19·6350	$13\frac{1}{2}$,,	143·139
$1\frac{3}{8}$,,	1·4848	$5\frac{1}{4}$,,	21·6475	14 ,,	153·938
$1\frac{1}{2}$,,	1·7671	$5\frac{1}{2}$,,	23·7583	$14\frac{1}{2}$,,	165·130
$1\frac{5}{8}$,,	2·0739	$5\frac{3}{4}$,,	25·9672	15 ,,	176·715
$1\frac{3}{4}$,,	2·4052	6 ,,	28·2744	$15\frac{1}{2}$,,	188·692
$1\frac{7}{8}$,,	2·7611	$6\frac{1}{4}$,,	30·6796	16 ,,	201·062
2 ins.	3·1416	$6\frac{1}{2}$,,	33·1831	$16\frac{1}{2}$,,	213·825
$2\frac{1}{8}$,,	3·5465	$6\frac{3}{4}$,,	35·7847	17 ,,	226·980
$2\frac{1}{4}$,,	3·9760	7 ,,	38·4846	$17\frac{1}{2}$,,	240·528
$2\frac{3}{8}$,,	4·4302	$7\frac{1}{2}$,,	44·1787	18 ,,	254·469
$2\frac{1}{2}$,,	4·9087	8 ,,	50·2656	$18\frac{1}{2}$,,	268·803
$2\frac{5}{8}$,,	5·4119	$8\frac{1}{2}$,,	56·7451	19 ,,	283·529
$2\frac{3}{4}$,,	5·9395	9 ,,	63·6174	$19\frac{1}{2}$,,	298·648
$2\frac{7}{8}$,,	6·4918	$9\frac{1}{2}$,,	70·8823	20 ,,	314·180
3 ,,	7·0686	10 ,,	78·5400	21 ,,	346·361
$3\frac{1}{4}$,,	8·2957	$10\frac{1}{2}$,,	86·5903	22 ,,	380·133
$3\frac{1}{2}$,,	9·6211	11 ,,	95·0334	23 ,,	415·476
$3\frac{3}{4}$,,	11·0446	$11\frac{1}{2}$,,	103·869	24 ,,	452·390
4 ,,	12·5664	12 ,,	113·097	25 ,,	490·875
$4\frac{1}{4}$,,	14·1862				

The area of a circle 8 inches in diameter is a little over 50¼ inches. A square inch of silver, size 12, weighs ·203 of an ounce. 50¼ multiplied by ·203 of an ounce gives 10·20 ounces (10⅕ oz.) which is the approximate weight of a circle of silver 8 inches in diameter, size 12.

The area of the surface of a sphere = the square of the diameter × 3·14159.

The solid contents of a sphere = one-sixth of the cube of the diameter × 3·14159.

The area of the curved surface of a cylinder = diameter × length × 3·14159.

The solid contents of a cylinder = square of the diameter × length × 0·7854.

APPROXIMATE WEIGHT OF 1 SQUARE INCH OF SILVER TO THE VARIOUS SIZES ON THE BIRMINGHAM METAL GAUGE

Gauge size	Approximate weight per square inch	Gauge size	Approximate weight per square inch
	Decimals of oz.		Decimals of oz.
1	·048	13	·215
2	·053	14	·243
3	·059	15	·272
4	·068	16	·289
5	·079	17	·311
6	·090	18	·334
7	·107	19	·351
8	·121	20	·368
9	·136	21	·387
10	·158	22	·416
11	·181	23	·435
12	·198	24	·458

WEIGHT OF METAL IN POUNDS PER SQUARE FOOT
Thickness in Standard Wire Gauge

S.W.G. of sheet	Thickness in decimals of an inch	Copper	Brass	Aluminium
0	·324	14·91	14·44	4·50
1	·300	13·82	13·38	4·17
2	·276	12·74	12·32	3·84
3	·252	11·60	11·26	3·51
4	·232	10·70	10·36	3·08
5	·212	9·78	9·47	2·81
6	·192	8·84	8·57	2·54
7	·176	8·11	7·85	2·34
8	·160	7·38	7·13	2·12
9	·144	6·62	6·41	1·91
10	·128	5·90	5·71	1·70
11	·116	5·33	5·18	1·54
12	·104	4·80	4·64	1·38
14	·080	3·68	3·57	1·06
16	·064	2·95	2·86	0·849
18	·048	2·21	2·15	0·637
20	·036	1·66	1·61	0·477
22	·028	1·29	1·25	0·371
24	·022	1·015	0·982	0·292
26	·018	0·830	0·804	0·239
28	·015	0·644	0·625	0·186
30	·012	0·552	0·536	0·159
32	·011	0·461	0·447	0·133
34	·009	0·415	0·402	0·120
36	·008	0·322	0·313	0·093
38	·006	0·276	0·268	0·079
40	·005	0·184	0·179	0·053

The Composition of Various Alloys

Alloy			Remarks
Aluminium bronze	9 parts copper	1 part aluminium	Best alloy for general purposes.
Bell metal	3 to 5 ,, ,,	1 ,, tin	
Brass	7 ,, ,,	3 parts zinc	For sheet metal and casting. Good colour.
,, white	7 ,, ,,	13 ,, zinc	Silver white colour.
Bronze coinage*	95 ,, ,,	4 ,, tin, 1 part zinc	English standard.
Bronze, malleable	19 ,, ,,	1 part tin	
Bronze, statuary	90 ,, ,,	6 parts tin, 3 zinc, 1 part lead	The best mixture for fine castings.
German silver	23 ,, ,,	17 ,, nickel, 10 parts zinc	Best alloy, but expensive owing to cost of nickel.
,,	20 ,, ,,	6 ,, nickel, 8 parts zinc	
Gilding metal	5 ,, ,,	1 part zinc	
Gold	9 ,, gold	2 parts silver, 1 part copper	18-carat gold. Rather pale.
,,	36 ,, ,,	7 ,, silver, 5 parts ,,	18-carat gold. Redder.
Gold coinage	22 ,, ,,	2 ,, copper	English standard (22-carat).
Gun metal	9 ,, copper	1 part tin	Strongest alloy. Zinc sometimes added.
Pewter †	4 ,, tin	1 ,, lead	Common. Other metal sometimes added.
,,	12 ,, ,,	1 ,, antimony	English standard.
Silver coinage ‡	222 ,, silver	18 parts copper	Good and strong.
Silver solder	3 ,, ,,	1 part brass wire	Good.
,,	2 ,, ,,	1 ,, brass wire or pins	
Soft solder	2 ,, tin	1 ,, lead	Plumbers'. For wiping joints.
,,	1 part ,,	2 parts ,,	
Speculum metal	2 parts copper	1 part tin	Perfectly white. Takes good polish.
Spelter for brazing	1 part ,,	1 ,, zinc	Strong.
,,	1 ,, ,,	2 parts zinc	More fusible. Weaker than the other.
Fusible metal for small casts	13 parts lead	3 ,, zinc, 6 parts bismuth	Very sharp casts.

* Modern bronze coinage no longer contains the tin content indicated.

† Modern pewter no longer contains lead, and is virtually tin with a small amount of antimony and copper.

‡ Modern silver coinage is a cupro-nickel alloy.

The Melting Points and Atomic Weights of Various Materials

Name	Cent.	Fahr.	Atomic weight
Aluminium . .	659·7°	1219·6°	26·97
Antimony . .	630·5°	1166·9°	121·76
Bismuth . . .	271·3°	520·3°	209
Brass . . .	1015° varies	1859°?	
Cadmium . . .	320·9°	609·62°	112·41
Copper . . .	1083°	1981·4°	63·57
Gold . . .	1063°	1945·4°	197·2
Ice . . .	0°	32°	
Iridium . .	2454°	4449°	193·1
Cast-iron . .	1100° varies	2012°?	
Iron (pure) . .	1535°	2795°	55·85
Lead . . .	327·4°	621·32°	207·21
Magnesium . .	649°	1200°	24·32
Mercury (solid) .	−38·87°	−37·966°	200·61
Nickel . . .	1455°	2619°	58·69
Platinum . . .	1773·5°	3192·3°	195·23
Silver . . .	960·5°	1728·9°	107·88
Steel . . .	1350° varies	2430°?	
Tin . . .	231·89°	417·5°	118·7
Water (boils) . .	100°	212°	
Zinc . . .	419·47°	787·1°	65·38
Common salt . .	801°	1441·8°	

The figures given above are for fine gold, fine silver, fine copper, etc. Those for alloys would differ.

Weight and Specific Gravity of Metals

	Troy oz.	Specific gravity
If platinum of given dimensions weighs . .	1·0	21·50
Fine gold of same dimensions will weigh . .	·900	19·33
22 carat	·820	17·60
20 ,, ...	·765	16·50
18 ,, ...	·725	15·55
15 ,, ...	·645	13·50
12 ,, ...	·590	12·75
9 ,, ...	·535	11·50
6 ,, ...	·505	10·90
Silver, fine	·495	10·70
Silver, standard	·490	10·50
Lead	·530	11·40
Bismuth	·455	9·80
Copper	·415	8·95
Nickel	·414	8·90
Brass	·375	8·10
Iron	·365	7·85
Tin	·340	7·30
Zinc	·335	7·15
Aluminium	·120	2·60

Whitworth Standard 55° Screw Threads for Bolts

Diameter of bolt		Number of threads per inch	Diameter at bottom of thread	Tapping Drill
Fractional sizes	Decimal sizes			
$\frac{1}{16}$	·0625	60	·0411	56
$\frac{3}{32}$	·09375	48	·0670	50
$\frac{1}{8}$	·125	40	·0929	40
$\frac{3}{16}$	·1875	24	·1341	$\frac{9}{64}$
$\frac{1}{4}$	·25	20	·1859	11 or $\frac{3}{16}$
$\frac{5}{16}$	·3125	18	·2413	D „ $\frac{1}{4}$
$\frac{3}{8}$	·375	16	·2949	N „ $\frac{19}{64}$
$\frac{7}{16}$	·4375	14	·3460	S „ $\frac{23}{64}$
$\frac{1}{2}$	·5	12	·3932	X „ $\frac{13}{32}$
$\frac{9}{16}$	·5625	12	·4557	$\frac{15}{32}$
$\frac{5}{8}$	·625	11	·5085	$\frac{33}{64}$
$\frac{11}{16}$	·6875	11	·5710	$\frac{37}{64}$
$\frac{3}{4}$	·75	10	·6219	$\frac{5}{8}$
$\frac{13}{16}$	·8125	10	·6844	$\frac{11}{16}$
$\frac{7}{8}$	·875	9	·7327	$\frac{47}{64}$
$\frac{15}{16}$	·9375	9	·7952	$\frac{13}{16}$
1	1·0	8	·8399	$\frac{27}{32}$
$1\frac{1}{8}$	1·125	7	·9420	$\frac{61}{64}$
$1\frac{1}{4}$	1·25	7	1·0670	$1\frac{5}{64}$
$1\frac{3}{8}$	1·375	6	1·1615	$1\frac{11}{64}$
$1\frac{1}{2}$	1·5	6	1·2865	$1\frac{19}{64}$
$1\frac{5}{8}$	1·625	5	1·3688	$1\frac{3}{8}$
$1\frac{3}{4}$	1·75	5	1·4938	$1\frac{1}{2}$
$1\frac{7}{8}$	1·875	4·5	1·5904	$1\frac{19}{32}$
2	2·0	4·5	1·7154	$1\frac{23}{32}$
$2\frac{1}{2}$	2·5	4	2·1798	$2\frac{5}{16}$
3	3·0	3·5	2·6340	$2\frac{41}{64}$
4	4·0	3	3·5731	
5	5·0	2·75	4·5343	
6	6·0	2·5	5·4877	

The standard Whitworth thread is inclined at an angle of 55°, one-sixth at top and bottom of thread being cut off and rounded.

NOTE: The threads in this table are too coarse for art metalwork.

BRITISH ASSOCIATION (B.A.) GAUGE FOR APPARATUS SCREWS

This is adopted as the Standard Screw Gauge by Post Office Telegraphs Department and most large Electrical Firms

BA No.	Threads per inch	Outside Diameter	Tapping Drill
0	25·38	·2362	12
1	28·25	·2087	19
2	31·36	·1850	26
3	34·84	·1614	30
4	38·46	·1417	34
5	43·10	·1260	40
6	47·85	·1102	44
7	52·91	·0984	48
8	59·17	·0866	51
9	64·94	·0748	53
10	72·46	·0669	56
11	81·97	·0591	58
12	90·91	·0511	63
13	102·0	·0472	65
14	109·9	·0394	70
15	120·5	·0354	72
16	133·3	·0311	74
17	149·3	·0276	76
18	169·5	·0244	77
19	181·8	·0213	79
20	212·8	·0189	
21	232·6	·0165	
22	256·4	·0146	
23	285·7	·0130	
24	323·6	·0114	

The thread is similar to the Whitworth, but the included angle is 47½ degrees.

AMERICAN STANDARD NATIONAL COARSE SCREW THREAD

This has an included angle of 60 degrees, and the top and bottom are flattened one-eighth of the full depth.

Diameter at top of thread		Diameter at bottom	Number of threads to inch	Tap drill size
Millimetres	Inches	Inches		
6·350	$\frac{1}{4}$	·185	20	7
7·937	$\frac{5}{16}$	·240	18	F
9·525	$\frac{3}{8}$	·294	16	$\frac{5}{16}$
11·112	$\frac{7}{16}$	·345	14	U
12·699	$\frac{1}{2}$	·400	13	$\frac{27}{64}$
14·287	$\frac{9}{16}$	·454	12	$\frac{31}{64}$
15·874	$\frac{5}{8}$	·507	11	$\frac{17}{32}$
19·049	$\frac{3}{4}$	·620	10	$\frac{21}{32}$
22·224	$\frac{7}{8}$	·731	9	$\frac{49}{64}$
25·399	1	·837	8	$\frac{7}{8}$
34·924	$1\frac{3}{8}$	1·158	6	$1\frac{7}{32}$
38·098	$1\frac{1}{2}$	1·283	6	$1\frac{11}{32}$
41·273	$1\frac{5}{8}$	1·389	$5\frac{1}{2}$	$1\frac{3}{8}$
44·148	$1\frac{3}{4}$	1·490	5	$1\frac{9}{16}$
47·623	$1\frac{7}{8}$	1·615	5	$1\frac{19}{32}$
50·798	2	1·711	$4\frac{1}{2}$	$1\frac{25}{32}$
57·148	$2\frac{1}{4}$	1·961	$4\frac{1}{2}$	$1\frac{29}{32}$
63·497	$2\frac{1}{2}$	2·175	4	$2\frac{1}{4}$
69·847	$2\frac{3}{4}$	2·425	4	$2\frac{1}{2}$
76·197	3	2·675	$3\frac{1}{2}$	$2\frac{3}{4}$

NOTE: The threads in this table are too coarse for art metalwork.

CHAPTER XLI

GAUGES

THE THICKNESS of a sheet of metal, or of a wire, is measured by a tool known as a gauge. This often takes the form of an oblong or circular sheet of steel with a number of slots cut round its edge. The slots are numbered, and they vary in width in regular order, from quite narrow ones, too small to admit the edge of a sheet of writing-paper, up to $\frac{1}{4}$ inch or more. In England there is, unfortunately, no standard gauge for all materials. In buying metal it is therefore advisable to mention which gauge you are using. For sheet gold, silver and copper, the " metal " gauge, that is to say, the Birmingham Metal Gauge, is generally, though not always, used. In the United States the Brown and Sharp (B. & S.) gauge is the standard gauge for sheet metal.

In the following pages, where the principal gauges in use for metalwork are printed in parallel columns, equal measurements are placed immediately opposite to each other.

To transfer a given thickness from one gauge to another it is only necessary to glance across the page, and the exact, or the nearest, equivalent will be found, in its proper column opposite. Thus, on the Birmingham Wire Gauge the nearest equivalent to 14 on the Birmingham Metal Gauge is 19 on the B.W.G. They differ by only a thousandth of an inch.

Size 11 on the Metal Gauge is the same thickness as No. 21, Standard Wire Gauge, or 21, B.W.G., or 66 on Stubs' Steel Wire Gauge, and 67 on the Morse Twist Drill and Steel Wire Gauge. It is 32 thousandths of an inch, or ·81 millimetre, in thickness.

In the first column the thickness is given in decimals of an inch. Thus ·500 represents a thickness of $\frac{1}{2}$ inch, or 500 thousandths parts of an inch; ·464 means 464 thousandths of an inch, and so on. A measurement like ·2055 represents 2055 ten-thousandths of an inch or $205\frac{1}{2}$ thousandths of an inch.

In the second column are given the sizes on the Birmingham Metal Gauge. This gauge is the one generally used for sheet gold and silver. It is also used for copper, brass, etc. Gold- and silver-smiths use it almost exclusively. Throughout this book it has been constantly referred to as " the metal gauge."

The third column gives the Imperial Standard Wire Gauge. It is very generally used for wire or sheet metal.

In the fourth column is the Morse Twist Drill and Steel Wire Gauge. Large numbers of American Twist Drills are made to this gauge.

The fifth and sixth columns give Stubs' Iron Wire Gauge and Stubs' Steel Wire Gauge. In using these gauges the difference between the two should be constantly borne in mind. The Stubs' Iron Wire Gauge is commonly known as the Birmingham Wire Gauge, sometimes as the English Standard Wire or Soft Wire Gauge. It is much used for iron, copper or brass wire. The Stubs' Steel Wire Gauge is used for measuring drawn steel wire or drill rods of Stubs' make, and has been adopted by many makers of American drills.

The last column gives the thickness in millimetres.

It is well to keep to one gauge as much as possible. A metal-worker, goldsmith or silversmith can get on quite well with the Birmingham Metal Gauge. It is in general use in the trade for measuring gold and silver. But he must not use it when buying steel wire or drills, or sheet iron, or aluminium, or many other things, unless he makes it quite clear to the salesman that he is using just that gauge. Gauges, again, get worn. The sheet of metal to be measured may fit tightly or loosely into the slot. Its extreme edge may be expanded by rough usage and so the sheet will appear to be thicker than it really is. All these things cause uncertainty as to the thickness of metal supplied you. The only way to make quite sure is by using a micrometer. These convenient tools measure thicknesses by means of a screw and vernier. If you have one of these you are independent of all the other gauges. The first column in the table below gives you the number of thousandths of an inch to which you must set the micrometer to correspond with any number on either of the other gauges. Thus ·250 means 250 thousandths of an inch, or $\frac{1}{4}$ inch; ·055 in the first column means 55 thousandths of an inch. If you set the micrometer to that, it will correspond with size 17 on the Birmingham Metal Gauge, and No. 54 on both the Morse Twist Drill Gauge and Stubs' Steel Wire

Gauge; ·0095 means 9·5 or 9½ thousandths of an inch. It is 95 ten-thousandths of an inch; ·0080 is 8 thousandths of an inch or 80 ten-thousandths of an inch—which is the same thing. Micrometers to measure in ten-thousandths of an inch are considerably more expensive than those which go only to thousandths. But they are unnecessary except for very fine scientific work.

COMPARATIVE TABLE OF THE VARIOUS GAUGES

Decimals of inch	B'ghm Metal Gauge	I. Standard Wire Gauge	Morse Twist Drill and Steel Wire Gauge	Stubs' Iron Wire Gauge or B'ghm Wire Gauge	Stubs' Steel Wire Gauge	Milli-metres
·500	—	7/0	—	—	—	12·70
·464	—	6/0	—	—	—	11·79
·454	—	—	—	0000	—	11·53
·432	—	5/0	—	—	—	10·97
·425	—	—	—	000	—	10·79
·413	—	—	—	—	Z	10·49
·404	—	—	—	—	Y	10·26
·400	—	4/0	—	—	—	10·16
·397	—	—	—	—	X	10·08
·386	—	—	—	—	W	9·80
·380	—	—	—	00	—	9·65
·377	—	—	—	—	V	9·58
·372	—	3/0	—	—	—	9·45
·368	—	—	—	—	U	9·35
·358	—	—	—	—	T	9·09
·348	—	2/0	—	—	S	8·84
·340	—	—	—	0	—	8·64
·339	—	—	—	—	R	8·61
·332	—	—	—	—	Q	8·43
·324	—	1/0	—	—	—	8·23
·323	—	—	—	—	P	8·20
·316	—	—	—	—	O	8·03
·302	—	—	—	—	N	7·67
·300	—	1	—	1	—	7·62
·295	—	—	—	—	M	7·49
·290	—	—	—	—	L	7·37
·289	—	—	—	—	—	7·34
·284	—	—	—	2	—	7·21
·281	—	—	—	—	K	7·14
·278	—	—	—	—	—	7·06
·277	—	—	—	—	J	7·04
·276	—	2	—	—	—	7·01
·272	—	—	—	—	I	6·91
·270	—	—	—	—	—	6·85
·266	—	—	—	—	H	6·76
·261	—	—	—	—	G	6·63
·259	—	—	—	3	—	6·58

COMPARATIVE TABLE OF THE VARIOUS GAUGES—*continued*

Decimals of inch	B'ghm Metal Gauge	I. Standard Wire Gauge	Morse Twist Drill and Steel Wire Gauge	Stubs' Iron Wire Gauge or B'ghm Wire Gauge	Stubs' Steel Wire Gauge	Milli-metres
·257	—	—	—	—	F	6·53
·252	3	—	—	—	—	6·40
·250	36	—	—	—	E	6·35
·246	—	—	—	—	D	6·25
·242	—	—	—	—	C	6·15
·238	35	—	—	4	B	6·04
·234	—	—	—	—	A	5·94
·232	—	4	—	—	—	5·89
·228	—	—	1	—	—	5·79
·227	—	—	—	—	1	5·77
·221	—	—	2	—	—	5·61
·220	—	—	—	5	—	5·59
·219	—	—	—	—	2	5·56
·216	34	—	—	—	—	5·48
·213	—	—	3	—	—	5·41
·212	—	5	—	—	3	5·38
·209	—	—	4	—	—	5·31
·207	—	—	—	—	4	5·26
·2055	—	—	5	—	—	5·22
·204	—	—	6	—	5	5·18
·203	—	—	—	6	—	5·16
·201	—	—	7	—	6	5·11
·200	33	—	—	—	—	5·08
·199	—	—	8	—	7	5·06
·197	—	—	—	—	8	5·01
·196	—	—	9	—	—	4·98
·194	—	—	—	—	9	4·93
·1935	—	—	10	—	—	4·91
·192	—	6	—	—	—	4·88
·191	—	—	11	—	10	4·86
·189	—	—	12	—	—	4·80
·188	—	—	—	—	11	4·78
·185	—	—	13	—	12	4·70
·182	32	—	14	—	13	4·62
·180	—	—	15	7	14	4·57
·178	—	—	—	—	15	4·52
·177	—	—	16	—	—	4·50
·176	—	7	—	—	—	4·47
·175	—	—	—	—	16	4·44
·173	—	—	17	—	—	4·39
·172	—	—	—	—	17	4·37
·1695	—	—	18	—	—	4·31
·168	—	—	—	—	18	4·27
·166	31	—	19	—	—	4·22
·165	—	—	—	8	—	4·19
·164	—	—	—	—	19	4·17

Comparative Table of the Various Gauges—*continued*

Decimals of inch	B'ghm Metal Gauge	I. Standard Wire Gauge	Morse Twist Drill and Steel Wire Gauge	Stubs' Iron Wire Gauge or B'ghm Wire Gauge	Stubs' Steel Wire Gauge	Milli-metres
·161	—	—	20	—	20	4·09
·160	—	8	—	—	—	4·06
·159	—	—	21	—	—	4·04
·157	—	—	22	—	21	3·99
·155	—	—	—	—	22	3·94
·154	—	—	23	—	—	3·91
·153	—	—	—	—	23	3·89
·152	—	—	24	—	—	3·86
·151	—	—	—	—	24	3·84
·150	30	—	—	—	—	3·81
·1495	—	—	25	—	—	3·80
·148	—	—	—	9	25	3·76
·147	—	—	26	—	—	3·73
·146	—	—	—	—	26	3·71
·144	—	9	27	—	—	3·66
·143	—	—	—	—	27	3·63
·1405	—	—	28	—	—	3·57
·139	—	—	—	—	28	3·53
·136	29	—	29	—	—	3·45
·134	—	—	—	10	29	3·40
·1285	—	—	30	—	—	3·26
·128	—	10	—	—	—	3·25
·127	—	—	—	—	30	3·23
·124	28	—	—	—	—	3·15
·120	—	—	31	11	31	3·05
·116	—	11	32	—	—	2·95
·115	—	—	—	—	32	2·92
·113	—	—	33	—	—	2·87
·112	27	—	—	—	33	2·84
·111	—	—	34	—	—	2·82
·110	—	—	35	—	34	2·79
·109	—	—	—	12	—	2·77
·108	—	—	—	—	35	2·74
·1065	—	—	36	—	—	2·70
·106	—	—	—	—	36	2·69
·104	—	12	37	—	—	2·64
·103	—	—	—	—	37	2·62
·1015	—	—	38	—	—	2·58
·101	—	—	—	—	38	2·57
·100	26	—	—	—	—	2·54
·0995	—	—	39	—	—	2·53
·099	—	—	—	—	39	2·51
·098	—	—	40	—	—	2·49
·097	—	—	—	—	40	2·46
·096	—	—	41	—	—	2·44
·095	—	—	—	13	41	2·41

COMPARATIVE TABLE OF THE VARIOUS GAUGES—*continued*

Decimals of inch	B'ghm Metal Gauge	I. Standard Wire Gauge	Morse Twist Drill and Steel Wire Gauge	Stubs' Iron Wire Gauge or B'ghm Wire Gauge	Stubs' Steel Wire Gauge	Milli-metres
·0935	—	—	42	—	—	2·37
·092	—	13	—	—	42	2·34
·090	25	—	—	—	—	2·28
·089	—	—	43	—	—	2·26
·088	—	—	—	—	43	2·24
·086	—	—	44	—	—	2·18
·085	—	—	—	—	44	2·16
·083	—	—	—	14	—	2·11
·082	24	—	45	—	—	2·08
·081	—	—	46	—	45	2·06
·080	—	14	—	—	—	2·03
·079	—	—	—	—	46	2·01
·0785	—	—	47	—	—	1·99
·077	23	—	—	—	47	1·96
·076	—	—	48	—	—	1·93
·075	—	—	—	—	48	1·90
·073	22	—	49	—	—	1·85
·072	—	15	—	15	49	1·83
·070	—	—	50	—	—	1·78
·069	21	—	—	—	50	1·75
·067	—	—	51	—	—	1·70
·066	—	—	—	—	51	1·68
·065	20	—	—	16	—	1·65
·064	—	16	—	—	—	1·63
·0635	—	—	52	—	—	1·61
·063	—	—	—	—	52	1·60
·062	19	—	—	—	—	1·57
·0595	—	—	53	—	—	1·51
·059	18	—	—	—	—	1·50
·058	—	—	—	17	53	1·47
·056	—	17	—	—	—	1·42
·055	17	—	54	—	54	1·40
·052	—	—	55	—	—	1·32
·051	16	—	—	—	—	1·30
·050	—	—	—	—	55	1·27
·049	—	—	—	18	—	1·24
·048	15	18	—	—	—	1·22
·0465	—	—	56	—	—	1·18
·045	—	—	—	—	56	1·14
·043	14	—	57	—	—	1·09
·042	—	—	58	19	57	1·07
·041	—	—	59	—	58	1·04
·040	—	19	60	—	59	1·02
·039	—	—	61	—	60	·99
·038	13	—	62	—	61	·97
·037	—	—	63	—	62	·94

Comparative Table of the Various Gauges—*continued*

Decimals of inch	B'ghm Metal Gauge	I. Standard Wire Gauge	Morse Twist Drill and Steel Wire Gauge	Stubs' Iron Wire Gauge or B'ghm Wire Gauge	Stubs' Steel Wire Gauge	Milli-metres
·036	—	20	64	—	63	·91
·035	12	—	65	20	64	·89
·033	—	—	66	—	65	·84
·032	11	21	67	21	66	·81
·031	—	—	68	—	67	·79
·030	—	—	—	—	68	·76
·02925	—	—	69	—	—	·74
·029	—	—	—	—	69	·74
·028	10	22	70	22	—	·71
·027	—	—	—	—	70	·69
·026	—	—	71	—	71	·66
·025	—	—	72	23	—	·63
·024	9	23	73	—	72	·61
·023	—	—	—	—	73	·58
·0225	—	—	74	—	—	·57
·022	—	24	—	24	74	·56
·0215	8	—	—	—	—	·55
·021	—	—	75	—	—	·53
·020	—	25	76	25	75	·51
·019	7	—	—	—	—	·48
·018	—	26	77	26	76	·46
·0164	—	27	—	—	—	·42
·016	6	—	78	27	77	·41
·015	—	—	—	—	78	·38
·0148	—	28	—	—	—	·38
·1045	—	—	79	—	—	·37
·0140	5	—	—	28	79	·36
·0136	—	29	—	—	—	·35
·0135	—	—	80	—	—	·34
·0130	—	—	—	29	80	·33
·1024	—	30	—	—	—	·31
·0120	4	—	—	30	—	·30
·0116	—	31	—	—	—	·295
·0108	—	32	—	—	—	·274
·0105	3	—	—	—	—	·267
·0100	—	33	—	31	—	·254
·0095	2	—	—	—	—	·241
·0092	—	34	—	—	—	·234
·0090	—	—	—	32	—	·229
·0085	1	—	—	—	—	·216
·0084	—	35	—	—	—	·213
·0080	—	—	—	33	—	·203
·0076	—	36	—	—	—	·193
·0070	—	—	—	34	—	·178
·0068	—	37	—	—	—	·173
·0060	—	38	—	—	—	·152

COMPARATIVE TABLE OF THE VARIOUS GAUGES—*continued*

Decimals of inch	B'ghm Metal Gauge	I. Standard Wire Gauge	Morse Twist Drill and Steel Wire Gauge	Stubs' Iron Wire Gauge or B'ghm Wire Gauge	Stubs' Steel Wire Gauge	Milli-metres
·0052	—	39	—	—	—	·132
·0050	—	—	—	35	—	·127
·0048	—	40	—	—	—	·122
·0044	—	41	—	—	—	·112
·0040	—	42	—	36	—	·102
·0036	—	43	—	—	—	·091
·0032	—	44	—	—	—	·081
·0028	—	45	—	—	—	·071
·0024	—	46	—	—	—	·061
·0020	—	47	—	—	—	·051
·0016	—	48	—	—	—	·041
·0012	—	49	—	—	—	·030
·0010	—	50	—	—	—	·025

JEWELLER'S GAUGE (SHAKESPEARE)

Numbers	.	.	0000	000	00	0	1	2	3
Decimals of inch		.	·0035	·004	·0045	·005	·0055	·006	·0065
Millimetres	.	.	·090	·102	·115	·127	·140	·152	·165

Numbers	.	.	4	5	6	7	8	9	10
Decimals of inch		.	·0075	·0085	·0095	·0105	·012	·014	·016
Millimetres	.	.	·191	·216	·242	·267	·305	·356	·406

Numbers	.	.	11	12
Decimals of inch		.	·019	·0215
Millimetres	.	.	·483	·546

The Brown and Sharpe (B. & S.) wire gauge is the standard gauge for sheet metal in the United States.

Number of gauge	Thickness	
	Inches	Millimetres
6/0	·580	14·73
5/0	·5165	13·119
4/0	·46	11·68
3/0	·409	10·388
2/0	·364	9·24
1/0	·324	8·23
1	·289	7·338
2	·257	6·527
3	·229	5·808
4	·204	5·18
5	·181	4·59
6	·162	4·11
7	·144	3·66
8	·128	3·24
9	·114	2·89
10	·101	2·565
11	·090	2·28
12	·080	2·03
13	·071	1·79
14	·064	1·625
15	·057	1·447
16	·050	1·27
17	·045	1·14
18	·040	1·016
19	·036	·91
20	·032	·81
21	·028	·711
22	·025	·635
23	·022	·558
24	·020	·508
25	·017	·431
26	·015	·381
27	·0148	·376
28	·012	·304
29	·0116	·29
30	·01	·254
31	·008	·203
32	·0079	·199
33	·007	·177
34	·006	·152
35	·0055	·142
36	·005	·127

Bibliography

AGRICOLA, GEORGIUS. *De Re Metallica.* 1556. (HOOVER translation reprinted by Dover.)

BIRINGUCCIO, VANNOCCIO. *De la pirotechnia.* 1540.

BOLAS, THOMAS. *Etching on Metals.*

CELLINI, BENVENUTO. *Treatises on Goldsmithing and Sculpture.* Translated by C. R. ASHBEE. 1898.

CUNYNGHAME, HENRY. *Enamelling on Metals.*

CUZNER, BERNARD *A Silversmith's Manual.* 1949.

EMERSON, A. R. *Handmade Jewellery.* 1953.

FIELD, S., and BONNEY, S. R. *The Chemical Colouring of Metals.* 1925.

" Improved Casting for Silversmiths." *Bulletin of the Design and Research Centre for the Gold, Silver and Jewellery Industries,* Nos. 3 and 5. 1948-9.

" Improvement in Method and Means of Casting, etc." British Patent Nos. 449062 (1934) and 503537 (1937).

" Investment Casting—Patent Position." *Bulletin of the Design and Research Centre for the Gold, Silver and Jewellery Industries,* No. 5. 1949.

" The Investment Casting of Jewellery." *Overseas Watchmaker, Jeweller and Silversmith,* Nos. 5 and 6. 1952.

MOSS, DR. A. A. " Niello, Studies in Conservation No. 2, 1953." *Journal of the International Institute for the Conservation of Museum Objects.*

NELSON-DAWSON, MRS. *Enamels.*

OTTEN and BERL. *Enamelling.*

RATHBONE, R. L. B. *Simple Jewellery.* 1910.

ROBERTS-AUSTEN, SIR W. C. " The Colours of Metals and Alloys." *Nature.* December 2nd, 1886.

Scientific and Technical Factors of Production of Gold and Silverware. A Course of Lectures at Goldsmiths' Hall, London. 1935-6.

SELWYN, A. *The Retail Jewellers' Handbook.* 1948.

SPON, ERNEST. *Workshop Receipts.*

THEOPHILUS, called also RUGERUS. *Essay on Various Arts.* Translated by ROBERT HENDRIE. 1847. Also: Edited by DODWELL. 1961. Edited and translated by J. G. HAWTHORNE and C. S. SMITH. 1963.

THEOBALD, W. *German Translation of the Treatise by Theophilus.* 1933.

WIGLEY, T. B. *The Art of the Goldsmith and Jeweller.*

WILSON, HENRY. *Silverwork and Jewellery.*

Notes on the Plates

B.M. = British Museum   S.K.M. = Victoria and Albert Museum, South Kensington.

PLATE

The Royal Gold Cup. Probably made in Burgundy or Paris about 1350. The finial and a band of ornament round the lid, once decorated with pearls, are missing. The two bands in the stem are later additions. The cup is decorated with bassetaille enamels, showing scenes from the life of St. Agnes. The preparation of the ground for the enamel was almost entirely by chasing, though some work with the scorper followed. The enamels are of great splendour on fine gold. See p. 187.

Frontispiece.
B.M.

1. *The " King John " Cup, King's Lynn, Norfolk.* It was made about 1325, and is the oldest piece of corporation plate in the country. Silver gilt, and decorated with bassetaille enamel. The tree-forms on base, bowl, and lid are cast. The silver panels for the enamels were chased in sheet metal. Each part of the design which was to be enamelled was outlined with the tracer and driven below the general level of the background: the folds in the draperies being suggested by gently modelled ridge and hollow. The chased recesses were then filled with enamel and the piece fired. Each panel is held in position by a band setting. For sheer beauty of line and colour I know of no equal to this splendid cup. See p. 187.
Photograph by Goodchild, King's Lynn.
KING'S LYNN.

2. *Candlestick of Bronze inlaid with Silver.* Venetian-Saracenic, about 1550. Perfect in form and treatment. This rich type of decoration originated with the Islamic craftsmen of the Near East: the earliest example being dated A.D. 1145.
S.K.M.

3. *A dish by Omar Ramsden* in the collection of the Worshipful Company of Goldsmiths. It was made from a single piece of silver, and illustrates the delightful way that a skilled craftsman, by repoussé work, may turn the surface of his work this way and that, and, as Nature does on shells and flowers, play fine patterns with the light and shade. Further fine examples of such relief work (cast in bronze, however) may be found on the Piccadilly Fountain and on many other works by Alfred Gilbert and other craftsmen whom he has inspired.

4. *The Bell Shrine of St. Conall Cael.* Irish, about Fifteenth Century, enclosing the sacred relic: the hand-bell of one of the early Irish ecclesiastics. The shrine was borne on legal and ceremonial occasions

319

by its hereditary keeper. The shrine is composed of various metals, the five lowest figures being of gilt bronze, the upper three of repoussé silver. Other parts of the shrine are of silver or of brass. The large crystal does not seem to have been part of the original design as it overlaps some of the other work rather awkwardly. But its position in relation to the rest of the design is very happy and it adds a touch of inspired magic to the whole. Notice the gradation from plain tubular angle members, with strongly modelled joints, through the flattish bands of lettering, the floral panels in higher relief, to the gilded figures in the round, reaching at last the central figure between the two crystals. At the sides are diapers of pierced crosses and the chain for suspension.

B.M.

5. *Golden Cover for a Copy of the Gospels.* Formerly at Sion Cathedral, Valais, Switzerland. French or German, about A.D. 1000. Central panel, end of Twelfth Century. The central panel and its floral border are worked in repoussé, with some chasing from the front. The metal panels in the outer border with the exception of those at the bottom corners, are constructed in an unusual manner. The scrolls were worked separately in high relief and then cut from their background. They were soldered to their present ground plate, and, naturally, appear to be more detached from it than would patterns worked from the plate itself. Cloisonné wire with grained edge was employed for the lighter parts of the design, and the animals' heads were given jewelled eyes. Some of the band settings to the stones and enamels have stamped quatrefoil patterns in relief on their vertical sides. Open coils or spirals of fine wire were run round some of the stone settings. Others have a section of closely coiled wire and then a section of open spiral wire, alternately, right round the setting. Others again have a narrow ribbon coiled like No. 67, Fig. 243 as an enrichment of the setting. The enamels are of gold cloisonné work, and are in band settings. The double border round some of the panels was formed from a ribbon of gold waved up and down, and soldered in position. It forms a very effective decorative border. The whole work is full of colour: a jewel of exceeding beauty.

S.K.M.

6. *The " Bacon " Cup*, 1574. Silver-gilt. A sturdy beautifully proportioned example of English craftsmanship.

B.M.

7. *The Birdlip Mirror.* A characteristic feature of Celtic art is the craftsman's interest in pure linear ornament: a quality well displayed in this beautiful mirror-back. The handle is of cast bronze with roundels of red enamel.

GLOUCESTER.

8. *The Ramsay Abbey Incense Boat.* Silver, parcel gilt. An exceptionally graceful example of English craftsmanship of the Fourteenth Century. The foot, down to the top of the mouldings, was raised from sheet

PLATE 1.   The " King John " Cup.   *King's Lynn.*

PLATE 2.   Candlestick of Bronze inlaid with Silver.   Venetian-Saracenic.   S.K.M.

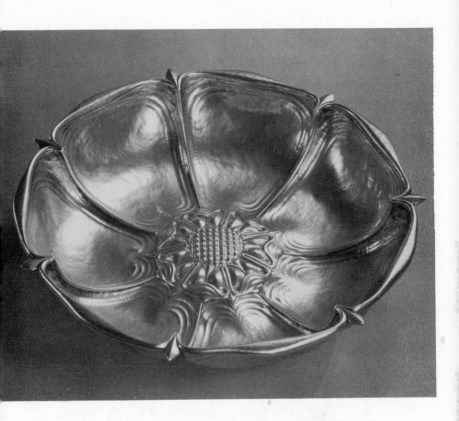

PLATE 3.   A Dish by Omar Ramsden.   *The Worshipful Company of Goldsmiths.*

PLATE 4. The Bell Shrine of St. Conall Cael.   B.M.

PLATE 5.   Golden Cover for a Copy of the Gospels.

Plate 6.   The " Bacon " Cup, 1574.

PLATE 7. The Birdlip Mirror. *Gloucester.*

PLATE 8.   The Ramsay Abbey Incense Boat.

PLATE 9. The Valence Casket.

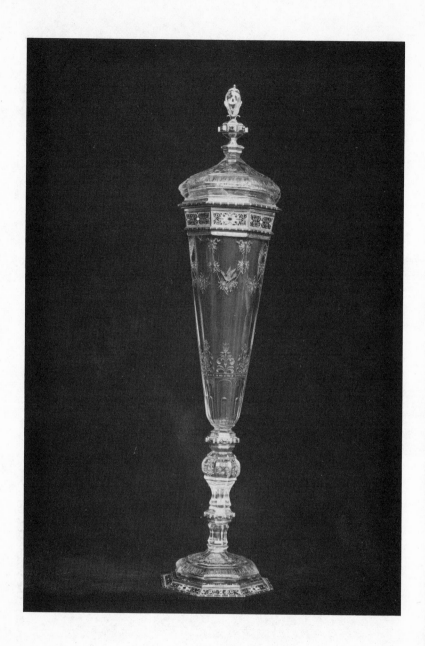

PLATE 10. Standing Cup in Rock Crystal. Italian. *B.M.*

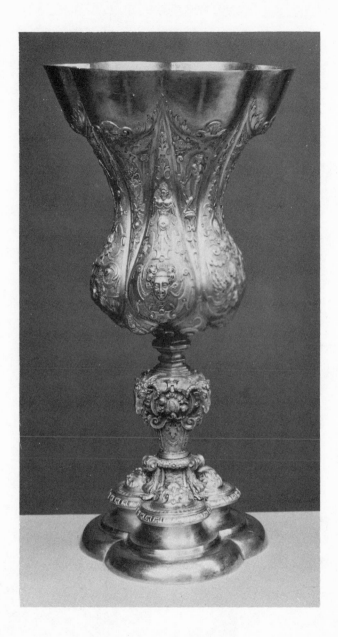

PLATE 11.   Silver Cup.   Nuremberg.   S.K.M.

PLATE 12.   A fine Golden Dagger Handle from China.

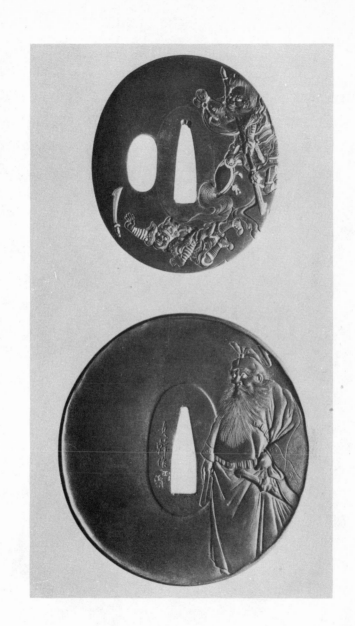

PLATE 13.   Two Japanese Sword Guards.   *Newman Collection.*

PLATE 14. Enamelled Bronze Trappings from Polden Hill, Somerset.

B.M.

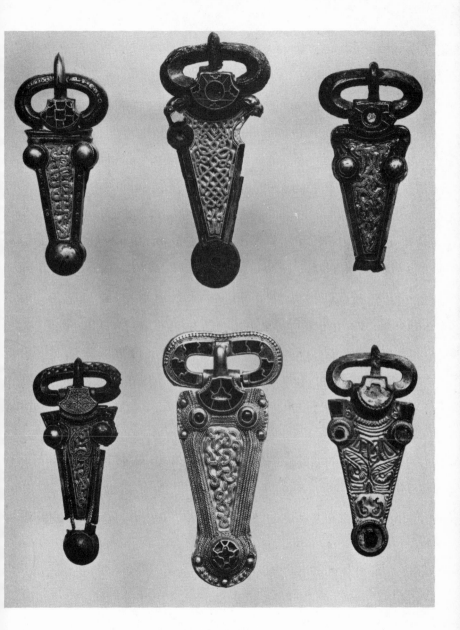

PLATE 15.   Anglo-Saxon Buckles from Taplow.   *B.M.*

PLATE 16.   The Tara Brooch.

PLATE 17.   Gold Bowl.   Etruscan.

PLATE 18.   An Inscribed Ewer.

PLATE 19. Two Golden Shoulder-clasps from the Sutton Hoo Ship Burial.

B.M.

PLATE 20. A French Wine Cup of the Sixteenth Century.

PLATE 21. Shoulderpiece from a Cuirass. *B.M.*

PLATE 22. Silver Bowl from Chaource. Roman. *B.M.*

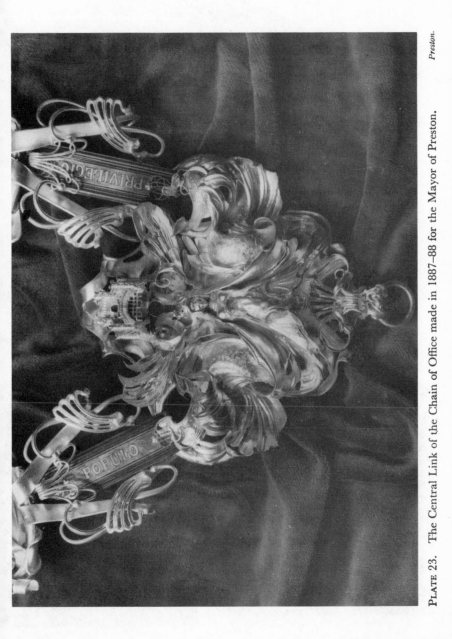

PLATE 23. The Central Link of the Chain of Office made in 1887–88 for the Mayor of Preston.

Preston.

PLATE 24.   The Kingston Down Brooch.

Liverpool.

PLATE 25.   A Panel in Champlevé Enamel and
Millefiori Work.

B.M.

PLATE 26.   Cire Perdue Work.

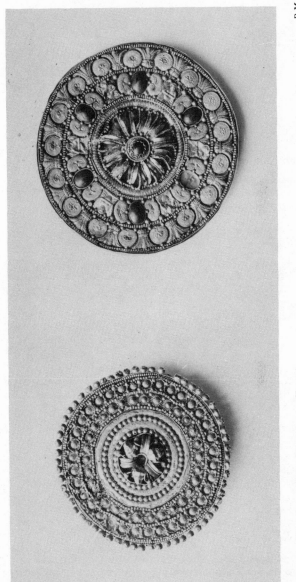

PLATE 27. Two Gold Brooches. Etruscan.

PLATE 28.   A Sampler of Granulation Work.

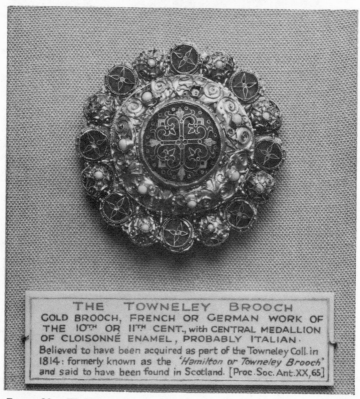

PLATE 29.   The Towneley Brooch.

B.M.

metal. The heavy base-plate and the six-pointed decorated mouldings were made separately and soldered to it. The bowl was sunk. The mouldings upon it were chased up from heavy strip: not swaged.

S.K.M.

9. *The Valence Casket.* English or French work of the end of the Thirteenth Century. Gilt copper with champlevé enamels. The recesses for the enamels were chiselled from the heavy sheet copper, some ¾ inch thick, of which the casket is made. The sides and bottom have butt joints, and are fastened together by copper pins whose heads, visible at the ends and underside of the casket, are riveted over. The top, front, back and sides of the casket are covered with a diaper of coats of arms. The enamel colours employed are red, blue, white, black and a purple produced by mixing the red and blue. All the ground between the enamelled areas is decorated with ornament executed with the tracer. The great decorative value of heraldry is manifest in this fine example.

S.K.M.

10. *Standing Cup in Rock Crystal.* Gold and enamel, from the collection of Viscount Lee of Farnham. Italian. Sixteenth Century. An example of graceful and restrained design. Perhaps the most beautiful cup in existence.

B.M.

11. *Silver Cup.* Originally belonging to the Nuremberg Goldsmiths' Guild. Believed to have been made by Martin Rehlein in 1572–3 as a model for trial works for candidates for the rank of master-craftsman of the Guild. A characteristic example of Sixteenth Century work.

S.K.M.

12. *A fine Golden Dagger Handle from China.* Late Chou period.

B.M.

13. *The Two Japanese Sword Guards* introduce us to craftsmanship of a kind practically unknown to European art. The work of our finest medallists is the nearest approach, for low relief work of unsurpassed excellence may be found occasionally among modern medals. The Japanese masters, however, besides their amazing variety and vitality show a sustained interest in the colour and the surface treatment of their material. The guard with the old man upon it is of iron, and the artist, not content with producing a striking character study in low relief, has given the surface of the work the texture known as pear-skin, graduated from an extremely fine raised grain to one which fades away at last into an almost imperceptible ripple. The old man's eyes and the lowest part of the inscription are inlaid with gold, and the colour of the iron is a rich chocolate. The artist was Sadamoto (Teikan) 1828–1878. School of Motozane I. The other guard is of a copper alloy containing about 25 per cent. of silver: an alloy which takes a very fine silvery patina. The colour scheme includes inlays of

321

gold, silver, and copper. There is great energy and skilful modelling in the figures of the warriors in combat. By Masayuki (1683–1769) School of Toshinaga.

COMMANDER NEWMAN.

14. *Enamelled Bronze Trappings from Polden Hill, Somerset.* British. First Century A.D.

B.M.

15. *Anglo-Saxon Buckles from Taplow.* Note how the gold filigree work is enriched by its repoussé background, and the lines of twisted wires form a worthy foil to the grain and garnet work.

B.M.

16. *The Tara Brooch.* Detail. Irish, about Tenth Century. A characteristic of this work, as of many others of its time, is the close association of modelling and metal casting, fine filigree in gold or silver, with engraving, niello, cut stones, amber and glass. Every branch of the metal worker's art is employed on a single work, and, quite probably, by a single hand. As a result we may examine the work and find new features of interest in every part: a concentration of fine design, clearly expressed ideas, and good workmanship, which holds us enthralled. How seldom, alas, has a modern work this power. Yet should we not look for it in a work of art?

DUBLIN.

17. *Gold Bowl.* Etruscan. *Circa* 600 B.C. About 4 inches in diameter. The design is carried out in double rows of gold grains soldered in position. It has been calculated that no less than 137,000 grains were employed on the work. The bold repoussé flutes provide a valuable contrast with the delicate granulation.

S.K.M.

18. *An Inscribed Ewer.* Made at Mosul in A.D. 1232. From the Blacas Collection. A beautiful example of inlaid work.

B.M.

19. *Two Golden Shoulder-clasps from the Sutton Hoo Ship Burial.* Their principal decorations are cloisonné panels and borders, with some filigree work. The panels are filled with stepped garnets over diapered gold foil, and blue, white and red mosaic glass, each piece having a slightly arched surface. The borders represent interlaced patterns, formed from shaped garnets against a ground of plain gold. Each piece of garnet is in a separate cloisonné cell. The background to the garnet pattern is constructed from a plate of gold soldered on top of the gold cloisonné cells. As a result the borders look almost like champlevé work, though the background is not of solid metal but of closed cloisonné cells. The filigree is formed from beaded wires and grain-edged cloisons.

B.M.

20. *A French Wine Cup of the Sixteenth Century.* A fine example, though one part of the stem looks weak.

S.K.M.

21. *Shoulderpiece from a Cuirass.* Greek. Found near the River Siris, South Italy. Fourth Century B.C. The figures were worked in repoussé from a sheet of bronze, originally size 16 on the metal gauge. The man's head is three quarters of an inch above the ground and almost in the round. It would be difficult to find a more beautiful and skilful example of repoussé than this fine work.

B.M.

22. *Silver Bowl.* Roman. Second Century A.D. Treasure of Chaource, France. See how the flutes play with the light. The turned-in lip helps considerably by giving the shadow at the top.

B.M.

23. *The Central Link of the Chain of Office* made in 1887–88 for the Mayor of Preston, Lancashire, by the late Sir Alfred Gilbert. The principal links are wrought in elaborately chased and pierced high relief repoussé work, in several superposed layers. The link shown in the illustration represents a mermaid holding two ships, symbolizing the ancient port of Preston. Between the principal links, which are of gilded and enamelled silver with jewelled devices, is a series of inscribed, rectangular links in laminated metals. These strike a strong note of silvery-grey. A mural crown, the seal and arms of the city of Preston, the arms of several of the sovereigns who granted charters to the town, and those of Queen Victoria, of whose jubilee the chain is a memorial, are represented in enamel. The chain is a remarkably original, practical, and beautiful example of English craftsmanship. See p. 167.

PRESTON.

24. *The Kingston Down Brooch.* Gold, set with pearl shell, garnets, opaque blue glass and filigree work of twisted, beaded and plain wires over repoussé work. Found in 1771 near Canterbury. The most beautiful brooch of the period. Seventh Century A.D.

LIVERPOOL.

25. *A Panel in Champlevé Enamel and Millefiori Work.* From one of the hanging bowls from Sutton Hoo. Note also the chased decoration of the silver frame.

B.M.

26. *Cire Perdue Work.* Wax casts for 20 finger rings set up ready for investment. Note: Even the claws to hold the stones are already completely formed. See Chapter XXXI.

27. *Two Brooches.* In the larger example the eye travels from the strong floral centre, each petal of which is worked in repoussé, past spirals of coiled wire and waved ribbons of gold foil to the next zone where,

between dark stones flanked by kidney-shaped bosses of granular ornament, are little seated figures. The outer zone has further, almost circular bosses of granular work between lotus flower patterns in low relief. The smaller brooch, with a similarly constructed centre, has rings of small bosses and grains decorated with the finest granular work, separated by lines of waved ribbon foil. The delicacy of workmanship in these brooches is almost miraculous, and the fineness of the granular work has never been excelled. Etruscan. See p. 53.

B.M.

28. *A Sampler of Granulation Work by the Author.* The 1-inch rule alongside reveals the minuteness of scale. See pp. 9, 53.

29 *The Towneley Brooch.*   B.M.

Workshop First Aid

BURNS AND SCALDS

Exclude air by a paste of baking soda (sodium bicarbonate) and water. Use vaseline, olive or castor oil, lard or cream—except for phosphorus burns. A good dressing is lime water with an equal part of raw linseed oil. After treatment with any of the above cover with a soaked pad of cotton wool and bandage lightly.

ACIDS AND ALKALI BURNS

Wash for several minutes under a water tap. Then for:

Acid Burns. Apply freely baking soda (sodium bicarbonate) in water, or lime-water or limewater and raw linseed oil. Then cover with a pad soaked with bicarbonate of soda and bandage lightly. Get medical aid.

Acid in the Eye. After thorough washing apply limewater. Get medical aid.

Alkalis. Wash well under tap, as for acids. Neutralize with weak vinegar or lemon juice. Get medical aid.

Alkali in the Eye. For lime and other strong alkalis wash with a weak solution of vinegar or olive oil or a saturated solution of boric acid. Get medical aid.

ANTIDOTES FOR POISONS

Acids (Glacial Acetic, Hydrochloric, Nitric, Sulphuric). Magnesia, lime, chalk or soda water. If not available, give plenty of water, and oil, milk, uncooked white of eggs. Get medical aid.

Acids (Carbolic). Give emetic, i.e. zinc sulphate, ipecacuanha or mustard and water, the uncooked white of several eggs, milk of lime, olive or castor oil with magnesia in suspension, ice. Wash out the stomach with equal parts water and vinegar. Give brandy or whisky and water, chloric ether, or 4 fluid ounces of camphorated oil in one dose. Get medical aid.

Arsenic, Rat Poison. Use stomach pump or an emetic. Give milk, raw eggs, sweet oil, limewater or flour and water, and small doses of stimulants. Keep warm by hot blankets, etc. Get medical aid.

Carbon Monoxide. Immediately remove to fresh air and send for pulmotor. Artificial respiration for at least one hour or till pulmotor in use. Inhalation of ammonia or amyl nitrite often useful. Get medical aid.

Methylated Spirit. Emetic or stomach pump. Give milk, white of eggs, or flour in water. Artificial respiration if necessary. Keep warm. Get medical aid.

Potassium Cyanide. Stomach pump or siphon, or emetic of mustard and water or sulphate of zinc. Hydrogen peroxide internally. Artificial respiration if required, breathing ammonia or chlorine from chlorinated lime, ferrous sulphate followed by potassium carbonate. Cool head but keep extremities warm. Get medical aid.

Zinc chloride, i.e. *Killed Spirits of Salt.* Give plenty of water in which bicarbonate of soda has been dissolved, white of egg, milk, strong tea. See also page 25.

Get medical aid.

FIRE AND CHEMICAL HAZARDS

Efficient gas mask essential in most cases. Use water or sand—except that for calcium carbide, magnesium, potassium or sodium no water must be used.

Index

Acid burns, 25, 325
  glacial acetic, 39
  hydrochloric, 37
  hydrofluoric, 174, 180, 194, 197
  muriatic, 37
  nitric, 7, 24, 48, 154, 287
  splashes, 25
  sulphuric, 7, 25
  tannic, 25
Æsthetic precedence, 282
  quality, 274
Ætna blowlamps, 31
Agate burnisher, 259
  pestle and mortar, 174
Agricola, 318
Airhole, 24, 238
Alcohre flux, 37
Alloys, 5, 6, 7, 8, 11
  fusible, 235
  removal, 24
  steel, 269
Alum, 262
Aluminium, 2, 37, 259
  bronze, 182, 304
Amalgam (of gold and mercury), 159, 262
American (Sellers) Screw Thread, 308
Ammonia, 266
Ammonium carbonate, 264
  chloride, 265
  sulphide, 263, 264, 265
Angle, grinding, 272
Anglo-Saxon buckles, 322
Annealing, 30, 93
  an enamel, 180
  wire, 42
Antidote for burns, etc., 25, 325
Antimony, 164
Aqua regia, 287
Arab mosque lamps, 169, 198
Ardagh chalice, 198
Arrow-head moulds, 201
Arsenic, 265
Asbestos, 21, 223
Ascending principle in metal-casting, 213, 222
Ashanti, 226
Assaying and hallmarking, 287
  final, 288
  preliminary, 288
Atomic weights, 305

Backgrounding, 116

Backing an enamel, 175
  a pearl, 78
" Bacon " cup, 320
Ball, 24, 53
  -faced hammer, 91
  joint, 146
Banded alloys, 166
Band setting, 81, 170
Barium sulphide, 263, 264, 265
Barthel blowlamp, 31
Bassetaille enamels, 171, 186, 319
Bath or dish (etching), 157
Bathbrick dust, 208, 260
Battersea enamels, 198
Bead, 24, 50, 58
Beading tool, 110
Bearers for hinge, 140
  for stones, 71, 82
Beeswax, 219
Bell casting, 236
  metal, 304
  shrine, 319, 320
Bellows, 3, 27, 28, 33, 48
Bench, 3
  jeweller's, 51, 52
  pin, 51, 52, 71, 74
Bending sheet metal, 241
  strip, 132
Benin, 226
Benzine, 260
Berl enamelling, 318
Bezel, 72, 73, 82
Bibliography, 318
Bick-iron or sparrow-hawk, 15, 51, 55, 88, 237
Binding wire, 17, 18, 26, 43, 48, 61
Birdlip mirror, 171, 320
Biringuccio, 216, 318
Birmingham, 7, 171
  metal gauge, 309
  wire gauge, 309
Bismuth, 235
Biting a plate (etching), 157
Black polish, on silver, 257, 258
  stone, 1, 68, 72
Blick, 288, 289
Blotting paper, 54, 193
Blowlamp, 31
Blowpipe, 3, 21, 27
  flame, 28
  mouth, 27, 28, 48
Blue stone, 257
Board for repoussé, 114, 117

" Boiling out," 23, 61
Bolas, Mr., 164, 318
Bone, powdered, 223, 224
Bonney, S. R., *Colouring of Metals*, 318
Borax, 18–20, 59
   dissolve to, 24
   glass, 10, 19
   slate, 19, 48
Boss, 55
Boring hole in stone, 243
Bosse's etching ground, 154
Bossing tools, 121–122A
Bottom stakes, 88
Bowl from five-shilling piece, 92
   hanging, Sutton Hoo, 323
   Roman, Chaourse, 323
Boxes, casting, 216
Box, iron, 54
Bracelets, 9, 199
Branches, filigree, 58
Brass, 2, 11–13, 23, 234
   colouring, 264
   tongs, 25
Brazing, 12, 26
   spelters, 12, 13
Breaking down mould, 236
Brickdust, 208, 222
Britannia Standard, 11, 291
British Association lecture, 166
   screw threads, 307
British Museum, 9, 149, 171, 187, 191,
   201, 263, 319
   Standards, 12
Bronze, 234, 304
Brooch catch, 147
   Etruscan, 324
   joint, 144
   Kingston Down, 323
   pin, 145
   Towneley, 324
Brown and Sharpe wire gauge, 317
Brunswick black, 156
Buckle or warp, 242
Bullstickers, 64, 71
Bunsen burners, 172
Burin or graver, 152, 153
Burnisher, 51, 259
Burns acid,, 25, 325
Burnt areas, 17, 39, 176, 253
   joints, 39
   steel, 268
Byzantine jewels, 86, 175

Cabochon cut, 63
Cadmium, 235
Candlestick, Venetian-Saracenic, 319
Calcium chloride, 266
Calor gas, 31
Carat, 6, 7
Carbon, 9, 10, 11
Carbon steels, 267

Carborundum wheel, 4
Carlungie, enamel, 199
Carron oil, 25
Case-hardening, 268
Casting, 200
   flasks or boxes, 216
   flexible mould, 210
   in metal, 200
   irons, 210, 211, 218, 221, 224
   mouldings in plaster, 133
Castor oil, 25
Cauldrons, Iron Age, 93
Cellini, 163, 191, 208, 220, 223, 285,
   318
Celtic enamels, 171, 320
Cement, 65, 243
   sticks, 65
Central America, 226
Centrifugal casting, 232, 318
Chain of Office, Preston, 167, 323
Chalice, 238
Champlevé enamels, 171, 184, 321, 323
Chaource treasure, 323
Chaplets, 265
Charcoal block, 14, 16, 22, 53, 203
   fire, 9, 33
   fumes, 33, 34
   powder, 54
Chasing, 113, 186, 236
   tools, 118, 122
Chenier or tube, 1, 44, 70, 140
China, 216
   colours, 197
Chinese dagger handle, 321
   enamels, 181
   piece-mould, 205
   wine vessel, 205
Chisel, 48, 58, 176, 243
Chloride of zinc, 37
Chucks for spinning, 105
Circles, areas of, 301
   properties of, 301
Cire perdue casting, 209, 219, 226, 228,
   323
   centrifugal, 232
Clamp, 68
Claws, 71
Claw setting, 70
Clay bands for piece moulding, 207
   or loam moulds, 200
Cloisonne enamels, 170, 175, 320
Cloisons, 170, 176
Closing tool, 74
Cobalt, 2
Coinage, 304
Coin, setting for, 85
Collet, 70
   hammer, 91
Colouring gold, 8, 25, 261
   metals, 260, 318
   silver, 25, 148, 161, 263
Colour of metals, 318

Colour in tempering steel, 270
Compo for moulds, 208, 225
Composition of various alloys, 304
Conall Cael, 319, 320
Cong, Cross of, 86
Construction, 237
Cope or mother mould, 207, 217
Copper, 2, 6, 7, 11, 23, 234
   annealing, 93
   nitrate, 265
   oxide, 9, 10
   salts, 9
   sulphate, 264
Core, 201, 209, 216, 218, 220, 236
   supports, 209, 218, 221, 224, 236
   vents, 210
Cornet, 289
Coronet setting, 70, 71, 73, 74, 229
Cow or horse dung, 223
Cramp setting, 83
Crocus, 257
Crucible, 15, 233, 234
   tongs, 236
Culet, 63, 71, 76
Cunynghame, H., 174, 318
Cup " Bacon," 320
   Enkomi, 161, 199
   French wine, 323
   King's Lynn, 187, 319
   Nuremburg, 321
   Rock Crystal, 321
   Royal Gold or St. Agnes, 187, 319
Cupel, 287
Curls (metal), 82
Cut-down setting, 74
Cuttlefish bone moulds, 202
Cuzner, B., 318
Cyprus, 170

Dagger handle, Chinese, 321
Damascening, 151
Decagon, 251
Decimals of inch, 299
   of ounce, 300
De la pirotechnia, 216, 318
De Re Metallica, 318
Descending principle in metal-casting, 213
Design, 274
Diamonds, 86, 296
Dies, 129
Directional quality, 111
Discs, 55
Doming block, 49, 55
Drawbench, 4, 131
   plate, 41, 46, 57
   swage, 46, 129
   tongs, 41
Drawing on metal, 246

Drill and drillstock, 49, 65
   stone, to, 243
Drop-stone, setting for, 85
Dublin Museum, 86, 135, 498
Duodecagon, 249

Ecuador, 226
Eggshell polish, 181
Egypt, 8, 170, 216
Electroplating, 158, 258, 262
Electrum, 8
Ellipse, 250
Emerson, A. R., 318
Emery, 257
Enamel, 169, 318
   alterations, 197
   Anglo-Saxon, 184
   backing or counter-enamel, 175, 176
   backplate or ground, 176, 186
   bassetaille, 171, 186
   Battersea, 198
   Belgium, from, 199
   Byzantine, 175
   Carlungie, 199
   Celtic, 171, 184
   champlevé, 171, 184
   china colours on, 197
   Chinese, 181
   cloisonne, 171, 175
   encrusted, 172, 190
   firing an, 178
   Greek, 171
   grinding and washing, 177, 193
   grisaille, 198
   Japanese, 177
   Limoges, 184, 192
   modern, 188
   painted, 172, 192
   plique-à-jour, 171, 182
   polishing, 180, 188
   samplers, 173
   setting for, 84
   tools required, 174
Enamelled glass, 169
Engraving, 153
Enrichment of surface, 8
Essay on various arts, 318
Etching, 154, 318
   biting, 154, 157
   ground, 154
   needle, 154
   stopping-out varnish, 154
Etruscan gold bowl, 322
   goldsmiths, 9
Ewer, Arabic work, 322
Eyeglass, 51

Ferric chloride, 40
Field, S., Colouring of Metals, 318

Files, 48
Filigree, 9, 41, 53, 58
Filings, 1, 52, 53
Finger-ring, 228
Fion, 67
Fire or firestain, 258
free silver, 259
First-aid, 25, 325
Fixing, wall-tablet, 243
Flasks for sand-casting, 216, 229, 231
Fletcher's furnaces, 172, 221, 233
Flint, 169
Flooding, 9
Flushing, 262
Flush setting, 80
Flux, 10, 12, 13, 18, 19, 36, 37, 39
" Alcohre," 37
for enamelling, 169
Foil, 79, 195
Folding iron, or tool, 241
Forme, for spinning, 104
Foxing, 257
Francis I salt-cellar, 191, 285
French chalk, 203, 217, 218, 229, 231
Frit (clear enamel), 169
Frosted surface, 260
Fryolux solder, 36, 39, 59
Furnace, 27, 33, 34, 223, 233
enamelling, 172
Fusible alloys, 235

GALENA, 164
Gallery, 74
Gallipoli oil, 40
Gas, blowpipe, 27
for soldering, 27
supply, 3
Gates or jets in a mould, 206, 221, 236
Gauges, 309
Birmingham, metal, 309
wire, 309
Brown and Sharpe, 317
Imperial wire, 309
Morse Twist drill and steel wire, 309
Stub's steel wire, 309
Shakespeare jewellers', 316
Geometrical drawing, 249
forms, 278
problems, 247
German silver, 2, 304
Ghiberti, Lorenzo, 286
Gilbert, Sir Alfred, 167, 274, 323
Gilding metal, 304
with mercury, 159, 181, 262
Gipsy setting, 80
Girdle of a stone, 63
Glacial acetic acid, 39

Glass, 169
enamelled, 198
Glasspaper, 256
Gloucester Museum, 171
Glue, 10
Gold, 1, 8, 23, 300
bowl, Etruscan, 322
colouring of, 261
fine, 6
plating, 262
smithing and sculpture, 318
solders, 6–11, 13
standard, 6
upon enamel, 196, 197
Goldsmiths' Hall Research Centre, 228
Gospel Cover, 320
Gothic setting, 79
Graining tools, 66, 78
Grains, 78, 300
Granulation, 1, 9, 10, 53, 324
Graver or burin, 152, 153
Greek bronzes, 125, 323
enamels, 171
goldsmiths, 9
soldering, 36
Greensand moulding, 204
Green stick, 235, 236
Grinding a tool, 271
Grindstone, 3
Ground for etching, 154
Grounding a plate (etching), 155
Growth, 278
Gum, 18, 19, 61, 217
Gunmetal, 304

HAEMATITE (iron) burnisher, 259
Half-round wire, 44
Hall-marking, 11, 289
Handle, hollow, 237
Handvice, 47, 56
Hardening Japanese sword blade, 266, 270
steel, 268
Hard solders, 5–12, 22
Hare's foot, 1
Head of metal, 236
Hearthstone moulds, 14, 15
Hendrie's Theophilus, 9, 162
Heptagon, 249
Hexagon, 249
High relief repoussé, 125
Hinges and joints, 140
Horn tip, 90
Horse, 88
trappings, Polden Hill, 322
Hydrocal, 228
Hydrochloric acid, 37, 40, 157
Hydrogen peroxide, 39

IMPERIAL Standard Wire Gauge, 309
Inches and millimetres, 299, 300
Ingot moulds, 13, 14, 15
Injector for wax, 230
Inkpot tops, 244
Inlaying, 148, 149
  coloured stones, 170
  electro-plated, 158
  fused, 158
  parquetry work, 149
  repoussé, 148
Inscriptions, 123
Iridium black, 195
Irish work, 86, 135, 158, 198, 319, 320, 322
Iron box, 54
  perchloride, 265
  supports, 221, 224, 236
  wire, 17, 18, 43, 48, 224

JAPANESE work, 102, 166, 168, 223, 263, 270, 321
Jets or gates in a mould, 206, 221, 236
Jewellers' bench, 51
  eyeglass, 51
  gauge (Shakespeare), 316
  jet, 27, 28, 48, 52
  mouth blowpipe, 27, 28, 48
  rouge, 257
Joint, brooch, 144
  file, 141
  hinge, 140
  tool, 142

KEYS or wedges, 208, 217
Killed spirit, 37
King's Lynn Cup, 113, 187, 319
Kingston Down Brooch, 323
Knuckles, 141
Kouklia, 170

LACQUERS, 159
Lamp, 52
Lathe, 3, 104
Lavender, oil of spike, 196
Lead, 24, 35, 39-40, 162, 234
  pipes, 37, 39
  red, 167
Leaves, 58
Lectures at Goldsmith's Hall, 318
Lemel, 1
Limoges enamel, 184
Line composition, 279
Lithium fluoride, 259
Littledale, Mr., 10, 11, 59
Loam, 19, 22, 61, 222
Lucca della Robbia, 286
Lugs, for fixing, 221, 236
Lycopodium as parting powder, 217

MAKING and sharpening tools, 267
Mallet, horn, 51
Materials for moulds, 14, 200, 204, 216, 222, 228
Matt surface, tools, 122
Measures of capacity, 296
  of lengths, 294, 300
  of surface, 294
  of temperature, 297
  of weight, 295
Melting point, 7-8, 12, 13, 23, 35, 235, 305
  wax model, 219, 222, 225, 227
Metal casting, 200, 318
  centrifugal, 232, 318
  cire perdue, 219, 318
  flasks or boxes, 216, 229
  ingots, 13-15
  pressure, 232, 318
Metal, colouring of, 260
Metal gauge, 309
  inlaying and overlaying, 148
  moulds, 201
Metallic oxides, 169
Methylated spirit, 30, 31
Metric measures, 294-300, 307-317
Mexico, 226
Mica backing for enamel, 182
Middle Ages, 9
Mildenhall Treasure, 115
Millefiori, 323
Millegriffe setting, 75
Milligrams, 300
Millimetres and inches, 299
Mirror, Birdlip, 171, 320
Mills, flatting, 44
Mixing plaster of Paris, 21, 133
Modelling tools, 122
Mokume, 167
Mond Nickel Co. Research Department, 228
" Mop," 22, 29, 48, 60
Mordants, 157
Morris's Geometrical Drawing, 250
Morse twist drill and steel wire gauge, 309
Moss, Dr. A. A. Niello, 318
Mother mould, 207, 209, 217
" Motifs " in jewellery, 53
Mouldings, 127, 238-240
  turning, 240
Moulds, 13-16, 43, 200, 219, 224, 235
  breaking down, 236
  cire perdue or waste wax, 219
  clay, 200
  cuttlefish bone, 202
  drying, 205
  firing, 225
  hearthstone, 14-15
  investment powder, 228, 231

Moulds, joined to crucible, 226
  materials for, 208, 222
  metal, 201
  moulding, 280
  outer or mother, 207
  piece, 205, 220, 222
  qualities required for, 204
  rubber, 228
  sand, 204, 216
  sticks in clay-, 201
  stone, 200, 201
Mouth blowpipe, 27, 28
Muffle furnace, 172, 260, 288
Muriatic acid, 37
Mycenæan daggers, 161
  gold rings, 170

Needle, 54
  etching, 154
  files, 48, 71
Nelson-Dawson, Mrs., Enamels, 318
National Art Library, 285
Nature, 275
Nickel, 2
  tongs, 25
Niello, 158, 161, 199, 263, 318
Nitric acid, 7, 24, 48, 154, 287
Nonagon, 249
Number and letter punches, 122
Nuremburg Cup, 321
Nymph of Fontainbleau, 223

Octagon, 249
Oil of spike lavender, 196
  turpentine, 196
Olive oil, 37, 111
  soap, 42
Ornamental wires, 135
Otten, Enamelling, 318
Oval, 250
Overlaying, 148, 150, 151
Ox bone, 223, 225
" Oxidized Silver," 263

Paillons, 19, 20, 59, 195
Painted enamels, 172, 192, 196
Pala d'Oro, 283
Paraffin wax, 42
Parting dust or powder, 201, 219
Patent, 11, 318
Pattern for metal casting, 201, 217, 229
  for spinning, 104
Pave setting, 79
Peaflour as parting powder, 217
Pearce, Mr. C., iii
Pearl, setting for, 84, 85
Pearlash, 13, 234
Pearls, seed, 58

Pennyweights, 300
Pentagon, 249
Perchloride of iron, 157
Perseus, 224
Persian repoussé inlays, 150
Petroleum jelly, 19, 37
Pewter, 2, 39, 304
Phosphorus, 13
Piccadilly Fountain, 275
Pickle, 7, 16, 23, 24, 25, 43, 48, 54, 61
Piece mould, 205, 216, 219, 228
Piercing saw, 48, 56
Pin, bench, 51, 52, 71, 74
  spinning, 104
Pitch, 114, 117, 219
  bowl, 118
  removal, 118
Planishing, 97
  hammer, 91
Plaque for enamelling, 176
Plaster of Paris, 21, 133, 190, 208, 228, 235
Plasticine, 18
Plastics, 159
Platinum, 1, 234
  chloride, 264
Pleats, 95, 111
Pliers, 47
Pliny, 9
Plique-à-jour enamels, 171, 182
Plon's Cellini, 285
Plumber's solder, 35, 304
Polden Hill horse trappings, 322
Polishing an enamel, 180
  head, 4
  materials, 256
Polythene, 181
Port-chenier, 143
Potash, 169, 260
Potassium chlorate, 206
  nitrate, 261, 262
  sulphide, 264, 265
Pour, 15, 200, 202, 218, 221, 226, 236
  plug, 226
  or sprue, 229
Powdered bone, 208
Precautions, acids, 25, 93, 325
  against loss, 1, 52
Precious quality, 282
  stones, 281
Pressure casting, 232, 318
Preston Mayor's Chain, 167, 323
" Proflavine," 25
Properties of circles, 301
Proportion, 276
Pumice, 21, 256, 260
Pumps, 28
Punches, cutting, 49, 55
  doming, 49, 50
Push tool, 68

QUALITY, æsthetic, 281
    of gold or silver, 1, 6, 11
Quartation, 288
Queen Elizabeth book cover, 191
Quenching, 93

RAGS, 224
Raising, 87, 94
    hammer, 89, 94
    mallet, 90
Ramsay Abbey Incense Boat, 320, 321
Ramsden, O., dish by, 319
Rathbone, R. L. B., *Simple Jewellery*, 53, 318
Red lead, 169
Refining, 1
Register marks, 201, 208, 217
    pins, 202, 216
Relief, mould for, 204
Remedy for burns, 25, 325
Removal of lead, 24, 39-40
    of soft solder, 39-40
Repoussé, 113, 114, 242
    high relief, 125
    lettering, 123
    tools, 119
    work on pitch, 114
        on wood, 114
Research Departments, 228
Resin, 37, 40, 219
Retsil Jewellers' Handbook, Selwyn, 318
Rhind's etching ground, 154
Ring, 54, 55, 59, 228, 239
    tools, 122
Roberts-Austen, Sir W. C., 166, 318
Rock crystal cup, 321
Rocked or wriggled cut, 154
Rolls, flatting, 44
Roman enamel, 199
    setting, 81
Rotaprint brush, 40
Rouge, 19, 22, 61, 257
Roulette, 67, 83
Royal Gold Cup, 187, 319
Rubbed-over setting, 81
Rubber for mould, 228, 230
Rubstone, 69
Ruby drawplate, 46
Rugerus, 9

SAL-AMMONIAC, 37, 40
Saltcellar, Cellini, 191, 285
Salt, bath, 258
    table or common, sodium chloride,
        13, 234, 261, 262
Sampler, enamel, 173
    granulation, 324
Sand, 169, 228
    bag, 50

Sand, blasting, 260
    mould moulding, 204, 216, 228
Sawdust, 211, 223
Saw, piercing, 48
Saxon hanging bowl, 171
Scandinavia, 227
Sceptre, 171
Scissors or snips, 48
Scollopers, 153
Scorpers, 48, 64
Scramaxes, 149
Scratch-brushing, 261
Scratches, removal, 256
Screw threads, American National
        coarse, 308
    British Association, 307
    Whitworth, 306
Seal stone, setting, 81
Seccotine, 10
Selwyn, A., *Retail Jewellers' Handbook*, 318
Setting out, 245
    inscriptions, 253
    tools required, 245, 246
    stones, 63, 70, 77, 80
    tool, 68, 72
Sezenius, Valentin, 199
Shaku-do, 168
Sharpening graver, 152
    tools, 272
Sheepskin, 52
Sheffield lime, 67, 259
Shibu-ichi, 168
Shoulder clasps, 322
    of a stone, 63
    piece from cuirass, 323
Shrinkage, 202, 236
Sieves, for grains, 54, 55
Silfos, 13
Silicate of soda, 203
Silver, 1, 7, 11, 23, 234
    annealing, 93
    Britannia, 11, 291
    chloride, 40
    German, 304
    new sterling, 11
    nitrate, 43
    oxidized, 263
    solders, 11, 13
    standard, 11
    sulphide, 263
    sulphurized, 263
    work and jewellery, 318
Simple Jewellery, Rathbone, 318
Sinking, 87, 102
    block, 88–89
    hammer, 91
    a tray, 243
Sion gospel's cover, 320

Siris bronze, 323
Slide tongs, 47, 56
Snarling-irons, 122
Snicks, 77
Society of Arts, 166
Soda (baking) bicarbonate, 25
    removal of acids or grease, 26, 260 261
    silicate, 203
    washing, 23, 208
Sodium cyanide, 268
Solder, 5–10, 11–13, 16, 19, 20, 36
    for enamels, 11
    gold, 6–11, 13
    plumbers', 35
    silver, 7, 8, 11–13
    tinman's, 35, 36, 39
Soldering, 5, 9–13, 22, 59, 60
    bit or iron, 36
    can, 10
    hearth, 3, 20, 21, 33
    jet, 27, 28
    lamp, 30, 31
    Roman, 9
South Kensington Museum, 186, 187,
    191, 199, 263, 285, 319
Sparrow-hawk, 51
Specific gravity, 305
Speculum metal, 304
Spelter, 12–13, 26, 304
Spinning, 104
    chucks, 105
    followers, 108
    forme, 104
    tools, 104, 109
Spiral, 248
Spirit lamp, 30, 48
    of salts, 37
Spitstickers, 64
Spon, *Workshop Receipts*, 165, 318
St. Agnes Cup , 187, 188, 319
St. Conall Cael shrine, 319
St. Mark's, Venice, 282
Stakes, 51, 87, 102
Standard gold, 6, 304
    silver, 11, 304
Star setting, 79
Starch, 25
Statuette, casting in metal, 207
Stearin, 40
Steel, 267
    to harden, 268, 270
    to temper, 269, 270
Stirrup, 125
Stone moulds, 200, 201
    setting, 63
Stopping-out varnish, 154, 262
Straighten an enamel, 197
    a wire, 46
Stripping, 258

Stropping a tool, 272
Stubs iron wire gauge, 309
    steel wire gauge, 309
Sulphur, 162, 164, 264
Sulphuric acid, 7, 16, 23, 25, 263
Sumeria, 8, 36
Surface-plate, 3
Sutton Hoo Ship Burial, 108, 171, 322,
    323
Swage, 45, 46, 130
Sweet oil, 40
Sword Guards, Japanese, 321
    mould, Viking, 201

Tables and Standards, 294
Tablet, fixing, 241
Talc, 231
Tallow, 37, 40, 111, 219
Tannic acid, 25
Tapping, sizes screw, 308
Tara Brooch, 322
Tarentum, 171
Temperature, measures of, 297
Temperatures, high, 298
Tempering steel, 269, 270
Theophilus, 9, 162, 165, 216, 318
Thickness of metal casting, 209, 210
Thio-urea, 40
Thread and grain setting, 76
    polishing, 259
Tin, 2, 35, 39, 235, 304
    canister, 38
    foil, 39
Tinman's solder, 35, 36
Tinning a " bit," 37
Tone, 282
Tongs, crucible, 236
    enamelling, 173
Tortoise brooches, 227
Tortoise-shell, 259
Touch needle, 1, 287
    stone, 1, 288
Tracers, 119, 120
Tracing, 119
    and transferring design, 123, 156,
        176, 192, 246
Triblets or mandrels, 50, 51, 57, 64
Tripoli, 19, 257
Troy weight, 300
T-stake, 87
Tube or chenier, 43
    drawing, 44
Tulip setting, 79
Turning-over tool, 127
    a moulding, 239, 240
Tweezers, 48, 58
Twisted stem, 252
    wires, 58, 135, 149
Typemetal, 235

UNDECAGON, 249
Undercut pieces, 217
Unity in design, 278
Unsoldering a joint, 5, 24

VACUUM chamber, 258
Valence Casket, 321
Vaseline, 10, 42
Venice, 86, 282
  turpentine, 65, 219
Vent, 24, 204, 207, 218, 220, 221, 224,
  236, 238
  for core, 210
Vertical or horizontal lines, 280
Vice, 3, 89
  hand, 47, 56
  pin, 47
Vienna, Cellini's saltcellar, 191, 285
Viking sword mould, 201
Vitriol (sulphuric acid), 25, 48
Vulcanizing, 229

WAIST of a stone, 63
Waste wax casting, 209, 219, 226
Water glass, 203
Water-or-Ayr stone, 256, 260
Wax, injector, 230
  Japan, 219
  lining of mould, 210, 220, 224, 225
  model, 219, 228

Wax, paraffin, 42, 156, 219
  sealing, 202
  stick, 65, 72
Weight of aluminium, brass, copper
  303
  of precious stones, 296
  of silver sheet, 302
  of various metals, 305
West Africa, 226
Whiting, 19, 22, 61
Whitworth screw threads, 306
" Wig," 22, 29, 48, 60
Wigley, T. B., *Art of the Goldsmith, etc.*,
  318
Wilson, H., *Silverwork and Jewellery*, 318
Wine cup, French, 323
" Wiping " a joint, 35
Wire, binding, 17, 18, 26, 60
  drawing, 41
  inside a moulding, 128
  or filigree, 9, 43, 58
  square, oblong, etc., 43
  twisted, 58, 135
Wood-grain, 167
Work-bench, 3, 4
Workshop First Aid, 325
Workshop Receipts, Spon, 318
Wriggled or rocked cut, 154

ZINC, 11, 12, 13, 36, 235
  chloride, 37, 40, 265